Praise for

The Story of Stuff

"Annie Leonard occupies a unique, vital place in the pantheon of leading social and political thinkers in American society today. Better than anyone before, she is able to explain, with simplicity, humor, and verve, the *intrinsic* problems of an economic system that destroys the Earth while delivering social and economic chaos. This is *must reading* for anyone seeking to grasp the interlocking crises of our time, what to do about them, and how to talk about them with others. An educational and organizing tool of the utmost importance."

—Jerry Mander, founder, Distinguished Fellow, the International Forum on Globalization, and author of *In the Absence of the Sacred: Failure of Technology* and *The Case Against the Global Economy—And for a Turn Toward the Local*

"Annie Leonard has a gift for teaching without preaching. *The Story of Stuff* is a brilliant and heartwarming book, a much-needed burst of energy directed toward solutions that stands out in a field of dire facts and laborious explanations about the state of our world."

—Maude Barlow, author of *Blue Covenant: The Global Water Crisis and the Coming Battle for the Right to Water*

"Annie Leonard journeys into the dark heart of consumerism and returns with a masterpiece. Part handbook, part manifesto, fact-packed and eye-opening, *The Story of Stuff* is essential reading for anyone concerned about the environment."

—Alan Burdick, author of *Out of Eden: An Odyssey of Ecological Invasion*

"Annie Leonard has done it again! The Story of Stuff video was a huge hit with my students and my family, and I plan on sharing this amazing book with everyone I know. Leonard expertly guides us through the hard truths of our materials economy, from extraction to disposal and she offers concrete and positive alternatives every step of the way. The most important thing I learned from this book is that if we build community and focus on what really matters, we can use our collective power and imagination to change the world. Let's get to work!"

—David Naguib Pellow, professor of sociology, University of Minnesota, and author of *Garbage Wars: The Struggle for Environmental Justice in Chicago* and *Resisting Global Toxics: Transnational Movements for Environmental Justice*

"Many of the problems facing the world today can be traced back to how we make, consume, and toss our mountains of stuff. Annie Leonard takes us on a much-needed journey into the heart of stuff, and brings us back again with the knowledge and optimism to change our lives and our society."

—Tim Kasser, Ph.D., professor & chair of psychology, Knox College,
and author of The High Price of Materialism

"Annie Leonard's marvelous new book could not have appeared at a better time, as people across the country (and the world), and young people in particular, grapple with the interconnected issues of consumption and our environmental, social, and economic crises. I recommend *The Story of Stuff* to students everywhere: it's a must-read for anyone looking to make a profound difference."

—Michael Maniates, professor of political science and environmental
science at Allegheny College, co-editor of Confronting Consumption
and The Environmental Politics of Sacrifice

"Annie Leonard's is the rare voice who can pose fundamental questions about our economic system without alienating or frightening her audience. With *The Story of Stuff*, she provides not only a comprehensive look at what's broken, but a bridge to a whole new economic, social, and environmental reality."

—James Gustave Speth, author of The Bridge at the Edge of the World:
Capitalism, the Environment, and Crossing from Crisis to Sustainability

"*The Story of Stuff* is a brilliantly argued triumph of common sense and optimism. A work of great courage, it offers the greatest possible public service: speaking truth to power. A compelling and vitally important book for our troubled times."

—Ellen Ruppel Shell, author of Cheap: The High Cost of Discount
Culture, professor and co-director of the Graduate Program in
Science Journalism, Boston University

THE STORY OF STUFF

HOW OUR OBSESSION WITH STUFF IS TRASHING THE PLANET, OUR COMMUNITIES, AND OUR HEALTH —AND A VISION FOR CHANGE

Annie Leonard

with Ariane Conrad

FREE PRESS

New York   London   Toronto   Sydney

Free Press
A Division of Simon & Schuster, Inc.
1230 Avenue of the Americas
New York, NY 10020

Illustrations by Ruben DeLuna and Louis Fox, Free Range Studios

First Free Press hardcover edition March 2010

FREE PRESS and colophon are trademarks of Simon & Schuster, Inc.

For information about special discounts for bulk purchases,
please contact Simon & Schuster Special Sales at
1–866–506–1949 or business@simonandschuster.com.

The Simon & Schuster Speakers Bureau can bring authors to your live event.
For more information or to book an event contact the Simon & Schuster Speakers
Bureau at 1–866–248–3049 or visit our website at www.simonspeakers.com.

Designed by Chris Brunell, Free Range Studios

Manufactured in the United States of America

10   9   8   7   6   5   4   3   2   1

Library of Congress Cataloging-in-Publication Data

Leonard, Annie.
   The story of stuff : how our obsession with stuff is trashing the planet,
our communities, and our health—and a vision for change / Annie Leonard
with Ariane Conrad.
      p. cm.
   1. Material culture.   2. Personal belongings.   3. Acquisitiveness—Moral
and ethical aspects.   4. Consumerism (Economics)—Moral and ethical aspects.
I. Conrad, Ariane.   II. Title.
   GN406.L46 2010
   306.4—dc22   2009042207

ISBN 978-1-4391-2566-3
ISBN 978-1-4391-4878-5 (e-book)

To Bobbie and Dewi

CONTENTS

INTRODUCTION

Growing up in the green and luscious city of Seattle during the 1970s was idyllic, but the real joy came in the summertime, when my family and I piled our camping gear into our station wagon and headed for the stunning North Cascades mountains. Since this was in the days before DVD players in the backseats, during the drive I'd look out the window and study the landscape. Each year I noticed that the mini-malls and houses reached a bit farther, while the forests started a bit later and got a bit smaller. Where were my beloved forests going?

I found my answer to that question some years later in New York City, of all places. The Barnard College campus where I went for my environmental studies classes was on West 116th Street on Manhattan's Upper West Side, and my dorm room was on West 110th Street. Every morning I groggily trudged up those six blocks, staring at the mounds of garbage that line New York City's streets at dawn each day. Ten hours later, I walked back to my dorm along the emptied sidewalks. I was intrigued. I started poking around to see what was in those never-ending piles of trash. Guess what? It was mostly paper.

Paper! That's where my trees were ending up. (In fact, about 40 percent of municipal garbage in the United States is paper products.[1]) From the forests I knew in the Pacific Northwest to the sidewalks of the Upper West Side to . . . where?

My curiosity was sparked. I couldn't stop there; I needed to find out what happened after the paper disappeared from the curb. So I took a trip to the infamous Fresh Kills landfill on Staten Island. Covering 4.6 square miles, Fresh Kills was one of the largest dumps in the world. When it was officially closed in 2001, some say the stinking mound was the largest man-made structure on the planet, its volume greater than that of the Great Wall of China, and its peaks 80 feet taller than the Statue of Liberty.[2]

I had never seen anything like Fresh Kills. I stood at its edge in absolute awe. As far as I could see in every direction were trashed couches, appliances, cardboard boxes, apple cores, clothes, plastic bags, books, and tons of other Stuff. You know how a gory car crash scene makes you want to turn away and stare at the same time? That is what this dump was like. I'd been raised by a single mother of the post-Depression era who instilled in her kids a sense of respect for quality, not quantity. Partly from her life philosophy and partly out of economic necessity, my youth was shaped along the lines of the World War II saying: "Use it up, wear it out, make it do, or do without." There just wasn't a lot of superfluous consumption and waste going on in our house. We savored the things we had and took good care of them and kept them until every last drop of usefulness was gone.

So the mountains of perfectly good materials that had been reduced to muck at Fresh Kills made no sense to me. It felt terribly wrong. Who set up this system? How could those who knew about it allow it to continue? I didn't understand it, but I vowed to figure it out. After two decades of sleuthing, when I'd figured it out, I called it the Story of Stuff.

Interconnections

The Story of Stuff journey took me around the world—on research and community organizing missions for Greenpeace, Essential Action, the Global Alliance for Incinerator Alternatives (GAIA), and other environmental organizations—not only to more dumps but also to mines, factories, hospitals, embassies, universities, farms, World Bank offices, and the halls of government. I stayed with families in Indian villages so isolated that my arrival would be greeted by desperate parents running up to me asking "Are you a doctor?" hoping I happened to be the international medic—on her *annual* visit—who would be able to cure their child. I met entire families who lived on garbage dumps in the Philippines, Guatemala, and Bangladesh and who survived on the food and material scraps they pulled from the stinking, smoldering heaps. I visited shopping malls in Tokyo and Bangkok and Las Vegas that were so big and bright and plastic that I felt like I was in *The Jetsons* or *Futurama*.

Everywhere I went, I kept asking "why?" and digging deeper and deeper. Why were dumps so hazardous? Because of the toxics in the trash. And why were there toxics in the trashed products to begin with? Answering that question led me to learn about toxics, chemistry, and environmental health. Why were dumps so often situated in lower-income communities where people of color live and work? I started learning about environmental racism.

And why does it make economic sense to move entire factories to other countries: how can they still sell the product for a couple of dollars when it's traveling so far? Suddenly I had to confront international trade agreements and the influence of corporations on governmental regulations.

And another thing: why are electronics breaking so fast and why are they cheaper to replace than repair? So I learned about planned obsolescence, advertising, and other tools for promoting consumerism. On the surface, each of these topics seemed separate from the next, unconnected, and a long way from those piles of garbage on the streets of New York City or the forests of the Cascades. But it turns out they're all connected.

The journey led me to become what people call a systems thinker. That means I believe everything exists as part of a larger system and must be understood in relation to the other parts. It's not an uncommon framework: think about the last time you came down with a fever. You probably wondered if it was caused by a bacteria or a virus. A fever is a response to a strange element being introduced to the system that is your body. If you didn't believe that your body was a system, you might look for a heat source underneath your hot forehead or some switch that accidentally got flipped and raised your temperature. In biology we easily accept the idea of multiple systems (e.g., circulatory, digestive, nervous) made of parts (like cells or organs), as well as the fact that those systems interact with one another inside a body.

In school we all learned about the water cycle, the system that moves water through its various states—as liquid, vapor, and solid ice—around the earth. And about the food chain, the system in which, as a simple example, plankton get eaten by small fish, which get eaten by bigger fish, which get eaten by humans. Between those two systems, the water cycle and the food chain—even though one's inanimate and the other is made of living creatures—there's an important interaction, as the rivers and oceans of the first provide the habitat for the creatures of the second. That brings us to an ecosystem, made up of interrelated inanimate physical parts and subsystems like rocks and water, as well as all the living parts like plants and animals. Again there are systems within systems. The earth's biosphere—another word for the planet's entire ecosystem—is a system that exists inside of that much larger thing that we call the solar system.

The economy functions as a system, too, which is why there can be a domino effect inside it, as when people lose their jobs and then reduce their spending, which means that factories can't sell as much Stuff, which means that more people get laid off . . . which is exactly what happened in 2008 and 2009. Systems thinking as related to the economy also explains a theory like "trickle-down" economics, in which benefits like tax cuts are given to the wealthy so that they'll invest more in businesses, which would hypothetically in turn create more jobs for the middle and lower classes. If you didn't believe these parts (money, jobs, people across classes) operated within a system, there'd be no basis for the trickle-down theory, or for beliefs about the interplay between supply and demand. All these examples assume interrelated parts within a larger system.

Another way to say that everything exists as part of a larger system (including systems themselves) is to say *everything is connected.*

It's funny: Most people's professional paths start with a general interest that becomes increasingly specialized with years of education, training, and on-the-job implementation. There's powerful social and professional validation for increasing specialization like this. I, however, took the opposite path: I started with a fascination—and outrage—about garbage, specifically about the bags of the Stuff piled up on New York City's Upper West Side. After getting a degree in environmental science, I got a job with Greenpeace International, which paid me to track the destination and the impact of all the waste loaded onto ships in the United States and sent abroad. My whole job was about investigating and stopping the international dumping of waste.

I will forever be grateful to Greenpeace. Founded on the Quaker principle of bearing witness—the idea that seeing wrong-doing with our own eyes creates a moral responsibility to inform others and take action—Greenpeace provided me with a laptop computer and rudimentary training and then set me loose upon the world to bear witness to waste trafficking and tell everyone what I saw. However, like most institutions, Greenpeace divided its work into specific issue areas that left us working in silos, disconnected from one another: toxics, oceans, forests, nukes, marine ecosystems, genetically modified organisms, climate, etc. The organization cultivated a strong culture of specific expertise. For example, the toxics people knew a scary amount about toxics—even the interns could rattle off the molecular structures of chlorinated organic compounds and explain their environmental health impacts—and they single-mindedly pursued their issue to the exclusion of everything else. Back then, we didn't spend much time understanding the connections between the problems we were each working so hard to solve.

In the early 1990s, I started traveling extensively to work with allies in other countries. At first, I prided myself on knowing more about international waste trafficking than anyone outside my team at Greenpeace. But the more I traveled, the more I realized how much I didn't know and didn't understand. I was initially shocked by the scope of work that I found others doing, in India, Indonesia, the Philippines, Haiti, and South Africa, for example. I met dozens of people who worked on a whole jumble of issues altogether: water and forests and energy and even women's issues and international trade. At first, I assumed that they had to cover so many issues because they were short staffed; I felt sorry for them having to do the jobs of multiple people while I had the luxury of devoting all my attention to one issue. After a while, I had a revelation: all those issues are interconnected. As I kept unraveling the strings of connections, I realized that garbage—or any single problem, for that matter—can't be solved in isolation. Focusing so exclusively on a single issue wasn't helping me; in fact it was retarding my ability to understand the context of the issue of garbage, to see the Big Picture. Learning about other issues wouldn't distract from my progress, it would enable breakthroughs.

And so it was that I went from poking in bags of garbage to examining the global systems of production and consumption of manufactured goods, or what academics call the materials economy. That means I cross back and forth between two disciplines that the modern world usually sees as not only sharply divided but at total odds with each other: the environment (or ecology) and the economy. But guess what? Not only are these two systems connected, one is actually a subsystem of the other, the same way that earth's ecosystem is a subsystem of the solar system.

Now, a lot of environmentalists don't really want to deal with the economy. Traditional environmentalists focus on that cuddly endangered bear or the majestic groves of redwoods or the nature preserves where they go to forget all about ugly things like the stock market. Endangered species and pristine places have nothing to do with pricing structures or government subsidies for mining or international trade agreements, do they? (Uh, actually, yes, they do.) Meanwhile, classical economists have acknowledged the environment only as an unlimited and cheap or *free* set of raw resources to fuel the growth of the economy. Oh, and the arena from which pesky activists sometimes pop up to challenge a new factory site based on protecting the habitat of the woodland shrew.

Yet in fact, the economy is a subsystem of the earth's ecosystem, its biosphere. You see, any economic system—like barter, slavery, feudalism, socialism, or capitalism—is a human invention. Since humans are just one of the earth's many species (albeit a powerful species, what with our written words and our weapons), any invention of ours is a subsystem of the earth's ecosystem. Once we understand that (which is not my opinion, but plain fact), it leads to other insights.

Nearing Limits

The most important of these further insights is about limits. For one system to exist inside of another, the subsystem needs to fit inside the constraints of the parent system. You've seen those pictures of our pretty blue planet from space, right? The surface area on this hunk of rock that we call home is 197 million square miles (roughly a third of that is land).[3] To wrap a (long) piece of string around the middle of the planet at the equator you would need 24,901.55 miles (40,075.16 kilometers) of it.[4] The total water supply—in all its states—measures about 326 million cubic miles.[5] That's what we've got. The earth's dimensions and capacity remain stable. That means there is a *limit* to the amount of land, water, air, minerals, and other resources provided by the earth. That's just a fact.

Believe me, I know that can be easy to forget, given the way most of us here in the United States or in other rich nations live. How would we know that the soil is degrading or the oceans are being emptied of fish? Few of us get to see our food growing or the nets pulling our fish out of the water. Let alone where and how our T-shirts, laptops, books, and other Stuff is made, halfway across the planet. From where I sit in my cozy Berkeley bungalow, the world looks pretty good: the weather's nice, the vast selection in the grocery store is undiminished by the fact that my state of California is in a multiyear drought. If our fruit harvest is low this year, apples still arrive from Chile. *Don't worry, be happy.*

But the reports of every credible scientist in the world tell a different story. Evidence of the environmental crisis is now so abundant that only those committed to serious denial continue to contest the facts. While mainstream economists and politicians seem blind to the very real physical limits, environmentalists, scientists, academics, and others have raised concerns for decades.

There are literally hundreds of books and reports, from countless reliable and trustworthy sources, that document how things are going on the planet. Here are just a few highlights:

- In July 2009, we reached 387.81 parts per million (ppm) of carbon dioxide (CO_2) in the atmosphere. Leading scientists around the world have identified 350 ppm as the maximum level that the atmosphere can contain for the planet to remain as we know it.[6]
- Toxic industrial and agricultural chemicals now show up in every body tested anywhere in the world, including in newborn babies.[7]

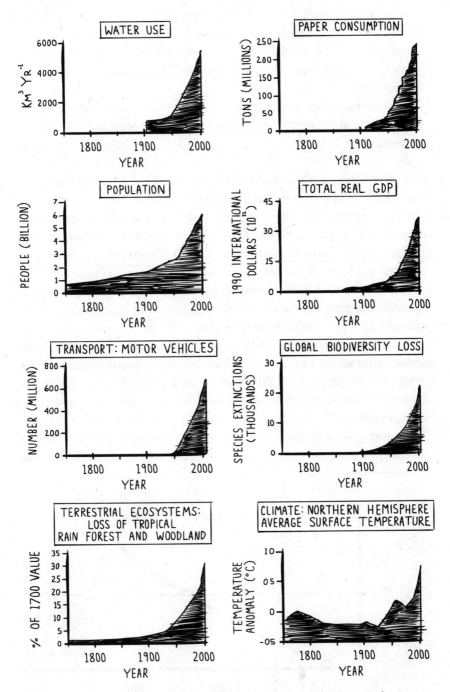

Source: W. Steffen at al, *Global Change and the Earth System: A Planet Under Pressure,* 2005.

- Indoor air pollution kills 1.6 million people per year, with outdoor air pollution taking another 800,000 lives each year.[8]
- About one-fifth of the world's population—more than 1.2 billion people—experience water scarcity, and this resource is becoming increasingly scarce.[9]
- Global income inequality is staggering. Currently, the richest 1 percent of people in the world have as much wealth and Stuff as the bottom 57 percent.[10]

So what happens when there's a subsystem like the economy that keeps growing inside of a system of a fixed size? It hits the wall. The expanding economic system is running up against the limits of our planet's capacity to sustain life. Economists project that, with current and projected rates of growth, developed countries will grow at 2 to 3 percent per year, and China and India at 5 to10 percent per year.[11] Already, in generating today's volume of goods and services across the world, we're producing more than five times (closer to six, actually) the level of CO_2 emissions to which we'll need to reduce by 2050 in order to avoid total climate chaos.[12]

So that's the conundrum. Then factor in the impact of raising the standard of living for the world's poor (which inevitably means increasing their carbon dioxide emissions). With carbon dioxide overloading our fragile atmosphere, and our demands on all the other life-sustaining services and resources that the earth provides, we're stressing the planet beyond its limits.

Put simply, if we do not redirect our extraction and production systems and change the way we distribute, consume, and dispose of our Stuff—what

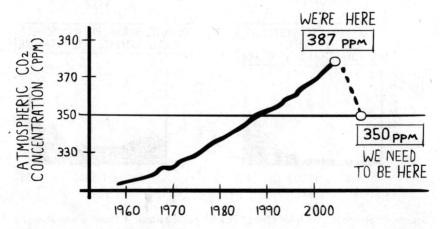

Source: J. Hansen et al, "Target atmospheric CO_2: Where should humanity aim?" 2008 350.org.

I sometimes call the take-make-waste model—the economy as it is will kill the planet. Look at the news coming through as I write these words: the financial markets have collapsed and were only partially resuscitated thanks to vast Wall Street/Washington bailouts; food prices are erratic and causing misery both for farmers and for the world's hungry; carbon dioxide levels are rising to life-threatening levels, and resources like oil, fish, and fresh water become scarcer every day.

In the face of the grim data and the stubbornness of the problem, I know it's tempting to tune out, give up, and resign oneself to the way things are. One friend told me that reading this kind of information actually makes her want to go shopping because it is such a relief to be in a situation where your biggest concern is if your shoes match your purse. People everywhere, but especially the poor, are experiencing crisis fatigue. Heck, there are flu pandemics, freak storms, unemployment, and foreclosures to worry about. The thing is, we don't have a choice. In the words of Joseph Guth, a lawyer, biochemist, and the legal director of the Science and Environmental Health Network: "*Nothing* is more important to human beings than an ecologically functioning, life sustaining biosphere on the Earth. It is the *only* habitable place we know of in a forbidding universe. We all depend on it to live and we are compelled to share it; it is our only home . . . The Earth's biosphere seems almost magically suited to human beings and indeed it is, for we evolved through eons of intimate immersion within it. *We cannot live long or well without a functioning biosphere, and so it is worth everything we have.*" [13]

Fragmented Solutions

While the challenges are interconnected and system-wide, the responses are often partial, focused on just one area—like improving technologies, restricting population growth, or curbing the consumption of resources.

Proponents of techno-fixes, for example, believe that cleaner, greener, and more innovative technologies will make our industrial and economic activity so efficient with energy and other resources that our problems can be solved this way. They point out that there's less and less environmental destruction per unit of activity (per dollar of gross domestic product or per ton of product made). They're not wrong. Many technologies are getting more efficient. But that progress is canceled out by the fact that—at least until the economic crash of 2008—there was more absolute growth overall: more people extracting, using, and disposing of more Stuff. (Even the decline in production from 2008 to 2009 was relatively small, and if past trends are any guide, we will revert to growth soon enough.) So the overall adverse environmental impact is still increasing, regardless of more efficient technology.

The reason that green technologies will not save us is that they are only part of the picture. Our collective impact on the planet—how fast we reach the limits of the earth's capacity to sustain us—results from a combination of how many of us there are, what kind of technologies we use, and how much we're consuming. In technical terms, this is often represented by the I=PAT equation, which was conceived in the 1970s during debates between the camp that believed that technologies and consumption patterns were the main driver of environmental destruction and the opposing camp, which argued that increasing population was at fault. The I=PAT equation—in which I is impact, P is population, A is affluence (aka consumption), and T is the technologies used—recognizes the interplay between all these factors. The equation helps us see how these factors can interact; *generally* we can decrease our impact by reducing population and/or improving technologies. Generally, but not always: not if other variables cancel out the change. Fewer people consuming much more Stuff, for example, still increases impact. More people consuming less Stuff could decrease impact. There are many ways these variables can relate to one another.

Of course total population growth is part of the problem: all you need to do is see those hockey-stick-like graphs on page xv to know that one of the big reasons that exponentially more of everything (trees, minerals, fresh water, fisheries, etc.) has been used up in the last fifty years is because there are exponentially more of us. It took us two hundred thousand years (until the early 1800s) to reach 1 billion people; then a little over a century (1960) to reach 3 billion; and we've more than doubled since then, with our current 6.7 billion and counting.[14]

Yet historically, interventions aimed at stabilizing global population have usually been driven by those in the overconsuming regions of the world and have often ignored the fact of vastly unequal consumption patterns. Often places with the most rapidly expanding populations are using very few (too few) resources. Meanwhile the very small slice of the global population that owns most of the world's wealth (the top 1 to 5 percent) is producing the lion's share of greenhouse gases and other environmental destruction. It's important that whatever strategies we democratically decide to employ in order to stabilize population must be grounded in an unshakable commitment to human rights, especially women's rights, and equity.

We don't know what the actual carrying capacity of the planet is, but we know it isn't one inflexible number; it depends on our levels and patterns of production and consumption. That raises huge issues about equity in resource distribution and value judgments about how much is enough. Should we be asking how many people the planet can sustain at the U.S. level of consumption or at the Bangladesh level of consumption? And, importantly, who decides the answer?

The questions are complicated, but we need to have the conversation and decide on our answers together. We need to do this because there is no doubt we will reach the planet's carrying capacity; we're heading in that direction now. And once we cross that line, it's game over: *We depend on this planet to eat, drink, breathe, and live. Figuring out how to keep our life-support system running needs to be our number-one priority. Nothing is more important than finding a way to live together—justly, respectfully, sustainably, joyfully—on the only planet we can call home.*

If what's getting in the way of that is this human invention gone haywire—the take-make-waste economic growth machine—then it's only logical to consider dismantling and rebuilding that machine, improved upon by all that we've learned over the previous decades.

It's the Economic Growth, Stupid

Economic growth generally refers to an increase in economic activity across the board (trade, services, production, consumption, everything), which also implies an increase in the amount of natural resources extracted from the earth, run through the economy, turned into products, and returned back to the earth as waste. Put simply, this means *more*. More Stuff. More money. Just like it sounds, growth means getting bigger.

Now, economic growth should be a value-neutral means toward the real goals: meeting everyone's basic needs and creating healthier communities, greater equality, cleaner energy, sturdier infrastructure, more vibrant culture, etc. For a long time, growth did contribute to those fundamental goals, although it's important to remember that growth in some places has too often required the exploitation of others. A century ago, when we still had vast stretches of open land, the growth model brought roads and houses and central heating and full bellies. Now, in much of the world, we have those things. In fact, we do have enough Stuff to meet the basic needs of everyone in the world; it's just not distributed well enough. We have a shortage of sharing rather than a lack of enough.

A big part of the problem we face today is that our dominant economic system values growth as a goal unto itself, above all else. That's why we use the gross domestic product, or GDP, as the standard measure of success. It counts the value of goods and services made in a country each year. But it leaves out some really important facets of reality. For starters, GDP doesn't account for the unequal and unfair distribution of wealth or look at how healthy, satisfied, or fulfilled people are. That's why the GDP of a country can keep rising at a good 2 to 3 percent clip while the incomes of its workers don't rise at all in the same time period—the wealth gets stuck in one spot in the system. Earth Economics director Dave Batker, a disciple of the great ecological economist Herman Daly, says the GDP is akin to a business owner adding up all her expenses and all her income and then adding them together into "a big dumb useless number." The fact that the number is big doesn't tell us a thing about how the business is really doing.[15]

Another huge problem with how the GDP is calculated is that the true ecological and social costs of the growth are not accounted for. Industries are usually permitted (both in the sense of being given permits by government as well as generally not being held accountable) to "externalize costs," which is a fancy phrase economists use to describe the fact that, while companies are busy producing and selling widgets, they're not paying for, or even tracking, the side-effects they cause, like contaminating groundwater, exposing communities to carcinogens, or polluting the air.

This is totally messed up: while on the plus side, GDP counts activities that cause pollution and cancer (such as factories making pesticides or polyvinyl chloride) as well as activities to clean up that pollution and treat the cancer (such as environmental remediation and medical care), there is no deduction in the GDP for the pollution released into the air or water or the loss of a forest. In his book *Deep Economy*, Bill McKibben gave this real world example of the failure of GDP to measure success: for years in Africa, the non-native water hyacinth was clogging waterways, and herbicides had done nothing to solve the problem. Then someone discovered that dried water hyacinth made great material for growing highly nutritious mushrooms, and that when the mushrooms broke down the cellulose in the hyacinths, it made a great medium for earthworms. The worms chomped that down and created high-quality fertilizer, then were themselves feed for chickens. The chickens, of course, provided people with eggs, while their droppings could be used to fuel biogas digesters that produced power, and this reduced the need to cut down more trees for firewood from the already deforested regions in that part of Africa. Because monetary transactions— like the purchase of fertilizer—were reduced, a solution like this actually shows up on a measure like GDP as diminished "growth."[16] Yet it's clear to anyone with eyes, a brain, and a heart that the hyacinth-mushroom-worm-chicken solution is true progress: healthy and sensible.

For the powers that be—the heads of government and industry—the undisputed goal of our economy is a steady improvement in the GDP, aka growth. Growth as a goal has supplanted the real goals, the things growth was supposed to help us achieve. What I and many others have come to see—and as I hope this book makes abundantly clear—is that too often, as a strategy, focusing on growth for growth's sake undermines the real goals. Too much of what gets counted toward "growth" today—tons of toxic consumer goods, for example—undermines our net safety, health, and happiness. Despite increasing growth and with all of our advances in technology, science, and medicine, more people than ever are hungry, half the world's people live on less than $2.50 a day,[17] and income inequity is growing within and between countries.

Our society's deep, unwavering faith in economic growth rests on the assumption that focusing on infinite growth is both possible and good. But neither is true. We can't run the expanding economic subsystem (take-make-waste) on a planet of fixed size indefinitely: on many fronts, we're perilously close to the limits of our finite planet already. Infinite economic growth, therefore, is impossible. Nor has it turned out to be, after the point at which basic human needs are met, a strategy for increasing human well-being. After a certain point, economic growth (more money and more Stuff) ceases to make us happier. I mean, if everyone were having fun and enjoying leisure, laughter, and well-being, we might decide that the pursuit of growth was worth the trashing of the planet. But the majority of us are not having fun; instead we are reporting high levels of stress, depression, anxiety, and unhappiness.

Alright. Are you ready? I'm going to say it: this critique of economic growth is a critique of many aspects of capitalism as it functions in the world today. There. I said the word: "capitalism." It's the Economic-System-That-Must-Not-Be-Named.

When writing the film script of The Story of Stuff, my intent was to describe what I saw in my years on the trail of trash, visiting factories and dumps and learning about how things are made, used, and thrown away around the world. I certainly didn't sit down to figure out how to explain the flaws in capitalism. It was trash, not economics, that was originally on my mind. So, at first it took me by surprise that some commentators called the film "an ecological critique of capitalism" or "anti-capitalist." Was it? Really? That inspired me to go back and dust off my old books on economics to revisit the core characteristics of capitalism. And I realized those commentators were on to something. It turns out that a hard look at how we make and use and throw away Stuff reveals some pretty deep problems caused by core functions of a specific economic system called capitalism. There's no way around it: capitalism, as it currently functions, is just not sustainable.

As lawyer and former presidential advisor Gus Speth wrote in his book *The Bridge at the End of the World*, "Inherent in the dynamics of capitalism is a powerful drive to earn profits, invest them, innovate, and thus grow the economy, typically at exponential rates . . . My conclusion, after much searching and considerable reluctance, is that most environmental deterioration is a result of systemic failures of the capitalism that we have today, and that long-term solutions must seek transformative change in the key features of this contemporary capitalism."[18]

Yet, in the United States, we're still hesitant to broach this unmentionable subject, fearful of being labeled unpatriotic, unrealistic, or insane. Elsewhere in the world, there's a widespread recognition that some aspects of capitalism aren't working well for the majority of the world's people or for the planet; people talk about it openly. Michael Cohen, Lecturer in American studies at the University of California, Berkeley, says that's because in other countries capitalism is seen as one option among many, whereas in the United States it's considered an inevitability.[19]

Can we put capitalism on the table and talk about it with the same intellectual rigor that we welcome for other topics? Can we examine the failures of capitalism without falling into generations-old stereotypes and without being accused of being un-American? Refusing to talk about it doesn't make the problems disappear. I believe the best way to honor our country is to point out when it's going astray, instead of sit here silently as many economic, environmental, and social indices worsen. Now would be a good time to start looking at what we could do differently, and what we could do better.

Take the Red Pill

The belief that infinite economic growth is the best strategy for making a better world has become like a secular religion in which all our politicians, economists, and media participate; it is seldom debated, since everyone is supposed to just accept it as true. People who challenge capitalism or growth are considered wackos, or as a recent article in *U.S. News & World Report* put it, "The growing anti-economic-growth movement [is] made up of extreme environmentalists, hand-wringing technophobes, and turn-back-the-clock globalization bashers . . ."[20] Even while taking over the reigns of a country steeped in social, environmental, and economic problems, during a troubled time ripe for the adoption of alternative strategies, President Obama and his team promised over and over that economic growth would return. The U.S. Treasury's $800 billion rescue package to stabilize financial markets in late 2008 was to protect this sacred idea of economic growth, and by 2009, Obama, Treasury Secretary Timothy Geithner, economic czar Larry Summers, and Federal Reserve chair Ben Bernanke had committed an estimated $13 trillion of public funds to bailing out Wall Street and kick-starting economic growth again.

What gives? Why are so few people willing to challenge, or even critically discuss, an economic model that so clearly isn't serving the planet and the majority of its people? I think one reason is that the economic model is nearly invisible to us.

"Paradigm" may be an off-putting word, but it's an important concept when considering different ways of organizing our economy and our society. A paradigm is like a framework, or like the operating system of a computer. It's made up of the dominant set of assumptions, values, and ideas that make up how a society views reality. It's our worldview. After a while we tend to forget that we're viewing the world through the paradigm, like it's a pair of contact lenses. "Your paradigm is so intrinsic to your mental process that you are hardly aware of its existence, until you try to communicate with someone with a different paradigm," said prominent systems analyst Donella Meadows.[21]

You're more likely to notice aspects of the paradigm when you view a culture from the outside. For example, living in Dhaka, Bangladesh, for five months in the mid-1990s provided me with many opportunities to see another culture's norms and also see my own from a new perspective. While there I lived in a house full of Bangladeshis and worked in an organization composed of Bangladeshis; there were no other westerners around. At first my housemates and co-workers were warm and friendly, but after about a week, they cooled toward me. I kept asking people if I had done something to offend them but got no response until one woman who had lived in the United States explained that I had insulted them by not going to their homes for dinner. "But they haven't invited me," I protested. She told me that I had to just go and show up at their homes at dinnertime and invite myself in.

Growing up in the United States, I never went to someone's house for dinner unless I was invited by them. In the back of my head was the understanding that it is rude to go to someone's house at dinnertime and expect to be fed without an invitation. "That's impolite," I told the woman. "No it isn't," she said. "Where you come from that is impolite. Not here." It was a simple thing, but it made me think. I started a mental inventory of all the beliefs, values, and concepts that I considered the truth without having ever questioned them: I started unpacking my paradigm.

Paradigms are so pervasive and invisible that they can be easily mistaken for truth. When this happens, we limit our creativity in finding solutions to the problems we face, since our thinking is cramped and predefined by society's dominant framework. For example, if your culture believes the earth is flat, you're unlikely to explore what lies beyond the horizon. If your paradigm views nature as a reservoir of supplies intended for meeting humanity's needs, you treat nature very differently than if your paradigm holds nature as a sacred, complex system of which humans are just one part. If your framework says that economic growth is the key to ending poverty and bringing about happiness, then you protect growth at all costs even when it makes many people poorer and less happy.

Unfortunately many organizations and political leaders working to improve environmental and social conditions operate unquestioningly from within the paradigm. However, to paraphrase Einstein, problems cannot be solved from within the same paradigm in which they were created. A prime example is the cap and trade approach to reducing greenhouse gas emissions. In this scenario, private companies are permitted to sell their "right" to pollute to other companies, which can then pollute more, in the belief that the free hand of the market will find the most efficient opportunities for greenhouse gas reductions. But viewing pollution as a "right" and relying on the market to solve environmental problems reinforces the very paradigm that got us into this mess. In a different paradigm, human health and ecological survival would be paramount, and industrial activities that undermine these goals would be prohibited outright. The right to clean air and a healthy climate would trump the right to pollute.

Before we can change a paradigm, we need to identify it as a paradigm rather than assume it is truth. In the film *The Matrix*, the dominant paradigm is the simulated reality that was created by machines in order to subdue the human population while their bodies' heat and electromagnetic activity are used as energy sources for the machines. The first thing that the band of rebels led by Morpheus does is "unplug": they take the red pill to see the Matrix for what it is. I believe that examining the hidden impacts of all the Stuff in our lives is a way to unplug, which is the first step toward changing things.

Donella Meadows worked for years to identify the leverage points where a "small shift in one thing can produce big changes in everything."[22] Over time she developed a hierarchy of leverage points, from those that make incremental but immediate change to those that can fundamentally change the entire system. At the top of the hierarchy is challenging and changing a paradigm itself, because a shift in the paradigm immediately changes everything.[23] For me, this fact is a huge source of hope and optimism. Although changing a paradigm can take generations, it can also happen in a second, when a person suddenly sees things in a new light, as I did standing aside the Fresh Kills landfill.

The Story of Stuff

My journeys led me to realize that the issue of garbage was related to the whole of the materials economy: to the extraction of natural resources, like mining and logging; to the chemistry labs and the factories where Stuff was designed and produced; to the international warehouses and stores where Stuff was shipped and trucked and then stuck with impossibly low price tags; to the clever television advertisements created with the help of psychologists to hook a consumer's attention. I learned about international financial and trade institutions like the World Bank, International Monetary Fund, and World Trade Organization; corporations like Chevron, Wal-Mart, and Amazon; indigenous tribes protecting rainforests in Ecuador, seamstresses making Disney nightgowns in Haiti, the Ogoni fighting Shell in Nigeria, communities along Cancer Alley in Louisiana, and cotton-field laborers in Uzbekistan—and all of these processes and institutions and communities turned out to be part of the same story! As environmental economist Dr. Jeffrey Morris explained when I asked about true cost accounting for my laptop, "Take any item and trace back to its true origins, and you find it takes the whole economy to make anything."[24]

As I pieced together the whole trajectory of the dysfunctional system, I discovered a number of different groups approaching these issues from many different angles. There are the super serious "wonks" in the fields of science, economics, or policy, armed with their true yet terrifying statistics and facts which, unfortunately, tend to inspire panic and despair that shuts people down as opposed to motivating them to take action. Then there are shrill voices waggling their fingers at bad consumers, relying on guilt to motivate mass change in resource consumption, rarely with much success. There are the downshifters, those who voluntarily live simply, unplugging from commercial culture, working and buying less. While they can effectively model a way to live besides take-make-waste, they're largely unable to get cultural traction beyond their communities. Similar to those who believe that technological improvements will save us, there are the conscious-consumption folks, who believe if we just provide enough of a market for greener products and processes, if we buy *this* instead of *that*, all will be well. (Those are the ones who inevitably ask at the end of my presentation, "OK, so what *should* I buy?") There are also green designers, working to make our products and homes safer while they're still in the idea stage. And of course there are all the activists and campaigners working on their issue of choice, as I did for many years.

For my part, I wanted to figure out how to talk about the materials economy and its underlying paradigm of economic growth by drawing on the best from each of the existing approaches and encouraging a broader systems perspective but without getting bogged down in technical jargon, guilt, or despair.

My goal with this book (and the film upon which it's based) is to unpack the Story of Stuff—the flow of materials through the economy—as simply as possible. My aim is never to make you feel guilty (unless you are the head of Chevron, Dow Chemical, Disney, Fox News, Halliburton, McDonald's, Shell, or the World Bank); it should be clear that the fundamental problem I identify here is not individual behavior and poor lifestyle choices, but the broken system—the deadly take-make-waste machine. I hope reading the Story helps inspire you to share information with people in your life about issues like toxics in cosmetics, the problems with incineration and recycling, and the flaws in the IMF's economic policies. I do my best to explain or just avoid the technical jargon of fields like chemistry, supply chain theory, and trade policies, which too often excludes people from this critical conversation.

In the face of so many tough challenges, there are many exciting and hopeful developments that I celebrate in these pages and that I see as steps toward a truly sustainable ecological-economic system. Above all, I invite the citizen in you to become louder than the consumer inside you and launch a very rich, very loud dialogue within your community.

A few points of clarification:

1. I'm not against Stuff.

In fact, I'm pro-Stuff! I want us to value our Stuff *more,* to care for it, to give it the respect it deserves. I want us to recognize that each thing we buy involved all sorts of resources and labor. Someone mined the earth for the metals in your cell phone; someone unloaded the bales from the cotton gin for your T-shirt. Someone in a factory assembled that pair of sunglasses, and they might have been exposed to carcinogens or forced to work overtime. Someone drove or flew this bouquet around the country or the world to get it to you. We need to understand the true value of our Stuff, far beyond the price tag and far beyond the social status of ownership. Stuff should be long-lasting, made with the pride of an artisan and cared for accordingly.

Like most average Americans, I have plenty of Stuff and I battle clutter. However, I do try to avoid buying Stuff, especially new Stuff, that I don't need. I buy furniture, kitchenware, sporting equipment, and just about everything I can from secondhand sources, which prevents new waste from being made during production. That also allows me to buy higher quality, longer-lasting Stuff than I could afford if buying it new. And then I take good care of it. I get my shoes resoled; I mend my clothes; I bring in my bike from the rain so it will last as absolutely long as possible.

2. I'm not romanticizing poverty.

When I point out the flaws in our overconsumptive U.S. lifestyle and praise the slower-paced and less materialistic countries that I've visited, I am not romanticizing poverty. Poverty is a wretched and intolerable reality, an outcome of the broken economic model that maldistributes resources. I don't wish that kind of existence for anybody, ever. I once visited an Indian boarding school that had just lost half a dozen kids to malaria, where I realized the medicine that could have saved them costs less than I pay for a cup of coffee at home. For those kids, and others without enough food, medicine, shelter, schools, and other basic goods, more money and more Stuff definitely helps. But once our basic needs are met, it's been proven that a focus on getting more and more Stuff actually undermines happiness. (See chapter 4 on consumption for details.)

In the United States we work more hours than folks in almost any other industrialized country in the world, and two of our main activities in our scant leisure time are TV watching and shopping. So we go to work, come home exhausted, and plop down in front of the TV; the commercials tell us we need new Stuff to feel better about ourselves, so we go shopping; and in order to pay for it all, we have to work even more. I call this the work-watch-spend treadmill.

What I'm appreciating about countries

that aren't as stuck on this treadmill as the United States has nothing to do with poverty. Instead, I admire societies where people work fewer hours, are guaranteed longer vacations, watch less TV, spend more time with their friends and neighbors . . . and waste less of their energy on Stuff. You could even say I romanticize that lifestyle: I'm OK with that.

3. I'm not bashing the United States.

There are some sweet things about life in the United States. Many of the technological advances and consumer options we have here have added to our quality of life. But after having traveled to forty countries, I also know that there are places from which we could learn a thing or two. I'm envious of my friends in Europe who aren't stressed about how to pay for their health care or their university education. I wish we had subway systems as clean, quiet, and prompt as the ones in Seoul and Montreal. I wish it was as pleasurable and safe to bike in U.S. cities as it is in the Netherlands. I wish our rates of obesity, diabetes, and other health problems weren't topping the charts. I don't believe it is U.S. bashing to point out that we're losing ground on some serious quality of life issues. On the contrary, I think it's patriotic to express a desire to aim higher and fix what's not working. I think of it as a tribute to my country's incredible potential.

A WORD ABOUT WORDS

Americans:

The Americas are, of course, far larger than the United States, including Canada, the Caribbean, and all of Latin America to our south. I'm therefore aware that it's inaccurate to refer to the citizens and residents of the United States as "Americans." But using "citizens and residents of the United States" repeatedly is a mouthful. Another term, *états-unisians* (French for "United Statesian") is catching on in international circles but hasn't made it to our own shores yet. So, with apologies to folks in the rest of the Americas, I use the word in this book to mean that mouthful: people living here in the United States. Similarly, all amounts given in dollars ($) refer to U.S. dollars.

Consumer/Consumption:

The word "consume" originally meant to destroy, as by fire or disease, to squander, to use up. That's where the old-fashioned term for the disease tuberculosis, "consumption," came from. That means that a consumer society is a society of destroyers and squanderers. No thank you.

Michael Maniates, a professor of political science and environmental science at Allegheny College, says perhaps we should rename most of what goes on in various life stages of Stuff—extraction, production, even distribution—and call it all consumption.[1] When we cut down a virgin forest to make disposable wooden chopsticks, wrapping them in paper and then burning fossil fuel to ship them halfway around the world, aren't all those processes, not really production but simply consumption, aka destruction? Yes. In fact, when we talk about national rates of resource consumption, all those things such as how much wood or oil the United States consumes, are included.

However, in the chapter in this book on consumption, I am using the common definition, focusing on the slice of consumption that involves consumers purchasing and using Stuff.

Corporations:

Some people have complained that the Story of Stuff film unfairly portrays all corporations as evil. For the record, corporations are not inherently good or evil. A corporation is just a legal entity. It's how the corporation is run that makes it an asset or a detriment to the broader society. I know that many people within corporations do care about the planet and people and are working to lessen their company's environmental impact. Some are going further, striving to be a force for positive change. Unfortunately though, there are some structural aspects of corporations that make them less than ideal neighbors—or planet-mates.

First, some have gotten so big and powerful that they have disproportionately large influence and impact, increasingly overwhelming the democratic process. Of the hundred largest economies in the world, over half are corporations—ahead of most countries.[2] When corporations control such a huge percentage of global resources, it's pretty hard to reign them in when they start trashing the planet, as far too many do. In 2007, the 60,000-plus multinational corporations controlled half the world's oil, gas, and coal and generated half the gases responsible for global warming.[3] In the United States, corporations are legally beholden above all else to make profit for their shareholders. So entities with a number one goal of short-term profit control much of the world's energy resources, the unbridled use of which is throwing our entire global climate into disarray.

In addition to their size and influence, corporations benefit from a number of legal and structural mechanisms that grant them powerful rights while allowing them to avoid many responsibilities. For example, U.S. corporations enjoy the same protection of rights under the U.S. Constitution as individuals—aka "personhood." At the same time, legal mechanisms exist that protect corporate shareholders with what's known as limited liability.

Even with these structural challenges, some corporations have taken steps to protect people and the planet while still making a profit (which, again, they are legally obligated to prioritize). Some corporations have made good progress toward using fewer resources, eliminating toxics, creating less waste, and respecting workers and host communities.

Yet voluntary codes of conduct or the good intentions of those currently in charge have proven not to be enough. Both the corporate structure and the surrounding regulatory system need to be changed: we should do away with limited liability and "personhood" under the Constitution and demand an increase in corporate accountability, stronger antitrust laws and international liability, the extraction of corporations out of the political process, extended producer responsibility, internalized (vs. externalized) costs, and total stakeholder responsibility (and it should be recognized that stakeholders include workers, fence-line communities, consumers, vendors, etc. All these will facilitate corporations becoming less of a problem and more of the solution).

Development:

Intuitively we understand that "development" has to do with things getting better. Unfortunately, too often development has come to refer to progress toward implementing a fossil-fuel-intensive, toxics-laden, consumption-driven economy. Thus, small towns in Costa Rica with high life expectancy, literacy, and life satisfaction may still be considered less "developed" than U.S. cities with higher rates of environmental degradation, social inequality, and stress.

The international "development" institutions, such as the United States Agency for International Development (USAID) and the World Bank's International Bank for Reconstruction and Development, have too often pushed policies and projects that promote a model of economic growth that makes things worse, not better, for people and the planet.

We need to keep our eye on the goals: human and environmental well-being. If new infrastructure, urbanization, and resource consumption contribute to those goals, great, that's real development. But if they start undermining well-being, then that's destruction, not development. Some advances, especially in medicine and communication, are clearly positive. Other things that generally come when a country advances down this path, like toxic body burdens and greenhouse gas emissions, are anything but.

Throughout this book, I've used the terms "developing" and "developed" as shorthand and as they are commonly used. I don't mean to imply a value judgment: so-called developed countries are not better than those designated as developing. The same global socioeconomic divide is sometimes described as the Global North or OECD countries (Organisation for Economic Co-operation and Development) versus the Global South or non-OECD. (North versus South are not strict geographical references; for example, the wealthy nations of Australia and New Zealand occupy the Southern Hemisphere. Likewise, in many countries in the Global South, some communities enjoy "Northern" levels of resource consumption.)

All the terms are imperfect. For simplicity's sake, I chose to use the "developing/developed" designation.

Externalized Costs (and Price versus Cost):

Bargains abound: rock-bottom prices at big-box stores, discount outlets, online auction sites, even 99-cent stores. Yet there's an unhealthy illusion at work there, a serious gap between the price you pay and the costs involved. The number on the price tag has very little to do with the costs involved in making Stuff. Sure, some of the direct costs like labor and material are included in the price, but those are dwarfed by externalized, hidden costs like the pollution of drinking water, health impacts on workers and host communities, even changes in the global climate. Who pays for these things? Sometimes it is the local communities, who now have to buy bottled water or filters or drink toxic water, since their local water is contaminated. Or the workers, who pay health care or disability costs themselves. Or future generations, who, for example, will pay by being unable to rely on forests to moderate the water cycles. Since these costs are paid by people and organizations outside the companies responsible for incurring them, they're called externalized costs. Economists define externalized cost as "an unintended or uncompensated loss in the welfare of one party resulting from an activity by another party."[4]

The good news is that a growing number of economists are attempting to capture these ecological and social costs in the price of consumer goods through approaches like full cost accounting or life cycle assessments so we can better understand the real cost of making all our Stuff. Prepare yourself for the sticker shock when those hidden costs become visible.

Organic:

These days we usually hear this word in reference to agriculture, to describe things like vegetables, dairy products, or cotton fibers raised without petrochemicals, sewage sludge, or genetically modified organisms, among other bad inputs. Although I sometimes refer to this agricultural meaning, more often I mean "organic" in the language of chemistry, where it indicates that a substance contains carbon. That's important for two reasons. First, because our human bodies (and the bodies of all living things), being carbon-containing themselves, have all kinds of biological/chemical interactions with and reactions to carbon-containing Stuff. So for example the pesticides made of organophosphates (parathion and malathion) and organochlorides (such as DDT) permanently deactivate an enzyme that is essential to the nervous system. That's why people with pesticide poisoning often twitch and shake, experience blurry vision, and lose control of their bladder and bowels.[5]

Second, the massive development of organic chemicals is relatively new, with many health and environmental impacts yet to be understood. Unlike the inorganic (i.e., non-carbon-containing) compounds like metal, stone, and clay, which we've been using for millennia, it's just in the last century, especially since World War II that scientists have been going nuts developing new organic compounds. The result, according to Ken Geiser, author of *Materials Matter,* "has been a near revolution in one century in materials production and consumption."[6]

Stuff:

When I say "Stuff" in this book, I mean manufactured or mass-produced goods, including packaging, iPods, clothes, shoes, cars, toasters, marshmallow shooters (this last from the SkyMall catalog). In the book I don't extend the meaning to include resources, like logs and barrels of oil. I focus here on Stuff we buy, maintain, lose, break, replace, stress about, and with which we confuse our personal self-worth. Stuff as I define it here is also known as "crap." You could substitute the word "goods" every time you see the word "Stuff," but since goods are so often anything but good—i.e., excessively packaged, toxics laden, unnecessary, and destructive of the planet—I don't like to use that term.

Sustainability:

This word gets thrown around all the time now, and it's not always clear what's intended. Perhaps the most common definition of sustainability evolved from the United Nations World Commission on Environment and Development's description of sustainable development: *meeting the needs of the current generation without compromising the ability of future generations to meet their own needs.*[7]

My definition of sustainability includes a couple of other key concepts. For one thing, sustainability must include equity and justice. As astrophysicist and writer Robert Gilman defines it, "sustainability is equity over time."[8] Also, sustainability requires looking at the big picture, not just the sustainability of a specific forest or the climate in isolation, not just our household or city or country, but the whole enchilada. The Center for Sustainable Communities says that sustainability "consider[s] the whole instead of the specific. Sustainability emphasizes relationships rather than pieces in isolation."[9]

KEY TO RECURRING GRAPHICS

A Sign of Hope:

This drawing indicates that progress is being made on this issue, for example that there is growing awareness of the problem, inspiring citizen action or legislation in progress that will improve the situation.

Another Way:

This symbol means I'm presenting a viable alternative to the problematic status quo, for example green chemists developing safe compounds to replace the toxins used in production processes.

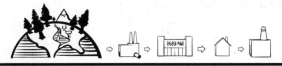

CHAPTER 1

EXTRACTION

In order to make all the Stuff in our lives, we first need to get the ingredients. Now, some of these don't occur naturally—the man-made synthetic compounds—and we'll cover them too. However, many ingredients for our Stuff exist inside the earth or on its surface. They only need to be harvested or extracted . . . Only!

Once we start examining them, we soon find that each key ingredient requires a lot of *other* ingredients just to get it out of the earth, processed, and ready for use. In the case of paper, for example, we don't just need trees. We need metals to make the chainsaws and logging machines; trucks, trains, and even ships to cart the logs to processing plants; and oil to run all those machines and the plants themselves. We need water (a lot of it) for making the paper pulp. We usually need a chemical like bleach (no!) or hydrogen peroxide (better) to get a desirably light shade of paper. All in all, making one ton of paper requires the use of 98 tons of various other resources.[1] And believe me when I say that's a pretty simple example. That's why we have to look at the whole materials economy, and often a map of the world, to get a clear picture of the ingredients that go into any one product on store shelves these days.

98 TONS OF MATERIAL

1 TON PAPER

There are lots of ways to think about the various resources that come from the earth. For simplicity's sake I'll use just three categories: trees, rocks, and water.

Trees

As I said in the introduction, having grown up in Seattle, a green city in an even greener state, I love trees. Half of the land area in Washington State is covered in forests,[2] and I visited them every chance I had. Over the course of my childhood I watched in dismay as more and more forests gave way to roads and malls and houses.

As I grew older, I learned that there are more than sentimental reasons to worry about the fate of our trees. Trees create oxygen, which—may I remind us—we need to breathe. That alone would seem sufficient motivation for us to keep them intact. As the lungs of the planet, forests work around the clock to remove carbon dioxide from the air (a process called carbon sequestration) and give us oxygen in return. These days scientists concerned about climate change research all sorts of elaborate, expensive, man-made schemes to sequester carbon from the atmosphere in hopes of moderating climate change. Seems like a waste if you ask me. We already have a natural system that not only sequesters carbon but also provides the exact kind of air we need to breathe: our trees. And their services are free! It doesn't get much better than that.

And there's more—forests provide other vital services. They collect and filter our fresh water, maintaining the planet's overall hydrologic cycle and moderating floods and droughts. They maintain soil health by keeping the nutrient-rich topsoil in place. What are we *thinking*, destroying these obvious allies?

To name just one more reason that it's a terrible idea to cut down forests: one-quarter of all our prescription drugs are derived from forests—rainforests in particular.[3] Curare, an anesthetic and muscle relaxant used in surgery[4]; ipecac, for treating dysentery[5]; and quinine, for malaria[6] are just a few examples. Not long ago, western chemists were turned on to a plant native to the tropical forests of Madagascar, the rosy periwinkle, after learning that the island's healers used it to treat diabetes. It turns out the pink-flowering plant has anticancer properties, and is now used to make the medicines vincristine and vinblastine. The former is used to treat Hodg-kin's disease, and the latter has proven to be a total wonder drug for those suffering from childhood leukemia, who now have a 95 percent chance of survival, up from their previous slim 10 percent chance before the plant was discovered.[7]

(Unfortunately, even though sales of the two drugs are in the hundreds of millions of dollars per year, almost none of this money winds up in the hands of the people in Madagascar, which is one of the poorest countries in the world.[8] This will be a recurring theme.)

It's nuts to be wiping out forests anywhere on the globe, but it's especially crazy to be clearing the tropical rainforests because they contain such rich-ness of biodiversity. Generally, the closer forests are to the equator, the greater the diversity of trees and other species they contain. A twenty-five-acre plot of rainforest in Borneo, for instance, can contain more than seven hundred species of trees, which is equal to the total number of tree species in all of North America.[9]

And the plants and other life we've discovered so far are just the begin-ning; most scientists estimate that only 1 percent of the species that exist in the rainforest (and only there) have been identified and examined for their beneficial properties.[10]

If the loss wasn't so tragic, it would be ironic that these invaluable repos-itories of not-yet-discovered useful chemicals are being cleared in the name of "progress" and "development." It seems to me a far wiser development strategy would be protecting these forests that will potentially heal our ills (as well as provide the air we breathe, clean our waters, and moderate our climate).

When I was kid savoring my time camping out in the forest, I hadn't ever heard of carbon sequestration, hydrologic cycles, or plant-derived pharmaceuticals. Instead, one big reason I loved forests was the many animals that lived in them. Forests provide homes for about two-thirds of the species on earth[11]—from koala bears, monkeys, and leopards to butterflies, lizards, parrots, you name it. Cutting down these homes, espe-cially in areas of rich biodiversity like tropical rainforests, leads to the extinction of as many as one hundred species a day.[12] One hundred species per day? For some perspective, think of all the dogs you've ever seen; worldwide, they make up fewer than ten species (genus *Canis*).[13] And there's only *one* species of human! Losing one hundred species a day is a big deal. Those species could contain miracle medicines or could play some vital irreplaceable role in the food chain. Wiping them out is like throwing out our lottery ticket before we have even checked if we had the winning number.

Imagine for a minute that some other species (maybe *Periplaneta fuliginosa,* aka the smokybrown cockroach) had control over the planet and was eradicating one hundred species per day to satisfy their appetites. What would we say about them? We might think their actions were a little unfair. What would we *do* about them? Lead an insurrection? Of course, we might not have a chance—from one day to the next we could just be extinguished, along with ninety-nine other lesser species.

And trees don't just house wildlife—around the world about 300 million *people* live in forests, while about 60 million indigenous people are almost wholly dependent on them.[14] Forests are the main source of life for more than a billion people living in extreme poverty.[15] Forests provide the "four F's" essential for survival: food, fodder, fiber, and fuel. From healthy forests, indigenous, tribal, or other forest-dwelling communities gather or hunt for food, feed livestock, obtain materials to build homes, and collect firewood for cooking and heat.

As I was growing up in Seattle, my primary relationship with forests was based on a fifth F: fun. I relied on the forests for hiking, camping, birding, and cross-country skiing, not for building materials. If I needed a snack, I'd head for the fridge, not the forest. Even after studying the issue, my understanding of the connection between forests and immediate survival was academic, not experiential. It wasn't until I went overseas that I realized how directly forests sustain life in other countries.

While traveling in the once lush Haitian countryside, I met families who had lost their homes after forests were cleared. After the destruction of the roots that held the soil in place and moderated water flows following a heavy rain, mudslides took the homes of those families. No forests, no flood control. In India, I saw women walking miles a day to collect branches to feed cows, patch roofs, or cook rice. No forests, no fodder, fiber, or fuel. Forests are essential to life. The values of all these kinds of services dwarf the price of timber from a felled forest.

In fact, economists are working to calculate the monetary benefits that forests produce. In October 2008, the European Union undertook a study to put a dollar value on the forest services that we're losing through deforestation each year. This study, published in *The Economics of Ecosystems and Biodiversity* report, warns that the cost to the global economy from the loss of forests is far greater than the economic losses incurred up to that point in the banking crisis that garnered so much media attention and government action that year. Further, the report points out, the losses from deforestation aren't a one-time fiasco, but continuous, year after year.[16] By evaluating the many services that forests perform and figuring out how much it would cost for humans to adapt to their losses and provide these services themselves, the study calculated the cost of forest loss at between $2 trillion and $5 trillion, or about 7 percent of global GDP *each year.*[17] Now, if that doesn't merit a bailout on both economic and environmental grounds, I am not sure what does.

Despite the implications, even though they provide frames for our houses and our lifesaving medicines, even though they filter our water and create the air we breathe, we're still cutting down forests at break-neck speed. Globally, we've been losing more than 7 million hectares a year, or 20,000 hectares—almost 50,000 acres—a day.[18] This is equivalent to an area twice the size of Paris each day, or about thirty-three football fields' worth every minute.[19] According to Rainforest Action Network, fifty thousand species of trees go extinct every year.[20]

Rates of forest loss are especially high in Africa, Latin America, the Caribbean, and much of Asia. According to reports, the exceptions are China and India, where large investments in forest plantations skew the data to hide the ongoing rates of loss of natural forests.[21] However, industrial timber plantations are very different from real forests. The goal of a plantation is to produce wood products, with little or no regard to the many other services, resources, and habitat that real forests provide. To this end, they are generally intensely managed, evenly spaced, monoculture fields of imported species with the highest wood yields. Such plantations simply don't hold a candle to the real thing in terms of biological diversity, resistance to disease, or provision of the many other nontimber forest products that people and animals depend on for survival. Tree plantations can generally only sustain 10 percent of the species that lived in the forests that preceded them[22] and are best described as "green deserts." They also provide relatively few jobs, increase the use of pesticides, and negatively impact local water cycles.[23]

So scientists, climatologists, and economists—not to mention all the animals and other people—concur that we need real nonplantation forests.

Yet we continue to cut those down—not only in the biodiversity hot spots in the tropics, but also right here at home, in the temperate forests of the Pacific Northwest.

I got to see this firsthand during the summer of 1980, when I spent more time in the forests than out of them. It was the summer after tenth grade, and I signed up to work for the Youth Conservation Corps, or YCC. The YCC was a federal program, established a decade earlier to get kids out of the city, in some cases off of the street, and into the woods for a summer of service and learning. We worked hard, learned about natural systems, and earned a modest salary as well as a sense of purpose. It was my first experience with what my colleague Van Jones would later call "green-collar jobs."

My YCC site was in the North Cascades National Park in Washington State, a breathtakingly gorgeous region with terrain ranging from alpine peaks and glaciers dotted with crystal blue lakes that literally sparkled in the sun to lowland forests, from mossy dark green water-soaked temperate rainforests to dry ponderosa pine ecosystems. Even for a forest connoisseur like me, this was truly a special place.

Jack Kerouac, who spent a summer there about twenty years before I did, does justice to the area in *The Dharma Bums*: "It was a river wonderland, the emptiness of the golden eternity, odors of moss and bark and twigs and mud, all ululating mysterious visionstuff before my eyes, tranquil and everlasting nonetheless, the hillhairing trees, the dancing sunlight . . . The pine boughs looked satisfied washing in the waters. The top trees shrouded in gray fog looked content. The jiggling sunshine leaves of Northwest breeze seemed bred to rejoice. The upper snows on the horizon, the trackless, seemed cradled and warm. Everything was everlastingly loose and responsive, it was all everywhere beyond the truth, beyond emptyspace blue."[24]

Amidst this incredible natural beauty, my new YCC friends and I spent our days clearing fallen tree limbs from hiking trails, burying campfire remnants from careless campers, tending to the local salmon hatchery, and learning about the forest ecosystem from college students whose expertise and worldliness awed me. The program worked—at least for me it did. I entered that summer loving forests because of the way I felt in them: secure, grounded, humbled in the presence of something that seemed divine. I ended the summer realizing that our rivers, the fish, and the planet as we know it depended on forests. I left with a solid commitment to protect them.

That summer, I saw my first clear-cuts up close. "Clear-cutting" is the term for aggressive logging that removes all the trees in an area. All the roots, all the wildflowers, all the life. The ground is shaved clean like the head of a prison inmate, so nothing but scattered stumps and drying brown brush remains. I've heard clear-cut sites compared to ravaged, pock-marked bomb sites like Baghdad. That's an apt description. Previously, I'd see them from the windows of a plane or just driving past, getting away as fast as we could. But that summer, we hiked in them to see how different they felt from a forest. We sampled water in the creeks that ran below them, to see the changes in temperature, oxygen, and aquatic life. It was shocking to me to see how far the damage spread, far beyond the scorched boundaries of the cut.

In contrast to forests, which act like giant sponges that hold water in their leaves and trunks and among their roots, regulating its flow into streams and rivers, clear-cut areas don't hold soil and don't absorb water. During heavy rains, water just runs off clear-cut hills, causing mudslides, flooding, and erosion. Waterlogged earth comes down in landslides, clogging waterways and burying communities. Downstream, the water and mud destroys property and sometimes injures or kills people. In some cases, millions of dollars of government money is required to repair the damage. In other places, the people just bear the cost themselves, sometimes losing everything they have. And of course the damage impacts the entire delicate web of life dependent on forests: the fungi that grow in the roots of trees feed small mammals, which feed birds like owls and hawks, and so on.

For me, that summer in the North Cascades gave new meaning to something that early wilderness advocate John Muir once said: "When we try to pick out anything by itself, we find it hitched to everything else in the universe." [25] I had heard that quote previously but had thought it referred to metaphorical connections. In fact, he meant it literally—the whole planet is, in fact, connected. The forests to the rivers to the ocean to the cities to our food to us.

The clear-cuts brought to mind the traditional folk hero image of a lumberjack: a smiling bearded guy wearing blue jeans and a plaid flannel shirt and holding an axe. His picture adorned local diners and bottles of maple syrup. If logging ever was like that, it sure isn't anymore. Nearly all the flannel-clad guys with axes have long since been replaced with huge belching machinery: massive bulldozers, cranes, gigantic pincher things that pick up the logs in their huge metal claws to pile them on huge trucks. And while machines have taken the place of many human workers, they haven't removed the risks for those workers who remain. Falling trees, heavy machinery, rough terrain, and weather all contribute to the International Labour Organization identifying logging as one of the three most dangerous occupations in most countries.[26]

And for what? There must be some darn good reasons why we are we undermining our planet's health, destroying potentially valuable medicines, driving plants and animals to extinction, eliminating a much needed carbon storage sink, and harming loggers. Right?

A whole lot of forests get cut down to make way for cattle ranches, soy fields, and other agricultural products. Ironically, a short-sighted quest for plant-based alternatives to fossil fuels, called biofuels, is now a major driver of deforestation around the world as forests are cleared to grow palm and other oil crops. "Biofuels are rapidly becoming the main cause of deforestation in countries like Indonesia, Malaysia, and Brazil," says Simone Lovera, who works in Paraguay with the international environmental organization Global Forest Coalition. "We call it 'deforestation diesel.'"[27]

Forests are also cleared to make way for sprawl and so-called development. Trees are taken for lumber that goes to build homes and furniture. In many places in the world, millions of people depend on wood for heating and cooking. But excluding the trees used for fuel, the number-one thing made from trees is paper. Seemingly simple paper, then, is the main nonfuel product of deforestation. That doesn't just mean newspapers, magazines, posters, books, and Lands' End catalogs. There are about five thousand other kinds of products made with paper,[28] including money, board games, microwave packaging, and even the inserts of fancy running shoes.

In the United States, we're consuming more than 80 million tons of paper per year.[29] For our books alone, a 2008 report calculated the amount of paper consumed in the United States in 2006 as 1.6 million metric tons, or about 30 million trees.[30] For every ton of virgin office or copier paper, 2 to 3 tons of trees were cut down in some forest somewhere.[31] And there's no end in sight. Globally, paper consumption has increased sixfold in the last fifty years[32] and is projected to keep rising, with the United States leading the way. A typical office worker in the United States now uses more than ten thousand sheets of paper a year[33]; together we Americans use enough paper each year to build a ten-foot-high wall from New York City all the way to Tokyo.[34]

While there is a growing movement to make new paper from recycled or sustainably managed sources, most of the world's paper supply, about 71 percent, still comes from forests, not tree farms or the recycling bin.[35]

The current trajectory of forest loss is bleak, but there are opportunities to turn things around. Over the past generation, paper recycling has increased at both ends: more discarded paper is being recovered for recycling, and more companies are using recycled paper. We're closer to closing the loop and producing paper from paper, not from trees. The Environmental Paper Network (EPN) is a coalition of dozens of groups using market-based strategies to promote paper production from postconsumer recycled paper, agricultural waste, alternative fibers, or sustainably certified trees rather than virgin forests. Their members engage internationally in activities as varied as dialoguing with corporate CEOs and organizing large protests at stores and industry trade shows.[36] One EPN member, ForestEthics, has been especially successful at getting high-profile companies—including Office Depot, Staples, and Home Depot—to source sustainable wood and recycled paper. They have also targeted high-volume catalog offenders, most notably Victoria's Secret, to increase the use of recycled stock in their catalogs. Now they're upping the ante by campaigning to establish a national Do Not Mail Registry, like the Do Not Call Registry, to stop the incessant flow of junk mail to our homes. According to ForestEthics, more than 100 billion pieces of junk mail are delivered to U.S. households annually—more than eight hundred pieces per household—almost half of which (44 percent) is thrown away before being opened.[37] This consumes more than 100 million trees, equivalent to clear-cutting the entire Rocky Mountain National Park every four months.[38]

The thing is, we don't just use a lot of paper; we also *waste* a lot of paper. Almost 40 percent of the Stuff in U.S. municipal garbage is paper,[39] all of which is recyclable or compostable if it hasn't been treated with too many toxic chemicals. By simply recycling, rather than trashing, all this paper, we would reduce the pressure to cut more forests for our next ream. (We'd also reduce our garbage by 40 percent.) Of course, preventing the use of paper in the first place, as in the case with junk mail and catalogs, is even better than recycling.

Also, there are ways to harvest trees from forests without decimating the ecosystem and the communities that depend upon them. These environmentally preferable timber practices limit the intensity of timber harvest, reduce chemical use, maintain soil health, and protect wildlife and biodiversity. The potentially lower short-term profitability of implementing these practices, as opposed to clear-cutting the whole landscape, is far out-weighed by long-term environmental and social benefits.

One attempt to track and certify forests that adhere to these higher environmental standards is the Forest Stewardship Council (FSC), which is active in forty-five countries. Over the past thirteen years, more than 90 million hectares around the world have been certified according to FSC standards; several thousand products are made with FSC-certified wood and carry the FSC trademark.[40] While forest activists generally agree that the FSC isn't strong enough and should not be seen as a label of eco-purity, it is a good start. "The FSC is the best forest certification system out there," says Todd Paglia, director of ForestEthics, "and it needs to continue to get stronger. Compared to other comparable systems, like the timber industry's greenwashed program called the Sustainable Forestry Initiative, FSC is the clear choice."[41]

 Additionally, there's a promising model of forest management known as community forestry, a new school of thought in which forests are managed by communities and maintained to protect the sum of their contributions, i.e., not solely for logging. Actually, this isn't really a "new school of thought," since many rural and indigenous communities around the world have a long tradition of managing forests through the collective efforts of community members. At last others are beginning to see the enormous benefits of this approach.

Water

The summer I worked in the North Cascades National Park taught me about more than trees. I also spent a lot of time around rivers. We waded—if you can call being in water up to your neck "wading"—in icy waters that had recently been glaciers to retrieve trash left by campers and branches that blocked river channels. Plunging into glacier melt to pick up an empty Coke can is a great way to solidify a commitment never to drop a piece of trash in a body of water, ever.

It was there I first saw the profound difference between a river at the base of a clear-cut and one below a healthy, intact forest. The rivers below a clear-cut were cloudy, full of muck and debris, with fewer fish, bugs, and life of any kind. When we took samples of the water, we learned that the rivers below the clear-cuts had a higher biological oxygen demand, or BOD, which is a measure of how much organic matter is in the water. A low BOD indicates healthy water, and a too high BOD means polluted water.

Now, in farming or in the produce aisle, the label "organic" is a plus. This is not always the case in the worlds of biology and chemistry, where "organic" doesn't mean the absence of toxic pesticides. In biology, an organic substance is one that comes from living organisms. In chemistry, it is something that contains carbon among its elemental building blocks.

Organic material is part of nature, rivers included, and its presence is not by definition good or bad. As in many things, the dose makes the poison. Organic matter (like leaves or dead bugs) doesn't become a problem in water unless it builds up faster than it can be decomposed. The tiny bacteria whose job it is to decompose all that organic stuff need oxygen; when their workload increases, their demand for oxygen outpaces the supply, leading to oxygen-deprived rivers, on their way to becoming dead ones.

Healthy forest floors are covered with organic matter known as "humus," which is held in place by tree roots and shrubby plants. Humus decomposes just fine in the presence of bugs and oxygen, constantly replenishing the soil with its nutrients. In a clear-cut, the forests are wiped clear of tree roots and shrubs, leaving an exposed surface, so that come a rainstorm, all that nice rich soil rushes downhill into rivers and turns into a pollutant.

The rivers in the North Cascades feed multiple watersheds from which Washington State's population draws water for drinking, washing, and irrigation. The water eventually makes its way to Puget Sound, where I dug clams and splashed in the waves as a kid. The health of those rivers impacts the health of bodies of water—as well as bodies of fish, birds, and people—hundreds of miles away.

Talk about being hitched to everything else in the universe. Water is the natural resource where we can most clearly see the interconnectedness of systems—as children we learn that the rain comes down, fills our groundwater reserves, rivers, and gutters, evaporates from lakes and oceans, and gets stored in clouds, only to reappear in the form of rain and snow. Water's also not something only found out there in "the environment," external to us: our own bodies are 50 to 65 percent water, 70 percent for babies.[42]

But somehow, as we grow into adulthood, we learn to think about water in a very disconnected way. Pat Costner, a retired Greenpeace scientist, expert in waste issues, and author of a book called *We All Live Downstream: A Guide to Waste Treatment that Stops Water Pollution*, believes that our water-based sewage systems do us a deep psychological disservice. From the age at which we get potty-trained, we begin to think of water as a waste receptacle and associate water with waste. Costner and many other water activists frequently point out the absolute absurdity of using our most precious resource—water—to transport bodily eliminations to expensive high-tech plants where the water has to be "treated" to remove the sewage. Costner has gone so far as to suggest, only half jokingly, that new parents potty-train their kids in a sandbox to prevent the association of water and waste.[43]

There is a much better, cleaner, and saner solution: it's called a composting toilet, and the simple, waterless technology is perfectly ready to be implemented everywhere on earth, preserving our water from contamination and turning a would-be pollutant and health hazard into a valuable soil additive (which we especially need in those clear-cut areas where the nutrient-rich topsoil has washed away). Composting toilets are a win-win-win scenario. Good for the water. Good for soil. Good for plants. All around good.

Living in the United States, where our toilets gobble up gallons of water (even the low-flow ones, although they're an improvement), and where both warm and cold water are on tap day and night in more than 95 percent of households,[44] it is easy to forget how valuable and limited a resource this is. Once you've spent a while in a place with limited water, as I have, it is impossible to ever turn on that tap without feeling a rush of gratitude.

In 1993, I moved to Bangladesh to work with a local environmental organization in the country's capital, Dhaka, for six months. Bangladesh experiences tremendous regular water crises. There's often too much and there's often not enough. It's a low-lying country, basically a giant floodplain where three major rivers—the Brahmaputra, Meghna, and Ganges—all enter into the Bay of Bengal. During the monsoon season each year, about a third of the country floods. Really floods. Millions of people lose their homes. Entire communities of char dwellers—people who live on the islands of silt and soil formed in the constant shifting geography of the rivers—disappear.

Bangladesh's floods are getting worse for the same reasons that other environmental problems are getting worse. The clearing of forests upstream in the river basin—as far away as the Himalayas in India—causes greater runoff after rainstorms. Without the tree roots to hold the ground in place, the runoff carries more silt and soil, which settles in the rivers, making them shallower and more susceptible to flooding. Global climate change is raising sea levels, which, in a low-lying country like Bangladesh, means that the water levels in the ground itself are also rising, making the land less able to absorb water in times of heavy rains and floods. If sea levels rise 30 to 45 centimeters, as many scientists predict, about 35 million people will literally lose the ground beneath them and be forced to migrate inland from coastal areas.[45] More than once during my time there, the roads between my house and office in Dhaka were flooded so deep that the bicycle wheels of my rickshaw were completely beneath water.

Paradoxically, in a country that is increasingly under water, it can be hard to get water to drink. Millions of people in Bangladesh rely on surface water, such as ponds and ditches, which are frequently contaminated with human waste as well as agricultural and industrial pollutants. More than one hundred thousand kids die each year from diarrhea, an easily preventable condition linked to dirty water. Meanwhile many of the wells have been discovered to be contaminated with arsenic, which occurs naturally in the region. In 2008, up to 70 million Bangladeshis were regularly drinking water that doesn't meet World Health Organization standards.[46]

While I lived in Dhaka I shared a house with eight Bangladeshis. They drank the tap water, but since my body wasn't used to it, the two women who did the cooking constantly boiled pots of water for twenty minutes just for me. I was acutely aware of the imposition of using so much of our household's precious cooking fuel to prepare water for me to drink. You can be darn sure I didn't throw even one half glass of water into the sink in six months there. After traveling through the country, seeing communities with no access to water, and experiencing real, all-encompassing thirst for the first time in my life, I savored every sip of water I had. I appreciated the fact that this water was in a glass and not flooding my home. It is a very different way to drink water: full of awareness and gratitude.

Bathing in Bangladesh was also different. Every other morning, I got one bucket of cold water. That was it. Sometimes it was so cold that I could only bear a sponge bath to wash those parts of me that most needed it. I did have one other emergency option: I could take a rickshaw down to the fancy part of town to one of two luxury hotels—the Sheraton or the Sonargaon. In the women's restroom I'd spend a good twenty minutes scrubbing my hands and face with hot water before indulging in the only thing— besides hot baths—that I missed in Bangladesh: a really good cup of coffee.

Then I'd sit in the little café sipping my café au lait, listening in on the conversations of businessmen and aid workers at neighboring tables, aware of the sparkling water in the pool, aware that my cup of coffee required about 36 gallons of water to produce, and acutely aware that the only reason that such a grubby person as me was permitted to spend twenty minutes in their fancy bathroom was the color of my skin and the American Express card in my pocket. I wondered how different life would be for those hundred thousand kids who would die from lack of clean water during the next twelve months, if they each had one of those cards, or even a safe tap in their yards.

36 GALLONS OF WATER

1 CUP COFFEE

Having experienced the level of scarcity that is the norm for most of the world's people, I am now more aware of the many ways that so-called advanced societies take for granted the one substance, after air, that we most need to survive. Remember we don't just need it for drinking and bathing, but for growing our food too! Still, we let it pour down the drain when we brush our teeth, we dump everything from our poop to our hazardous waste in it, and we feed millions of gallons of it to our golf courses and lawns.

Did you know that in the United States we spend more than $20 billion a year on our lawns?[47] On average, we spend twenty-five hours a year mowing them, often with power mowers so notoriously inefficient that they consume 800 million gallons of gasoline a year.[48] And that's before we even get to the water use. We're pouring humongous amounts of this liquid treasure onto our lawns: about 200 gallons of water per person, per day during the growing season is used just to water lawns. In some communities, that amounts to more than half of the total residential water use![49] In the United States, the lawn, or "turfgrass," is the single largest irrigated crop, three times larger than corn.[50] Simply by replanting lawns with native plants that use less water and allow more rainwater to seep into the soil, rather than run off into drainage systems, U.S. homeowners could drastically reduce their water use at home.

As you may have guessed, we also use up a lot of this vital, precious resource to make our Stuff.

In fact, from my short list of key ingredients, water is the most fundamental one of all, because it's a necessary input for virtually every industrial production process. Consider the fact that paper-making plants use 300 to 400 tons of water to make 1 ton of paper, if none of the water is reused or recirculated.[51] Growing the cotton for one T-shirt requires 256 gallons of water.[52] To get your morning cup of coffee, 36 gallons of water are used to grow, produce, package, and ship the beans.[53] Producing a typical U.S. car requires more than fifty times its weight in water, or more than 39,000 gallons.[54] Much of the water used in producing these goods is badly contaminated by the chemicals used in the production processes, like bleach (for paper or white T-shirts), lead, arsenic, and cyanide (for mining metals). There is always the danger that these toxins will leach into groundwater or overflow from holding containers into rivers and seas—if the water's not dumped there directly, as is still too often the case.

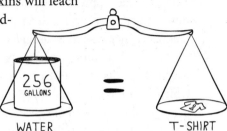

WATER   T-SHIRT

Water is also necessary to power the machines that make our Stuff. I'm not just talking about hydropower (electricity derived from the force of moving water); all power generated from fossil fuels such as coal, fuel oil, and natural gas is converted in thermal power plants that need water to cool them down. Together these make up the great majority of the world's energy sources, and they all use water.

So for all these purposes we need water, and we're running out of it. Maybe you're asking how can that be, on a blue planet that's way more than half covered in water? Of all the water on earth, 97.5 percent is salt water; and most of the 2.5 percent that is fresh water is frozen in the icecaps or so deep underground in aquifers that we can't reach it.[55] Only about 1 percent of the world's water is accessible for direct human use.[56] This includes the water we see in lakes, rivers, and reservoirs as well as those underground sources that are shallow enough to be tapped affordably. Only this 1 percent is regularly renewed by rain and snowfall and is available to us on a sustainable basis. So we're in trouble if we use too much.

It is that same 1 percent of water we use to meet all our needs for drinking, sanitation, irrigation, and industrial use. Increases in population, urbanization, industrialization, and consumption all mean that demand for water also increases. We're using and wasting more water than ever before while the supply of clean available water is shrinking. During the last century, our use of water globally increased sixfold, which was twice the rate of population growth.[57] There are more of us using more water. This is not a sustainable trajectory.

Already, about one-third of the world's population lives in countries that are experiencing water stress.[58] Despite all our technological know-how, at least one in six people doesn't have access to safe drinking water. Every day, thousands of people—mostly children—die from preventable diseases contracted because they do not have access to clean water.[59] In Asia, where water has always been regarded as an abundant resource, the amount of it available for each person declined by 40 to 60 percent between 1955 and 1990.[60] Experts predict that by 2025, fully three-quarters of people on earth will experience water scarcity, a condition in which the demand for water outstrips the supply.[61] Overuse of water, along with droughts, contamination, climate disruption, diversion for industrial or agricultural uses, and inequality in access to water all contribute to water scarcity.

As water becomes increasingly scarce, conflicts are emerging all over the world about its use, and perhaps more important, about the process by which its use is determined. Many people—myself included—fear that the growing phenomenon of private business interests managing water systems for profit is incompatible with ensuring everyone's right to water and sustainable water management. Too often, the privatization of water systems has been followed by rate hikes, service interruptions, and an overall decline in access to water because there is often not money to be made in delivering water to the poorest communities.

Because water is absolutely essential to life, including the lives of future generations, it should be shared and allocated fairly. Programs to manage water must be developed in this context, prioritizing long-term sustainability, ecological integrity, community participation in decision making, and fair access rather than individual private gain. A global movement is calling for water to be managed publicly rather than by private firms, while a network of "water justice" activists are working for a binding United Nations convention that secures every person's right to water. Already, General Comment No. 15, adopted in 2002 by the UN Committee on Economic, Social and Cultural Rights, recognized that the right to water is a prerequisite for realizing all other human rights and for living in dignity.[62]

Still, a number of giant multinational companies are working to privatize public water systems in the United States and around the world, making decisions based on market opportunities and potential profit rather than meeting basic human needs and ensuring ecological well-being and social justice. These corporations are working to expand the market for bottled water and to sell "bulk" water, which will be transported miles to its new market. As communities run out of their own water, they'll be forced to pay for it from other regions if there is no other option. For this reason, *The Economist* magazine has predicted that "water is the oil of the 21st century."[63]

The fact is, as with most of our dilemmas around diminishing natural resources, there is no one solution to the growing global water crisis; we need action on multiple fronts. Some experts recommend billion-dollar infrastructure and megadams, but I prefer what the Pacific Institute calls the "soft path" solutions to the global water crisis. In their words: "Soft path solutions aim to improve the productivity of water rather than seek endless new supply . . . [and] complement centrally-planned infrastructure with community scale projects; and soft path solutions involve stakeholders in key decisions so that water deals and projects protect the environment and the public interest."[64] Such solutions include improved technology, improved conservation, and truly democratic, just decision-making processes, all done in concert.

One major step in the right direction is just uncovering and identifying where water is being used and wasted, which often includes uses invisible to us on a day-to-day basis. Hardly anyone looks at a cotton T-shirt, a car, or a light switch and thinks about water. To bring this "invisible" water to light, a British professor named John Allan came up with the concept of "virtual water" to track the use of water in global industry and trade.[65] Virtual water is the amount of water embedded in food or other products based on how much water was needed to extract and produce that item. Countries that grow and export water-intensive crops, like cotton and coffee, can be thought of as virtual water exporters.

Another helpful concept is a "water footprint," which calculates the total volume of fresh water used for the goods and services produced by a business or used by an individual or a community. If you're curious, you can go to www.waterfootprint.org and get a rough 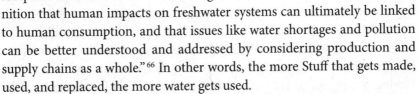 calculation of your own water footprint. Professor Arjen Hoekstra of the University of Twente in Holland explains his creation of the "water footprint" tool as "rooted in the recognition that human impacts on freshwater systems can ultimately be linked to human consumption, and that issues like water shortages and pollution can be better understood and addressed by considering production and supply chains as a whole."[66] In other words, the more Stuff that gets made, used, and replaced, the more water gets used.

When I calculated my personal footprint, I found that my total water footprint is about 500 cubic meters per year. I played around with the numbers and saw that I could reduce it by drinking less coffee, eating fewer animal products, and buying less Stuff.

I'd like to think that my grey-water system, which waters my garden with my washing machine drainage, after filtering it through a simple multi-tiered planter full of specifically chosen filtering plants, makes a difference. Variations of this system are used around the world to filter and reuse grey water in homes, universities, hotels, food processing plants, and other sites. My garden loves it, but I know that the water diverted is just a drop in the bucket compared to the water that was needed to make the Stuff I use every day. The use of water in agriculture, energy production, and as an ingredient in industrial production is where the greatest potential exists to reduce water use.

The true cost of water is another one of industry's huge externalized costs, meaning the costs they don't actually pay. The prices of Stuff don't reflect water's real value (which economists are only now beginning to calculate) or the costs of the degradation of water resources through pollution and contamination, or the ecosystem services that are impacted. To capture its true value, some people are beginning to use what's known as a total economic value framework, which includes direct uses (like drinking water) and indirect uses (like the level and flow of a river) as well as the so-called bequest value (use by future generations) and "existence value" (the right simply to be present on earth).[67] Along these lines, government representatives and NGOs from around the world created the Dublin Principles at the International Conference on Water and the Environment in 1992 to recognize the value of water and set standards for water management.[68]

This shift could motivate improved water productivity. If those hidden or "virtual" externalized costs of using and polluting water actually started showing up under "costs" on the balance sheets of businesses, companies would be highly motivated to reduce the amount of water they use or pollute. At the same time, we need to be sure that calculating the economic value of water doesn't obscure our recognizing access to water as a basic human right. Assigning economic value to water is a strategy to better understand its overall value, not a step toward privatizing and selling it.

The hope is that if we make industries responsible for the full costs of water use, they will start employing the technological fixes to use and waste less. The tricky thing about economic, or market-based, strategies is that forcing companies to factor in externalized costs will invariably raise the price tags of goods, as industries pass the higher costs on to consumers. While in many instances that might not be all bad (after all, do we really need yet another 256-gallon-of-water T-shirt that we couldn't resist because it cost $4.99 at Target?), increased prices for basic commodities can be devastating to the poorest people around the world.

There are people already at work on this very issue to ensure that everyone, even those too poor to pay, get enough water for their basic needs, while those who use (waste) water for luxury consumption or excessive industrial use are charged extra. An international coalition of human rights activists, progressive municipal leaders, trade unions, and environmental organizations—collectively known as water warriors—are collaborating to achieve the recognition of water as a human right, improved access to water for poor people, the decommodification of water, taxes for excessive water use, and the defense of elected municipal governments as the key institution in water delivery, rather than private businesses.

On the technological front, many companies are already improving their processes so they use and waste less water through innovations like closed-loop factories, which continuously recycle all the water they use. As companies shift away from toxic inputs into their production processes, the water leaving the plant won't be contaminated and so can be safely used again: this is a huge improvement. One company undertaking these kinds of practices is the carpet manufacturer Interface. Since 1996, under the visionary leadership of CEO Ray Anderson, the company has reduced water intake by 75 percent per production unit in its facilities.[69] And they say they aren't done yet!

Meanwhile, professionals in regional planning, industrial ecology, urban design, and architecture are redesigning our built environment—from individual homes to factory complexes to entire cities—to mimic rather than disrupt natural water systems or "watersheds." Replacing lawns with native plants that demand less water; replacing solid surfaces with permeable ones that allow more rainwater to seep into the soil; removing industrial tie-ins that allow factories to dispose of hazardous waste in the municipal sewers; and many other shifts can help protect water supplies. Not to mention (again) the composting toilet.

In addition to market-based and technological solutions—which are ready to be implemented as soon as we decide to do so—we also need changes in our cultural approach to water that would prioritize sustainable usage and access for all. Like the oxygen we breathe, water is absolutely essential to survival, and there's no substitute waiting in the wings.

Rocks

The most elusive ingredients needed to make our Stuff are underground. Metals, gems, and minerals—and their organic cousins petroleum and coal—are basically nonrenewable, unlike trees (renewable, as long as our rate of replanting is faster than our rate of use) or water (replenishable, which means a resource at risk of being depleted, but which can be restored in a healthy ecosystem over time). They're also harder to reach. That's where mining comes in.

You're unlikely to hear someone wax sentimental about rocks. They're not grand, awe-inspiring living creatures like trees or a serene, healing, cleansing substance like water. You don't hear appeals from nonprofits to save the poor silver or uranium from being removed from its native habitat. You *are* likely to run in to people who are emotionally attached to their rock-based Stuff, though. Threaten someone's wedding ring, cell phone, and car, and you're likely to wind up underground yourself.

So what's the big deal about removing these inanimate and uncharismatic resources from the earth in the name of our most cherished possessions? Well, for starters, there's the issue of availability of these materials for future generations. What we use up today isn't going to grow back. The fact that our primary economic model is based on using up nonrenewable resources, like minerals, is one of the main blind spots of the GDP as a viable measure of progress.

And then there's the whole story of how we get at those materials—mining. No matter how you slice it, mining is a serious drag—for people and the planet. Open-pit, strip, shaft, above the surface, below it, it doesn't matter: these are energy- and water-intensive, waste-spewing, often poisonous, and all-around dirty processes. Communities are evicted, workers' rights are violated, and the toxic by-products endanger everyone's health, all in the name of mining. And the trauma doesn't stop when a mine gets shut down—it continues for years afterward.

Underground, or subsurface, mining involves tunnels dug deep down into the earth. Although this is probably the image—along with headlamps and canaries—that most people have in their heads when they think of mining, most mining today occurs in gigantic open-air pits. In the United States, open-pit mining provides the bulk of the minerals extracted; globally, two-thirds of all metals are from open pits.[70] Diamonds, iron, copper, gold, and coal are all commonly extracted from open pits, which can be huge. The Bingham Canyon copper mine in Utah, for instance, covers about 3 square miles (7.7 square kilometers) and the Chuquicamata copper mine in northern Chile covers about 4.5 square miles (12 square kilometers).[71] There's also mountaintop removal, usually used to get at deposits of coal found deep inside mountains (see the box on coal on page 35). Particularly in developing countries there are also still small-scale "artisanal" operations that employ workers in mining accessible surface deposits using their hands and basic tools.

Creating an open pit means chopping down trees (more trees!) and clearing off the land's inhabitants, whether they walk on four or two legs. A report on the mining industry in India compared the mineral and forest maps, only to find that the highest concentrations of coal, bauxite (used for aluminum), and iron ore are all located in forest areas that are home to most of the country's biodiversity and indigenous people as well.[72]

And the living things atop a mine only make up the first layer of what gets scraped off. All the stone and soil covering up the valuable ores— what the mining industry terms "overburden"—also have to be removed using heavy duty tools like bulldozers, drills, explosives, and trucks (all of which require their own long lists of ingredients to create and operate). This rubble gets piled up, sometimes skyscraper high. In fact, open-pit mines produce eight to ten times as much waste rubble as underground mines.[73]

Getting at the ore is only the beginning. Because even high-grade ore only contains a little bit of the pure metal or mineral being sought, it has to be processed, which involves more machinery as well as loads of water and chemicals. Most of the ore—and an ever-increasing amount, as high-grade sources disappear—ends up as waste. According to a report by Earthworks and Oxfam America called *Dirty Metals*, in the United States, "the copper ore mined at the beginning of the 20th century consisted of about 2.5 percent usable metal by weight; today that proportion has dropped to 0.51 percent. In gold mining, it is estimated that only 0.00001 percent [that's one hundred thousandth of 1 percent] of the ore is actually refined into gold."[74] Chemicals used in processing contaminate at least 90 billion tons of waste ore per year globally, equivalent in weight to almost nine times as much trash produced annually by all U.S. cities combined.[75]

Of course mine workers suffer disproportionately from the toxins, as well as from injuries caused by using dangerous heavy equipment and from events like explosions, fires, mudslides, etc. The International Labour Organization reports that although mining accounts for only 0.4 percent of the global workforce, it is responsible for more than 3 percent of fatal accidents at work (about eleven thousand per year, about thirty each day).[76]

In Rajasthan, India, for example, miners—many of them women and children—toil long days to extract the marble and sandstone that furnishes fancy bathrooms and kitchens worldwide. GRAVIS, a nongovernmental organization inspired by Gandhi that works with Rajasthani miners, reports that about half of the mineworkers in the state have developed lung disease, such as silicosis. "The mineworkers work in deep open pits where the air is thick with dust from dry drilling, and safety equipment is nonexistent. There is no drinking water provided, no shade to rest in, no toilets, no first aid kits, and no worker's compensation for accidents. Accidents occur frequently and often mineworkers have no extra money to pay for medical treatment."[77]

You would think, given all the costs, from contamination of water, air, and soil to the health care of workers, that mining companies would be hard-pressed to turn a profit. But only a smidgen of the true costs is borne by those companies; their balance sheets rarely factor in things like water or air quality. In fact, get this: it is virtually free to mine on U.S. federal lands. Under the General Mining Act, passed in 1872, any U.S. citizen eighteen years or older has the right to prospect and mine for minerals, such as gold, silver, platinum, copper, lead, and zinc, on federal lands. For *free*. The argument of the day was that miners and prospectors were performing valuable services by promoting commerce and settling new territory, particularly out west.[78]

Since the passage of the act, it is estimated the federal government has given away minerals worth more than $245 billion.[79] This not only deprives the government of revenue, it also encourages use of virgin materials instead of recycled. One study found that in the United States fifteen federal subsidies—averaging $2.6 billion each—annually benefit resource extractive industries,[80] again guiding them toward virgin rather than recycled metals. When minerals are basically free, there is little incentive to conserve them or to go to the effort to recover the gold, silver, lead, and other metals in all the electronics and other Stuff we throw out.

Thankfully, efforts are underway to update the antiquated mining law. In early 2009, the Hardrock Mining and Reclamation Act was reintroduced, after the 2007 version failed to pass the U.S. Senate. The new law would impose a royalty of 4 percent of gross revenues on existing mining from unclaimed mines and place an 8 percent royalty on new mining operations. Seventy percent of the royalty money would go to a cleanup fund for past abandoned mining operations, and 30 percent would go to communities impacted by mining.[81] While a step in the right direction, that law only pertains to mining on U.S. public lands. Meanwhile, the subsidies encouraging the use of virgin materials still exist; they need to go!

If I wanted to examine every kind of metal and mineral that gets extracted to make our Stuff, it would take several books' worth of stories. So let's look at a select handful of rocks that get dug up or blasted out of the ground. They're pretty representative of the way all the metals and minerals needed for our Stuff are extracted.

Gold and Diamonds

Gold is used for a lot of things, from dentistry to glassblowing to stock-piling wealth. Gold is also used in electronics; virtually every modern electronic device—cell phones, laptops, televisions, GPS systems, MP3 players—has a bit of gold in it. But the biggest use, dwarfing all the rest, is jewelry. Jewelry accounts for more than 75 percent of the total amount of gold consumed today.[82]

Maybe you have a piece of gold jewelry that's very dear to you. You're not alone. I don't have much of it, but I do have one little gold ring, given to me by a long-ago love.

When he wanted to buy me a ring, I insisted on an old one and a small one. I'd seen gold mines in South Africa. I knew that gold mining is horribly polluting, is routinely linked to human rights violations, and that more than three-quarters of the gold mined around the world ends up in jewelry. Since there is a lot of gold in jewelry rattling around in old ladies' dresser drawers and increasingly in piles of e-waste, why fuel the market for mining more? So he got me an antique ring from the Tiny Jewel Box store in Washington, D.C. It's inscribed "16 Mai 1896" and has a fleck of sapphire surrounded by tiny pearls not much larger than pencil dots.

I love that my ring has a past from long before me. Given the spelling of "May," it was likely presented to someone in France or Germany. And given its tiny size, it seems unlikely to have been an engagement ring: perhaps a sweet-sixteen ring? I've often gazed at it and imagined its life on the finger of a young European woman and wondered who gave it to her. And of course the metal had a life before her, before being shaped into a ring.

Where was the gold for my sweet little ring mined? Maybe South Africa? For years, South Africa has supplied much of the world's gold and still provides more than a quarter of today's demand. When I visited South Africa in the mid-1990s, I looked out the window of the car in which I was riding and wondered aloud what geologic processes could have created so many randomly spaced small hills that covered the countryside. "Those aren't hills," my South African host explained. "Those are piles of mining waste."

Mining enough gold for an average gold wedding ring creates about 20 tons of hazardous mining waste,[83] which is sometimes dumped in rivers or the sea, sometimes just left right where it was created, as I saw in South Africa. The reason it's toxic is that to get the gold from the ore, mining companies use a process called heap leaching, which means piling up the gold-containing ore and pouring cyanide over it to let it slowly drip through, extracting the gold on its way. At the same time, the cyanide also extracts toxic metals, including cadmium, lead, and mercury. The cyanide and toxic metal liquid runoff ends up in a big pool, from which the gold is extracted, leaving behind a heavy metal and cyanide contaminated pond next to a heavy metal and cyanide contaminated hill of leftover ore. Cyanide, I probably don't need to remind you, is a deadly poison. An amount about the size of a grain of rice is enough to off a human being, and one-millionth of a gram of it in a liter of water kills fish,[84] which is a big problem since much mine waste ends up in rivers and lakes.

But my ring was so tiny! I reassured myself that it must have only created half the average amount of waste. Then I realized that's still 10 tons.

I hope my ring wasn't made by pouring cyanide over heaps of earth. Cyanide wasn't widely applied to gold ores until 1887.[85] And maybe the gold in my ring is American, maybe even Californian, like me. Since early Californian gold miners didn't use cyanide, this would free my ring from that toxic legacy but would unfortunately bring another equally problematic one.

Gold was discovered in Northern California forty-eight years before my ring was inscribed. In 1848, a man named James Marshall working on a sawmill in Northern California found the shiny metal in the American River in Coloma. Marshall's discovery led to the Gold Rush of 1849: hundreds of thousands of people arrived in hopes of striking it rich.[86] As a result the white population in California soared from 13,000 to 300,000 by 1854, while California's native American populations were decimated, declining from a pre-gold rush population of 150,000 to about 30,000 by 1870. Sixty percent of those deaths were linked to diseases introduced by the invading gold miners, while others were hastened by forced relocation onto reservations or happened in outright massacres.[87]

In that era, the ore wrested from riverbanks and mountains was soaked with mercury to extract the gold. Mercury, which I'll discuss more fully in the upcoming chapter on production, is a potent neurotoxin that can affect the brain, spinal cord, kidneys, and liver. (The term "mad hatter" comes from the neurological damage done to those who cleaned felt hats, which used to be done with—you guessed it—mercury.[88]) During the gold rush, an estimated 7,600 tons of mercury were deposited into the rivers of the central Sierra Nevada alone.[89] That mercury remains in the California environment, in rivers and in sediments, much of it being continuously transported to the San Francisco Bay, where people swim and fish.

The unfortunate fact is, I can't tell you where the gold in my little ring came from, or who was harmed by its creation. All I know is that when it came to me, it was already secondhand—and that's a plus. Since the great majority of gold is used for jewelry and since two-thirds of gold in use is newly mined, old gold is a good choice for people who believe that gold is the best way to symbolize love or commitment.

 Buying previously owned or recycled gold, or forgoing it altogether, is the best way to ensure we're not contributing to the devastation caused by gold mining. However, for those who are stuck on buying new gold, there are still ways to lessen the impact. There are a number of jewelers who have committed to ensuring that the gold in their wares wasn't produced at the expense of local communities, workers, or the environment. The No Dirty Gold campaign has developed a set of voluntary guidelines called the Golden Rules that jewelry retailers can sign on to in order to promote environmental, worker, and community rights. You can find out which jewelers are on board at www.nodirtygold.org.[90]

Conflict Minerals

Unfortunately the story of gold has a lot in common with the stories of almost all of the minerals or metals needed for our Stuff. Unfortunately, it gets even worse than gold.

"Conflict minerals" is the term for valuable rocks that fuel violent conflict when the profit from their control, sales, taxation, or protection funds criminal gangs, brutal regimes, and weapons. These minerals and metals are usually mined under oppressive conditions, with workers paid little to nothing. According to Global Witness, a London- and Washington, D.C.-based organization leading the campaign on conflict diamonds, these rocks "have funded brutal conflicts in Africa that have resulted in the death and displacement of millions of people. Diamonds have also been used by terrorist groups such as al-Qaeda to finance their activities and for money-laundering purposes."[91]

The role of "conflict diamonds" or "blood diamonds" in Sierra Leone's civil war has received global attention, in large part thanks to Global Witness' Combating Conflict Diamonds campaign, launched in 1998. The situation was also brought to light through the 2006 film *Blood Diamond*. The film does a pretty good job of illustrating the brutality of both the rebel forces that run the mines (kidnapping villagers to make them into miners and young boys to serve as child soldiers) as well as the government forces, which indiscriminately kill civilians and villagers alongside the rebels.

In real life, during Sierra Leone's eleven-year civil war from 1991 to 2002, a vicious rebel army called the Revolutionary United Front (RUF) utilized violence and terror, including rape, the systematic amputation of victims' limbs, and mass murder. Tens of thousands of Sierra Leoneans were killed.[92] In early 2009, three senior commanders of the RUF were convicted of war crimes and crimes against humanity. They had participated in seizing diamond mines, forcing kidnapped citizens to mine diamonds, and then trading the diamonds for money and military support.[93] "Trade in diamonds and other natural resources has underwritten some of the worst war crimes of the past two decades," said Mike Davis, who campaigns for Global Witness, an international nongovernment organization (NGO). "Yet despite cases such as Sierra Leone, there is still no comprehensive international approach to this problem. Natural resources continue to fuel conflict to this day, notably in eastern Democratic Republic of the Congo, where armed groups are financing themselves through the trade in minerals and committing atrocities against the civilian population."[94]

In 2000, the South African government hosted a meeting of major diamond trading and producing countries, diamond industry representatives, and NGOs in Kimberley, South Africa, to launch an international diamond tracking and certification program, which became known as the Kimberley Process. Formally launched in January 2003, it aims to guarantee a "clean" source of diamonds, free of conflict and violence. In order for a country to be a participant, it must ensure that none of its diamonds have financed a rebel group or other entity seeking to overthrow a UN-recognized government, that every diamond has official certification, and that no diamond is imported from or exported to a nonmember country.[95] As Sierra Leonean

Martin Chungong Ayafor testified to the UN, "'Diamonds are forever,' it is often said. But lives are not. We must spare people the ordeal of war, mutilations, and death for the sake of conflict diamonds."[96]

Unfortunately, the Kimberley Process has not lived up to its potential, and the diamond industry continues to be rife with human rights abuses and links to conflict. Global Witness reported that after the agreement's first five years, "the trafficking of conflict and illicit stones is looking more like a dangerous rule than an exception."[97]

The best way to avoid fueling conflict and civil war is to not buy diamonds. Period. The diamond industry does a fabulous job marketing these rocks as a symbol of love, commitment, wealth, and status. But we don't have to buy into it. There are plenty of better ways to demonstrate one's love. If you are really compelled to go spend a month's salary on a rock, then consult the diamond buying guide produced by Global Witness and Amnesty International, which includes a number of important questions to ask a jeweler.

Coltan

There's another conflict mineral that's in all of our cell phones, MP3 players, remote controls, and PlayStations: tantalum, derived from an ore known as "coltan" in miner slang. It's known for its resistance to heat and to corrosion by acids—even when actually submerged in acid.[98]

Although coltan has mostly been sourced from other countries like Australia, Brazil, and Canada, 80 percent of the world's supplies are in the politically unstable and violence-plagued eastern part of the Democratic Republic of the Congo.[99] Congolese coltan mining has funded brutal guerilla forces and their backers in neighboring countries like Rwanda, Burundi, and Uganda. Coltan can be mined with very basic methods: simply dug up and sifted through pans, just as the forty-niners in the California Gold Rush worked. So when the global price of the metal shot up in 2000 to three hundred dollars per pound of the refined mineral (in part due to the huge launch of Sony's PS2 game console), thousands of Congolese scrambled into the country's lush green forests to get at it, destroying national parks and other pristine land, killing gorillas for food, and ruining the animals' habitat.[100] Various armies (official and rebel) rushed in to take over the trade, often employing children and prisoners of war, brutally raping local women (the UN estimated 45,000 raped in 2005 alone[101]), and bringing prostitution and illegal arms trade with them. Oona King, a member of the British Parliament at the time, said about the situation: "Kids in

Congo were being sent down mines to die so that kids in Europe and America could kill imaginary aliens in their living rooms."[102]

Coltan mining has been an enormously lucrative business for both the rebels and the armies of the Congo and its neighbors. By some estimates the Rwandan army, which has occupied parts of the Congo off and on for the last decade, made $500 million just between April 2007 and October 2008 on Congolese coltan.[103] And, of course, the corporations selling all these coltan-containing products are making massive profit too, with most investing far more in advertising the latest gadget than in ending the trail of violence that too often follows this metal.

Congolese human rights activist Bertrand Bisimwa summarized the way far too many people perceive his country: "Since the 19th century, when the world looks at Congo it sees a pile of riches with some black people inconveniently sitting on top of them. They eradicate the Congolese people so they can possess the mines and resources. They destroy us because we are an inconvenience."[104]

Some electronics manufacturers have publicly declared their ban on African-mined tantalum altogether, although, as depicted in the film *Blood Diamond,* tracing the source through so many dealers and handlers means this is far easier said than done. A solution with more promise is a database of "coltan fingerprints" that scientists are creating, which is feasible because each mining site has a distinct geological history and produces metal with a specific composition.[105] This database would allow an international certification system like the Kimberley Process to be established for coltan, so that electronics manufacturers could source their coltan from legitimate mines with decent working conditions and environmental standards.

But the best solution of all—not just for coltan but also for gold and other metals contained in today's array of electronic products—is to increase the durability and expand the life span of today's electronics so we don't have to keep chucking and replacing them so quickly. We also need to require manufacturers to take back electronics when we are done with them. Take-back programs, like those now mandated throughout the European Union, allow manufacturers to recover the tantalum (and other ingredients) for reuse, thus keeping electronic waste out of landfills and decreasing the pressure to mine more.

Earthworks, a Washington, D.C., based environmental advocacy group specializing in mining issues, estimates that if 130 million phones were recycled, they would yield about 202,000 ounces of gold alongside other precious metals. Every year 150 million cell phones are thrown out in the United States, along with over 300 million other electronic devices. It's estimated that there are another 500 million unused cell phones sitting around in people's drawers.[106] That's a lot of perfectly good rocks for the (re)taking.

Petroleum

No discussion of wars fueled by natural resources is complete without mention of oil. In our current system petroleum is used to power many of the processes by which our Stuff is made. Powering machines and vehicles and heating our buildings takes 84 percent of the petroleum used every year.[107] Petroleum itself is also an ingredient in a lot of Stuff: the remaining 16 percent of it goes into making plastics, pharmaceuticals, and fertilizers, as well as Stuff like crayons, bubble gum, ink, dishwashing liquid, deodorant, tires, and ammonia.[108]

Drilling, processing, and burning oil is dirty and damaging to the health of people everywhere, not to mention the health of the planet. The other big problem with oil is that we're running out. "Peak oil" is the term used to describe the point at which we've used more oil than what's left available to us because of technological and geological limitations. Once peak oil is reached, oil production declines. The International Energy Agency (IEA), which tracks energy supplies around the world, believes we may reach peak oil by 2020 but are likely to experience an "oil crunch" even earlier as demand outpaces supply and oil becomes increasing expensive to extract.[109]

In August 2009, Dr. Fatih Birol, chief economist at the IEA, said that "global production is likely to peak in about ten years—at least a decade earlier than most governments had estimated."[110] After assessing eight hundred major oil fields around the world (three-quarters of global reserves), the IEA reported that oil is being depleted more quickly than the agency had estimated even a couple of years ago and concluded that current energy use patterns are "patently unsustainable." According to Dr. Birol, if oil demand remains steady, the world would have to find the equivalent of four Saudi Arabias to maintain production and six Saudi Arabias if it is to keep up with the expected increase in demand between now and 2030.[111]

"We have to leave oil before oil leaves us, and we have to prepare ourselves for that day," Dr. Birol said. "The earlier we start, the better, because all of our economic and social system is based on oil, so to change from that will take a lot of time and a lot of money."[112] Yet despite the facts, many governments have been slow to invest in alternatives, and some—like our own—have instead invested in costly wars to protect access to it.

We've all heard about the connection between oil reserves and American military engagement in the Middle East. Meanwhile the extraction of oil from places like Ecuador and Nigeria has gotten less attention, but has been just as devastating.

In Ecuador, Texaco (now Chevron) spent nearly three decades between 1964 and 1992 extracting oil from a chunk of the Amazonian forest three times the size of Manhattan, destroying much of the area's life. Violating environmental standards, Texaco dumped toxic water and sludge by-products from the drilling, saturated with carcinogens like benzene, cadmium, and mercury, in local waters. They left more than six hundred unlined and uncovered waste pits that leak chemicals like hexavalent chromium (remember Erin Brockovich?) into rivers and streams used by more than thirty thousand people for drinking water, cooking, bathing, and fishing. The local population is suffering from skyrocketing rates of cancer, severe reproductive problems, and birth defects.[113] In a David versus Goliath protracted legal battle that is still underway, local people are demanding Chevron clean up the mess and pay for the tremendous devastation it caused.

The future looks slightly more hopeful; in 2007, Ecuadorean president Rafael Correa's government announced that it intended to protect the oilfields located in the extraordinarily rich Yasuní rainforest. The Yasuní houses a million hectares of pristine rainforest, indigenous tribes, and glorious species of wildlife and plants, many of which are endangered. It's also home to one of the world's largest undeveloped oil reserves—close to 1 billion barrels' worth. Not extracting that oil would prevent the release of an estimated 400 million tons of carbon into the atmosphere.[114]

Taking a stand for the Yasuní oilfield's protection is a bold move, considering that about 70 percent of Ecuador's income is from oil.[115] So how do they plan to accomplish it? They asked the international community to pay them half of the income that would result from the extraction over the likely lifetime of the oil fields, or $350 million a year for a decade.[116] This is a big deal: a really innovative idea that other developing countries could employ to protect their own resources and help combat climate change. Unfortunately, although the governments of Spain, Norway, and Italy voiced support for Correa's plan, no one offered cash until Germany did in June 2009, with a promise to pay $50 million in grants annually.[117] It remains to be seen how the Yasuní will fare.

In Nigeria, the villain has a different name (Shell), but the story is similar. Starting in 1958, Shell went into Ogoniland, one of the most fertile regions of the country. The five hundred thousand Ogoni who live there are an ethnic minority group; they are basically unrecognized by the Nigerian constitution and have few protections under it. They don't have mineral rights to their land either, since all mineral rights are owned by the state.[118] As in Ecuador, their land has been trashed by spills, sludge, and other by-products from the drilling.

After decades plagued with poverty, public health crises, and environmental devastation, while Shell extracted millions of dollars' worth of oil from under their homes, the Ogoni began to organize themselves to fight for their rights and their land. In 1990, they formed MOSOP, the Movement for the Survival of the Ogoni People, a peaceful resistance group under the leadership of a charismatic writer, businessman, TV producer, and environmental activist named Ken Saro-Wiwa.[119] A brilliant public speaker, Ken traveled the world raising awareness about the little-known environmental and public health catastrophe that oil drilling had wreaked upon his homeland. His work created a strong international network of people inspired and committed to pressuring Shell to improve its operations, clean up past environmental damage, respect human rights, and share oil profits more fairly with host communities. Around the world, students began protesting at Shell stations. Filmmakers interviewed Ken and visited Ogoniland, ensuring that even more people would see the atrocities Ken described. Faith-based and corporate-accountability activists raised questions and eventually introduced resolutions at Shell's annual meetings. Greenpeace, Project Underground, Essential Action, and other groups developed campaigns in support of the Ogoni.[120]

At that time, Nigeria was controlled by a military dictatorship led by the infamous Sani Abacha. Shell was by far the largest oil company in a heavily oil-dependent economy and had a close, even symbiotic relationship with the government. Neither was pleased with Ken's work at home and around the world. Shell had pulled out of Ogoniland in 1993, at least partly because of MOSOP, but they—and the Nigerian government, which gets more than 85 percent of its revenue from oil—still wanted the troublesome group silenced: correspondence between Shell and the Nigerian government revealed Shell's desire to stop MOSOP.[121] Even in the face of growing threats and government harassment, Ken didn't give up his struggle for environmental justice and human rights, right up to his very premature end.

"Appalled by the denigrating poverty of my people who live on a richly endowed land, distressed by their political marginalization and economic strangulation, angered by the devastation of their land, their ultimate heritage, anxious to preserve their right to life and to a decent living, and determined to usher to this country as a whole a fair and just democratic system which protects everyone and every ethnic group and gives us all a valid claim to human civilization, I have devoted my intellectual and material resources, my very life, to a cause in which I have total belief." [122] That's from Ken's closing statement to the military-appointed special tribunal that heard his case after he and fifteen other Ogonis were arrested on bogus charges. He was convicted of a murder that happened in an area that had been blocked off by the military—with Ken irrefutably outside the barricades, nowhere near it. As it turned out, Ken did devote his "very life" to the cause: he was hanged on November 10, 1995.

There was an international outcry over his wrongful execution. I remember exactly where I was when I heard: in New York City, in Riverside Church, at a gathering of international environmental and human rights activists discussing economic globalization. Many of the people there had followed the Ogoni case because it was so dramatically emblematic of the intersection of environmental, human rights, and economic abuses too often linked to extractive industries. I knew that Ken had been charged with murder in a secret, widely discredited trial. Yet I honestly didn't believe he would be hung. He had too many international friends. Amnesty International had spearheaded a campaign on his behalf. Governments, human rights organizations, and prominent writers around the world had called on the Nigerian government to spare Ken and his colleagues. He had written one of the most-watched soap operas in all of Africa. He was charming and educated and internationally recognized. Many of the people in the church that day had met him, seen him speak in person, and considered him a friend. He wasn't the kind of activist whose death could just be swept under the rug, unnoticed except by friends and family.

Yet it happened. When we heard the news, literally hundreds of people rushed out of the church into the streets to march to Shell's office in Midtown Manhattan. Some were crying. Some were so angry that they lay down in the entranceway, blocking the door and disrupting Shell's business until the police came and dragged them away. I was just in shock. I had overestimated the Nigerian government's vulnerability to international pressure and underestimated the strength of their desire to silence Ken. They didn't really silence him though; his memory continues to inspire people to take action against destructive oil projects. Ken's last words are reported to have been "Lord, take my soul, but the struggle continues."[123]

And that it does. It continues in the courtroom as well as in the streets. The lawsuit *Wiwa v. Shell* charged Shell with providing arms and transportation, collaboration and direction to the Nigerian military to suppress the Ogoni opposition. The plaintiffs included surviving relatives of Ken and his executed colleagues—now known as the Ogoni 9—as well as other Ogoni who were tortured, and in some cases killed, for their resistance to Shell and their support for MOSOP.[124]

Just days before the federal court trial date in June 2009 in New York City, Shell agreed to an out-of-court settlement of $15.5 million for the relatives of Ken and the other victims. However, Shell denied any wrongdoing or responsibility for the deaths, calling the settlement money a "humanitarian gesture" toward the families for their losses and their legal expenses. Some of the money will also go into a trust to benefit the Ogoni people.[125] While the settlement was meager compared to the extent of Shell's wrongdoing, it's still a step forward in holding all corporations accountable for crimes they commit in other countries.

Although Shell hasn't been back to Ogoniland, it still pumps more than 250,000 barrels a day from Nigeria.[126] And in June 2008, the Nigerian government announced plans to give rights to drill in Ogoniland to the Nigerian Petroleum Development Company, so operations there will begin anew.[127]

Even should Shell be forced to reform its ways, such disregard for both people and the environment in drilling areas continues to be an industry norm. In May 1998, less than three years after Ken's execution, members of another Nigerian community—the Ilaje—were shot and two were killed while engaging in a nonviolent protest on a Chevron oil platform off the Nigerian coast.[128] According to EarthRights International, which serves as counsel for *Wiwa v. Shell* and another case related to the killing of the platform protestors, Chevron called in the Nigerian military and police, flew them to the platform on Chevron-contracted helicopters, and supervised their attack against the protesters.[129]

The crazy thing is, we have perfectly good alternatives to petroleum for both energy and materials. There's no need to continue such widespread environmental destruction and violence to meet our energy needs. As many scientists and business leaders now agree, solar and wind power can pick up much of our energy needs. Combining renewable energy with a much needed reduction in demand through greater energy efficiency and improvements in everything from land use planning to transportation systems to consumption patterns, we could have enough energy to just leave that oil in the soil.

And the oil used for plastics and other products is also replaceable with other materials, including bio-based ones. David Morris at the Institute for Local Self-Reliance has documented the technical potential and environmental benefits of shifting from a petro-based to a carbohydrate-material economy for more than a decade.[130] A number of green chemists, sustainable agriculture activists, and environmental health advocates have formed a Sustainable Biomaterials Collaborative. This body has established criteria to ensure that the transition from petro-based to plant-based materials is done in a way that supports ecological health, healthy farms, good farm jobs, and other criteria for a safe, healthy, and just planet.[131]

Rethinking Extraction

Perhaps, as some people claim, it is possible to take metals or oil out of the ground without widespread environmental and human rights abuses, but I sure haven't seen it. The scale of investment and hard work it will take to turn those industries around is huge. And, in the case of the toxic heavy metals—like lead and mercury—or oil, getting it out of the ground is only the first problem. Use of these resources adds to a whole second generation of problems. Many heavy metals are neurotoxins, carcinogens, and reproductive toxins (which diminish your ability to have healthy children and your children's ability to have healthy children).

While some extractive industries can be improved—the Golden Rules and Kimberley Process are examples of potential steps in that direction—attempting to fix others just won't work. It is impossible to safely and sustainably extract resources that are, by definition, environmental and health problems themselves.

In the case of the toxic metals, like lead and mercury, we should leave them in the ground and redesign our industrial processes and products to eliminate their use. Both lead and mercury have been eliminated from the many common uses of just a generation ago. Remember leaded paint and gasoline? Mercury thermometers?

I am not saying it is going to be easy. It's a big job to redesign everything from consumer products, to sustainable energy systems, to cultural norms around diamond rings set in gold as the ultimate expression of love. But with the stakes so high—our very planet plus all our fellow planet-mates depending on us—we can do it.

Imbalanced Benefits

Maybe you noticed a common thread in the stories of Madagascar's periwinkle, Sierra Leone's diamonds, the Congo's coltan, Nigeria's oil, and Appalachia's coal. In all of these places there's an abundance of valuable

---

COAL

Coal doesn't make my list of rocks because it's used less often as a direct ingredient in consumer goods. Like water and oil, however, it powers the machines that make our Stuff, so it deserves mention.

Coal is used to generate a lot of electricity (40 percent of the world's and approximately 49 percent of the United States'[132]), even though it's hard to imagine a dirtier source. Back in the early days when coal was abundant and easier to reach, people didn't necessarily know how bad it was. You'd think they'd have realized the mining of it wasn't a great idea based on the fact that they had to send those poor little canaries in to make sure the air wasn't poisonous! Or when mine roofs kept collapsing, fires and explosions occurred relentlessly, and black lung disease shrank the life expectancies of miners. But no.

And now we know so much more. Creating and running a coal mine destroys vegetation, soil, and groundwater; displaces and destroys wildlife and habitat; degrades air quality with ash and dust; and permanently scars the landscape, especially in the case of mountaintop removal mining. Mines produce tons of waste like ash and sludge that contains mercury, uranium, arsenic, and other heavy metals. The December 2008 tragedy in which a billion gallons of toxic sludge burst out of a holding pond into the rivers, towns, and land of Roane County, Tennessee, is just the latest in a litany of disasters associated with coal mines.[133]

Meanwhile, *burning* coal constitutes the largest human-generated contribution to atmospheric carbon dioxide and is a major source of methane; both gases are proven causes of climate change and global warming. In his book *Big Coal*, Jeff Goodell notes that "between 1975 and 2001, the annual releases of toxic metals from coal plants nearly doubled, from about 350 tons to 700 tons . . . Toxic emissions from coal-fired power plants account for over 40 percent of all air toxins reported to the EPA."[134] And there are many more ecological impacts of burning coal that I don't have room to cover in a short section devoted to its extraction.

Of all the impacts from coal mining, blowing the tops off mountains, the method prevalent in Appalachia, takes the prize for most vile. Coal mining companies started this practice when there were no more veins of coal near the surface and using tunnels and shafts became prohibitively expensive. The crazy thing is that even deep in those mountains there's not that much coal— there's just enough profit in it for the mining companies to do it, and only because they don't have to pay anything for the ecological damage and havoc they're wreaking.

Plus, there's actually much more accessible coal in states like Montana and Wyoming.[135] So why are we even mining for it in Appalachia? The mining companies there—and the local residents who've bought into the story—claim that the region will collapse without those mining jobs. But the truth is otherwise. For example, despite *13 billion tons* of coal being pulled out of West Virginia in the past 150 years, West Virginians have the lowest median household income in the country, with the literacy rate in the southern coalfield region about that of Kabul, Afghanistan.[136]

I wanted to investigate any links between my own lightbulbs and blowing the tops off of mountains in Appalachia, so I went to the www.ilovemountains .org website, which allows anyone in the United States to type in a zip code and see which mountains were destroyed for your power. My search showed two power plants serving my area that purchase coal from companies blowing up mountains in Appalachia. Also on that site, I visited the powerful National Memorial for the Mountains, which identifies more than 470 destroyed mountains.[137] The combined horror of mountaintop removal and massive climate disruption inspired me to put solar panels on my own house, so I can rest assured that no more mountains are destroyed to power my home.

Unfortunately, we don't have time for every household to install solar panels and, even if we did, that doesn't address the massive coal used to fuel industrial uses. The extraction and burning of coal is so devastating that there's really only one solution: keep the coal in the hole. Leave it there. There's a growing global consensus that the climate simply can't sustain coal-fired power plants.

natural resources, but somehow the local people get the short end of the deal, environmentally and economically. In fact, many places with valuable, nonrenewable resources like forests, metals, and minerals wind up as impoverished noncontenders in the global economy, with their citizens often left hungry and sick. This paradox is known as the resource curse.

Some economists and social scientists say the resource curse is caused when a country or region blessed with valuable resources relies too much on them, with its best people drawn to extraction-related work, so that other economic sectors just can't compete. Meanwhile the prices for those native resources can fluctuate wildly based on the whims of the global economy, creating grave instability. Other observers point to the role of conflict minerals in sustaining political, and thus economic, chaos. American University professor Deborah Bräutigam suggests that governments in natural-resource-based economies don't rely on taxes from citizens, which means that the contract between government and its citizens is weak; citizens can't hold their leaders accountable. If ordinary folks complain about government in those situations, leaders can always use the money from the resources to fund a military presence that silences the grumbles.[138] The practice of externalizing costs—which allows multinational companies to trash the environments in which they drill, mine, and extract, without financial consequences—compounds the local devastation.

The unfortunate fact is that a resource curse experienced by a single country is just one facet of a complex global situation riddled with unfairness and lack of equality. The benefits and costs of international extraction are not equitably distributed and, as we'll see in the coming chapters, involve a messy web of often greedy and corrupt players, including multinational industries, national governments, and international development banks. As for the many millions of people who live and work on the land from which those resources are taken—they're pretty much left out of the equation.

In particular, indigenous communities bear disproportionate impacts from extractive industries. Around the world, many indigenous communities are located in resource-rich areas that are targeted for logging, mining, oil and gas drilling, and other kinds of extraction. Indigenous peoples' livelihoods and cultures often depend on access to land and natural resources, which they've respected and protected in sustainable relationships for hundreds if not thousands of years. Yet indigenous communities are often discriminated against and shut out of decision making about projects that affect their resources and their communities.

I'm happy to report that indigenous communities are gaining ground in securing their rights to participate in environmental planning processes, even though it still irks me that this is something for which they need to fight. On September 13, 2007, after more than twenty years of advocacy and negotiations, the United Nations adopted a Declaration on the Rights of Indigenous Peoples, which is a huge step toward protecting the environmental, economic, and other rights of these individuals and communities. The declaration was adopted by an overwhelming majority of 143 votes in favor, with only 4 votes—from Canada, Australia, New Zealand, and the United States—against it.[139]

While the official international political recognition helps, there's still a long way to go. As the International Working Group for Indigenous Affairs explains, "Translating this political recognition into concrete advances locally, nationally, regionally and internationally remains a big challenge for indigenous peoples."[140] Indigenous communities continue to be targeted for destructive extractive projects around the world, often with little or no opportunity to engage meaningfully in the decision-making processes.

In our increasingly globalized economy, more and more extraction projects are run by multinational companies and financed by international financial institutions like the World Bank or the International Monetary Fund (for more on these institutions see chapter 3 on distribution), whose decision-making centers are far from the impacted communities. Having distant and often unresponsive decision makers running these projects makes it even harder for local communities to have a substantial voice in project planning. Too often, the most heavily impacted communities have the least say in the projects and gain the least from the downstream benefits of the resource use.

Many organizations around the world are working to influence these financial backers—both public and private—to get them to adhere to higher environmental, social, and human rights standards. To a limited extent, advocacy and activist groups have been able to force some public and private lenders to adopt policies that protect or promote environmental and social issues.

For example, the World Bank Group, one of the biggest financial backers of extractive, infrastructure, and policy projects around the world, loaning an average of $20 to $25 billion to developing country governments annually—including more than $1 billion specifically for extractive industries[141]—did not even have mandatory environmental review procedures until 1987.[142] It adopted the inadequate review process it now uses after lengthy, heated campaigns by coalitions of environmental, human rights, and other nonprofit organizations in countries that both lend to and borrow from the World Bank. In June 2003, the World Bank endorsed the Extractive Industries Transparency Initiative (EITI), a voluntary program promoting greater transparency and civil society participation in extractive industries in resource-rich countries.[143] Even with these policies in place, the World Bank continues both to fund devastating extractive industry projects and to fail to utilize its significant leverage in developing countries to promote transparency by industries or community involvement.

Appealing to these huge financial institutions to change their ways is a slow process and has so far proved inadequate in both pace and scale. Many groups have abandoned efforts to reform them, believing that the structures and programs of the World Bank, along with its sibling organization the International Monetary Fund (IMF), are too deeply flawed. Instead, these groups focus their efforts on restricting the reach and influence of these institutions. "The record of the IMF and the World Bank is one of unmitigated failure. Their . . . failed megaprojects have disqualified them from any future role in development. It is time to shrink these institutions," explains Njoki Njoroge Njehu, a Kenyan activist who has focused on the World Bank and IMF for more than a decade.[144]

 After witnessing many devastating World Bank projects in Asia and Africa with my own eyes, and getting inadequate responses from World Bank officials each time I marched up to their Washington, D.C., offices with my latest data and concerns, I have to agree that the best approach is restricting these institutions' reach. Through an international campaign called the World Bank Bonds Boycott (WBBB), many individuals are ensuring that their pension funds, labor unions, churches, municipalities, and universities do not buy World Bank bonds. By withdrawing financing for its bonds, the WBBB exerts pressure on the Bank to, among other goals, stop environmentally destructive projects in oil, gas, mining, and dams.[145]

It's clear that the risks and negative impacts of extractive projects are not shared equitably. The same holds true for the benefits—the profits and the actual resources. Some people are using way more than their share while others are using far too little. Jared Diamond, author of *Collapse,* notes that "the average rates at which people consume resources like oil and metals, and produce wastes like plastics and greenhouse gases, are about 32 times higher in North America, Western Europe, Japan and Australia than they are in the developing world."[146] The United States consumes the highest percent; with only 5 percent of the world's population, it accounts for about 30 percent of all resources consumed. Overall, the 25 percent of the world's population in industrialized countries consume about 75 percent of global resources.[147]

In fact, all of us on the planet collectively are consuming more resources than the planet produces each year; we're consuming about 1.4 planets' worth of bio-capacity resources annually.[148] It seems impossible: we're consuming an amount equivalent to more than the total resources produced by the planet each year. In fact, it's only possible because the planet's been around a little longer than we have and has had time to accumulate extra. Now the extra is running out. It's as though a household saved income for years before ramping up its spending. It could spend more than it earned for some time, eating away at the savings, but eventually there's nothing left. That's what is happening with the planet.

And if all countries used resources at the rate that the United States does, we would need about 5 planets to sustain us.[149] That's clearly a problem, since we only have one. Two European-based organizations, BioRegional and World Wildlife Fund, have launched the One Planet Living program to reduce overall resource use, sustain ecological and community health, and ensure that the resources used are shared equitably. In order to achieve these goals, One Planet Living promotes a vastly reduced materials economy alongside new cultural norms that are proportionate to the resources we have.[150]

The equity piece means it's not as simple as saying that everyone should cut their resource use—because that would be grossly unfair. Some parts of the world, like the United States and Europe, need to consume fewer resources, while other countries need to *increase* their consumption in order to meet even their basic needs. We've got to meet somewhere in the middle. And the total amount of extraction needs to stay within the planet's ecological limits.

Transforming Extraction

In order to turn things around, we need to extract less and ensure that the extraction processes we do use support environmental, community, and worker well-being. We need to utilize what we extract more efficiently, more wisely, and more reverently. And we need a much more equal distribution of both the harms and the benefits generated by resource extraction.

While advancing sustainability standards (like the Forest Stewardship Council) and integrating worker and community voices into the planning process for extractive projects (as in community forestry initiatives) can help lessen the impact of specific projects, if we're going to seriously address the crisis of global resource depletion as well as the public health and environmental consequences of extraction, we need deeper changes.

We need to radically reduce the overall demand for the materials being extracted. We need to increase the efficiency or productivity of resources used and ramp up reuse and recycling programs. Finally, we need to seek out alternative ways to meet our needs, which, for many, means less focus on a constant flow of new Stuff.

There is another way. There are three places we can change the system so it uses fewer natural resources: at the front end, the back end, and in our hearts and minds.

1. At the Front End

At the design stage we must redesign our production systems to use fewer resources in the first place, thereby decreasing the need for more extraction.

From a materials and energy viewpoint, our current economy and industrial models are vastly inefficient. We could use less and waste less, starting right now. In the United States the materials used by industry amounts to more than twenty times each person's weight per day—more than 1 million pounds per American per year.[151]

A growing number of scientists, activists, economists, government officials, and businesspeople are calling for a massive increase in our resource productivity—in other words, to get way more out of each pound of material or unit of energy consumed.

A German think tank called the Wuppertal Institute for Climate, Environment and Energy convened a group of designers, economists, development experts, and materials geeks and launched the Factor 10 Club. In 1994 they issued a declaration calling for an increase in resource productivity by a factor of ten within fifty years, which they believe "is technically feasible if we mobilise our know-how to generate new products, services, as well as new methods of manufacturing."[152]

There are loads of examples of making intense resource efficiency a design goal, such as reduced packaging or redesigning products to contain fewer materials, which is known as "light-weighting." Other design strategies include making Stuff more:

- Durable: So products last longer and don't need to be discarded and replaced so quickly.
- Repairable: This has the added benefit of producing jobs.
- Recyclable: Materials should be chosen for their ability to maintain their integrity when recycled. Some materials degrade quickly, while others can be recycled many times.
- Adaptable: Instead of chucking our cell phones, laptops, etc. when new features become available, these items can have removable, update-able components, like lenses on a camera. The initial extra material or financial investment to make this change systemwide will be far outweighed by the costs saved on reduced extraction of new materials.

Our most brilliant minds can and should be let loose on cutting-edge industrial design that focuses not on improving just speed and style, but on dematerializing—using fewer resources. For example, digital music has replaced tons of vinyl records, plastic cassettes, and CD jewel cases. Sleek flat-screen TVs and monitors are replacing old washing machine-sized ones. Packaging has been made thinner, lighter. In lots of arenas, resource use per product is decreasing. (Unfortunately this progress can be canceled out if overall consumption rates don't likewise slow down.)

2. At the Back End
Vast amounts of metals, paper, wood, and water wasted each year can be recycled or reused. Once materials have been extracted and processed, it is far better to keep them in use than to chuck them and go blow up more mountaintops or clear-cut more forests. (This is not true for toxic compounds, like PVC plastic, or heavy metals like lead and mercury, which should not be recycled but should be pulled out of use and replaced with nontoxic, ecologically compatible materials.)

3. In Our Hearts and Minds
We can and should always be asking the question, are there nonmaterial ways to meet our needs? For example, a diamond set in a gold ring doesn't equal love—love equals love! Listening well, being respectful, offering to help out, tenderness and intimacy: that's what equals love in my book. How can we show our affection, engage our kids, and amuse ourselves without using more and more resources? Rather than our status being signaled by the clothes we wear, the cars we drive, and the size of our homes, can't status be based upon kindness, experience, and wisdom? Let's get creative, people!

And we can get back to that essential social activity known as *sharing*. Car-sharing programs such as Zipcar, tool-lending libraries like the one offered by the City of Berkeley, and good old-fashioned borrowing between neighbors are great strategies for less resource intensive ways to meet our needs. This approach has the added benefit of building community and strengthening interpersonal relationships, which psychologists and social scientists have proven to be an important factor in mental health and happiness.

CHAPTER 2

PRODUCTION

If you were surprised by how complicated it turns out to be to assemble a list of natural ingredients from the forests and rivers and mountains, and how extractive industries have impacts that you never considered (civil wars!), just wait. The next stage—production—might make your head spin. "Production" is the term for taking all the separate ingredients, mixing them together in processes that use lots of energy, and turning them into our Stuff.

In the previous chapter I described how we get most of the materials and all the energy needed for production. However, there's one last category of ingredient that isn't found on top of the earth, or even underneath its surface: synthetic materials. Chemists combine molecules to create polymers, which make things harder, stretchier, softer, stickier, glossier, more absorbent, longer lasting, or flame or pest or water resistant. They also make alloys, or combinations of metals mixed together to give them specific properties—for example, stainless steel combines the strength of iron with the anticorroding qualities of chromium. Other common synthetic materials include plastics, polyester, and ceramics.

Today, there are about one hundred thousand synthetic compounds in use in modern industrial production.[1] They are so ubiquitous that most of the Stuff we're used to having in our lives can't be made without synthetic ingredients, or it can't be made with quite the same qualities (not quite as shiny or stretchy or what have you). Now, synthetics aren't inherently good or bad. Some are even made from natural ingredients while others are wholly developed in a laboratory. The distinction is simply that the new compound is something that didn't exist naturally on earth.

The trouble with synthetics is that most of them are a big unknown in terms of their impacts on our health and the health of the planet. Because few of them have been tested in the half century or so that most of them

with total global production at more than 25 million tons per year, or enough to make fifteen T-shirts for every person on earth.[4]

Cotton plants love water—in fact it's one of the world's most heavily irrigated crops.[5] And irrigation—with the exception of drip irrigation, currently used in a mere 0.7 percent of world irrigation systems—wastes a lot of water through seepage and evaporation.[6]

One of the big issues with cotton and water brings us back to the concepts of virtual water and the water footprint introduced in the last chapter; cotton-buying countries are using up tons of water outside their borders. For example, about half of the 176 cubic yards (135 cubic meters) of water used per year for cotton consumption per person in the United States come from outside the United States.[7] In Europe, a full 84 percent of the cotton-related water footprint comes from elsewhere in the world,[8] which means U.S. and European consumers are essentially soaking up the water of cotton-producing countries elsewhere, decreasing the water available to people in those places, and leaving them to figure out how to handle the resulting water scarcity problems. (Note that the water footprints refer to water use not just in growing but also processing cotton, as well as the water pollution caused by both.) With global water scarcity increasing and impacting public health in a huge way, this scenario is downright unfair and is reason enough to pause before adding yet another cotton t-shirt to our already full drawers.

One of the most tragic examples of water depletion is the former Soviet state of Uzbekistan, where state-run cotton farms drained the rivers that flowed into the Aral Sea, the world's fourth-largest inland sea, reducing its volume of water by 80 percent between 1960 and 2000 and creating a near desert out of the once green and fertile area.[9] The shrinking of the Aral Sea has literally changed the climate of the area, causing shorter, hotter summers and colder winters, less rainfall, and tremendous dust storms. The dust carries salt and pesticides including DDT, which are resulting in a host of public health crises. Growing cotton is not just depleting the *quantity* of water, it's also damaging the *quality* of water that remains; there's less water overall and what remains is increasingly polluted by agricultural chemicals.[10] And we're talking about a ton of chemicals.

Though it takes up just 2.5 percent of the world's croplands, cotton uses 10 percent of the world's fertilizers and 25 percent of its insecticides[11]; agribusiness spends nearly $2.6 billion worth of pesticides on cotton plants every year.[12] Farmers in the United States apply nearly one-third of a pound of chemical fertilizers and pesticides for every pound of cotton harvested.[13] Many of the pesticides (which include insecticides, herbicides, and fungi-

have been around,[2] we run a risk by using them and exposing ourselves to them. The old thinking about chemical ingredients was that low enough exposure prevented health risks. But as was proved in the groundbreaking research of Dr. Theo Colborn and Dr. John Peterson Myers, environmental scientists and coauthors (with Dianne Dumanoski) of the 1996 book *Our Stolen Future*, low-dose exposures over time can have tragic outcomes, with the worst fallout from even infinitesimal levels of chemical contamination showing up in the next generation(s) as reduced intelligence, lowered immunity, ADD, infertility, cancer, and other potential effects of which we're not even yet aware.[3] In the upcoming section on dangerous materials I'll talk about the negative impacts of some of the synthetics that we've already been able to track.

But first, now that we've got the gamut of necessary ingredients—stacks of logs, tankers of water, mounds of metals, barrels of petroleum, piles of coal, yards of synthetic fibers, vats of chemical compounds, etc.—it's time to peer into some factories and witness our Stuff being made.

Of course, the process of production looks different for different kinds of Stuff. But there are also similarities—for example, every single production process requires an input of energy, and right now this is nearly always provided by burning coal or oil. I decided to approach the overwhelming number of production processes that are out there by investigating just a few of my favorite things, along with a few of my least favorite.

My Cotton T-Shirt

What a great invention, right? It's comfy, breathable, washable, absorbent, and versatile. I can wear it under a blazer to an important meeting, over a swimsuit at the beach, or with my jeans—plus or minus a sweater—in just about every season. I can pick one up almost anywhere, even the grocery store or drugstore, and I'll only have to spend $6.99 or $4.99 or maybe even $1.99 if I get a multipack or catch a sale. What's not to lov let's see . . .

I intentionally leave out agricultural products and food in t Story of Stuff; there are plenty of other people, books, and film those issues. But to unravel the story of my T-shirt, which prov dow into the whole textiles industry, we have to start out i Fluffy, thirsty, toxic: that could be the tagline for cotton, a sh the tropics but today grown in the United States, Uzbekis China, India, and small African countries like Benin and

cides like aldicarb, phorate, methamidophos, and endosulfan) are among the most hazardous chemicals and carcinogens in existence and were originally developed by scientists for simultaneous use as nerve agents in warfare alongside their use as insecticides.[14]

In conventional cotton farming, chemicals are first sprayed on the fields before planting to fumigate the soil. The cotton seeds themselves are often dipped in fungicide. Then the plants are sprayed with pesticides several times over the course of the growing season.[15]

These chemicals are indiscriminate: they kill beneficial insects and microorganisms in the soil in addition to bugs that eat the cotton plants. Snuffing out the good bugs means eliminating the natural predators of bad bugs, which creates the need for yet more pesticides. Meanwhile more than 500 species of insects, 180 weeds, and 150 fungi have developed resistance to pesticides.[16] All of this keeps chemical companies busy developing more, while farmers get stuck on "pesticide treadmills." Further compounding the problem, industrial agriculture has whittled hundreds of diverse species of cotton down to just a handful of varieties; the common practice known as monocropping (planting farms with just one variety) makes farms even more vulnerable to pests, which love to feed on big fields of one consistent meal.

Even when used according to instructions, pesticides drift into neighboring communities, contaminate groundwater and surface water as well as animals like fish, birds, and humans—and, above all, the farmworkers. Cotton workers frequently suffer from neurological and vision disorders. In one study of pesticide illnesses in my state, California, cotton ranked third for total number of pesticide-caused worker illnesses.[17]

In many developing countries where environmental regulations are less stringent, the amount of pesticides, and their toxicity, is even greater, while workers are provided with even fewer safety precautions. The UN Food and Agriculture Organization points out that farmers in many developing countries use antiquated, dangerous equipment, which is more likely to result in spills and poisonings.[18] According to the Pesticide Action Network's Organic Cotton Briefing Kit: "In India, 91% of male cotton workers exposed to pesticides eight hours or more per day experienced some type of health disorder, including chromosomal aberrations, cell death and cell cycle delay . . . Pesticide poisoning remains a daily reality among agricultural workers in developing countries, where up to 14% of all occupational injuries in the agricultural sector and 10% of all fatal injuries can be attributed to pesticides."[19]

To top it all off, at harvest time the plants are sprayed with toxic chemical defoliants that strip off the leaves so they don't stain the fluffy white bolls and so the bolls are more accessible to the mechanical pickers or "strippers." [20]

We've now left the cotton fields, but we're still not even close to the finished product: my T-shirt. Taking the raw cotton and turning it into fabric requires a whole litany of industrial processes. The energy-sucking machines involved include a cotton gin that separates the fiber from the seeds, stems, and leaves, followed by machines that bundle the fibers into bales so they can be transported elsewhere, where more machines undo the bales, fluff the cotton, and press it into sheets called laps. Then come carding, combing, drawing, and spinning machines, which produce cotton thread. Finally weaving or knitting machines transform the cotton thread into fabric. But it's still not the soft, bright fabric of my white T-shirt. It needs to be "finished." This can involve "scouring," which means boiling the fabric in an alkali like sodium hydroxide to remove impurities. [21]

Next up: the color. Since my T-shirt is white, it's going to get an especially strong dose of bleach—but even colored T's get bleached before being dyed. (The dying process often uses benzene, heavy metals, formaldehyde fixing agents, and a whole host of chemicals, and because cotton naturally resists dyes, one-third of them run off into wastewater.) But back to my white one: to bleach its fabric, I can only hope hydrogen peroxide was used, but many companies outside the United States and Europe, where most garments are produced, are still likely to use chlorine. [22] Chlorine is toxic on its own, but if it gets mixed with organic (carbon-containing) material, as can happen once the chlorine leaves the factory in wastewater, it becomes a carcinogen and neurotoxin.

In the last stage before the fabric is trundled off to the sewing machines (or sometimes after it is sewn and assembled) it's usually treated to become what the textile industry calls "easy care," which means soft, wrinkle resistant, stain and odor resistant, fireproof, mothproof, and antistatic. Here we have one of the fabulous legacies of our post-1950s infatuation with science's capacity to "simplify" our lives. So which magic potion did scientists find would keep fabric so carefree? Formaldehyde. [23] This dangerous chemical (usually used as a building block of materials like resins and plastics) not only results in respiratory problems, burning eyes, and cancer, it can cause allergic contact dermatitis when it touches the skin. [24] Um, I don't know about you, but my clothes come into contact with my skin *all the time*. Other popular ingredients in this stage are caustic soda, sulfuric acid, bromines, urea resins, sulfonamides, and halogens. [25] These can cause problems with sleep, concentration, and memory . . . and more cancer.

Needless to say, it's not only we wearers of cotton whose health is at risk: factory workers processing the fabrics are especially impacted, and the contaminated wastewater from these factories ultimately affects the entire global food chain. In fact, about one-fifth of the global footprint of cotton consumption is related to pollution from wastewater from fields and factories.[26]

At last my T-shirt is ready to be born, and the finished cotton fabric is shipped off to the factory where this will happen. This is the stage we've heard the most about, on account of all the bad press that sweatshops have received. Sadly, despite the attention, the conditions for most garment workers are still horrendous. Many big brand clothing companies tend to seek out factories that pay the absolute lowest wages. Today this means places like Bangladesh and the "special economic zones" or "export processing zones" of China, where workers—squeezed into underlit, under-ventilated, deafening factories to perform mind-numbing, repetitive drudgery, sometimes for eleven hours a day—receive wages as low as ten to thirteen cents per hour.[27] Free speech and the right to form a trade union are routinely repressed as well. Child labor, though officially outlawed pretty much everywhere, still exists in shadowy pockets, most often employed when deadlines are tight.

When I visited Port-au-Prince, Haiti, in 1990, I met with women who worked in sweatshops making clothing for Disney. This was six years before the New York–based National Labor Committee released its 1996 film *Mickey Mouse Goes to Haiti*, exposing the hardships these workers face, but the plight of garment workers was already getting international attention and some of the women were nervous about speaking freely. Others weren't shy, hoping their stories would be heard by people like me who might be able to shift Disney's practices. Least shy of all was Yannick Etienne, the firebrand organizer from Batay Ouvriye ("Workers Fight"), who facilitated the meeting and translated the women's stories.

In the Haitian heat, we crowded into a tiny room inside a small cinder-block house. We had to keep the windows shuttered for fear that someone might see the workers speaking to us. These women worked day in and day out, sewing Disney apparel that they could never save enough to buy. Those lucky enough to be paid minimum wage earned about fifteen dollars a week for a six-day workweek, eight hours per day. Some of their overseers refused to pay minimum wage unless a certain number of garments were completed each shift. The women described the grueling pressure at work, routine sexual harassment, and other unsafe and demeaning conditions. Through international allies in the workers rights movement, they had learned that Disney's CEO Michael Eisner made millions. In the year that *Mickey Mouse Goes to Haiti* was released—1996—he made $8.7 million in salary plus $181 million in stock options, which comes out to $101,000 an hour.[28] In contrast, these women were paid *half of 1 percent* of the sales price of the garment in the United States.

Yet even with the horrible working conditions and starvation wages, the women feared losing their jobs, because they had no other opportunities. One told me that working for Disney allowed them to starve slowly, which was better than a quick starvation. The women wanted fair pay for a fair day's work. They wanted us to use our voice as U.S. consumers and citizens to pressure Disney into improving the wages and living conditions for the workers, so they could have a healthy, decent life. They wanted to be safe, be able to drink water when hot, and to be free from sexual harassment. The mothers wanted to come home early enough to see their children before bedtime and to have enough food to feed them a solid meal when they woke. Since that visit, I've never been able to look at Disney products without thinking of the women of Port-Au-Prince.

In August 2009, Etienne e-mailed me to say, "The working conditions have not changed much in the industrial park in PauP [Port au Prince]. We are still fighting for the same changes and now the battle for an increase of the minimum wage is waging fiercely."[29] It's been nineteen years since I first met the determined organizer and she is still fighting for worker rights in Haiti. In August 2009, the Haitian government did increase the minimum wage, but it still fell short of the five dollars a day that many workers were demanding. The new minimum wage is three dollars and seventy-five cents a day.[30] A *day!* Three dollars and seventy-five cents for a full day sewing our T-shirts and jeans and pajamas.

Back to my T-shirt: a final impact to consider is its carbon dioxide (CO_2) footprint, or its contribution to climate change. To grow the cotton for just my one shirt, about 2 pounds of CO_2 are generated—to make petrochemical-based fertilizers and pesticides, and for the electricity used in pumping irrigation water. The cleaning, spinning, knitting, and finishing processes add another 3 pounds. So in total my little T-shirt generates about 5 pounds of CO_2. That's *before* it gets transported to and from the store and then gets washed and dried over its lifetime, which at least doubles its carbon footprint.[31]

When I visited the website of the clothing company Patagonia recently, it allowed me to calculate the footprints of several of their items, including one of their organic cotton T-shirts. The site told me where "nearly half" of the cotton came from (Turkey); that's a long way away. The next stop listed was Los Angeles, for knitting, cutting, and sewing in one factory and dyeing in another, using oil-based dyes, some of which are not PVC free. Patagonia explains: "Although plant-based dyes would seem to be more environmentally benign, they can be hard to harvest in sufficient quantity for commercial use. Plant-based dyes often lose their colorfastness after very few washings." Then the shirt was driven up to their distribution center in Reno, Nevada. According to their calculations, Patagonia's T-shirt travels about 7,840 miles and generates 3.5 pounds of carbon dioxide, even before it gets sent to your local store.[32]

Now, I don't mean to imply that organic cotton T-shirts (and other clothes) aren't worth the extra dollars you'll likely need to spend on them. Organic cotton avoids the use of pesticides and chemical fertilizers, which avoids the carbon involved in making those chemicals, keeps the groundwater and soil cleaner, and safeguards the health of animals and humans (farmworkers, residents of neighboring communities, and consumers). Organic farmers claim that the healthier soil (with the aerating services of earthworms that have not been killed by chemicals) causes less water to be lost in runoff, although biotech proponents say their genetically modified crops use less water. Factories like the ones Patagonia uses for the spinning, weaving, and sewing processes are at the forefront of energy conservation and also minimize toxic runoff. And if you see a fair trade logo, it means that the cotton farmers got fairer prices and the fabric workers got better than sweatshop conditions and were compensated more fairly than the women I met in Haiti.

For all these reasons, organic and fair trade cotton products are the better choice. But the best choice of all? Cherish the T-shirt you have. Wear it and care for it with the same persevering love you have for an heirloom piece of jewelry. Resist the urge to replace it with the newest color or neckline. I keep my T-shirts until they're too worn to wear even to the gym, and then I turn them into rags. It's what my grandparents did, and it's good enough for me. Because even though the price tag said $4.99, or even $12.99 at Patagonia, that doesn't come close to reflecting all the hidden costs of one plain white cotton T-shirt.

A Book

I have shelves and shelves of books. An entire wall in my bedroom is books. I have books on the kitchen counter, books spilling off my daughter's shelves, books piled by the unused fireplace. Books occupy an odd space in my relationship to Stuff: while I feel uncomfortable buying new clothes or electronics, I don't hesitate to pick up the latest recommended title. I asked my friends about it and found I'm not alone in feeling like books are some-how exempt from the negative connotations of too much Stuff. Do we feel the value of knowledge and creativity embodied by a book justifies its foot-print? Do we just not think about the footprint? In writing this book, I real-ized that I knew far more about the environmental and health threats of my laptop, cell phone, or even my T-shirts than I did about the far more numerous books in my house-hold. So I was eager to find out how books are produced.

Today, when we think of paper, we think of it com-ing from trees. However, paper has only been made from wood pulp since the 1850s.[33] Before then—and still to some extent today—paper was made from agricultural crops like hemp and bamboo, and from rags and old textiles. The word "paper" comes from the Greek word (*papyros*) for papyrus, a writing material they developed by mashing strips of the papyrus plant. The first known piece of paper was made almost two thou-sand years ago by a Chinese court official, Ts'ai Lun, who used mulberry bush fiber, old fishing nets, hemp, and grass. In the fifteenth century, some books were printed on parchment, which is made from the specially pre-pared skin of sheep or goats, or on vellum, made of calfskin. It took the skins of three hundred sheep to print one Bible back then. Later, in the six-teenth century, cloth rags and linen were also frequently used as the fiber in papermaking.[34] It wasn't until much later—around the mid-nineteenth century—that large-scale wood pulp processing was developed, allowing trees to become the primary source for fiber with which to make paper, and hence books. (Not every book today is made from plant fibers: One excep-tion is Bill McDonough's book *Cradle to Cradle*, which was printed on plas-tic. E-books, of course, aren't printed at all.) Paper can also be made from previously used paper. That's recycling.

During all these hundreds of years, the basic steps of papermaking have remained the same. The fiber is mashed, flattened, and dried, and presto, you have paper. It's not unlike art projects I do with my daughter where we put old paper, flower petals, and wrapping paper scraps in the blender with water, whir it up, pour the slurry onto a window screen, squish it flat, and lay it in the sun to dry. Just four categories of ingredients are needed: fiber, energy, chemicals, and water.

But this simple list is a little bit misleading. First, of course, there's the problem of deforestation (see chapter 1 on extraction), including the less visible form of deforestation in which natural forests are replaced with plantations. Today, nearly half of the trees cut in North America go to making paper for everything from newsprint to packaging to stationery.[35] Each year, about 30 million trees are used to make books sold in the United States.[36] To give you a visual, there are about 26,000 trees in Central Park,[37] so to make our books we use more than 1,150 times that number. Papermaking also uses vast amounts of energy and is among the top five emitters of greenhouse gases of all manufacturing industries.[38] It requires huge amounts of water and toxic chemicals, which get mixed and released together into the environment.

No matter which source you start with—virgin trees, managed forests, agricultural crops, or recovered paper—part of the substance is useful and part is not. The desired part is the fiber. What are not wanted are the lignin, sugars, and other compounds found in wood and other plants. If the source is paper that's being recycled, then most of the lignin is already removed, but the inks, staples, perfume inserts, and other contaminants have to be taken out.[39] Unfortunately, each time the paper goes through this process, the fibers get worn down and shortened, so they can't be recycled more than a handful of times.

The process of separating the useful fibers from the unwanted parts is called pulping. There are two main technologies used to make pulp: mechanical and chemical. Mechanical pulping involves chopping, grinding, or mashing the source material to separate the cellulose fibers from other compounds. Mechanical pulping is twice as efficient as chemical pulping, but the resulting fibers are short and stiff, which limits their use to a lower quality paper, mostly for newsprint, telephone directories (when was the last time you needed one of these?), and packaging.[40]

Chemical pulping, the more widespread process, takes chemicals, heat, and pressure to separate the fibers. More chemicals are used later in the process as dyes, inks, bleach, sizing, and coatings. "The art of modern papermaking lies in the specialty chemicals used," explained one chemical journalist. "Like spices for food, they give the paper that certain something."[41] And as paper use goes up, so does demand for those chemicals used in production. In the United States, the demand for chemicals for pulp and paper production is projected to reach 20 billion tons in 2011, with the chemicals valued at $8.8 billion.[42]

The most notorious and controversial chemical used in papermaking is chlorine, which is added to help with the pulping and also to bleach the paper. By itself, chlorine is a powerful toxin—so toxic that it was used as a weapon in the First World War. But when chlorine gets mixed with organic compounds (those that contain carbon)—which, in a slush made of mashed plants, happens a lot—the chlorine bonds with them to create nearly a thousand different organochlorines, including the most toxic persistent pollutant in existence, dioxin.[43] The U.S. Environmental Protection Agency and the International Agency for Research on Cancer have both confirmed that dioxin causes cancer.[44] It's also linked to endocrine, reproductive, nervous, and immune system damage[45]—which really don't seem worth it for having white paper. Me, I'd take slightly brown—or tree colored—paper over carcinogens any day.

In Europe, much of the paper—from toilet paper to book pages—is off-white in color. Many of their paper mills have switched to totally chlorine free (TCF) processes, using oxygen or ozone and hydrogen peroxide instead of chlorine to bleach paper.[46] In the United States and Canada, many of our mills prefer elemental chlorine free (ECF) processing, which replaces chlorine gas with chlorine derivatives, such as chlorine dioxide. True, this beats dousing our paper with chlorine gas, and it reduces dioxin formation by about half. But any amount of dioxins is too much, even a speck. So TCF is definitely preferable. There is one last variation on the chlorine front: processed chlorine free (PCF) refers to paper made from recycled paper sources. This means the mill can't guarantee that no chorine was used in the original paper production but promises that no chlorine was used in the recycling process.

Getting rid of chlorine requires some investment, but is a small price to pay compared to all those costs that get externalized onto the environment and people, such as the dioxin discharged into rivers that threatens fishing grounds, livelihoods, and community health.

One of the other toxins involved in papermaking is mercury, the potent neurotoxin that harms the nervous system and brain, especially in fetuses and children. Mercury has a backstage presence in papermaking, "upstream" at so-called chlor-alkali plants where chlorine and caustic soda (lye) are produced. The pulp and paper industry is the single largest consumer of caustic soda worldwide.[47] Even though competitive, cost-effective, nonmercury alternatives exist to making chlorine and caustic soda, a number of chlor-alkali plants in the United States and the rest of the world still use mercury in their manufacturing. And once it's been released into the environment, mercury doesn't go away.

However, things are looking up: there has been enough sustained concern about mercury (see the section "Dangerous Materials" later in this chapter) that these plants are increasingly becoming a relic of the past, gradually being replaced with mercury-free alternatives.

So, back to the paper mill. Once the pulping process is finished, the pulp is mixed with water and sprayed onto a moving mesh screen. These screens get vacuumed, heated, and pressed to get them to dry into a consistent paper product—all processes that consume energy. Now the paper is ready to be printed.

At the press, there's another slew of toxic petroleum-based chemicals added to the mix, which are used to make inks, clean the presses, and wash the so-called blankets (used to transfer ink-filled images to paper). At the top of the list comes toluene, which accounts for 75 percent of all toxic chemicals used in printing.[48] These chemicals get released into the environment at frightening levels. Many escape as vapors known as volatile organic compounds (VOCs), which not only smog up the air, causing respiratory, allergic, and immunity problems, but also drop into soil and groundwater.

There are viable alternatives to petrochemicals for inks and cleaners, however, in the form of vegetable-based "biochemicals." Although most are still made with some percentage of petroleum, they represent a huge improvement. They avoid a lot of the initial upstream pollution from the processes by which crude oil is extracted and refined into chemicals. They are much safer for workers at printing presses to handle and inhale and mean less investment in safety training and protective equipment. They are far less flammable. And they create far less toxic solid waste and emissions: while petroleum-based inks contain 30 to 35 percent VOCs, soy inks range from 2 to 5 percent.[49]

Soybean-oil-based inks have become the most popular of the vegetable-based inks and are now used by about one-third of the commercial printers in the United States.[50] Although they're priced slightly higher, soy inks turn out to perform better, producing brighter colors and requiring less ink to cover the same space, so they end up being more cost-effective than traditional chemical inks. They also make paper recycling easier, because they can be more easily removed from the old paper.

Once the pages are printed, they are stitched and/or glued together inside a hard cover (made of cardboard) or a soft paper cover. A final aspect of a book's footprint involves its distribution and shipping, which I'll examine in the next chapter.

Thanks to the work of advocacy organizations such as the Environmental Paper Network and the Green Press Initiative, and to sustainable business leaders like Inkworks Press, EcoPrint, and New Leaf Paper, both the papermaking and the publishing industries have become greener. A lot more books are being printed on recycled paper stock, using fewer petroleum-based inks. When they are made in processes that have a lighter footprint, today's books often include a page explaining the source of the paper (recycled, virgin, from certified sustainable forests), the bleaching process, and the type of inks used, allowing readers a glimpse into the production process.

I took a look at the five books sitting on my nightstand as I wrote this. Two didn't mention their fiber source at all, leading me to assume the worst. One said its pages are "printed on recycled paper" but didn't provide specifics—what percentage recycled? Preconsumer (meaning trimmings from the paper factory that have never been touched by consumers) or postconsumer (meaning it was used and discarded by consumers)? Another confirmed its pages came from FSC-certified "well managed forests, controlled sources and recycled wood or fiber." The last book was made from postconsumer recycled content, which is a higher form of recycling than using preconsumer paper because it diverts would-be municipal waste back into useful products. Only one of my bedside books mentioned the chlorine issue, proudly displaying both the TCF logo on its cover and the PCF status of the interior pages.

When I was initially approached about creating a book based on the twenty-minute animated film of *The Story of Stuff*, I was a little bit reluctant, thinking of the resources it would involve. Yet thousands of people were asking me for more information about what I'd touched on in the film, wanting to hold discussion groups, create curricula, and learn more about positive alternatives to the current system and actions they could take. And, as I know from my travels around the world, there are still a lot of people in a lot of places who simply don't have access to the technology that would allow them to watch the film and access more detailed information online or as a DVD. So I agreed to do this book, but I held out for a publisher that committed to minimizing resources and toxic inputs in the book's production. You'll find an environmental impact statement for this very book on page 307.

My Computer

Collectively, Americans own more than 200 million computers, 200 million TVs, and around 200 million cell
phones.[51] I do have a laptop and a cell phone, but the
truth is, I'm one of those people who is just not
attracted to new electronic gizmos. The incessant beep-
ing annoys me, and the thought of losing all my contact information or
documents in a single zap gives me hives. I staunchly rely on my fifteen-
year-old refillable paper appointment book, which has accompanied me to
at least thirty countries, even though each year that passes it becomes
increasingly difficult to find replacement pages, an endangered species. I
love this well-worn, very unhip appointment book so much that once I
even entered an essay contest sponsored by the company that made it. The
first stanza of the poem I composed read: "It doesn't light up; it doesn't plug
in. It doesn't need batteries, has no secret PIN." I prefer it to high-tech alternatives for all those reasons.

But before you write me off as a total Luddite, let me assure you I appreciate the positive contributions that electronics and computer technology
make. I would be hard-pressed to manage without my cell phone today. I
know electronic devices can help find lost kids and stranded hikers. In the
hands of activists around the world, they document human rights abuses
and disseminate alerts and warnings. Text messages and tweeting have
alerted the media and support networks when people have been unjustly
detained or harmed. And I would be a very unhappy camper without my
computer, which helps me find and organize information, communicate
with friends and colleagues, and write this book.

Yet the story of our electronics is extremely complicated. Those Apple
advertisements make their products look so clean, simple, and elegant,
don't they? High-tech development is often cast as an improvement over
the belching smokestacks of old-fashioned industries, but it actually just
replaces the highly visible pollution of old with a less visible version.

The truth is, electronics production facilities are ecologically filthy, using
and releasing tons of hazardous compounds that poison the workers and
surrounding communities. Silicon Valley, less than fifty miles south of my
home in Berkeley, has so many toxic contaminated sites linked to former
high-tech development that it has among the highest concentration of
Superfund sites in the country.[52] (Superfund is the U.S. government's list of
sites so contaminated with toxins that they qualify for priority cleanup programs.) Much of the high-tech production has now moved out of Silicon

Valley—seeking the lower wages and less stringent worker safety and environmental regulations in Asia and Latin America—but it has left behind a toxic legacy.

The famed high-tech wonderland of Silicon Valley is also a place of social extremes, with the mansions where Internet tycoons live butting up against rundown neighborhoods inhabited by the people who actually make electronic components—or who used to before the factories moved overseas. As computer companies strive to offer lower prices to consumers while maintaining their hefty profits, they increasingly focus their cost-cutting efforts on the stops along the supply chain. Big name brand computer companies are infamous for pressuring manufacturers and suppliers to lower expenses and prices and to lengthen working hours in order to make and sell the components cheaply. Michael Dell of Dell computers once said, "Our job is to be absolutely the best in the world at driving costs down."[53]

Then there's the back-end problem of electronic waste, or e-waste. As I'll discuss further in the chapter on disposal, e-waste is a global nightmare, with between 5 and 7 million tons of electronics becoming obsolete each year, their trashed toxic components poisoning the land, air, water, and all of the earth's inhabitants.[54]

In trying to gather information about the specific materials that went into my computer and the processes by which it was made, I ran up against some insurmountable barriers. Ted Smith at the Electronics TakeBack Coalition shook his head when he heard that I wanted to uncover the story of my computer in the same way as I'd tracked the production of my T-shirt and this book. "A computer is more complex than those items by several orders of magnitude," he told me, like the difference between the biological makeup of, say, an earthworm and the entire planet. Smith points out that more than two thousand materials are used in the production of a microchip, which is just a single component of my machine! And because the industry moves so fast, continuously introducing new materials and processes, regulators and heroic watchdog groups like Smith's can't keep up. They haven't yet completed their analyses on the health and environmental impacts of electronics from several years ago, and a new crop of products has already been introduced.[55] On top of that, what makes telling the full story truly impossible is the secrecy the industry mandates, claiming their processes and materials are proprietary. That mentality is reflected in the title of a book by former Intel CEO Andy Grove: *Only the Paranoid Survive*.[56]

It is impossible to know the exact locations where all the components of a laptop were drilled for, mined, or made, because of the increasingly complex supply chain of the electronics industry, which the UN reports has the most globalized supply chain of all industries.[57] But we do know that all the problematic mining practices described in the chapter on extraction—for gold and tantalum, as well as copper, aluminum, lead, zinc, nickel, tin, silver, iron, mercury, cobalt, arsenic, cadmium, and chromium—are involved. The brand name company—Dell, HP, IBM, Apple, etc.—may have little immediate knowledge of, or even control over, how materials are derived or components are made, because these companies outsource to hundreds of other companies all over the world that provide and assemble the pieces. But that doesn't exonerate those big brands from their responsibility for the environmental contamination, health problems, or human rights violations that their products cause.

There *is* a fair amount of information available about the manufacturing of microchips, so we can at least take a look at how these are made. Chips, being the brains of the computer, are very complex. A chip is a thin wafer, usually made from silicon, onto which they etch tiny, fussy pathways made of metal that enable an electrical current to be transmitted and transformed into digital information. One of these chips is smaller than the fingernail of your pinky, and they're getting smaller all the time.[58]

The silicon for the wafers can be derived from nearly anyplace on earth; silicon is a kind of sand, very common and not inherently toxic. Fortunately wafer production does not require large amounts of silicon, which is good because exposure to silicon in mines or factories at greater levels can lead to respiratory problems and an incurable lung disease known as silicosis. According to the World Health Organization, thousands of people die from silicosis every year.[59] Later in the chip-making process, the toxic elements antimony, arsenic, boron, and phosphorus are added to make the silicon conduct electricity.[60]

To create the wafer, the silicon is ground to a powder, then dissolved in a flammable, corrosive, highly toxic liquid. In energy-intensive steps (there will be more than 250 of them before the chip is finished), this liquid is heated until it evaporates, is allowed to crystallize, and is baked again to form cylinders. The cylinders are cleaned and polished in a series of acidic and caustic solutions. Finally, the wafers are sliced from these cylinders. "Imagine a seriously high-tech, ultrapure silicon crystal roll of refrigerated cookie dough," writes Elizabeth Grossman in her comprehensive book *High Tech Trash*.[61]

It's onto these wafers that circuits will be etched, a process that involves another whole set of toxic metals, gases, solvents, and "etchants." "Altogether, one individual semiconductor fabrication plant may use as many as five hundred to a thousand different chemicals," writes Grossman, "acids, including hydrofluoric, nitric, phosphoric, and sulfuric acid, as well as ammonia, fluoride, sodium hydroxide, isopropyl alcohol, and methyl-3-methoxyproprionate, tetramethylammonium hydroxide, and hydroxyl monoethanolamine, along with acetone, chromium trioxide, methyl ethyl ketone, methyl alcohol, and xylene."[62] And that's only a partial list.

All of this takes place in so-called clean rooms, which use vast amounts of toxic solvents to keep microscopic particles of dust from landing on the chips. The term "clean" refers to protecting the product, not the workers. In fact, workers in clean rooms are among the most contaminated of all high-tech workers. The materials to which they're routinely exposed have been proven to cause respiratory diseases, kidney and liver damage, cancers, miscarriages, and birth defects like spina bifida, blindness, and missing or deformed limbs.[63] Many of these adverse health impacts likewise affect the communities around fabrication facilities, whose groundwater, soil, and air are contaminated.

And yes, the toxics threaten us even as we work on our computers. In 2004, two nonprofit organizations promoting safer materials in the electronics sector—Clean Production Action and the Computer TakeBack Campaign—collected dust from computers to test for the presence of toxic flame retardants. The scientists found these potent neurotoxins in every sample tested.[64] Flame retardants, such as PBDEs (polybrominated diphenyl ethers), are chemicals added to materials in an attempt to slow the time needed to reach ignition. But it isn't even proven that these chemicals deter flames: so they may not even help. When electronics that are encased in plastic treated with PBDEs heat up (as happens when a computer's been running for a few hours), the chemicals break off in the form of dust or as a gas that can leach out of the product into the environment (i.e., our desks).[65] The particular form of PBDEs used in computers persists in our bodies for years. Beyond their neurotoxicity, further studies have linked them to problems with immunity and reproductive systems, as well as to cancer, which is why PDBEs have been banned in Europe, are being listed under the Stockholm POPs Convention, and why computer manufacturers everywhere have come under pressure to phase them out.[66]

The public health implications of electronics production are matched by its impacts on the environment. Take the production of just one of these finished wafers, this tiny thing weighing in at about 0.16 grams.[67] According to Eric Williams of United Nations University, coauthor of the book *Computers and the Environment,* a wafer's production involves about 5 gallons (20 liters) of water, about 45 grams of chemicals—or more than 250 times the weight of the finished wafer—and enough energy to run a 100-watt lightbulb for 18 hours, or 1.8 kilowatt hours.[68] Additional energy is needed for the heating, cooling, and ventilation of the clean room. A factory making semiconductors can consume as much electricity in a year as ten thousand homes and up to 3 million gallons of water per day.[69] Annual utility bills can be as high as $20 to $25 million.[70] Finally, making a single chip results in 17 kilograms of wastewater and 7.8 grams of solid waste.[71] The wastewater contains a lot of nitrates, which in turn cause an explosion of aquatic plant growth in bodies of water that upsets the balance of ecosystems. Air pollution also results from the release of ammonia, hydrochloric acid, hydrogen fluoride, and nitric acid—toxins one and all.[72] And that's all just the microchips.

Then there's the monitor—the glass, especially in older models, often contains lead, the lights behind the flat-panel display often contain mercury—and the housing, which is composed of various petroleum-based plastics treated with flame retardants and other chemicals for color and texture. Noxious PVC, which I'll describe in more depth in an upcoming section, insulates the wires. The lithium batteries usually used to power laptops contain some toxic substances—for example, the lithium itself. These hundreds of materials, many of them hazardous, are all enmeshed and

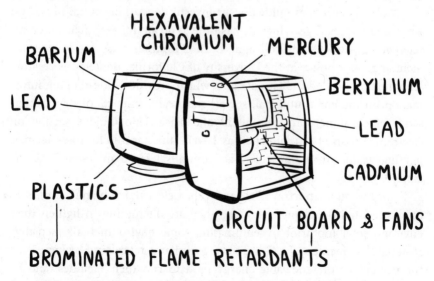

HAZARDOUS MATERIALS IN A PC

HEXAVALENT CHROMIUM
BARIUM
MERCURY
BERYLLIUM
LEAD
LEAD
CADMIUM
PLASTICS
CIRCUIT BOARD & FANS
BROMINATED FLAME RETARDANTS

Source: Silicon Valley Toxics Coalition/Electronics Take Back Campaign, 2008.

entwined, which is why recycling the components and materials from my laptop later, after its eventual disposal, will be such a hassle.

My laptop—the one on which I'm writing this book—was made by Dell. In 2006, when I was in the market for a new computer, I chose it because of Dell's high ranking in Greenpeace's regularly-updated *Guide to Green Electronics*, which rates electronics manufacturers on three areas: toxic chemicals, recycling, and climate change/energy consumption. Since 2006 Dell has dropped to a much lower ranking due to its backtracking on a commitment to eliminate toxic PVC and brominated flame retardants by 2010.

There's also some upsetting news in terms of worker safety at Dell. Their company policies discuss their commitment to ensuring safe working conditions, both at their own factories and for contractors that produce materials for Dell computers. Unfortunately, a number of investigations by labor and human rights organizations have found ongoing labor violations at factories producing for Dell. The Centre for Research on Multinational Corporations (SOMO), a nonprofit Dutch research and advisory bureau, investigated eight Dell suppliers in China, Mexico, the Philippines, and Thailand. SOMO uncovered "violations including dangerous working conditions, degrading and abusive working conditions, excessive working hours and forced overtime, illegally low wages and unpaid overtime, denial of the right to strike, discrimination in employment, use of contract labor and 'trainees,' workers without a contract, and lack of freedom of association and unionization."[73]

Uh-oh. Greenpeace's guide doesn't investigate working conditions. And who but a materials geek like me has time to do all this research and cross-referencing? Luckily, my colleague Dara O'Rourke, professor of environment and labor policy at the University of California, Berkeley, is creating an online tool called the GoodGuide, which provides wide-ranging information on the environmental, social, and health impacts of many thousands of consumer products all in one place. GoodGuide's section on electronics hasn't been launched as I write this (and O'Rourke's team is fighting against the same corporate firewalls I faced in researching my laptop).[74]

I don't want to portray Dell and other electronics manufacturers as totally resistant to change, though. They are attempting to lighten their environmental footprint by eliminating some environmentally sensitive materials like mercury, PVC and some toxic flame retardants; by increasing the percentage of renewable energy used to run their facilities; and by reducing packaging and increasing the recycled content of packaging.[75] I applaud these efforts, but I'm afraid they just don't go far enough.

It seems ludicrous that electronics can't be made differently. Electronics designers and producers are smart people—it's mind-blowing how fast they come up with improvements in speed, size, and capacity. The oft-quoted Moore's law predicts that computing capacities can be doubled approximately every two years. So these guys can figure out how to fit thousands of songs on a device the size of a matchbook, but they can't eliminate the most toxic plastic—PVC—from their high-tech wonders or reduce packaging waste by more than 10 percent? Please! These brainiacs should be able to figure out how to phase out toxics, reduce waste to a minimum, and expand the durability and life span of their products too.

Environmental health activists tracking the industry have challenged the high-tech manufacturers to achieve the same level of improvement in environmental and health impacts as those Moore predicted for technical capacity. More than a decade ago, in May 1999, the Trans-Atlantic Network for Clean Production adopted the Soesterberg Principles, which added environmental, health, and social issues to the quest for technical innovation in the industry. The Electronic Sustainability Commitment of the principles reads:

> *Each new generation of technical improvements in electronic products should include parallel and proportional improvements in environmental, health and safety as well as social justice attributes.*[76]

If semiconductor capacity can double every two years, how about likewise halving the number of toxic chemicals and doubling the usable life span of these same devices every two years? Sadly, more than ten years since the Soesterberg Principles were adopted, technical improvements continue to get far more attention and make far greater progress than corresponding environmental and health improvements. And the vast majority of the environmental health advances that computer companies have made have only come after sustained campaigns by NGOs. Those NGOS—Silicon Valley Toxics Coalition, Clean Production Action, Electronics TakeBack Coalition, Good Electronics, Greenpeace, Basel Action Network, and others—are going to continue to work hard to press the electronics industry for improvements; but it would be a lot easier for us all if electronics producers embraced sustainability and social goals as seriously as technological and economic goals.

In the meantime, what I do is resist the impulse to trash my old electronics and replace them with the latest, shiniest versions. My appointment book and 2006 laptop do just fine.

Stupid Stuff

Some consumer products are so inherently toxic or wasteful or energy intensive that improving production just isn't a viable option and it would be better to just stop making and using them. If I could wave a magic wand and do away with two everyday items in order to have a huge positive impact on human health and the well-being of our planet, those two things would be aluminum cans and PVC. And if you're looking for some really easy, immediate things you can do to lessen your own impact, start by eliminating these two toxic and totally unnecessary materials from your life.

Platinum—I Mean *Aluminum*—Cans

As I was walking along in downtown San Francisco the other day, two enthusiastic promoters were handing out freebies of some new caffeinated drink. "Try it! It's fair trade! It's made with organic ingredients! It's good for you *and* the earth!" I declined the offer and decided not to rain on their feel-good parade by telling them what a joke it is that a fair-trade organic drink is packaged inside one of the most energy-intensive, CO_2-producing, waste-generating products on the planet: a single-use, single-serving aluminum can.

In the United States we consume about 100 billion cans per year, or 340 per person: almost one a day. That's ten times more than the average European and twice as many as the average Canadian, Australian, or Japanese. In places like China and India, people are only consuming about 10 cans per person per year on average (with wide disparities between social classes), although that number is expected to rise as their economies explode.[77] People like cans because they're light, they don't break, they chill quickly, and they have a reputation for being widely recycled. If the real story were more widely known, people might stop using aluminum cans so carelessly.

A can starts its life as a reddish ore called bauxite, which gets strip-mined in Australia, Brazil, Jamaica, and a few other tropical spots.[78] The mining displaces native people and animals and cuts down legions of those brave soldiers in the war against global warming—the trees.

The bauxite is transported elsewhere to be washed, pulverized, mixed with caustic soda, heated, settled, and filtered until what's left is about half the weight of the original ore in aluminum oxide crystals. But something else is left over: a waste slurry known as "red mud," made of the extremely alkaline caustic soda, as well as iron from the bauxite. The mud is often just held in huge open-air pools.[79] Were a major storm to flood these reservoirs, the environmental damage to the surrounding environment would be devastating. Incidentally, we could be using the iron in that sludge, but no one has figured out an economical way to extract it yet.

Next, the aluminum oxide is transported to smelters, and this is where the truly gross aspects of aluminum production kick in. There's a reason scientists call aluminum "congealed energy": making one aluminum can takes energy equivalent to one-quarter of the can's volume in gasoline.[80] Aluminum smelting requires more energy than any other metal processing on earth.[81]

At the smelter, the aluminum oxide crystals are dissolved in a bath of something called cryolite (sodium aluminum fluoride) and zapped with enormous jolts of electricity (100,000 to 150,000 amps), which strips the oxygen from the aluminum. This process also breaks off bits of the fluorine from the cryolite, which escapes the smelter in the form of perfluorocarbons (PFCs)—these are the most noxious of greenhouse gases, trapping thousands of times more heat than carbon dioxide. What remains is pure aluminum, which gets poured into molds and cooled into bars. Then these bars are shipped elsewhere, rolled into super-thin sheets, and shipped to another factory that punches and forms those sheets into cans. They are washed, dried, primed, painted with the brand and product information, lacquered, sprayed inside with a noncorrosive coating, and finally filled with a beverage.[82]

After all that, the can's contents are consumed in a matter of minutes, and the can is trashed in a matter of seconds. "I don't understand my countrymen. They import this product, drink the garbage, and then throw away the valuable resource," says Puerto Rican activist Juan Rosario, bemoaning the high levels of soda consumption and low level of recycling on his island.[83]

Globally, about a third of aluminum smelters use coal-generated electricity. In addition to carbon dioxide emissions, this pollutes our air with tons of carbon monoxide (the gas that'll kill you if you leave your car running in a closed space), sulfur dioxide, and nitrogen dioxide.[84]

Most of the smelters in the United States and other developed countries have been shut down, and those that are still operational probably won't be up and running much longer. Since 20 to 30 percent of aluminum's total production cost is electricity, while the transportation costs from mines to refineries to smelters constitutes less than 1 percent,[85] it's common to ship the raw materials around the world to take advantage of the cheapest power. Rio Tinto, a huge Australian mining concern, has plans for a new smelter in Abu Dhabi.[86] Why there? Because now that Australia's coming on board with international carbon emissions policies (the Kyoto Protocol's follow-up), that old coal-fired plant will become too expensive, while Abu Dhabi will remain a carbon free-for-all zone.

Worldwide, smelters in rich countries where energy is becoming more expensive are being abandoned in favor of building new ones (plus the power plants needed to fuel them, usually dam projects) in farther-flung places like Mozambique, Chile, Iceland, and along the Amazon River in Brazil.[87] Construction of the dams, roads, and other necessary infrastructure (plus the waste and emissions once the plants are up and running) seriously threatens lives—human, animal, and vegetable—and the climate. For example, a planned site in Iceland would flood a pristine area that contains more than one hundred breathtaking waterfalls and habitat for reindeer and other vulnerable wildlife.[88] Glenn Switkes, the Amazon Program Director of International Rivers, an organization dedicated to protecting rivers around the world, explains that aluminum companies are the principle force behind the Brazilian government's plans to dam the major rivers of the Amazon: "Aluminum companies are relocating to the tropics because governments in developing countries are providing them with subsidized hydroelectricity. These dams have irreversible impacts on biodiversity, and displace thousands of riverbank dwellers and indigenous peoples."[89]

What's that? You're waving the white flag of recycling? Well, the fact is, all the attention paid to recycling in the past few decades has given Americans an inflated idea of how much aluminum is being recycled. That, and some clever manipulation of the numbers by the aluminum industry.*

While it's true that cans are 100 percent recyclable, aluminum recycling in the United States has been on the decline for decades. We're recycling

---

*There are inconsistencies in calculations of the "recycled" sources of the aluminum supply. The U.S. Geological Survey, for example, differentiates between "old," or postconsumer, scrap, and "new," or preconsumer, scrap, which consists of leftover shreds from the production process that never leave the factory. The Aluminum Association, an industry trade group, lumps these streams together in its calculations, which gives the impression that a higher percentage (close to a third) of aluminum comes from "recycled" (or "recovered") sources, when in truth real recycling (postconsumer) accounts for less than one-fifth of the supply. (Jennifer Gitliz, *The Role of the Consumer in Reducing Primary Aluminum Demand*, a report by the Container Recycling Institute for the International Strategic Roundtable on the Aluminum Industry (São Luís, Brazil, October 16–18, 2003, p.9).

about 45 percent of cans today, down from 54.5 percent in 2000 and the peak rate of 65 percent in 1992.[90] In part this is because Americans are spending ever more time commuting and consuming beverages on the go, while there are few recycling bins in places away from home like the mall, the movie theater, the airport, etc. It's also because we still only have bottle bills, which place a 2.5- to 10-cent deposit on each can and bottle, in a mere ten states across the country.[91] In Brazil, meanwhile, there's an impressive 87 percent recycling rate for beverage containers because many people rely on the income from collecting them.[92] Given rising levels of unemployment stateside, you'd think we might follow Brazil's example.

As the Container Recycling Institute points out, widespread subsidies for virgin aluminum also detract from recycling: "Because of long-term, cut-rate energy contracts, below-market water rates, the easy acquisition of government lands for mining, and a myriad of tax breaks and infrastructural assistance, aluminum companies have perhaps been less vulnerable to global economic forces than some other primary industries. [This has] enabled the world aluminum primary industry to expand capacity ahead of demand. As long as excess primary aluminum production capacity exists on the global market, and as long as the cost of making virgin ingot remains low, scrap prices will remain suppressed."[93]

In fact, it's estimated that more than a trillion aluminum cans have been trashed in landfills since 1972, when records started being kept. If those cans were dug up, they'd be worth about $21 billion in today's scrap prices.[94] In 2004 alone, more than 800,000 tons of cans were landfilled in the United States (and 300,000 tons in the rest of the world).[95] As a Worldwatch report pointed out, "that's like five smelters pouring their entire annual output—a million tons of metal—straight into a hole in the ground. Had those cans been recycled, 16 billion kilowatt hours could have been saved—enough electricity for more than two million European homes for a year."[96]

I saw a great depiction of the irrationality of aluminum beverage cans when I was working on waste issues in Budapest in 2007. HuMuSz, an organization there that raises awareness about waste, had made a series of short, entertaining films that play before feature films in Hungarian movie theaters. My favorite film took place in a *WALL-E*-like, totally trashed planet Earth of the future, where aliens arrive to conduct research. They find one remaining human being and grill him for answers about the incredibly valuable and widely dispersed pieces of aluminum strewn about the planet, convinced these were used for communications, military, or medical purposes. When the human replies that they were for single-use servings of sugary, carbonated drinks, the aliens berate him for lying:

"No one would be so stupid, so irrational to use such a highly valuable, energy-intensive metal to hold a simple beverage!" I'm with the aliens on this one.

For once, the solution is incredibly straightforward. If we cut out the absurd, frivolous use of aluminum as a container for our beverages, we can put the tons of aluminum already in circulation into Stuff that makes sense, like to replace some steel to lighten up our modes of transportation, especially while these are still running on CO_2-spewing fossil fuels. And instead of disposable cans, we could be drinking out of refillable bottles, which will take a little advance planning but will cut air and water pollution, energy use, and the production of CO_2 and waste.

PVC, aka Pernicious Vile Compound

Plastic is pretty much universally recognized as a problem these days, from the oil needed to produce it to the virtually immortal debris it leaves floating in our oceans. But not all plastics are created equal; some are more problematic than others. PVC plastic (polyvinyl chloride), commonly referred to as vinyl, is the most hazardous plastic at all stages of its life: from its production in the factory; to its use in our homes, schools, hospitals, and offices; to its disposal in our landfills or, worst of all, our incinerators. It's also a cheap and versatile plastic, which are two reasons it continues to be widely used in spite of its negative environmental health impacts.

PVC has a variety of forms and textures and shows up in all kinds of places: fake leather shoes and purses, waterproof raincoats and boots, shiny bibs and aprons and tablecloths and shower curtains; garden furniture and hoses; food containers and wrapping; plastic-coated dish drying racks; vinyl siding and windows and pipes. It's in medical supplies (tubing) and office supplies (binders). And it's all around our kids in their toys and clothes.

Again we see toxic chlorine, which shows up in much of our Stuff. During PVC's multistage production, chlorine gas is used to produce ethylene dichloride (EDC), which is converted into vinyl chloride monomer (VCM), which is converted into the PVC.[97] This is a horrifically poisonous list of ingredients. Many studies have documented high rates of diseases among workers in vinyl chloride production facilities, including liver cancer, brain cancer, lung cancer, lymphomas, leukemia, and liver cirrhosis.[98]

PVC's production process also releases a lot of toxic pollution into the environment, including dioxins. As I've mentioned, dioxins are a group of noxious chemicals that persist in the environment, travel great distances, build up in the food chain, and then cause cancer, as well as harm the immune and reproductive systems.

Additionally, because in its pure form PVC is actually a brittle plastic with limited use, further chemicals, or additives, need to be mixed in to make it pliable and expand its uses. These include neurotoxic heavy metals, like mercury and lead, and synthetic chemicals, like phthalates, which are known to cause reproductive disorders and are suspected to cause cancer.[99] Since most of these additives don't actually bond to the PVC at the molecular level, they slowly leak out, a process called leaching or off-gassing. Sometimes quickly, sometimes slowly, these additives seep out of the PVC plastic, migrating from toys into our children, from packaging into our food, and from our shower curtains into the air we breathe.

In 2008, the Center for Health, Environment and Justice (CHEJ) released a study testing toxic chemicals that off-gassed from a new PVC shower curtain. CHEJ's tests found 108 different volatile compounds released from the shower curtain into the air over twenty-eight days. The level of these compounds was sixteen times in excess of the indoor air quality levels recommended by the U.S. Green Building Council.[100]

But before you start a massive PVC purge of your surroundings, consider the last part of PVC's miserable lifecycle: its disposal. We Americans toss out up to 7 billion tons of it per year, with 2 to 4 billion tons of that going to landfills.[101] When PVC winds up in a landfill, it leaches its toxic additives into the soil, water, and air.

Dumping PVC is bad, but burning is even worse, since burning PVC produces the super toxin dioxin.[102] Despite this fact, much burning of PVC isn't accidental. It generally gets burned in one of four places: backyard or open burning, medical waste incinerators, municipal waste incinerators, or copper smelters (often scrap wire is coated in PVC, so burning to reclaim the copper inevitably also burns more PVC[103]). Also, as more PVC is used in construction materials, building fires have become a new source of dioxin and other toxic emissions. When PVC building materials heat up in fires, they release toxic hydrogen chloride gas or hydrochloric acid, which is deadly if inhaled by firefighters and others trapped inside.[104]

And what about recycling? There's that white flag again, eager to quell our concerns about using too much Stuff and making too much waste. With PVC, recycling simply isn't a solution: it just adds to the problem, because recycling a poison perpetuates the hazard and exposes yet another round of workers and future consumers. The only answer is to stop making new PVC and get the existing PVC out of circulation.

So what to do with the PVC you do have? First off, don't beat yourself up if it's around you and your family: even in my household, despite my vigilance, insidious PVC infiltrates. Sometimes it arrives in the form of small toys in goodie bags my daughter brings home from birthday parties. Occasionally I get something, like the new extension cord I just bought, that I didn't realize was PVC until I opened the package and its stench filled up the garage. Once I ordered a rain jacket for my daughter; again, although the online description didn't say it was PVC, its odor did. So what to do? In all of these cases, I pack up the product and send it back to the manufacturer with a letter explaining why the product is unacceptable, giving them the rundown on PVC, and demanding a refund. (There's a sample letter in appendix 3 you are welcome to copy). If I can't identify the manufacturer, the offending product goes into a box in my garage that, when full, I mail off to the Vinyl Institute, an industry trade group in D.C. (Their address is also in appendix 3.) Since these guys make big bucks to defend the producers of PVC, I figure they can deal with it. You could also invite your neighbors to send theirs back with yours, and if you get enough people to participate, invite a local TV, radio, or newspaper reporter. The more we can raise awareness about how unacceptable PVC is, the better.

As for avoiding future PVC purchases, this material isn't too hard to identify. The two easiest clues are the label and the smell. If you turn a plastic container over and find a number 3 inside the little chasing-arrows recycling logo, put it back on the shelf.

If you can, make a quick call to the customer service number on the container, or send an e-mail or letter when you get home, telling the company you're not buying their Stuff as long as it's packaged in the most toxic plastic on the planet. Some containers don't display the number but say "vinyl" or "PVC" or may even have just a little "V." Look carefully. It's worth the extra minute to make sure you're not bringing PVC home.

The other way to identify PVC—often from yards away—is the smell. You know that smell of a new shower curtain, a new car, or the shoe section at a Target store? That is PVC. Or more accurately, it's some of the additive chemicals that are off-gassing. At a Halloween-time birthday party my daughter attended recently, plastic vampire fangs were handed out as favors. As soon as she got a whiff of them, she started running around the party grabbing them from the other kids, yelling, "Don't put them in your mouth!" In other words, even your kids can be on guard against it. If you think this is a sad situation to put our kids in, you're right. It stinks—both in terms of odor and in terms of whoever made the decision to use this supertoxic material when safer alternatives exist.

It's more of a challenge to figure out how to get all the PVC pipes out of our houses, but we can easily eliminate the packaging, plastic bottles, and containers, as well as all the junky vinyl Stuff PVC is so often used for, like plasticky backpacks or inflatable kiddie pools. There are safe, cost-effective alternatives to so much PVC crap! In my bathroom, I have a cotton shower curtain that I can launder. In my kitchen, I use sturdy reusable containers instead of ever letting my family's food touch that foul plastic wrap.

Unfortunately, other choices are harder to make. For example, when I wanted to replace three old windows in my house with more energy efficient ones, I found that the price of PVC window frames is about half that of traditional wood. Knowing about PVC's lifecycle, I know that the true costs of producing those PVC windows include nearly insurmountable health and safety impacts, while wood window frames can be made from sustainably harvested or salvaged wood and can be painted without heavy metals or other toxics. The PVC windows just *seem* cheaper because someone else (the workers, the fence-line communities, the environment) is paying the real costs. My current solution is to just make do with some less-than-perfect-looking window frames for a few more years and to install far less expensive insulating curtains instead.

As more people learn about the dangers of PVC and refuse to buy it, some companies are beginning to respond. Organized consumer-citizens have pressured Bath & Body Works, Honda, IKEA, Johnson & Johnson, Microsoft, Nike, Toyota, Victoria's Secret, and even Wal-Mart to commit to phasing out PVC at different levels. While I am glad every time these organizers add another store to their victory list, I don't think we can solve this problem going store by store, forcing each one to stop using PVC. We simply don't have time. We need a combination of leadership from within the business community, strong citizen watchdog groups, and government action to stop PVC at its source.

Sweden, Spain, and Germany have all restricted PVC in some locations or uses. In Spain, more than 60 cities have been declared PVC free, and 274 communities in Germany have enacted restrictions against PVC.[105] Many government actions have focused on the specific concern about endocrine-disrupting phthalates in PVC toys, in response to which some restrictions or bans have been adopted by the European Union, Japan, Mexico, and elsewhere.[106] Meanwhile, the United States has not even considered a national ban, opting instead for a *voluntary* agreement with manufacturers to remove two phthalates from PVC rattles, teethers, pacifiers, and baby bottle nipples.[107]

Can you detect the problems with this approach? First, every parent knows that kids don't limit their playthings to items labeled as "toys." Second, we can't limit our concerns to children: that leaves the rest of the population exposed to phthalates as well as all the other toxins in PVC. The only solution is to go 100 percent PVC free, as quickly as possible.

Key Questions About Production

By investigating just these five items, we start to get a sense of how production plays out. Even with Stuff that seems simple, there are a mind-blowing number of ingredients, machines, by-products, not to mention impacts on the environment and human health. Imagine what goes into making your car or home.

Therefore, before buying anything, I've developed the habit of asking myself: Is all the effort to extract ingredients for and produce this thing, combined with my hours of work to pay for it, worth it? Can I borrow one from a friend? Deborah loaned me a baking pan for last Thanksgiving dinner. Andrea loaned me her pickup truck to move furniture. Nick loaned me his ladder. I loaned Jane my extra-warm down coat when she went back east last January. The benefits to borrowing and lending aren't just environmental, they're social as well. It's fun, and it builds community.

Of course there are times when I do need or want to purchase something new. In that case there are a couple key parts of the production process that I focus on. I ask: Were toxic ingredients used to make it? What was it like to be one of the factory workers who helped create it? Was any part of the production so distasteful that rich countries with higher standards refused to do it?

Here's a little of what I've learned along the way by asking those very questions.

Dangerous Materials

Industrial production facilities today use a mind-boggling array of hazardous chemicals. Some are part of the production process, like solvents employed for diluting other compounds, or cleaning and drying machinery, while others are mixed into the product, like lead or phthalates, which help to create a certain texture or color.

Chemists and industrial designers and activists use all sorts of complicated systems to classify materials. But I figure that what's really important to us as individuals is whether or not any of the materials used in our Stuff are dangerous. So although it's unorthodox by scientific standards, I'm going to lump all the toxic materials together—heavy metals mined from the earth, like lead, cadmium, arsenic, chromium, and mercury, alongside synthetic organic compounds, like the organochlorines (dioxin, DDT), perfluorooctanoic acid (PFOA, used as a water repellant), and polybrominated diphenyl ethers (PBDEs, the flame retardants).

Another term you'll frequently hear is POPs, or persistent organic pollutants. To decode that: "Persistent" means they don't break down. They stay inside the tissues of living creatures, often bioaccumulating, which means they lodge in fat cells and get passed up the food chain at ever-increasing concentrations. "Organic" means they contain carbon, which means they can interact with the cells of living things (all of which contain carbon) in a variety of insidious ways. "Pollutant" means that they're toxic—disruptive to the endocrine, reproductive, and immune systems and also a source of neurobehavioral disorders.*

Let's look at the naturally occurring heavy metals. Even though these all occur in nature, the scale at which we're extracting them, putting them into consumer goods, and distributing them around the planet is unnatural and devastating. As a case in point, global emissions of lead from industrial sources are twenty-seven times higher than lead emissions from natural sources.[108] There's a reason nature secured these metals underground rather than circulating them in biological systems: they are supertoxic to all life forms. Scientists have amassed piles of studies concluding beyond a doubt that even low-level exposure to these chemicals is causing widespread neurological, developmental, and reproductive problems. Many of the heavy metals are biopersistent, which means that once they are inside a living organism, they remain there for a really long time—we're talking decades—before passing out of the body. Many of them also bioaccumulate.

Lead, for example, is a neurotoxin, which means it poisons the brain and

---

* POPs are so bad that a United Nations Convention was created to target them, outlawing some and severely restricting others. To start with, the Stockholm Convention identified twelve top-priority POPs: eight pesticides (aldrin, chlordane, DDT, dieldrin, endrin, heptachlor, mirex, and toxaphene); two industrial chemicals (the hexachlorobenzenes (HCBs) and the polychlorinated biphenyls [PCBs]); and two groups of industrial by-products (dioxins and furans). In May 2009, additional chemicals were included: HCH/Lindane, HBB, Penta and Octa DBE, Chlordecone, PFOS and pentachlorobenzene. Source: Stockholm Convention on persistent organic pollutants, http://chm.pops.int.

the nervous system. It's been linked to learning disabilities and reproductive disorders. "We've learned that virtually any level of lead is associated with neurodevelopmental impacts. It's a continuous impact beginning from non-zero levels and on up. So, for any of us, if we are exposed to lead, there's an impact. It may be small in the lower exposure range, but it's there," says scientist Ted Schettler of the Science and Environmental Health Network.[109] In spite of this, lead is still in widespread use in Stuff like car batteries, PVC plastic, roofing materials, lipstick, and toys. In their 2007 study, the Washington Toxics Coalition found lead in 35 percent of 1,200 children's toys tested, with 17 percent of the products containing lead levels above the 600 ppm federal recall level for lead paint.[110] Brain-harming poison in children's toys: it sounds like a bad horror movie, except it's real.

Another notorious toxin we surround ourselves with is mercury. There is a reason my mother warned me not to touch the irresistible silver liquid that oozed out of broken glass thermometers. Mercury exposure impairs cognitive skills; in large doses it messes with your lungs and eyes and can cause tremors, insanity, and psychosis. It's also been linked to cancer, cell death, and diabetes.[111] Children and babies are especially vulnerable to mercury because their nervous systems are still developing. A baby exposed to mercury in the womb can be born with neurological problems, physically deformities, or cerebral palsy. The United States government estimates that more than 15 percent of children born in the United States could be at risk for brain damage and learning difficulties due to mercury exposure in the womb.[112] According to a 2005 study, the IQ of 316,000 to 637,000 children per year is lowered by mercury exposure.[113]

We've heard a lot about mercury contamination from fish in recent years. Already in my daughter's kindergarten, these tiny kids matter-of-factly explained to one another that they couldn't have any tuna fish sandwich because they'd already had one that week. The reason that mercury in fish is such a big deal is that when mercury emissions from factories, coal-burning power plants (which provide power for the factories), and incinerators (which burn the Stuff made in factories) sink into the sediment of lakes, rivers, and oceans, anaerobic organisms turn those emissions into methylmercury.[114] This form of mercury is a far more powerful toxin than even the original mercury, and it bioaccumulates, meaning it builds up from small fish to larger and larger ones, with concentrations becoming much higher near the top of the food chain, ending with humans.

While it's true that we metabolize and move mercury out of our bodies, the ubiquity of it means we're re-exposing ourselves and taking in more every day. There's also significant disparity between individuals as to how fast that clearing-out process can go—for some people it's 30 to 70 days, but for others it can be nearly 190 days![115] The difference in clearing time appears to be written in your genes, and until the brand-new field of envirogenetics (which studies the interplay of genetics and environmental factors like diet or toxics exposure) matures, it's hard to know what your body's mercury timeline is.

Meanwhile, government warnings and stark statistics about mercury-contaminated fish have become so routine that we barely take note. I have to ask: why have these warnings been aimed at getting people to cease eating fish, rather than at getting the industries to stop putting mercury into our environment? Finally in February 2009, near-global consensus was reached: more than 140 countries convened by the United Nations Environment Programme (UNEP) unanimously agreed to create an international mercury treaty. They also urged immediate action through a voluntary Global Mercury Partnership while the treaty is being finalized.[116] Getting mercury out of our production processes will be hard work and it will cost money, for sure. But investments in eliminating mercury are investments well spent. UNEP estimates that every kilogram of mercury taken out of the environment can lead to up to $12,500 worth of social, environmental, and human health benefits.[117]

It's high time, because about 6,000 tons of mercury are released into our environment every year.[118] Some of this is a by-product of a primary process, as with coal-fired plants, chlor-alkali plants involved in papermaking, and the especially stupid practice of burning municipal waste. But much is also released consciously in the primary process—in gold mining, as I mentioned in the last chapter, as well as in the manufacture, use, and disposal of medical equipment, fluorescent and neon lighting, dental amalgams, vaccines and other pharmaceutical products, and even mascara. Yes, mascara.

Synthetic Offenders

In addition to the naturally occurring heavy metal poisons, there are the synthetic ones. While synthetic compounds have been made since cavemen experimented with mashing materials together, the large-scale development and use of synthetics has really exploded since the mid-twentieth century. Sometimes the drive to invent new materials has come from a specific requirement for the product, such as the need for paint that won't wash off in the rain. Other times the production of synthetic compounds has been motivated by the need to find a use for the by-product of another

THE MAKEUP OF YOUR MAKEUP

I'm not huge on makeup, perfume, or "beauty products" myself. Maybe you are, and maybe you're not. But at the very least I bet you use soap, shampoo, conditioner, and lotion. I do. Collectively this Stuff is also known as personal "care" products—but I put "care" in quotes because it's pretty questionable how much "caring" is going on here.

Here we are, rubbing these products into our pores, sometimes on our lips and eyes. So what's in them? A lot of nasty surprises and industry secrets is what. Have you ever turned your shampoo bottle or tube of sunscreen around to read the ingredients? Once you get your magnifying glass out, it might as well be written in Klingon, right?

It turns out that every day of her life, the average American woman uses a dozen products that contain 168 chemical ingredients. The average guy is using six products a day, with 85 chemicals in them—with the use of products among men rising.[119] Whether they're drugstore purchases, indulgences from the ritziest cosmetics counter, or even "natural" and "organic" products from your local health food store, they're almost certain to contain hazardous chemicals.

A 2005 study of thousands of personal care products found that:

- One-third of them contained at least one ingredient linked to cancer
- Nearly half of them contained an ingredient that is harmful to the reproductive system and to a baby's development
- 60 percent of them contained an ingredient that mimics estrogen or can disrupt hormones
- More than half of them contained "penetration enhancer" chemicals, which help other chemicals move into the body deeper and faster.[120]

By law, companies are allowed to keep their trademark scents a secret; they show up on ingredient lists as the mysterious "fragrance." One example of what's lurking behind the word are phthalates—proven to disrupt the production of testosterone and cause babies of contaminated mothers to be born with malformed and malfunctioning testicles and penises.[121] Even with what we know about these chemicals, in 2002 researchers still found (unlabeled) phthalates in three-quarters of the seventy-two products they randomly tested, including hair spray, deodorant, hair gel, body lotion, and perfumes.[122]

Other surprises: as the Campaign for Safe Cosmetics put it in a Valentine they sent me last February, "Roses are red, Lipsticks have lead . . ." In 2006, random tests of lipsticks (again, at all price ranges) found lead at two to four times the levels permitted by the FDA for candy.[123] There is absolutely no reason a product that gets applied, eaten away, and then reapplied to our lips should have a neurotoxin like lead in it! Meanwhile, *baby* shampoos often contain a carcinogen called 1,4-dioxane—it's in most adult shampoos too, often hidden as an ingredient called sodium laureth sulfate.[124]

There are particular dangers for specific populations, too. Nail salons overflow with potent toxins; the women who work in them are overwhelmingly nonwhite, often Asian, with an average age of thirty-eight—which means many are of childbearing age.[125] The skin-whitening products so popular in Asia frequently contain a carcinogen called hydroquinone, as well as the heavy metals chromium and mercury.[126] And the hair relaxers aggressively marketed to African-American women are very toxic. Products that change the shape and color of your hair are right up there at the top of the most hazardous list.[127]

Isn't someone regulating this Stuff? The 2005 study found that 87 percent of ingredients have not been assessed for safety by the Cosmetic Ingredient Review (CIR) panel.[128] Now, the CIR is the *only* body responsible for testing the safety of these products. The FDA doesn't have the authority to require companies to do safety tests; it can't even recall personal care products when they've been proven to be defective or harmful! As it turns out, the CIR is funded and run by the cosmetics industry through its trade association, the Cosmetic, Toiletry, and Fragrance Association. Their tests focus on immediate health effects like rashes and swelling. Unfortunately, they really need to test for long-term effects, as well as what happens when different chemicals interact with one another and with genes.

This information gets overwhelming fast. Thank goodness some activists have created powerful resources that enable us to inform ourselves and to push for change. The Environmental Working Group created and maintains Skin Deep, a huge database of more than forty thousand products and their ingredients.[129] You can enter in the name of many cosmetics and personal care products and find out what's in them. Visit their site at cosmeticsdatabase.com so you can avoid as many chemicals as possible, especially if you are pregnant or planning on getting pregnant.

You can also look out for companies that have signed the Compact for Safe Cosmetics, a pledge to replace ingredients linked to cancer, birth defects, and hormone disruption. More than one thousand companies have signed it to date.

chemical reaction or industrial process (often the refining of petroleum and natural gas). This type of material is often called a sink—someplace to pour what you don't want.

For example, in making ethylene, which is needed to produce the plastic product polyethylene, the by-product propylene is created. If this by-product can be put to use as a sink, or a raw material for something else, the cost of making ethylene goes way down. So inventors cast around for something to do with propylene and discovered it can be turned into something called acrylonitrile, which can be made into those acrylic outdoor carpets. And so acrylic outdoor carpeting was born as a substitute for natural ground covers.[130] It's not like we needed a replacement for mosses or grass and set our most brilliant minds to come up with one. Instead there was a strange backward development process, driven by profit.

TOXINS GET PERSONAL

In the summer of 2009, I had my own "body burden" tested to find out which of the chemicals that I'd been investigating for years were present in my own body.[a] The testing was organized by Commonweal's Biomonitoring Resource Center and the results were analyzed by Dr. Ted Schettler from the Science and Environmental Health Network.

Not surprisingly, the test uncovered dozens of toxic chemicals, including heavy metals, pesticides, and the chemicals used in industrial production that are present in everyday items. While certain lifestyle choices, like avoiding nonstick pans and eating organic food, have likely reduced my exposure to some compounds, there is still a disturbingly high level of toxins inside me. Even more unsettling, no one can say for sure how they got there, because it's impossible to link contaminants to a specific route of exposure. For example, although I avoided a toxic source like a vinyl raincoat, I may have been exposed to the same chemicals it contains and offgases—through the air, the water, or my food.

Here is an overview of some of the chemicals in my body, along with some of their most widely known sources:

Bisphenol A (BPA)—BPA is an endocrine disruptor, which means that it can interfere with the body's hormones. It causes a variety of health problems, particularly to the reproductive system. BPA is used in many everyday products from baby bottles to plastic water bottles to the linings of most canned food containers. When buying your refillable water bottle, make sure to check for the BPA-free label.

Lead—(see pages 73–74) a neurotoxin that was once widely used in gasoline and paint and is still used in many consumer products, from lipstick to electronics to children's toys.

Perflorinated compounds (PFCs)[b]—a probable cause of many cancers as well as liver and kidney damage, and reproductive problems, PFCs are used to make Stuff resist sticking and staining. They are found in microwavable popcorn bags, Teflon pans, and in some waterproof clothing and carpets.

Triclosan—linked to endocrinological problems, asthma, and allergies in animal studies. The Environmental Protection Agency (EPA) has listed triclosan as "could be" and "suspected to be" contaminated with dioxins.[c] Triclosan is used in many antibacterial products including soaps, cosmetics, household cleaners, and increasingly in a host of products advertised as "antibacterial," like socks, toys, and blankets, even though it isn't needed to fight disease causing microorganisms and may even be helping to develop stronger strains of those very organisms it seeks to destroy.

My body also carries organochlorine pesticides, some with names you may recognize **(DDT, Chlordane, Mirex)** alongside others that are less familiar (including **Hexachlorobenzene, beta-hexachlorocyclohexane, Oxychlordane, t-Nonachlor, Heptachlor epoxide**). They are neurotoxins and carcinogens and are associated with a range of chronic diseases. Many of the organochlorines were banned decades ago, yet they break down so slowly that they persist in the environment, our foodchain, and our bodies. My levels of these toxins were actually relatively low. When I asked Dr Schettler why, he guessed that I don't eat much meat—which is a primary route of exposure for fat-soluble pesticides. He was right. Starting at age fourteen, I didn't eat meat for twenty-four years. Today I occasionally eat chicken or fish but never red meat.

Mercury is devastating to the brain and nervous system (see pages 74–75). So it's bad news that the levels in my body are far higher than average; in fact I'm in the top 10 percent of people studied by the Center for Disease Control. After his many questions about potential exposure routes, Dr Schettler surmised that the mercury entered by body via my periodic tuna sushi splurges. Since receiving my test results I've renewed my commitment to avoiding eating large fish. Because our bodies eliminate mercury faster than more persistent pollutants, I should be able to lower these levels.

The highest-ranking chemical in my body is **Deca-BDE,** a flame retardant at the center of a major environmental health battle right now.[d] Lucky me. Super toxic, Deca-BDE is another probable carcinogen that damages the liver, kidney, and thyroid. My levels are as high as those of workers at those nasty electronics recycling facilities in developing countries, where toxic-laden electronics are destroyed by hand with little or no protective gear.

There's no way to know why my Deca levels are so high. One possible reason is that I live in California. California law—influenced by the powerful interests of flame-retardant producers—currently requires flame retardant use far beyond what is necessary for fire safety. This in turn motivates producers in other places to use excessive flame retardants so their products can be sold in California. Every state considering legislation that would ban Deca-BDE needs our support: even with mounting evidence of serious health impacts and the strength of alternative fire prevention approaches (like self extinguishing cigarettes), the industries producing Deca-BDE and other flame retardants are fighting hard to keep using them.[e]

My own body burden tests underscore one of the morals of the Story of Stuff: It's time for comprehensive, prevention-focused reform of how we use chemicals. As vigilant as we can be on the individual level, we'll never rid our bodies or the environment of toxins as long as we're still using them in our factories and our Stuff.

---

[a] To learn more about body burden testing, or biomonitoring, see www.commonweal.org/programs/brc/index.html
[b] To learn more about perflorinated compounds, see www.pollutioninpeople.org/toxics/pfcs
[c] U.S. EPA. 1994. Estimating exposure to dioxin-like compounds, Vol. II: Properties, sources, occurrence and background exposures. Office of Research and Development. Review draft. Washington DC, June. pp. 3–54.
[d] To learn more about Deca-BDE, see cleanproduction.org/Flame.Scientific.php and envi ronmentalhealthfund.org/documents/Deca%20Claims-Facts.pdf
[e] Environmental Health Fund, "Claims and Facts about Deca-PBE Flame Retardant," http://environmentalhealthfund.org/documents/Deca%20Claims-Facts.pdf

---

Often it's cheaper for industries to use synthetics, but that's only because they rarely have to bear all the costs of making, using, cleaning up after, or disposing of these materials—in other words, the costs of paying for their ultimate ecological and health impacts. More externalized costs!

Only a handful of the tens of thousands of synthetic compounds in use have been screened for health and environmental impacts. Not one has been screened for full synergistic health impacts, which means the impacts on us when we're exposed to more than one of these compounds at the same time.[131] And these days, for those of us living in industrialized countries, that kind of multiple-compound exposure is pretty much constant.

The terrible truth is that once we make them (or, in the case of the heavy metals, extract and disperse them), it's very difficult, often impossible, to get rid of these materials. They travel vast distances, carried by wind and water and within animals. Many of them bioaccumulate or biopersist. We breathe tiny particles of them right into our lungs, drink them in with our water, absorb them from our Stuff. Our sunscreen, our furniture, our non-stick frying pans, our foam fire-retardant cushions, and our waterproofed fabrics, to name just a few sources, are all leaching toxins.

Toxics are everywhere now. Many scientific studies report they are ubiquitous. Scientists seeking an unexposed population tested native people in the Canadian Arctic, far from major industrial sources, and still found very high body burden levels of synthetic chemicals.[132] NGOs in the United States and Europe have vacuumed household dust, tested it, and found that it is full of toxic substances.[133] No wonder crawling babies and household pets often have such high body burden levels, even though they haven't been around long enough to come into contact with all the various sources of toxins or to be affected by what the chemical industry apologists call "lifestyle choices." In a study of umbilical cords, the Environmental Working Group found they contained an average of 287 agricultural and industrial chemicals each.[134] And, in a shocking violation of the sanctity of human life, breast milk, which is at the top of the food chain, now has alarmingly high levels of toxic contamination.[135]

The fundamental truth about all these dangerous materials is captured in one simple phrase: *toxics in, toxics out.* As long as we keep putting any of

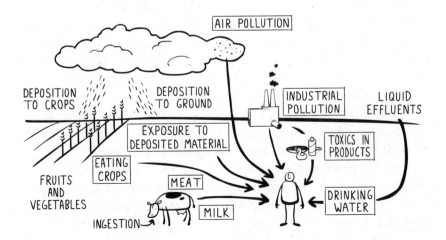

EXPOSURE PATHWAYS OF TOXIC POLLUTANTS

these toxic ingredients into our production processes, toxics will continue coming out: in the products, and via pollution.

 It seems like a lightbulb has gone off in the European Union, where in 2006 they passed the REACH act, which stands for Registration, Evaluation, Authorisation, and Restriction of Chemicals. Essentially, REACH means that companies have to prove that chemicals are safe before they get used and spread around,[140] as opposed to the "innocent until proven toxic" mentality that continues to reign in the United States. That mentality is illustrated by our ancient and notoriously weak Toxic Substances Control Act (TSCA), which has not been updated since its adoption in 1976. At its adoption, TSCA allowed 62,000 chemicals in use to continue without testing them; it has since allowed another 20,000-some chemicals to enter the market, resulting in tens of thousands in wide use today despite growing evidence of serious health risks.[141] To begin to rectify the situation, lawmakers introduced the Kid-Safe Chemicals Act (KSCA)

INTO THE MOUTHS OF BABES

Toxics in breast milk? Talk about a controversial issue.

This is a hard one to talk about for many reasons. It is the last thing that a new mother wants to think about while holding that precious little bundle of joy. It is scary. It feels overwhelming. It may discourage mothers from breast-feeding, which is still, by far, the best food for babies.

But we've got to talk about it. Silence only serves the polluters who, I am sure, would be grateful if no one ever brought up the issue of toxics showing up in human breast milk. So let's talk about it. Let's talk about it often, and loudly.

As I've said, every person alive today carries in his or her body a diverse range of toxic chemicals, thanks mostly to modern industrial processes and products. Pregnant and nursing women, and developing fetuses and newborn children—the littlest, most vulnerable members of society, with their rapidly growing brains and bodies—are no exception.

There have been a number of studies by medical professionals, government health agencies, environmental health groups, and others to track pollutants in breast milk. The Environmental Workgroup Group (EWG), for example, tested for toxic flame retardants in milk from twenty first-time mothers across the United States.[136] These flame retardants are linked to neurological problems, including reduced learning, attention, and memory. EWG's results showed some of the highest levels of flame retardants in breast milk ever found globally, with average levels seventy-five times higher than averages found in Europe, where some of these flame retardants have been banned.[137]

In the face of all the anguish and fear that this news brings with it, there are some important things to remember:

- The problem is not the mother, but the broader industrial system. We wouldn't have toxics in our breast milk if we hadn't developed an industrial model that permeates our communities with toxins, overseen by a regulatory model that really has no clue what's going on with these chemicals.

- Breast is still best. Breast-feeding provides nutrients, minerals, antibodies, and powerful emotional bonding for new babies. It helps mothers recover from pregnancy, and mothers who breast-feed have lower rates of ovarian and breast cancer later in life. (Breast-fed daughters may also have lower rates of breast cancer.[138]) Even in light of the scary news about toxics, environmental health and medical experts continue to recommend breast-feeding.

- The problem is not irreversible. Long-term testing of breast milk has shown that once toxic chemicals are removed from use, their levels in breast milk decline. The data comparing U.S. levels to those in Europe, where some flame retardants have been banned since 2004, proves there's lower contamination in places where the use of chemicals has been effectively restricted.[139]

---

in May 2008. KSCA takes Europe's REACH approach, placing the burden of proof on chemical companies to demonstrate that chemicals are safe *before* being introduced into commercial use.[142]

"When babies come into this world pre-polluted with hundreds of dangerous industrial chemicals already in their blood, it's clear that the regulatory system is broken," says Ken Cook, president of the Environmental Working Group. "The Kid-Safe Chemicals Act will change a lax, outdated system that presumes chemicals are safe into one that requires makers of toxic chemicals to prove their safety before they're allowed on the market. This bill is a long-overdue move to put public health ahead of chemical industry profits."[143] The chemical industry is rallying its troops of public relations specialists and lobbyists to defeat KSCA, so to get on board and help turn this bill into law, contact the Safer Chemicals, Healthy Families Campaign, working in Washington, D.C., and in communities across the country to pass laws to reform industry practices with regard to chemicals. Visit www.saferchemicals.org and saferstates.org to learn more.

Rather than focus on reducing any one population's (like children's) exposure to hazardous chemicals, the simplest solution to phase out toxics altogether and replace them with safe materials. This approach is far more effective, since the level of hazard in a chemical is controllable, while exposure is not, especially with chemicals that persist, disperse, and build up throughout ecosystems. This is where green chemistry comes in. Pioneering green chemists are design-ing new materials from the molecular level up to satisfy all our requirements (for things to be sticky, strong, colorful, flame-resistant, etc.) while also being fully compatible with ecological and human health. To learn more about green chemistry, visit Clean Production Action at www.cleanproduction.org.

The Front Lines

Up to now I've mostly been talking about how consumers like me are exposed to toxins through Stuff in stores and in daily life. But consumers are actually the third and last group of people to be affected by the toxins used in production processes. First come the workers actually making and assembling our Stuff.

The lyrics to one of my favorite songs, *More Than a Paycheck,* by the a cappella group Sweet Honey in the Rock, go like this: "We bring more than a paycheck to our loved ones and families . . . I bring home asbestosis, sili-cosis, brown lung, black lung disease, and radiation that hits the children before they've really been conceived."[144] It's true. Workers are on the front line, routinely exposed to toxic chemicals by touching them, inhaling them, and sometimes carrying them home on their clothing to share with their families. They bear the heaviest, unfiltered brunt of exposure to toxic inputs and dangerous processes and products. As Dr. Peter Orris, chief of environ-mental and occupational medicine at the University of Illinois Medical Center, laments, "These diseases and deaths are completely preventable. Civilized society should not tolerate this unnecessary loss of life either on the job or in our communities."[145]

The National Institute for Occupational Health and Safety (NIOSH) is the government entity focused on safety and health in the workplace. NIOSH believes that millions of workers in the United States are routinely exposed to substances found to be carcinogenic in animal studies and that millions more may be exposed to yet-undetermined carcinogens, since more than 98 percent—nearly all—of the substances used in our factories today have not yet been tested for carcinogenicity.[146] NIOSH estimates that work exposure to carcinogens causes about twenty thousand cancer deaths and forty thousand new cases of cancer each year.[147] And cancer is only one of a number of diseases linked to exposure of toxic substances at work; there's also cardiovascular disease, reproductive and neurological disorders, skin problems, respiratory diseases including asthma, and more. Maybe Sweet Honey should rewrite their song: "I bring home more than a paycheck to my loved ones and family, but I can't tell you what else I bring home since no one has bothered to study these chemicals that I inhale and handle all day at work."

But at least in the United States today there's growing awareness of the risks that workers face and increased safety regulations in the workplace. Back when environmental health activists first started raising concerns about industrial chemicals, many companies brushed aside concerns and focused their employees' attention on how environmentalists threatened to close factories and risk jobs. Corporate managers often framed the issues as "jobs versus environment." For a while this served to divide the two groups—representatives of labor versus environmental defenders. Ultimately it became clear that a healthy environment and good jobs that protect workers' health are integrally connected and mutually dependent.

In large part this shift in understanding came about through the work of one of my heroes, the late great Tony Mazzochi, a labor leader with the Oil, Chemical and Atomic Workers Union, who is frequently referred to as the

Rachel Carson of the labor movement. Throughout the 1960s Mazzochi informed workers about toxic threats, exposed information about workplace dangers to the public and policymakers, and, very important, built alliances between labor and environmentalists, defeating the attempts to keep these two powerful constituencies isolated. Today's movement for green jobs—dignified employment that is good for workers and for the planet—owes a debt to Mazzochi's tireless efforts.

We still have a ways to go in the United States before our factories are entirely green and toxics free, but meanwhile one of the tragic side effects of our cleaning things up at home has been exporting the nastiest production processes to poor countries around the world. I've seen many a dismal factory on nearly every continent, but my most gut-wrenching experience was in Gujarat, India, a region the Indian government calls the "golden corridor" because of the influx of international investment dollars. In my circles it's known as the "cancer corridor," because it's full of life-threatening chemical production plants, some of which were relocated from Western countries with stricter standards.

In 1995 my friends and I took the train from vibrant Delhi to the hot, dry, and dusty town of Ankleshwar, which is just one of about two hundred "industrial estates" in the Gujarat region. There, hundreds of factories crowded the area as far as the eye could see, sharing the same roads, power plants, and, as an afterthought, the same inadequate waste disposal sites. The air was thick with a stinky toxic stew from the plastics, petrochemicals, pesticides, and pharmaceuticals being manufactured. And in every free space between the factories, workers had built makeshift homes out of scraps of metal and wood. I tried not to think the about how these homes would fare during the annual monsoons.

Running right alongside the shacks and the roads were small ditches filled with foul-smelling reddish-brown liquid waste. From the look and smell of it alone we could tell this gunk was toxic—and my colleagues' tests would reveal that the wastewater contained mercury, lead, and many other chemicals that cause reproductive disorders and liver, brain, and kidney damage. Life went on around these ditches with no precautions— I watched barefoot children leap back and forth over them as they played, and women in bright saris squatted and cooked nearby. I followed the ditches to where they ended in a gigantic holding pond. There the young man who managed the pond's pump emerged from a utility shed to greet us, proud to explain his work to a group of curious foreigners.

What we learned was that he actually lived with the pump. Night and day without a break, he monitored the level of liquid in the holding pond.

When it neared capacity, his job was to turn on the pump. This drained some of the waste liquid out of the pond, from where it was transported by more open-air ditches to a local river, then to the sacred Narmada River, and eventually to the Gulf of Cambay (now known as the Gulf of Khambhat) where the local fishermen fished. Everything—the pump operator's T-shirt, his thin cotton sleeping mat, and the walls of the tiny five-foot by six-foot space in which he coexisted with the deafening pump machinery—was splattered with the gunk. A dark flood mark lined the walls: the place had been flooded knee-deep with the waste at least once.

Then, in front of my very eyes, he turned on the pump and, finding it wasn't running smoothly, he casually reached his bare arm up into the hose and pulled out a fistful of twigs and other debris drenched in the toxic liquid. The pump sputtered and started working. As he smiled, pleased with his successful repair, my friends and I were hit by the sickening realization that the problem went way beyond toxic waste and pollution: this was also clearly a human rights violation, a health threat, a tragedy of poverty, and an outrageous injustice. It was a scene no consumer ever imagines when he or she takes a product off the shelf in a Wal-Mart or Target thousands of miles away.

Fence-line Communities

In addition to the people who buy Stuff (consumers) and those who make Stuff (workers), there is one more group of people deeply affected by production processes: the people who live, work, and play near factories. These communities, whose children grow up in the shadows of giant factory smokestacks, are often called host communities or fence-line communities. They are virtually never consulted or informed when faraway CEOs make decisions about how and where dirty facilities will be operated. Rampant rates of cancers, birth defects, respiratory diseases like asthma, lowered attention and IQ, and radically shortened life spans plague these communities, no matter where in the world they are. And there's something else these communities have in common: they are usually poor, and the people in them are usually not white skinned.

This phenomenon is known as environmental racism—that is, the placement of the most toxic facilities in communities of color, zoning and other practices or policies that result in disproportionate burdens being placed on communities of color, and the exclusion of people from these communities from environmental planning and decision making. In the 1980s, the environmental justice (EJ) movement emerged in the United States in response to these fundamentally unfair practices and offered an alternative vision—one of environmental health, economic equity, and rights and justice for all people.[148]

In 1987, the budding EJ movement was bolstered by the first study to solidly document that the racial composition of a community was the most significant factor in determining whether or not a toxic waste facility was likely to be located nearby: *Toxic Wastes and Race in the United States,* published by the United Church of Christ (UCC). This astounding report showed that three out of every five African Americans and Hispanic Americans lived in communities with uncontrolled toxic waste sites.[149]

I remember when UCC released the findings, during my first year working at Greenpeace in its Washington, D.C., offices. The report sent shock waves through traditional environmental organizations, most of which didn't have industrial environments and racial justice on their radar screens. It was impossible to deny that the bulk of the issues that major environmental groups addressed—whales, forests, baby seals—utterly ignored the thousands of people living in the shadows of gigantic polluting industrial facilities and dumpsites. Sadly, some traditional environmental groups chose to downplay the report or to respond defensively. For others, the findings inspired some serious self-reflection. Some groups woke up to the fact that their boards, their staff, and their members were largely white, which meant they'd left a large segment of the U.S. population out of their strategic discussions and efforts. That is a pretty big oversight.

The UCC report helped inspire a powerful, diverse movement that saw environmental sustainability and social justice issues as inseparable. As civil rights and environmental justice activist Cora Tucker said, "People don't get all the connections [when] they say the environmental is over there, the civil rights group is over there, the women's group is over there and the other groups are here. Actually, all of them are one group, and the issues we fight become null and void if we have no clean water to drink, no clean air to breathe and nothing to eat."[150]

With the movement gaining momentum globally, the first ever National People of Color Environmental Leadership Summit was held in Washington, D.C., in 1991. Soon after, in 1993 President Clinton signed an executive order that created the National Environmental Justice Advisory Council to the EPA.[151] So by then, there was solid evidence of a racial bias in the choice of locations for polluting and hazardous facilities; there was a growing broad-based movement for environmental justice; and there was a presidential executive order and a special advisory council to the national Environmental Protection Agency. But while all that ought to have solved environmental racism, at least in the United States, that's not what happened.

Twenty years after the release of the first report, the UCC released *Toxic Wastes and Race at Twenty, 1987–2007,* which found the problems persisting and, in some areas, growing worse. "Race continues to be an independent predictor of where hazardous wastes are located, and it is a stronger predictor than income, education and other socioeconomic indicators. People of color now comprise a majority in neighborhoods with commercial hazardous waste facilities." [152] As Steve Lerner, an author and research director at the environmental health institute Commonweal, writes, "More remains to be done to keep America from being divided into livable communities, where the environment is relatively clean; and "sacrifice zones," where residents are exposed to the toxic by-products of a production process that keep goods artificially cheap and corporate profits rising. Many Americans do not realize [this is] part of the reason they are able to buy goods so cheaply." [153]

The fact that twenty years later, environmental racism persists and, in fact, has increased is shameful for all of us. This cannot continue. Of course, the answer to environmental racism is not some sort of "equitable pollution" in which we all share the toxic burden equally; the answer is to clean up our production processes and environmental governance so that no one—regardless of age or race or income, regardless of whether they are living now or in generations to come—has to subsidize the creation of Stuff chock-full of chemicals with his or her health and well-being.

We need to demand strong environmental health laws for everyone and the elimination of double standards in which whiter or richer communities get preferred treatment. And when I say for everyone, I don't just mean Americans. One of globalization's worst trends has been wealthy (often predominantly white) nations exporting the filthiest, most poisonous factories and facilities to countries that have weaker environmental, health, and worker protection laws; less capacity to monitor and enforce those standards that do exist; and, very important, less public access to information and involvement in the decision process. Hazardous industries follow the path of least resistance; they go to those places perceived as lacking the political, economic, educational, or other resources to resist them. Metals smelting, electronics production, PVC production: all these industries are increasingly being shut down in the United States while the number of facilities is expanding in developing nations. We're happy to take the products; we just don't want the mess. That's what is happening. And that is not okay.

If a particular industrial process is too toxic for U.S. communities, for American children, then it is too toxic for any community, for every child. Motivated both by a sense of global responsibility and justice, as well as by growing evidence that exported pollution still comes back to haunt us via air currents, food, and products, a growing number of communities are moving beyond NIMBY (not in my back yard) to NOPE: not on planet Earth. I'm right there with them.

Union Carbide on the Other Side of the Fence

From the massive chemical facilities in New Orleans to the diesel-exhaust-filled neighborhoods of the Bronx to the slums of Port-au-Prince to the belching refineries of Durban, I've seen for myself how communities that are poor, illiterate, and nonwhite are treated as expendable. But probably nowhere on earth is it more dramatically in evidence than in Bhopal, India. Bhopal, the City of Lakes and the City of Mosques, is best known today as the site of the world's largest chemical industrial disaster ever. What a claim to fame.

Late on the night of December 3, 1984, the poisonous gas methyl isocyanate (MIC) leaked from a factory owned by the U.S. multinational Union Carbide Corporation. The gas killed more than eight thousand people immediately, with a death toll now at twenty thousand and still counting, as people continue to succumb to related health impacts, averaging one more death each day over the last two decades.[154]

The stories I heard from survivors about "that night" haunt me: People woke in the darkness to the sound of screams, with the invisible gas burning their eyes, noses, and mouths. At first some thought a neighbor was burning too many chili peppers. Others thought the day of reckoning had arrived. Many began vomiting and coughing up froth streaked with blood. Not knowing where the gas was coming from, they just ran. Whole neighborhoods fled in panic, families were separated, many who fell were trampled, and others convulsed and fell dead. Within hours, thousands of dead bodies lay in the streets. Many people never found their missing family members and could only assume the bodies were among those hastily thrown into mass graves.

Some accounts call what happened that night an accident, but I call it an inevitability. Cost-cutting measures and overall sloppy management at the plant led to reduced staff safety training, ignored warnings about dangerous chemical storage practices, and no community warning mechanism. That night, not one of the six safety systems designed specifically to protect against a gas leak like this was functioning. Not one! You can't have a factory storing huge amounts of toxic chemicals and expect nothing bad to happen, especially if you run the place like you just don't care.

The factory was located in a densely populated part of the city, with small huts jam-packed full of sleeping families just meters from the factory walls. When the gas began leaking from the facility, Union Carbide staff did not notify police or warn community residents; in fact, they denied being the source of the leak for those first critical hours, during which the community members frantically ran to escape the suffocating gas and authorities scrambled to understand what was happening. Many believe that had the company admitted the leak and shared basic information, such as the importance of covering one's face with a wet cloth, many deaths could have been avoided.

Unbelievably, today, twenty-five years after the disaster, the company still refuses to share its information on the toxic health impacts of MIC, calling it a "trade secret," thwarting efforts to provide medical care to victims of exposure.[155] To add insult to injury, the abandoned Union Carbide factory, now owned by Dow Chemical, still sits there, leaking hazardous chemicals and waste left behind in the aftermath of the disaster. On the gates local residents have painted skulls and crossbones with dollar signs for eyes and have scrawled "killer Carbide" and "The Real Face of Globalization." Soil and water samples from around the plant, tested by Greenpeace fifteen years after the disaster, were full of heavy metals and other toxins.[156] A February 2002 study found mercury, lead, and organochlorines in the breast milk of the local women.[157] The children of gas-affected women are subject to a frightening array of debilitating illnesses, including retardation, gruesome birth defects, and reproductive disorders.[158]

Even having read a lot about that night, as soon as I arrived in Bhopal in 1992 for the first of many visits, I realized I'd underestimated the depth of the horror that occurred there. And I definitely was not expecting the many rays of strength and hope that abound among the survivors. They don't call themselves victims, because they aren't just sitting there taking it—they're fighting back. In fact, a Bhopali friend, Satinath Sarangi, and I call the city the "Fight Back Capital of the World." Two survivors, Champa Devi Shukla and Rashida Bee, were awarded the prestigious Goldman Environmental Prize for outstanding courage and tenacity in the struggle for justice in Bhopal. In the award acceptance speech, Bee said proudly, "We are not expendable. We are not flowers offered at the altar of profit and power. We are dancing flames committed to conquering darkness and to challenging those who threaten the planet and the magic and mystery of life."[159]

Each year, on the anniversary of the disaster, the survivors hold a commemorative protest. I was there again in 1994 for the tenth anniversary of the disaster. Poets sang *ghazals* about the loss of loved ones and the fight for justice. Colorful banners demanded justice and called for "No More Bhopals" anywhere on earth. Heart-wrenching photo exhibits showed large black and white images of the morning after the disaster, with dead bodies, many of them children, lining the streets awaiting identification. I saw a haunting photo of a small girl being buried, her father wiping away the soil from her face for one last look. As a parent myself, it is almost unbearable to look at that picture and allow myself to feel what that must have been like. I know that as long as we continue to rely on the toxins in, toxins out model of production, disasters like this one are inevitable.

The culmination of the anniversary events each year is the construction of a giant papier-mâché effigy of Warren Anderson, the CEO of Union Carbide at the time of the disaster. Survivors demand that Anderson come to Bhopal and face charges for his role in the management decisions that lead to the disaster. The Indian courts have a warrant out for his arrest, which he ignores from his comfortable home in Connecticut. The year I was there, the two-story-tall effigy of Anderson resembled a villain from an old movie, in a grey suit and hat, with a sinister mustache. When evening came, thousands of people took to the streets, chanting, yelling, and marching to the gates of the Carbide factory, where they lit the effigy on fire. Disoriented by the masses of shouting people and watching huge chunks of the burning effigy break off and float over the crowded, highly combustible slum, I began to imagine what it must have been like that night in the dark and chaos and fear.

Meanwhile all year long, every year since the disaster, the local community and allies globally in the International Campaign for Justice in Bhopal work to provide health care to the gas-affected and to fight for justice in Bhopal. The survivors' demands include: a cleanup of the abandoned, leaking factory; the provision of clean drinking water, since theirs has been contaminated; long-term health care and economic and social support for those who lost family members or are unable to work due to gas-related illnesses; and justice for those responsible for the shoddy factory maintenance.[160]

Elsewhere, news of the Bhopal disaster made headlines internationally and got a lot of people worried, from corporate executives of other chemical companies to residents of communities living near chemicals plants.

Union Carbide had a factory in Institute, West Virginia, which it had previously said was nearly identical to the Bhopal plant.[161] After the Bhopal disaster, workers and residents in Institute and other chemical-industrial communities began asking questions. Which toxic chemicals was the local factory using? Were toxic emissions coming from the plant, and if so, how much? Was a Bhopal-like disaster possible elsewhere?

Then in 1985, U.S. representative Henry Waxman, chairman of the House Health and Environment Subcommittee, released an internal Union Carbide memo that stated that a "runaway reaction could cause a catastrophic failure of the storage tanks holding the poisonous [MIC] gas" at the West Virginia plant.[162] The EPA confirmed that the Institute plant had experienced twenty-eight smaller gas leaks between 1980 and 1984.[163] Understandably, people freaked out.

The Chemical Manufacturers Association (CMA), now called the American Chemistry Council, responded with something they called the Responsible Care program and announced that its members were committed to a global voluntary safety program that would be self-audited and would "continuously improve their health, safety and environmental performance."[164] Based on this, CMA argued that more stringent regulations of their facilities weren't needed. As one NGO working to increase public access to information put it, the program basically had zero measurable goals, timelines, or external validation for reducing chemical hazards and essentially said to the public: "Trust us, don't track us."[165]

 The U.S. government's response, by contrast, was surprisingly useful. In order to help residents find out what chemicals are being used and released into their communities, the feds established the Toxics Release Inventory (TRI), which is a database of information about toxic chemicals releases, both via air and in waste. The TRI was created as part of the Emergency Planning and Community Right-to-Know Act of 1986.[166] This law requires companies to report the amount and location of toxic chemicals they use in order to assist emergency workers in the case of an accident. In addition, the law requires that companies producing or using toxic chemicals above specific threshold amounts provide data on toxic chemicals released via the air or in waste. Currently about 22,000 industrial and federal facilities are covered in the TRI. In 2007, those facilities reported that 4.1 billion pounds of 650 different toxic chemicals were released into the environment, including both on-site and off-site disposal.[167]

The data compiled in the TRI is available to the public through both government and nongovernmental websites. My personal favorite is Score-card (www.scorecard.org), which allows you to look up major pollution sources and chemicals by zip code. Scorecard provides information on health impacts, factory profiles, and even lets viewers send a message to their local polluters via the website.

I regularly check Scorecard to see how my own town is doing on the tox-ics front. It is a sobering experience. Berkeley is a city that prides itself on its high level of environmental awareness. Our public schools serve organic food. There are free parking places downtown for fully electric cars. Yet, my county ranks among the dirtiest 20 percent of all counties in the United States![168] The top polluters in my zip code include manufacturers of machinery and plastics as well as the stinky steel refinery just down the road from my house. The top twenty pollutants reported for my area are glycol ethers, xylene, n-butyl alcohol, toluene, 1,2,4-trimethylbenzene, methanol, ammonia, methyl isobutyl ketone, ethylene glycol, methyl ethyl ketone, styrene, barium compounds, m-xylene, N,N-dimethylformamide, lead, zinc compounds, ethylbenzene, cumene, n-hexane, and formalde-hyde.[169] Yuck.

The TRI is a great source of information on local pollution sources and on trends in different industrial sectors, but it still needs to be stronger. Scorecard describes TRI's five biggest limitations: (1) it relies on self-reporting by the polluters, rather than actual monitoring; (2) it doesn't cover all toxic chemicals; (3) it omits some major pollution sources; (4) it does not require the companies to report the amount of toxic chemicals used in products; and (5) it does not provide information about the possi-ble exposures people may experience as a result of the releases.[170] Once these shortcomings are addressed, the TRI could be an even more powerful tool for the public, one we can use to pressure companies to find alterna-tives to the toxic chemicals they use.

Watching Out for Us (Or Not)

Maybe the TRI has you contemplating the role of the government in all this. Haven't we elected or appointed someone to be in charge of making sure that we're safe from dangerous chemicals? What about the Food and Drug Administration? The Environmental Protection Agency? The Occupational Safety and Health Administration? Well, the very sad and very scary fact is, our government's regulation of toxic materials is riddled with holes.

For starters, the government's regulation takes a fragmented approach. We regulate chemicals in consumer products, air, water, land, our food, and our factories separately. A fundamental problem with this division of roles is that it approaches the environment as if it were a collection of discrete units, rather than one complex interrelated system. Often the agency staff who regulate the same chemical compound in water, air, our products. and the workplace don't even talk to one another, and when they do, they sometimes vehemently disagree.

Take fish, for example: the EPA has authority to monitor pollution in fish you catch from a stream, while the FDA has authority over a fish that someone else catches and you buy at the grocery store. The two agencies are supposed to work together and sometimes they do, like in 2004, when they jointly released guidelines recommending that pregnant women, women of childbearing age, nursing mothers, and young children not eat more than 12 ounces of fish each week in order to limit mercury intake.[171] Then, in late 2008, the FDA drafted a new report recommending that women now eat *more* than 12 ounces of fish each week.[172] The *Washington Post* reported that the FDA did not consult the EPA until the report was nearly completed. EPA internal memos called the new FDA recommendations "scientifically flawed and inadequate" and said that they fell short of the "scientific rigor routinely demonstrated by EPA."[173] The watchdog organization Environmental Working Group went even further, declaring the FDA's report "an astonishing, irresponsible document. It's a commentary on how low FDA has sunk as an agency. It was once a fierce protector of America's health, and now it's nothing more than a patsy for polluters."[174]

If these two agencies can't get on the same page about something as critical and basic as keeping neurotoxins off our dinner plate, what can we expect of the whole mess of government measures? Just take a look at the various agencies, commissions, and laws we're relying on:

GOVERNMENT LAWS & AGENCIES

Executive Branch

National Environmental Policy Act (NEPA) (1969)
A broad national framework to assure that all branches of government give proper consideration to the environment.

Council on Environmental Quality (CEQ) (1969)
Within NEPA, ensures that environmental amenities, services, and values are considered in decision making. Administered by the Office of Environmental Quality.

Food and Drug Administration (FDA) (mandated by the Federal Food, Drug and Cosmetic Act 1938)

Within the Department of Health and Human Services, the FDA is responsible for protecting the public health by assuring the safety and efficacy of our nation's food supply, medicines, cosmetics, etc. Amended in 2002 to authorize the EPA to set maximum limits for pesticide residues on foods.

Occupational Safety and Health Administration (OSHA) and National Institute for Occupational Safety and Health (NIOSH) (1970)

Created within the Department of Labor by the Occupational Safety and Health Act (1970) to assure safe and healthful conditions for workers. OSHA handles enforcement while NIOSH (now part of the Department of Health and Human Services' Centers for Disease Control and Prevention) conducts research, education, and training on occupational hazards.

National Oceanic and Atmospheric Administration (NOAA) (1970)

Within the Department of Commerce, a science-based agency responsible for predicting changes in the oceanic and atmospheric environments and living marine resources. NOAA encompasses the **National Environmental Satellite, Data and Information Service, the National Marine Fisheries Service** (responsible for the management, conservation, and protection of living marine resources), the **National Ocean Service** (maintains safe, healthy, and productive oceans and coasts, for example by ensuring safe and efficient marine transportation), the **National Weather Service,** and the **Office of Oceanic and Atmospheric Research** (provides research for NOAA).

Consumer Product Safety Commission (CPSC) (created by the Consumer Product Safety Act, 1972)

Protects the public from risks associated with consumer products such as electrical, chemical, or mechanical hazards.

Consumer Product Safety Improvement Act (2008)

Establishes consumer product safety standards and other safety requirements for children's products (modernizes the original act).

Environmental Protection Agency (EPA) (1970)

EPA's mission is to protect human health and to safeguard the natural environment—air, water, and land—upon which life depends. EPA coordinates research, monitoring, standard-setting, and enforcement activities to ensure environmental protection.

Laws Administered within the EPA

Federal Insecticide, Fungicide, and Rodenticide Act (FIFRA) (1947)
Registers (licenses), or exempts from registration, the sale and use of pesticides, including antimicrobials, for control of pests that threaten crops, animals, and humans.

Food Quality Protection Act (1996)
Sets safety standards on pesticide tolerances, especially for infants and children.

Toxic Substances Control Act (TSCA) (1976)
Addresses the production, importation, use, and disposal of specific chemicals including polychlorinated biphenyls (PCBs), asbestos, radon, and lead-based paint.

Clean Air Act (CAA) (1963, extended 1970, amended 1977 & 1990)
Limits certain air pollutants, including from sources like chemical plants, utilities, and steel mills. Individual states or tribes may have stronger air pollution laws, but they may not have weaker pollution limits than the federal standard. The 1990 revisions address emissions trading and clean fuel standards.

Clean Water Act (CWA) (1972)
Regulates discharges of pollutants into the waters of the United States and regulates quality standards for surface water.

Safe Drinking Water Act (1974, amended 1986, 1996)
Protects the quality of all waters actually or potentially used for drinking, from both above-ground and underground sources, and requires public water systems to comply with these primary (health-related) standards.

Comprehensive Environmental Response, Compensation and Liability Act (CERCLA) (aka Superfund, 1980)
Provides a special fund (originally $1.6 million) for cleaning up uncontrolled or abandoned hazardous-waste sites as well as accidents, spills, and other emergency releases of pollutants and contaminants into the environment. Seeks out parties responsible for any releases and assures their cooperation in the cleanup.

Superfund Amendments and Reauthorization Act (1986)

Updates CERCLA to increase states' involvement and citizen participation, increase the focus on human health impacts, revise the Hazard Ranking System, and increase the size of the trust fund to $8.5 billion.

Emergency Planning and Community Right-to-Know Act (1986)

Designed to help local communities protect public health, safety, and the environment from chemical hazards. The Community Right-to-Know provisions increase the public's access to information on chemicals at individual facilities, their uses, and releases into the environment.

Oil Pollution Act (1990)

Provides resources and funds to clean up oil spills as well as mitigation requirements for the polluter.

Resource Conservation and Recovery Act (RCRA) (1976, 1986, plus 1984's Hazardous and Solid Wastes Amendments)

Gives EPA the authority to control hazardous waste from "cradle to grave," including generation, transportation, treatment, storage, and disposal. Amendments focus on waste minimization and more stringent standards for hazardous wastes.

Pollution Prevention Act (1990)

Focuses on reduction of industrial pollution at the source, alongside resource efficiency and conservation, as part of pollution prevention.

Endangered Species Act (ESA) (1973)

Protects threatened and endangered plants and animals and their habitats.

Marine Protection, Research, and Sanctuaries Act (aka Ocean Dumping Act, 1972)

Prohibits ocean dumping.[175]

Notice something that all these have in common? Many were created before any of us had cell phones or Internet access; some were established even before fax machines. Lots were created before Rachel Carson's *Silent Spring*, before the Bhopal disaster, before climate change was a household topic. While the intentions at their founding were good, many of these agencies and laws are now simply out of date. Even the more recent amendments are often out of date. Environmental health threats have changed and continue changing while our understanding of those threats has evolved greatly, but the laws and regulatory agencies haven't kept up. Many of these laws were made back when people still believed that "dilution is the solution to pollution." Back then, folks thought that taller smokestacks or longer discharge pipes would solve the problem. No longer.

To further confuse matters, implementing the federal regulations set by many of these agencies is often a state-level responsibility. That means that compliance and enforcement varies from state to state depending on the priorities and powerful interests within each state. "States dominated by specific industry types (chemicals, mining, specific types of manufacturing) tend to be more tolerant of noncompliance by those sectors than other states with more heterogeneous industrial mixes," writes Professor Ken Geiser of the University of Massachusetts Lowell.[176] And since laws are only as strong as compliance and enforcement, this means that the effectiveness of these laws can look very different in different places.

Another huge issue is that so-called independent advisory committees that provide policy recommendations or scientific advice to government are stacked with people who have financial interests in the very activities on which they are advising. Isn't that what people mean when they say "the fox is guarding the henhouse"? In the United States there are about nine hundred advisory committees that provide peer review of scientific research, develop policy recommendations, evaluate grant proposals, and serve other functions to support good governance.[177] These committees are so active in providing advice to Congress, federal agencies, and the president that they are sometimes referred to as the "fifth arm of government."

Federal law requires that these independent committees have members who represent a balanced diversity of views and who are free from conflicts of interest (that is the "independent" part). In spite of that mandate, however, industry influence continues to dominate these committees, undermining their value and credibility as sources of independent and unbiased expertise. For example, in 2008, the FDA released a report that found that bisphenol A (BPA), a plasticizer used in food packaging and many water bottles, is safe.[178] This report followed growing concern about BPA's links to neurological, developmental, and reproductive harm to children. Then the Integrity in Science Project reported that the two main studies on which the FDA based its analysis were funded by a unit of the American Chemistry Council, an industry trade group that includes companies that produce or use BPA.[179] This is just one example from a long list of suspect information sources and appointments among government advisory committees. (And there's still no federal ban on BPA, despite proof that it causes reproductive damage in animals. To help get BPA out of food packaging, visit www.saferstates.com/2009/06/safer-cans.html.)

The nonprofit Center for Science in the Public Interest (CSPI) is one organization that researches and campaigns against corporate influence on science-based public policy. CSPI scrutinizes more than two hundred science-based federal advisory committees for undisclosed conflicts of interest and posts the results in a searchable online database (www.cspinet .org/integrity). In early 2009, CSPI released a new report, *Twisted Advice: Federal Advisory Committees Are Broken*, which revealed that government advisory panels continue to be skewed toward industry, largely through an overrepresentation of industry members with direct financial interest in the outcome of the committees' work.[180]

It's clear that the current approach to regulating toxic chemicals, worker safety, and broader environmental issues is not functioning to protect us. In some cases—like the chemical industries stuffing advisory panels with their people—the intent is bad. In other cases—like the mix-and-match collection of laws and agencies with overlapping areas of jurisdiction—the structure is bad. In either case, we clearly need another way. We need regulators and scientists who are working for the well-being of people, not for specific industries. And we need laws and agencies that understand and reflect the complexity of the planet, including the natural environment, the built environment, communities, workers, kids, mothers—the whole package.

Professor Ken Geiser, who is also the director of the Lowell Center for Sustainable Production, laid out a vision for a different approach in his 2008 paper *Comprehensive Chemicals Policies for the Future.* According to Geiser, a new chemicals policy would consider chemicals as components of the broader system of production in which they are used, not as isolated individual entities, which is never how they actually show up. A more successful approach to chemicals policy would include researching and disseminating more complete information on whole classes of chemicals, ramping up development of less toxic alternatives, and converting industry sector by sector from using high-hazard chemicals to using ones that represent a low hazard. With an integrated systems perspective, it will be possible to transform electronics, transportation, health care, and other sectors away from a reliance on toxic chemicals. As Geiser notes, "We need to think less about restriction and more about conversion." [181]

It Wasn't Always This Way

The problems with the production of Stuff seem nearly intractable. If you were born anytime in the last sixty-odd years, it's hard to imagine that things could possibly be any different. But it wasn't always like this. The most toxic parts of today's production processes have been with us for less than a hundred years. And that is cause for hope.

For a long time, the production of all our Stuff caused far less environmental harm. There were definitely some negative health impacts in early production, especially around the use of heavy metals like mercury and lead before people realized they were as dangerous as they are. But it was insignificant compared to today's global environmental destruction and persistent toxics, their reach extending from seemingly pristine wilderness areas to the fat cells of every person on the planet.

When we look back through history, we see two periods of change that fundamentally transformed production processes, with devastating effects. Before the Industrial Revolution, nearly all production was powered by elbow grease—meaning we humans, and the animals we could enlist to help, provided the energy needed to make Stuff. That meant there was a limit to how many resources we could collect and how much Stuff we could make. Then in the late eighteenth and early nineteenth centuries we developed the steam engine, and soon machines could replace a lot of people, toiling harder and longer, without demanding things like safe working conditions or breaks to eat or rest.

Suddenly the limits on how much Stuff we could extract and process disappeared, under the motto "more, faster, better." It was definitely more and faster, but not always better. The volume of resources moving through the system—both those used to power processes and those used as materials in production—increased dramatically. For example, in 1850, U.S. coal production was just under 8.5 million tons; by 1900 it increased to 270 million tons; and by 1918, it had reached 680 million tons.[182] A frontier mentality reigned: there would always be more forests to cut, more valleys in which to dump the waste. It seemed that there was no need even to think about limits back then.

Yet despite using more natural resources and making more Stuff faster, we needed less human labor. This raised a dilemma: if factories kept all the workers *and* introduced these new output-increasing machines, they would soon be producing more Stuff than people would need. (Economists call this overproduction, when production outpaces consumption.) There were two options: to ramp up consumption (more Stuff) or slow down production (more leisure). As I'll explain fully in the upcoming chapter on consumption, at that juncture America's business and political leaders unequivocally chose more Stuff.

The next wave of major change came in the early to middle twentieth century. This time it was on the materials front, as scientists began developing a whole new set of chemical compounds that hadn't previously existed. Many naturally occurring materials were replaced with synthetic petrochemicals. The volume and toxicity of chemical compounds used in production skyrocketed.

Of course the Industrial Revolution and modern synthetic chemistry have benefited us. I appreciate many things in my life that wouldn't have been possible without them. Refrigeration. A heated home. Medicine. The Internet. A tiny little device that brings music wherever I go. I don't want to do without these things and I don't want others to either. But it's time for another set of advances—another revolution.

Today we are running out of resources, while our population continues to grow. Yet our productive technologies have not kept up with this reality. We are still using processes that consume and waste huge amounts of energy and materials, acting as though both the supply of resources and the planet's ability to assimilate waste and pollution are endless. We're still celebrating economic activity that undermines the planet's very ability to support life. We have to figure out how to transform our production systems yet again: to make far less Stuff and far better Stuff.

Starting Upstream

The very first stage of production—way before we start the physical production—is the most important and least visible step: design. The design determines:

- which ingredients need to be extracted or created
- the amount of energy used in making and using the product
- the presence or absence of toxic chemicals
- the length of the product's life span
- the ease or difficulty of repair
- its ability to be recycled
- the harm caused by burying or burning the product if it's not recyclable

Architect Bill McDonough, an internationally renowned sustainability guru, calls design the "first sign of human intent." [183] Is our intent to make the cheapest-possible electronic gizmo to feed the latest consumer frenzy? Or is our intent to make a nontoxic, durable product made of ecologically compatible materials that provides a needed service, adds to society's well-being, can be easily upgraded and repaired as technology advances, and can ultimately be recycled or composted at the end of its life?

Changes in design can involve incremental improvements, like removing a particular toxin from use in one product line. Or the changes can be truly transformational, as a result of rethinking some of our long-held, and limiting, assumptions—our paradigms. For example, the assumptions that "pollution is the price of progress" or that "we must choose between jobs and the environment" have long limited our creative thinking about innovative solutions that can be good for the environment, the workers, and a healthy economy. We can't transform the system of Stuff unless we transform the way we think.

That said, it's good to remember that even incremental changes, when replicated over millions of consumer products, can make a difference. Getting lead out of gasoline, for example, had enormous benefits in protecting public health, especially the developing brains of children. That one change saved millions of IQ points worldwide. In February 2009, a group of mobile phone manufacturers and operators announced a commitment to design mobile phone chargers to be usable on any phone regardless of make or model, and to be far more energy efficient. [184]

I received news of this commitment while visiting Washington, D.C. Rushing to get ready for the trip, I had left my cell phone charger at home. I had a jam-packed week of meetings and was relying on my phone to ensure smooth logistics. Not wanting to buy a replacement charger for just a week's use, I asked the hotel if any previous forgetful guest had happened to leave behind a charger that would fit my phone. The desk clerk brought out a cardboard box with literally dozens of cell phone chargers, each neatly wrapped with their cords. I tried twenty-three chargers before finding one that fit my phone!

Changing the shape of the charger's jack is a small thing, but mobile phone industry representatives expect this simple design change could reduce the production of phone chargers by half, which in turn could reduce greenhouse gases in manufacturing and transporting replacement chargers by at least 10 to 20 million tons per year.[185] The mobile phone companies' press releases made interchangeable chargers sound revolutionary, but really, it could have been part of the original intent when cell phones were first being designed and developed.

One of the most exciting trends in truly revolutionary design is called biomimicry, in which design solutions are inspired by nature. After all, as the Biomimicry Institute notes, "nature, imaginative by necessity, has already solved many of the problems we are grappling with. Animals, plants, and microbes are the consummate engineers. They have found what works, what is appropriate, and most important, what lasts here on Earth. This is the real news of biomimicry: After 3.8 billion years of research and development, failures are fossils, and what surrounds us is the secret to survival."[186]

Biomimicry experts have identified the following list of core principles in how nature functions. Nature:

- runs on sunlight and uses only the energy it needs
- uses a water-based chemistry
- fits form to function
- recycles everything
- rewards cooperation
- banks on diversity
- demands local expertise
- curbs excesses from within
- taps the power of limits

Biomimicry takes these principles and figures out how to make human technologies, infrastructure, and products that adhere to them as well.[187]

What might this look like in practice? Janine Benyus, founder of the Biomimicry Institute, has endless examples. Rather than using toxic inks and phthalates to color Stuff, why don't we imitate the peacock, which creates the brilliant colors we see in its plumage through shape—layers that allow light to bounce off it in ways that translate as color to the eye. Instead of burning fossil fuels to heat up kilns for firing high-tech ceramics, we can mimic mother-of-pearl, which self-assembles a substance twice as strong as those ceramics in seawater: no heat required. The threads that hold a mussel to a rock dissolve after two years; the packaging we design can likewise be engineered to dissolve when it's no longer needed or wanted. Rather than mining virgin minerals, we can copy microbes that pull metals out of water.[188] Engineers and green chemists are already experimenting with all of these alternatives with success. They just need funds for continued research and development and government regulations on their side to achieve a full breakthrough.

Another revolution in the production of our Stuff is both necessary and possible. With existing and developing approaches, within a decade we could transform today's most destructive processes and eliminate the most toxic ingredients from our factories and products. With the government mandating this level of change, business people putting their money where their souls (and grandkids) are, and designers and scientists doing what they do best—innovate and improve!—we could be there in no time.

CHAPTER 3

DISTRIBUTION

Once upon a time it was simple: the only Stuff available to us was made locally or regionally. We picked it up in town, or it was transported to us in a horse-drawn wagon, often by the same person who made it. Unusual items—silks or spices, for example—occasionally arrived from faraway sources via one of three routes: returning armies loaded down with plundered loot, explorers returning from exotic lands, or the rare international traders who braved the dangers and shouldered the costs of overseas travel. By the fifteenth century, Europe had entered the Age of Exploration, and rich people were financing ventures specifically to acquire valuable Stuff like minerals (especially gold), textiles, spices, fruit, coffee, sugar. But even then, the elite consumers who could afford such treats had to exercise immense patience waiting while the goods made the voyage back and had to pay dearly for them once they arrived.[1]

Today nearly everyone on earth is able to consume Stuff made on the other side of the planet. Stuff travels at lightning speed around the world. We expect to have everything at our fingertips in the exact color and the exact style we want, and not just fast but immediately. In just a couple of generations, humankind has accelerated and complicated the distribution of goods at a mind-boggling rate. It's kind of like our grandparents were playing checkers, able to move their simple round pieces one or two steps forward or diagonally. Then our parents were playing chess, with a whole new array of two-dimensional moves by sophisticated bishops, knights, and rooks, not to mention the queen. And in my generation? It's like we're moving Stuff in the three-dimensional space-age version of chess that Spock plays in *Star Trek*.

To look at this stage in the story of our Stuff we need to go way beyond investigating the modes of freight (via land, water, and air) or the routes Stuff takes around the globe, in and out of factories and containers and warehouses. Distribution includes vast information technology systems (Wal-Mart, for example, supposedly has a computer network that rivals the Pentagon's, in order to keep tabs on the Stuff it moves). It encompasses the immense multinational retailers whose economies of scale are a key ingredient in making modern distribution systems feasible. And all of this activity happens against the backdrop of economic globalization, international trade policies, and international financial institutions, which set the larger context for how Stuff moves around the planet.

The Skinny on Supply Chains

To understand the path our products have taken to reach us, we need to understand their supply chains, which involve far more than merely getting something from point A (where it is made) to point B (where we buy it) but encompasses all the suppliers, component producers, workers, middlemen, financiers, warehouses, loading docks, ships, trains, trucks—basically every stop along the way from natural resource to retail outlet. In today's globalized economy, a product's supply chain can cover multiple continents and scores of businesses, each of which is trying to maximize its profit at that link in the chain. To that end, a whole complex science of supply chain

SUPPLY CHAIN OF A LAPTOP

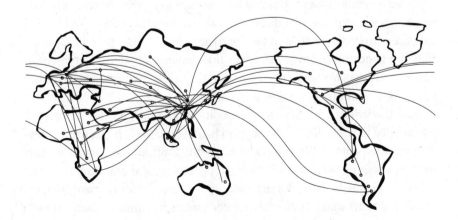

management has evolved that fine-tunes every detail, to make and move things as quickly and cheaply as possible.

Probably no one has more knowledge about supply chains than Professor Dara O'Rourke. During the years I was visiting polluting factories and dumps around the world, O'Rourke was investigating garment and shoe factories—sweatshops—in Honduras, Indonesia, Vietnam, and China. He says that while much has changed since the Age of Exploration, even more radical change happened in just the last decade. O'Rourke boils the revolution of the last ten years down to two ideas: lean manufacturing and lean retail.[2]

O'Rourke points to Toyota as the prototype for lean manufacturing; the company is famous for reconfiguring work stations so that assembly line workers wouldn't waste an extra second or use one ounce of extraneous energy in reaching for a part they needed. Toyota kept refining their assembly, shaving off seconds at each step along the way, until the process was airtight. An important breakthrough in their model was empowering any worker along the line to pull the "stop cord" if they detected a problem with the product. Immediately the root cause of the problem (faulty machine, sick worker, bad design) would be investigated and fixed; this kind of troubleshooting is way more cost-effective than waiting until an inspector at the tail end of the assembly line finds flaws in the finished products. This innovation is credited for giving workers a greater sense of responsibility and job satisfaction, although it led to some workers accusing one another of "speeding up the line" and negated many of the pro-worker concessions that the labor movement had won in prior generations' struggles.[3]

Over the years, lean manufacturing has gotten uglier. Manufacturers analyzed assembly line production ad nauseam to figure out every possible way to cut any expense that didn't add value to the end product. When that expense is toxic waste created by a particular technology, then its elimination is a good thing. However, when that expense is safety equipment or bathroom breaks for workers—as is often the case—then reworking factory operations to eliminate it is just plain scary.

And this efficiency-über-alles mentality spread beyond the factories. It was applied to the whole of the supply chain. How? Well, here's the key revelation: most companies from which we buy Stuff are no longer actually making anything themselves but are simply buying and branding Stuff that other people made. Nike doesn't make shoes. Apple doesn't make computers. Gap doesn't make clothes. These companies buy those shoes, computers, or clothes (and the parts to assemble them) from multiple factories all over the world. In fact, a given factory often makes goods for competing brands that only get differentiated once the label gets slapped on.[4]

What companies like Nike, Apple, and the Gap do produce are brands, and these brands are what shoppers are buying. Nike founder Phil Knight explained, "For years, we thought of ourselves as a production-oriented company, meaning we put all our emphasis on designing and manufacturing the product. But now we understand that the most important thing we do is market the product."[5] Companies spend billions on brand promotion, often not to advertise details of any actual product, but to maintain the image they want consumers to identify with their brand. As O'Rourke puts it, "When Apple sells you an iPod, it isn't selling an MP3 player; it is selling a fashion statement."[6]

Because the focus is on developing the brand, rather than on making any actual items, the place where Stuff is produced is increasingly irrelevant. In fact, the actual costs of making an item—the materials, the workers, running the factory—and then getting it to the store account for only a fraction of the price charged for that item. Most of the money goes to the brand, which means that the more costs are lowered along the supply chain, the more profit the brand holder makes.[7]

Because consumers play along and value the brand so highly, the balance of power along the supply chain has shifted from the manufacturers to the brands and retailers (who are sometimes but not always the same entity: at the Nike store, Nike is both brand and retailer, but if the Nike shoe is sold at Nordstrom's, then they're separate). It is they who now call the shots along the whole supply chain. They—not the actual manufacturers—decide what gets made, how fast, and for how much. If one manufacturer isn't able to meet their demands, that's fine, because there are plenty of other manufacturers ready to make the same product without complaint, often for a lower price.[8] "This is the 'treadmill' that ensnares developing countries," explains *The Nation*'s political correspondent William Greider. "If they attempt to boost wages or allow workers to organize unions or begin to deal with social concerns like health or the environment, the system punishes them. The factories move to some other country where those costs of production do not exist."[9] And David Korten writes in *When Corporations Rule the World*, "With each passing day it becomes more difficult [for factories] to obtain contracts from one of the mega-retailers without hiring child labor, cheating workers on overtime pay, imposing merciless quotas, and operating unsafe facilities."[10]

Removing themselves from the actual production of Stuff also allows the big brand-name companies to claim a level of ignorance about conditions—they can shrug and say, "Hey, they aren't our factories." This frees them from the responsibility and challenges and costs inherent in running real factories that employ real workers around the world.

All of these developments led O'Rourke to call this the "*mean* lean" system.

And that's only the half of the new leanness. The other half is lean retail. Like lean manufacturing, lean retail also seeks to cut costs at every turn. The ways to do this include all the obvious: lower workers' salaries in stores and refuse to provide health care benefits; stifle union organizing; and build gigantic stores in the suburbs where real estate is cheap, rather than in city centers where shoppers could access the store via public transportation.

But the biggest way to cut costs associated with retail is to eliminate inventory. In the lean retail model, inventory is the ultimate waste. Traditionally, inventory was costly because it incurred storage expenses and consisted of materials temporarily not on the market. However, with today's fast-changing fashions and speedy obsolescence, the wastefulness of inventory has taken on new proportions. It's not just clothes that are in fashion one week and out of fashion the next—it's now electronic gadgets, toys, even furnishings and cars.[11] That means holding Stuff in warehouses for even a few days is a risky act that could waste a lot of money (and product).

Michael Dell once famously said that "inventory has the shelf life of lettuce."[12] His company has been an industry leader in reducing inventory time. Dell computers aren't made en masse and stored as inventory until they are sold, as in the old distribution model. With complex computer tracking systems, any purchase or order from a customer is communicated back to the factory where the components are waiting. The specific kind, color, and style of computer that's desired is assembled and shipped; production is now based on individual demand. (This model is often called just-in-time, or JIT, in business lingo.)[13]

The attempts to reduce superfluous production through more surgical, "small batch" production, "niche marketing," and associated distribution all sound good, and from a business perspective they are, and even from an environmental perspective they might be, but the system is terrible for the workers. The combination of constantly changing styles plus consumers' expectation of immediate gratification adds to the already sharp pressure on workers. Under these circumstances, a rising share of the workforce can pretty much forget any hope of safe, steady, sustainable work and instead end up in short-term or part-time contracts, or "casualized," as political economists term it. This means reduced or completely eliminated benefits, lower wages, and less job security overall.[14]

The toy industry is among the worst examples. Most toys are sold during the Christmas season. Every retailer wants to stock plenty of whatever the hot toy is, but each year's hot toy isn't identified until just before Christmas. Manufacturers can't keep workers occupied steadily throughout the year preparing for the Christmas season: they have to wait until the hot toy is declared. Workers in toy factories end up working grueling long hours in the weeks before Christmas—and with this kind of time crunch all kinds of corners are cut in terms of factory conditions and workers' ages. There is built-in motivation for the workers not to complain since they don't want to be among the one-half to two-thirds of the workforce that gets cut in the offseason.[15]

Lean doesn't have to be mean, O'Rourke says. There could be a "green lean" instead of a "mean lean" system. In the same way that Toyota workers were empowered to pull the stop cord on their assembly lines, we could have an entirely transparent system of supply chains in which all the stakeholders are encouraged to identify flaws throughout the system and halt production until that problem has been taken care of. The stakeholders include not just workers but members of communities who live near factories. Under such a model, if they saw stinky brown gunk flowing into their fresh-water source, they could "pull the cord." The stakeholders also include consumers who, if they found out that a product contained toxic ingredients, could cry foul and give their feedback. And until the problem had been dealt with, the supply chain for that product would come to a screeching halt (which would provide incentives for brand-name companies to respond quickly). "Imagine a system in which firms would be pressured to produce goods not as cheaply as possible, but in ways that optimize labor, social and environmental benefits," O'Rourke says.[16]

That vision led him to take a sabbatical from his tenured Berkeley professorship to focus on realizing a long-term dream. For years, as O'Rourke visited factories and analyzed health and safety data on consumer products, he wondered what kind of information, delivered at what point in a purchase decision, could change a consumer's action. He explored ways to deliver this information to people in an easily accessible way, preferably at the point of purchase. Now O'Rourke has created the GoodGuide, a free online searchable database that allows you to get current data on the environmental, social, and health impacts of more than 75,000 (and growing) everyday products and their parent companies.[17] In late 2009, GoodGuide launched its iPhone application that allows shoppers to simply point their phone camera at a product's bar code and immediately receive environmental and health data on the product, far beyond what any label will reveal. It may look like just another green shopping site, but it's not. O'Rourke's goal is "not to help consumers buy less toxic shampoo (although that would be good), but to send market signals up the supply chain to the people making the decisions about what is in these products and how they are made."[18] The GoodGuide has regularly updated information on the companies' labor practices, corporate policies, energy use, climate impact, pollution track record, and even supply chain policies. It identifies ingredients in products and suggests less toxic or higher-scoring alternative products. Most important, it allows individuals to send messages to the companies behind the products.

When I first got onto the GoodGuide site, I looked up Pantene Pro-V hair conditioner, which I used for years until I found out about the crummy chemicals inside it. On GoodGuide, I read about other reasons not to love the parent company (Procter & Gamble), to whom I then sent a message: "Why does my hair conditioner have toxic chemicals? Why does your company have such a lousy air pollution score? I am not buying this anymore!" One message is easy to ignore, but not thousands. O'Rourke says that "send a message to the manufacturer" is the second-most-clicked button on GoodGuide and that a handful of companies have already switched away from toxic ingredients since receiving overwhelming consumer responses.[19]

O'Rourke's project provides all of us massively increased access to information about the supply chains of the products we use, so we can make better choices—better choices for our families, the workers making this Stuff, and the global environment. Some people call this "voting with our dollar."

While I am a big fan of GoodGuide and recommend we all make a habit of scouring its pages, I also want to add that what's really needed is to vote with our votes, not just our consumer dollars. Informing and convincing every parent on the planet to use GoodGuide to learn how to avoid toxic chemicals in children's shampoo is an impossible task, but uniting with a group of parents to lobby to change the laws that allow toxic chemicals in children's shampoos is possible. That is why I see GoodGuide, and other efforts at promoting supply chain transparency, as great transitional tools. They educate. They inspire. They encourage healthy and fair products and companies over nasty ones. They allow us to send messages up the supply chain to decisions makers to, I hope, inspire change for the better. But ultimately, we must remember—as Allegheny College political science professor Michael Maniates says—the choices available to us as consumers are limited and predetermined by forces outside the shopping market. Those forces can best be changed through social and political activism.[20]

Trucks and Container Ships and Planes, Oh My!

Ships, trucks, roads, planes, and trains are needed to move Stuff along this globalized supply chain. The transportation infrastructure consumes enormous quantities of fossil fuels and spews out waste, but these are some of the most hidden of externalized costs in consumer goods, and most people are completely unaware of them. Even those shoppers who are aware of the source of the materials in products, the ones who know to ask whether diamonds fueled violence in Africa or whether the cotton fields in Turkey used pesticides, rarely know what to ask about how goods are transported.

For starters, most Stuff imported from Asia comes across the ocean in containers loaded on gigantic barges. Water carries 99 percent of American overseas trade by weight.[21] Annual water freight was about 1.5 billion tons in 2004, worth nearly $1 trillion, and container traffic is expected to triple in the next twenty years, with most of that coming from China, India, and other places in Asia.[22] The global shipping business consumes more than 140 million tons of fuel per year and contributed 30 percent of developed countries' CO_2 emissions from fossil fuel combustion in 2005 (and 23 percent of the world's emissions, including developing nations).[23]

"Ship Sulfur Emissions Found to Strongly Impact Worldwide Ocean and Coastal Pollution: Trade-carrying cargo ships powered by diesel engines are among the world's highest polluting combustion sources per ton of fuel . . ."[24] "Pollution from Marine Vessels Linked to Heart and Lung Disease: Marine shipping causes approximately 60,000 premature cardiopulmonary and lung cancer deaths around the world each year . . ."[25] "Commercial ships emit almost half as much particulate pollutants into the air globally as the total amount released by the world's cars . . ."[26] "Large Cargo Ships Emit Double Amount of Soot Previously Estimated . . ."[27] These are just a few of the headlines based on research by scientists at Carnegie Mellon and other prestigious institutions related to the damage that cargo ships cause.

I've boarded these ships a couple of times in New York and Manila, when I worked for Greenpeace tracking hazardous-waste cargo. The word "ship" doesn't remotely convey the reality of these monsters. Think gigantic apartment building lying on its side. I remember the first time I boarded one. Our team was wearing hard hats and official-looking black jackets that said "Toxic Trade Patrol," with a pair of handcuffs dangling from our belts just in case we had to lock ourselves to an anchor chain to prevent the ship from setting off with hazardous cargo. When we insisted there was toxic waste hidden aboard the enormous vessel, the crew led us to the captain. We had to take an elevator to the eleventh floor to meet him.

Ships were huge then and they're actually getting bigger now. In order to accommodate ever-growing heaps of Stuff crossing the ocean, a whole new class of container ship has been developed: the jumbo vessel. Many of these are longer than three football fields and big enough to contain thousands of containers, each of which could hold all the contents of a three-bedroom house.[28] One little hitch is that most of the ports around the world can't actually accommodate these supersize ships, meaning that harbors will have to be dredged and enlarged. Plans have already been approved to expand the Panama Canal to allow these vessels to move through it.[29]

It's not just our hemisphere that is expanding its Stuff-distribution infrastructure. Between 2005 and 2010, China is planning to spend $70 billion annually for roads, bridges, and tunnels; $18 billion per year for railways; and $6.4 billion per year for ports.[30] Three of the four highest-volume container ports in the world are in China already; Shanghai is at the top of the list, moving more than 350 million tons in 2007.[31] Forty-three new airports were built there between 2001 and 2005, twenty-three of them in industry-heavy parts of western China.[32] A primary goal of this new infrastructure is to lubricate the distribution of Stuff out of the country to international markets.

Once Stuff arrives in the United States, it generally moves around in trucks. In 2005, 77 percent of the total weight of freight moved within the United States was carried on trucks that racked up more than 160 billion miles, a number that, at least prior to the economic crisis, was expected to double in the next thirty years.[33] Particularly around highway interchanges, in crowded sections of highways, and while waiting in line to enter or leave ports, those trucks often get caught in traffic and sit there, idling, for hours on end. In fact, a recent study found that American freight trucks spent 243 million hours per year stuck in congestion.[34] Delays like these cost the shippers between $25 and $200 per hour.[35] But what about the costs to air quality and the climate, not to mention the public health impacts on asthma rates and cancer? The Air Resources Board in California estimated the costs to public health (including treatment of asthma and lung diseases) from freight trucks at $20 billion annually[36]; in New Jersey, environmental groups say it's $5 billion per year.[37] Old brakes and tires and frequent overloading increase the likelihood that these vehicles will have accidents, creating further costs in highway patrol and emergency services, traffic delays, etc.

Finally, there's air freight: this is the royal treatment in terms of consumer goods and is reserved for high-value and/or time-sensitive cargo, like designer clothes and some electronics. Although it doesn't carry much of the total weight, 35 percent of the *value* of goods traded internationally travels by air, according to Giovanni Bisignani, the CEO of the International Air Transport Association.[38] And that's not all that's disproportionate about air freight. A study in Europe showed that while planes carried just 3 percent of all European cargo's weight, they contributed a whopping 80 percent of the total CO_2 emissions from freight.[39]

 With the recent spikes in oil prices and looming regulations and/or taxes on CO_2, some businesses and governments have already begun to address the energy use and greenhouse gas production from shipping. The U.S. EPA operates a program called SmartWay Transport, through which it works with shippers to reduce emissions. That means combining more sustainable railroad transport with trucking, for example; ensuring that trucks are loaded to full capacity and not wasting any space; improving truck aerodynamics by making sure tarps aren't flapping around and that loads are packed low and as streamlined as possible; monitoring and maintaining the air pressure of truck tires and replacing them with wider tires; training drivers in techniques like coasting when possible or limiting idling; and mandating slower speeds.[40]

Some companies that specialize in freight have taken steps to green themselves. United Parcel Service, or UPS, has launched trucks with hydraulic hybrid technology that are supposed to "increase fuel efficiency by 60–70% in urban use and lowers greenhouse gas emissions by 40%, compared to UPS's conventional diesel delivery trucks."[41] Not to be outdone, FedEx has peppered its fleet with hybrid electric vehicles that decrease particulate emissions by 96 percent and go 57 percent farther on a gallon of fuel than a conventional FedEx truck, reducing fuel costs by more than one-third.[42] DHL has launched its own version of carbon offsets, offering customers the ability to tack on a 3 percent extra fee that DHL promises to invest in "green projects like vehicle technology, solar panels and reforestation."[43]

Nice as those efforts sound, they don't get to the crux of the problem, which is this set of massive global supply chains (as long as ten thousand miles, according to some experts[44]), the consumer demand for more cheap Stuff delivered faster and faster, and the economic rules governing the whole show, which make it more profitable to make Stuff on the other side of the planet than close to home.

With all of the above in mind, let's look at the retail distribution of the same three items we zeroed in on last chapter. Although these aren't the retailers I bought my Stuff from, for the sake of discussion let's say the white T-shirt was sold by the low-end Swedish fashion giant H&M, that the book was bought via Amazon.com, and the computer was purchased at Wal-Mart (although it wasn't, I promise). Studying these three megavendors will shed some light on the role of retailers in global distribution.

H&M

In addition to little white T-shirts, the Swedish clothing giant H&M sells more than 500 million items every year, from more than 1,700 stores.[45] It's the world's third-largest clothing retailer, after Gap Inc. and Spain's Inditex group, netting more than $440 million even in the relatively sluggish year of 2008.[46] H&M is best known for its speed and reaction time—its "fast fashion." Its clothes can be designed, produced, and distributed (from the drawing board to the hanger) in just twenty days.[47] They are not made to last. Trendiness, combined with ridiculously low prices, is the secret to H&M's success.

Here's lean manufacturing in play: like so many other well-known brand retailers, H&M contracts with the cheapest suppliers available, mostly in Asia and Eastern Europe, where it leverages its size to push wages ever lower and timelines ever shorter. It uses lots of suppliers simultaneously, which reduces the risk should one factory fall behind schedule and makes it easy to break off relations with one in favor of another without disturbing the flow of product. It's constantly scouting for factories that undercut existing suppliers, prepared to jump without any sense of loyalty to the previous relationship.[48] Trade protection laws, tariffs, and quotas also affect which suppliers and manufacturing locations H&M chooses. H&M's speed and trendiness, meanwhile, has to do with its distribution machine. Many retailers of clothing (and increasingly also electronics, toys, and other items) reduce time in the supply chain by importing what are known as "greige goods." These are partially prepped and assembled pieces produced overseas in the lowest-wage factories (think undyed fabric roughly precut for sleeves or torsos but not yet sewn together). Greige goods are shipped to factories close to the retail stores to be finalized, which could mean being given the neckline or sleeve length or specific color that consumers are snapping up that week.[49]

In the United States, greige goods are usually brought by ship from Asia and then trucked from ports to assembly and distribution centers, and from there to stores. To keep the whole supply chain running, an enormous information technology brain and nervous system keeps track of the various suppliers, inventories, orders, means and routes of transport, weather, traffic, labor available for shipping and handling, etc. This IT system is under constant refinement, which, although an expensive endeavor, pays off by making distribution swifter every day.[50] Flip back to the section on the impacts of producing my one laptop computer to get an inkling of what the true costs of an IT system of this magnitude must be.

When consumer interest points to a certain trendy color or cut, H&M responds nearly instantaneously and floods their stores to meet the demand (that's the lean retail piece). Dara O'Rourke, who tracks this so closely that he calls himself a "supply chain geek," told me that trendy clothing stores used to have five distinct fashion seasons: each actual season (spring, winter, summer, fall), plus vacation. Now some retailers offer up to twenty-six distinct fashion "seasons," which means that each "season" is just two weeks.[51]

Every H&M store is restocked daily, while high-volume stores can receive as many as three truckloads a day.[52] It is a constant mad rush getting those clothes in the back door and out the front door, with each sale automatically sending data back to the factories as to what's hot. Even reading about the speed of their business makes me feel anxious; it's like retailers on crack. I mean, really, what is all the rush about? Don't we get more joy out of things like reading a great book or enjoying a meal with friends than from spending our money on this week's hottest clothes? Does wearing last month's or (gasp) last year's T-shirt really make such a difference? H&M and many consumers clearly believe it does.

H&M is an extreme example of the hypervelocity of today's distribution systems. As fast-fashion consumers get addicted to the ever-changing offerings that blare at them from TV and movies, store windows and ads, H&M is only to happy to keep supplying the Stuff. We'll see many of the same economic drivers with other products and retailers.

Amazon

When Internet shopping was just beginning, a lot of people thought this development would be good for the environment and amazing for small, independent businesses. After all, suddenly you could open a business without needing a physical storefront—you didn't even need inventory, because things could be produced when an e-mail came in from a customer, assuming you could fulfill the order in a reasonable amount of time. And of course that's all true. But overwhelmingly online retail has wound up supporting the same huge, insensitive companies that dominate in the brick-and-mortar world. In spite of the new potential for smaller companies to reach prospective consumers directly, about one-third of the $70 billion that Americans spent online in 2003 (that number had already topped $100 billion by 2006[53]) went to just the top twenty Web retailers, with twelve of those being major chains.[54]

Amazon.com is the undisputed emperor of this realm, priding itself on offering the world's biggest selection of items, at prices below, or at least competitive with, what they cost elsewhere. To broaden inventory even further, it partners with other vendors (even large ones like Target) and provides them with warehousing and distribution. Technology is Amazon's strongest suit and greatest investment (dwarfing H&M's logistics system by umpteen degrees). Not only for the customer interface—the programs that create a personalized shopping experience and recommend products to users (as founder and CEO Jeff Bezos says, with so many items to choose from, they had to create ways to not only "enable customers to find products, but also enable products to find customers"[55])—but also for the logistics of "fulfillment," or processing an order and getting it to a customer. Imagine tracking a couple of million different products, as opposed to a couple of thousand. Amazon had to create its own "inventory optimization" software that Bezos compares to airline routing: complex algorithms create an optimal "pick path" through multi-million-square-foot warehouses so machines can find and fetch the specific items on order.[56] It's this enormous selection and the technological whiz-bang behind the personalized experience that the Amazon brand is all about.

For most people, it takes a will of steel to resist Amazon and instead choose a local bookstore, which charges the price that's actually on the cover of the book and may well have to special-order a book because of its limited on-site inventory. Of course, as a result, the ranks of local, independently owned bookstores have been entirely decimated, which is a terrible loss.

However, there's still lively, ongoing debate among environmentalists about whether online shopping has a lighter footprint than traditional retail. Retail stores consume resources in their building, lighting, cooling, heating, etc., and consumers usually have to climb into their cars to reach them. However, e-commerce uses more packaging and is more likely to rely on air freight for at least part of the product's journey. An in-depth study done specifically on book sales compared the two forms of distribution. In the traditional model, books are trucked from the printer to a national warehouse, then to a regional warehouse, and from there to the retail outlets. The customer travels to the store to buy the book and brings it home. In the online model, the book is trucked from the printer to a central warehouse. After the customer orders it, it's packaged, flown to a regional hub, and trucked to the customer's door.

The study raises an interesting point in terms of unsold books (an average of 25 to 55 percent of what gets printed, depending on the genre[57]), which are usually either trashed, recycled, or sold to a discount bookstore—all of which at least means further transport, if not also waste. Because in the online model the central warehouse is a single inventory point, there are fewer unsold books, meaning less wasted paper and less transport. In the end, using average fuel consumption rates for the planes, trucks, and cars, average packaging for an average-sized book, and the average rate of books that go unsold, the study found that online shopping was more efficient and sustainable in terms of energy used, conventional air pollutants generated, waste generated, and greenhouse gas emissions.[58] This efficiency might even increase as print-on-demand technology is more widely available—where a book with a small readership would not even be printed until a reader puts in an order, using the printing press closest to the consumer. Some industry observers predict that by 2010, half of the books sold around the world will be printed on demand at or near the place of sale.[59]

However, as the online environmental magazine *TreeHugger* points out, details matter when evaluating today's online and in-person shopping options. If you take public transit, bike, or walk to your local bookstore, it's definitely a better choice than online shopping. They recommend shopping online only if "you live in the suburbs, or are surrounded by Mega-Marts, have to drive more than six or eight miles each way to go shopping, are scrupulous about bundling online orders, and choose ground shipping rather than overnight air."[60]

Then there's the whole issue of the digitization of books and devices like Amazon's Kindle. While there's no question that paperless books will slow the destruction of forests, this technological development means yet another electronic gadget on the market. And as we've seen with every other kind of electronics out there—be it cell phones, computers, cameras, what have you—that will likely mean a new version every few years, with the attendant mining of minerals, toxics in and toxics out during production, and ever higher mountains of e-waste.

Myself, I'm a fan of the following model: Local bookstores that I can walk or ride my bike to, with a friendly face behind the counter who can personally recommend titles to me. Once I'm finished with a book, I lend it to everyone I know, if I can recommend it; otherwise I Freecycle it (Freecycle is a 7-million-strong online network of people who post Stuff— and get Stuff—for free, in order to reduce waste[61]) so it finds a second life with someone else. My ten-year-old daughter churns through books very quickly, so every so often, we invite her friends over for a "book swap brunch" to empty out our overflowing shelves, get some new ones for free, and keep building community. The leftovers from the brunch (the books, not the waffles) get donated to local schools. And then there are libraries— in every place I've lived, the library has been one of my favorite places to find books, as well as to meet neighbors, attend public seminars, weigh in on community issues, and sometimes even hear live music. Amazon may be easy and fast and impressive in its scale, but it just doesn't provide those quality-of-life extras.

Wal-Mart

Almost 20 percent of the consumer electronics purchased in the United States is sold by Wal-Mart,[62] so it's not unreasonable to imagine that the laptop I described in the last chapter was distributed through the Godzilla of retail.

If H&M's special powers are speed and trendiness (in addition to rock-bottom prices), and Amazon's is unlimited choice (and lower than cover prices), Wal-Mart's is a combination of reach, breadth, and low prices. Wal-Mart is truly vast—in comparison, pretty much every other retailer in the world is a tiny pipsqueak. In fact, you could lump together Gap Inc., Target, Sears, Costco, JCPenney, Best Buy, Staples, Toys "R" Us, Nordstrom, Blockbuster, and Barnes & Noble, and all of them combined don't add up to the scope of Wal-Mart,[63] with its revenues of $401 billion in 2008.[64] It's one of the top economies in the world, bigger than the GDP of countries like Austria, Chile, and Israel and one of China's top-ten trading partners, ahead of the United Kingdom or Germany.[65]

There are more than eight thousand Wal-Mart stores worldwide, over

four thousand of them in the United States, each of which averages nearly three football fields in size.[66] Stacy Mitchell, author of *Big-Box Swindle*, comments that "with 600 million square feet of floor space in the United States, Wal-Mart could fit every man, woman, and child in the country inside its stores."[67] The stores' ubiquity in the United States means that virtually no one is ever farther than sixty miles from the nearest one, and the chain is constantly expanding, by about 50 million square feet every year.[68]

As for their breadth, what *can't* you get at Wal-Mart? It's now the number-one seller of groceries, clothing, home furnishings, toys, and music in the United States.[69] Americans are buying many of their DVDs, cameras, home appliances, and common household items like toothpaste, shampoo, and diapers there too. It sells gas. It's even opened health clinics. And it has been trying to overturn laws that keep it from offering banking services.[70] Remember the corporation in the film *WALL-E* that basically owned the planet, providing every good and service on, and then beyond, earth? It's really not that far-fetched; Wal-Mart seems to be headed in that very direction.

In contrast to Amazon, however, Wal-Mart offers at most only a couple of varieties of any given product. About 40 percent of products sold are its own private label brands, meaning they're produced exclusively for Wal-Mart.[71] Yet, even without the variety available at Amazon, the "always low prices, always" promised in these huge one-stop-shopping emporia are enough to keep people coming back again and again.

The funny thing about those "always low prices" is that they're actually not always so low. Sam Walton's whole shtick, starting with his very first store in Arkansas in 1962, was to stack popular items like shampoo and toothpaste at the front of the store, marked with ostentatious price tags that were well below cost. These are known as "loss leaders": they lured customers into the store and away from competing vendors. Once inside, people would usually buy additional products that were priced to make a profit.[72] A 2005 *Consumer Reports* analysis showed that big retailers like Wal-Mart rely on tricky pricing structures that make customers think their prices are lower, but that's not always the case.[73] Also, Wal-Mart often opens a new store in a new market with steep discounts to snuff out the competition and then raises its prices when there's no place else to shop.[74] That practice has earned Wal-Mart massive criticism from activists across the country, who blame the retail giant for undermining diverse local economies and communities.

And regardless what the price tag says, the true cost of every single product at Wal-Mart is actually much, much higher. The real costs start with raw materials that are often pillaged from poor countries or subsidized by the government and which leave behind a trail of tragic consequences for the earth's water, animals, air, forests, and people. The costs continue with hot, poorly ventilated factories in Asia, where thousands of workers slave away for less than five dollars per day, often exposed to toxic chemicals without adequate protection or health care, forced to work unpaid overtime, with little hope of rising out of their dismal situations. And the costs culminate in the stores, where many employees earn so little that they fall underneath the federal poverty line. According to WakeUpWalmart.com, a U.S. campaign working to make the megastore improve its operations, the average full-time associate (as Wal-Mart workers are called) earned $10.84 an hour in 2008. The annual salary of $19,165 (for a thirty-four-hour work week) is $2,000 below the U.S. federal poverty line. By contrast, in 2007 Wal-Mart's CEO, Lee Scott, earned $29.7 million, or 1,550 times the annual income of an average full-time Wal-Mart associate.[75]

Watchdog groups report that stores are regularly understaffed to save the corporation even more money, and managers have been caught secretly deleting hours, especially overtime, from time cards.[76] Employees are paid so little that most can't afford the company health care program, resulting in about half of Wal-Mart's 1.4 million U.S. employees not being covered by the plan.[77] Often workers are outright encouraged by Wal-Mart management to get federal assistance like Medicaid, food stamps, and subsidized housing. In fact, according to the Washington, D.C., based organization Good Jobs First, in the twenty-one out of twenty-three states for which data is available, Wal-Mart forces more employees to rely on taxpayer-funded health care than any other employer.[78]

So instead of Wal-Mart providing many employees with health care coverage, the American taxpayer does. Nor does taxpayer support of the company end there. We unwitting taxpayers have heavily subsidized Wal-Mart's success. Good Jobs First maintains a project called Wal-Mart Subsidy Watch that tracks and exposes how U.S. taxpayer money supports Wal-Mart's operations, like the "more than $1.2 billion in tax breaks, free land, infrastructure assistance, low-cost financing and outright grants from state and local governments around the country."[79]

And just try to put a dollar value on the social fabric of a community, which Wal-Mart megastores have repeatedly undermined. What's the value of pedestrian-friendly town centers and neighborhoods, bustling with a diverse and locally-based retail mix, with storekeepers who know our names leaning over their counters to ask our kids how school is going or willing to let us pay tomorrow when we accidentally left our wallet at home? Priceless.

Not to mention the wetlands, farmland, and forests which are often cleared for the twelve-acre plots that an average big-box retailer plus its mandatory parking lot takes up.[80] Wal-Mart also operates over 100 distribution centers in the United States, vast warehouses churning away 24/7, each with *five miles* of conveyor belts that pump nine thousand different tracks of Stuff into waiting trailers.[81] Each of these distribution centers takes up 400,000 to 1 million square feet of space.[82] To put that in perspective, 1 million square feet is about twenty football fields. Across the country, Wal-Mart has eviscerated thousands of small towns and natural landscapes; those losses are part of the true cost of the "always low prices" too.

And the costs don't end there. What comes between the raw materials, factories, distribution centers, and stores? Those trucks, container barges, and airplanes I mentioned earlier. Not surprisingly, no company has more trucks on America's roads than Wal-Mart, with more than eight thousand drivers racking up more than 850 million miles per year.[83] Wal-Mart, like most major retailers, frequently deals with trucking brokers who sell their services as independent contractors. This means Wal-Mart doesn't have to buy or maintain the trucks, pay for fuel, or provide benefits for these contracted drivers—no health insurance, unemployment insurance, workers' comp, Social Security, pension plans, vacations, or sick days. This also means they're not required to ensure compliance with federal OSHA (Occupational, Safety and Health Administration) regulations for drivers.[84] A study in New Jersey found that 75 percent of truckers (statewide, not Wal-Mart's alone) were independent contractors, earning just $28,000 per year on average, with zero employer-paid benefits.[85] Like Wal-Mart's store employees, these drivers have to rely on public health care programs, so taxpayers are essentially also subsidizing Wal-Mart's and other retailers' transport systems.

Given all of this, it's hard to take Wal-Mart seriously when it broadcasts its commitment to sustainability. Yes, Wal-Mart has made some real environmental improvements in its operations. Sources that are closer to the company than I am swear there's a sincere environmental awareness growing among many within the company leadership. Wal-Mart has switched its corporate fleet of cars to hybrids, made more of its packaging biodegradable and recyclable, installed solar panels on some stores, and even committed to eliminate PVC shower curtains and kids toys containing the toxic chemical phthalates.[86] The question is whether, in the big picture, these steps even matter. Wal-Mart still has a major problem with scale. It is moving so much non-durable toxic-laden Stuff so fast and so far that all the hybrid cars and solar panels in the world couldn't negate its enormous footprint.

I mean really: consider Wal-Mart's boasting that "by reducing the packaging on one of our patio sets we were able to use four hundred fewer shipping containers to deliver them."[87] How many shipping containers must be required to ship the patio furniture around the world if there was an excess of four hundred containers just from tightening up some of the packaging? There's something wrong with a distribution system that constantly ships everything from T-shirts to patio furniture halfway around the world. In the era of increasing resource scarcity and climate change, this model just doesn't make sense.

Superstores: Superbad

Wal-Mart is the epitome of the larger phenomenon of the rise of big-box stores. Although maybe you can hardly remember—and certainly kids today can't imagine—a time when stores like Target, Costco, and Wal-Mart didn't exist at every turn, they are a relatively new phenomenon that really only took off in the 1980s. Chain stores like Woolworth's started in the late nineteenth century, followed by stores like Sears, Roebuck and Montgomery Ward. By 1929 chains like these controlled 22 percent of the retail market. But by the mid-1950s they'd hardly grown, to less than 24 percent. That was partially because many people boycotted them, especially in the wake of the stock market collapse, believing (correctly) that chains drove down wages and undermined democracy by concentrating power in the hands of a few.[88]

But then in the 1950s came the explosion of suburban homes and with them the development of suburban shopping malls. Taxpayers paid hundreds of billions of dollars for the interstate highways that made this new style of life possible, while banks favored new suburban developments over established neighborhoods in their lending practices. Then, in 1954, Congress changed the tax code to make it more profitable for developers to create shopping malls, basically making a tax shelter out of shopping mall construction.[89] As Stacy Mitchell writes in *Big-Box Swindle,* 6 million square feet of shopping centers were constructed in 1953; just three years later that figure had increased by 500 percent; and over the next twenty years, eighteen thousand shopping centers were built across the United States.[90] And the owners of these shopping centers often preferred to make chain stores their tenants (considered a better bet for a landlord), some actually going so far as to bar independently owned stores.[91]

Today, cashing in on local municipalities' eagerness to have one in their community, big-box stores receive local and state subsidies and tax breaks. Local municipalities hope that having a local big-box store will increase economic growth, provide new jobs, and boost tax revenues, but unfortunately that isn't always borne out. Instead, big-boxes siphon money out of the local economy so those lucky Walton family members (and other chains' shareholders) can acquire another private jet for their extensive fleet and build a new wing on their nuclear-disaster-ready underground fortress (it's true).[92] Big-box payroll typically accounts for less than ten cents of every dollar spent at a given store,[93] and, in a domino effect, their low wages (16 percent less for Wal-Mart workers than the average retail worker in 2008, for example[94]) help suppress the wages of retail workers everywhere. Meanwhile, big-box chains have massive budgets and even specially trained response teams to counter any attempts of workers to unionize and improve their situations. According to WakeUpWalmart .com, the company has even created "A Manager's Toolbox to Remaining Union Free." The toolbox lists warning signs of potential organizing activities such as "frequent meetings at associates' homes" and "associates who are never seen together start talking or associating with each other."[95]

Because of their size, big-box stores and other chains are able to hold prices artificially low for as long as it takes to drive local independently owned enterprises out of business, even if this takes years. Other local economic activity is also hampered: for example, rather than hiring local accountants or graphic designers and placing ads in local newspapers as locally owned smaller stores do, the big-box headquarters handles it. Commercial real estate prices have been shown to drop the minute there's a plan for a new big-box in town, because people foresee hardships for existing businesses and difficulty finding new investors for the emptied-out storefronts.[96]

Obviously, because so much of their manufacturing-related work has been outsourced overseas to lower-wage factories in regions with weaker environmental regulations and enforcement, the big-boxes have effectively eliminated thousands if not millions of jobs in American manufacturing. That was the "giant sucking sound" that U.S. 1992 presidential candidate Ross Perot claimed NAFTA would create as scores of jobs disappeared from the U.S. economy and relocated to Mexico.[97] (More recently, *New York Times* columnist Thomas Friedman opined that "the Mexicans . . . are hearing 'the giant sucking sound' in stereo these days—from China in one ear and India in the other."[98])

All of this has fundamentally changed the landscape of this country. I mean that physically, with the total amount of retail space doubling between 1990 and 2005, from 19 to 38 square feet per person, and for every new square foot of store space, another 3 to 4 square feet paved for cars.[99] But I also mean it socioeconomically: this country's middle class, traditionally sustained by manufacturing jobs and small business ownership, has lost one opportunity after another while the rich accumulate unprecedented profits. So even with the nation's overall economic growth, the gap between rich and poor keeps widening. CEO pay versus worker pay is just one indicator of this: In the 1970s, for example, the head of a large corporation earned 30 times as much as the average worker. By 1997, CEOs earned 116 times as much as the average worker. And by 2007, CEOs were earning nearly 300 times as much as the average worker.[100]

And in a cruel turn of a self-perpetuating cycle, as ordinary people have less income, the bargains promised by big-box stores are even more inviting, and so consumers support the very entity that is sucking the life out of their local economy and communities.

There's some hope, though. Local communities have gotten hip to the deception and destruction of big-box development and have been organizing to fight new big-box stores in favor of local businesses, which provide more secure jobs and keep more of the money circulating in the local economy. The highly publicized case of Inglewood, California, going up against Wal-Mart itself was one such victory. In 2003, Wal-Mart planned to build a superstore covering an area the size of seventeen football fields in the town of Inglewood in Los Angeles County. After the city council effectively blocked Wal-Mart's proposal, the company decided to bypass them and take the issue directly to the voters. To win folks over, Wal-Mart spent $1 million—a huge amount for a city with a population just over 110,000—and even went as far as handing out free meals to city residents. Yet to Wal-Mart's surprise, in April 2004 Inglewood voters overwhelmingly rejected Wal-Mart's plan, preventing the store from being built.[101] While there were those who had looked forward to better access to bargain shopping, the community as a whole prioritized environmental, economic, and community well-being.

The victories in Inglewood and other communities remind me of one of the seminal events in establishing our independence as a country—the Boston Tea Party. To support local enterprise in the colonies, our plucky foremothers and forefathers boycotted tea from the East India Company, possibly the world's most powerful transnational corporation at the time. Then they boycotted all British goods (even though it meant a little bit of hardship and the loss of access to some Stuff they were used to) as a step toward independence.

In fact, there are those who compare today's huge multinational corporations to colonizers. Just like colonial powers, the corporation's central aim is not to foster local economic development, happiness, and prosperity but to enrich itself. In Africa, for example, colonizers built the railroads not so they would connect local African towns with one another, but as tracks that ran in single lines from the interior to the ports on the coast, so that resources and slaves could be extracted as efficiently as possible. And that's exactly what the major chains, with the help of international trade policies, have done: they've built tracks for the wealth of local communities (whether that wealth comes from natural resources in Africa, toxic goods produced by exploited workers in China, or the sweat of underpaid retail employees in America) to flow in one direction—into their pockets.

The Rule Makers

None of what I've described thus far happened in a vacuum. It has all been made possible by the massive development of information technology over the last twenty-five years: the evolution of computers, semiconductors, fiber optics, satellites, etc., which have laid the foundation for the elaborate management systems that have enabled companies to find the cheapest, fastest path to making and distributing products. Then there's the physical infrastructure of power plants, factories, ports, and roads—especially in rapidly developing countries like China and India.

A final huge piece of this puzzle involves the structure of the global economy, a group of global regulatory institutions, and a set of agreements that have been worked out between countries to promote trade and "growth." Uncovering the pervasive role of trade agreements and international financial institutions, or IFIs, is crucial. There is no way to comprehend the Story of Stuff without them, because they establish the rules by which not only the global distribution system but the whole of the take-make-waste economic model operates.

To understand how these IFIs came to be, we have to delve briefly into history, especially the financial crash of 1929 and the resulting Great Depression that lasted through the 1930s and led up to World War II. For decades up to that point, governments had relied on the supposedly free market to take care of business with minimal government involvement. Even during our so-called Progressive Era between the 1890s and 1920s, when early protections like antitrust legislation and food-safety regulations were adopted, big corporate interests, not government, were dominant.[102]

Then, in response to the Great Depression, national governments worldwide scrambled to protect their own workers and businesses by imposing tariffs on foreign Stuff, which led to a collapse in international trade and worsened unemployment and poverty for people across the globe. Even large increases in government spending for public works didn't solve the problem. In this international atmosphere of extreme political and economic stress, Adolf Hitler launched World War II, which got the U.S. out of the Depression but trashed the industrial base of Europe and much of Asia. As the war drew to a close in 1944, the Allied powers, led by the United States, decided they needed a way to rearrange global economic relations around the new de facto world currency, the U.S. dollar, while also facilitating investment in the economies freshly destroyed by the war.[103]

And so two superinfluential international agencies were born at a hotel in Bretton Woods, New Hampshire. The "Bretton Woods Institutions"—the International Monetary Fund (IMF) and World Bank (the nickname of the International Bank for Reconstruction and Development)—were later joined by the World Trade Organization, or WTO (which evolved from the 1948 General Agreement on Tariffs and Trade, or GATT). The IMF was created to deal with financial imbalances between countries: its primary role was to keep the world's currencies stable and exchangeable in order to support international trade and to provide emergency loans to any country whose economy was in such bad shape that it couldn't participate in global trade. The World Bank was created specifically to loan money to the governments of countries devastated by World War II so they could rebuild their economies and rejoin global trade. Soon, the World Bank shifted its focus to countries and European colonies in Latin America, Africa, and Asia. The GATT was a complicated treaty set up to reduce national barriers to trade; in 1995 it was replaced by the international organization known as the World Trade Organization (WTO), which has even broader-reaching powers. Note that these are only the three largest of these organizations; there are dozens of additional multilateral banks, government agencies, and trade agreements that replicate the IMF/World Bank/WTO model in regional or sector-specific forms.[104]

Although some of the original intentions behind these institutions may have been good, their evolution over the past half century has had disastrous results for the great majority of people on the planet, and for the planet itself. Dominated by the biggest players (especially the United States), the IMF, World Bank, and WTO have created and perpetuated huge imbalances in global wealth while trashing the natural environment and destroying communities all the way from Argentina to Zimbabwe and everywhere in between.

While most of us in the United States have few occasions to confirm this harsh truth regarding the negative impacts of IFIs, ordinary folks all over the developing world have extensive hands-on knowledge: these institutions influence their ability to do everything from make a living as farmers, get much-needed medicine, send their kids to school, or escape the grips of poverty.

In Singrauli, India, I met villagers who had been kicked off their land ("involuntary resettlement," in World Bank speak) in order to make room for a World Bank–funded coal-fired power plant complex. I was struck by the constant background shade of grey caused by the coal ash from the facility. A generation ago, Singrauli was richly forested, with wildlife and clean water and small subsistence farming; today, the coal mining and burning and ash has devastated the air, water, and landscape so intensely that some Indian journalists have dubbed it "the lower circles of Dante's *Inferno*."[105] The compensation given to the displaced families was nowhere near enough to make up for their increased distance to fresh water, the loss of farmland, and the destruction of the social fabric due to the relocation.

The problem is not just the actual projects, like highways to nowhere, greenhouse-gas-spewing coal plants, or dioxin-emitting incinerators, but the broader development model that is forced on borrowing countries as well. While the IMF, for example, does loan money to countries in need, these loans too often come with ruthless strings attached, requiring borrowing countries to further deplete their natural resources in order to ramp up exports and to divert funds from public health, education, and other social needs to ensure loan repayment. In other words, they have to lower their already low standard of living in order to meet international debt payments. And if a country refuses these conditions, it finds itself blacklisted from other international lenders, unable to access desperately needed funds.

The World Bank and IMF work hand in hand. Once the IMF requires borrowing countries to export more natural resources, the World Bank is happy to provide the technical expertise and loans needed to extract those resources, using technologies like those described in chapter 1 on extraction. Generally charging interest rates higher than those of local lenders, the World Bank finances roads, ports, power plants, factories, megadumps, incinerators, and dams all over the world. Its projects have been plagued with controversy, from the forced—sometimes violent—displacement of local residents to large-scale destruction of forests, aquifers, and entire ecosystems, as well as systemic corruption. The World Bank's stated mission is to "to help developing countries and their people . . . alleviate poverty." [106] A noble goal, sure enough, but the real issue is how the World Bank goes about achieving it. What values and beliefs guide the strategy to meet these goals? For the World Bank, it is pretty clear. The World Bank—like the other IFIs—believes that more economic growth, more globalization, more unhindered capital flow, and more natural resource exploitation will reduce poverty.

In fact, there's a ton of empirical evidence that proves otherwise. In spite of (actually, partly because of) all these required economic "reforms," loans, and "development" projects targeting developing countries, there's still a massive net flow of wealth out of them into the richest countries. This is partly because each time the World Bank or IMF loans a developing country money, some of that money goes right back to the lender countries via the purchase of technologies or international consultants from the lending countries. Then there are interest payments, often at crippling rates, and the payment of the loan principal, which becomes more onerous when developing countries' currencies decline in value (which happens most of the time). Zambia's 2004 loan repayments to the IMF alone, for example, amounted to $25 million, more than the education budget for the entire country.[107] In 2005–06, Kenya's budget for debt payments was as much as for water, health, agriculture, roads, transport, and finance combined.[108] Overall in 2006, the world's poorest countries (with annual average incomes of less than $935 per person) paid more than $34 billion in debt service (payments of interest and principal), which works out to $93 million a day. If you include all developing countries, the amount was $573 billion.[109] According to the Jubilee Debt campaign, which provides those numbers, although there was some debt cancellation in 2007 and 2008, today's figures are likely similar; there were also plenty of new loans.[110]

Finally, there's the transfer of wealth from the export of valuable natural resources—remember the resource curse I mentioned in the extraction chapter? So the World Bank and IMF have contributed to a situation where most borrowing countries pay way more than they ever receive in international aid.

But why is this our concern? These are international institutions, right? Actually, the United States provides 18 percent of the World Bank's funding. And the United States controls 18 percent of the voting power at the IMF—in effect a veto power, since an 85 percent majority is required for a decision.[111] This means the United States has a disproportionate share of influence over both the IMF and World Bank. And it means we U.S. citizens are involved by providing our tax dollars, as well as by benefiting from interest repayments the World Bank makes on its bonds that are bought by our pension funds, municipalities, and church or university endowments. We're paying for all these environmentally destructive projects, ruthless economic reforms, and bad loans that are suffocating many developing countries' economies. So we have both the responsibility and the right to check out what the IMF and World Bank are doing, and to rein them in.

It is simply not possible for developing countries to pay back the crippling debt on these international loans, many of which were made under misleading or coercive terms for poorly planned projects. Or were made with undemocratic and corrupt leaders who diverted the funds for their personal use, or spent them on arms to secure their hold on power. And it is even more impossible to expect poor countries to be able to chart a path of sustainability, of just and healthy economic development, while being held hostage to decades-old debt. If the World Bank and IMF are even remotely interested in improving the life of the world's poor, these debts need to be canceled. Instead, the Bank and IMF should offer ecological-debt repayments to communities worldwide to compensate for the social and environmental damages these institutions caused with their projects and policies over previous decades.

 The Jubilee movement—inspired by the biblical concept of a Jubilee year in which debts are forgiven and equity is restored—is active in many countries around the world, uniting faith-based communities with advocates for human rights, the environment, labor, and economic justice. It calls for a cancellation of international debts and the restoration of healthy relationships between nations. Some progress is being made. There is proposed legislation before the U.S. Congress called the Jubilee Act, which would cancel debt among the poorest countries in

the world and promote more transparency and responsibility in future lending. In 2008, this act passed in the U.S. House of Representatives and the Senate Foreign Relations Committee but didn't make it to the full Senate for a vote.[112] Even while waiting for the Jubilee Act to move forward, there are other signs of hope, such as the April 2009 promise by the Obama administration to provide $20 million to cancel Haiti's absolutely crippling debt payments to the World Bank and its regional ally, the Inter-American Development Bank.[113]

The last of the big three is the World Trade Organization. The WTO was created in 1995 as the successor to the General Agreement on Tariffs and Trade (or GATT). First aimed at reducing trade tariffs, it later turned to "trade liberalization"—that is, removing obstacles to increased trade. Now, I am not against trade, which has been happening since the beginning of time and has brought many good things. But trade should take place when it supports a thriving environment, good jobs, healthy communities, and cultural diversity. Trade can support all those things when those things are the end, and trade is one (just one) means by which to achieve them. The fundamental problem with the WTO is that it acts as though trade itself is the goal and that therefore trade must be given preference over pesky little things like public health, worker rights, and strong and vibrant local economies.

The trade-trumps-all approach of the WTO is demonstrated in its highly controversial provision which prevents nations from discriminating against any product based on how it was produced. It doesn't matter if the technology involved in making the product is horribly polluting or unsafe to workers. Any country—driven by its corporate interests—can challenge a law in another country by claiming it's a "trade barrier." Such disputes are decided by three-person arbitration panels that meet in secret and are not screened for conflicts of interest.[114]

In the late 1990s, I worked in Ralph Nader's office in Washington, D.C. One of my colleagues there, Rob Weissman, a Harvard-trained lawyer and leading critic of the WTO, used to chide me for my obsession with factories and dumps, urging me to join those fighting the WTO instead of, or more accurately in addition to, working on garbage. He pointed out that every law that I worked tirelessly to strengthen, and every victory against a dirty production process could get wiped out, or rendered illegal, by the WTO.

Weissman was right on: many of my local-level campaigns, for example to prevent a certain incinerator or polluting factory, were won as battles but then lost in the overall war as macro-level policies determined a different

longer term outcome. Under the WTO, environmental laws, labor standards, human rights legislation, public health policies, protection of native
cultures, food self-reliance—all of these can and have been attacked and
overturned as impediments to free trade. For example, the WTO overruled
the European Union's law banning beef raised with artificial growth hormones when beef producers outside Europe claimed the public health law
constituted a trade barrier.[115] Under the WTO, government laws made in
the public interest can be overturned just like that. Obviously, many companies that extract resources and produce Stuff love this, since it means
fewer obstacles to their business. For those of us who are working to promote higher standards and better practices for how resources are extracted,
Stuff is produced, and workers and communities are treated, it's a huge
problem. All our goals become secondary (at best) to more, faster, cheaper
trade.

Despite its implicit threat to the well-being of people and the planet,
the WTO (and international trade agreements leading to it) somehow
managed to keep itself off the radar screen of the American public for half a
century. And then 1999 happened. In 1999, some doofus at the WTO
decided to hold the annual ministerial conference in Seattle, Washington.
What were they thinking? Were they unaware of the city's demographics
and pro-environment politics? That meeting marked a major turning point
in public awareness about the WTO. An estimated seventy thousand people
from all over the world descended on Seattle[116] to make their opposition
to the WTO known, with nonviolence, teach-ins, strategy sessions, and
marches. The protest was amazing in both its scale and its diversity. Alongside representatives from rich and poor countries alike, environmentalists
and labor activists—two communities with a history of misunderstandings
and tension between them—joined forces against an international regime
that prioritizes trade over the planet, communities, and workers.

Of course I was there: how could I not be when this was going down in
the town where I was born? My mother and my childhood neighbors were
kind enough to open their doors and guest rooms and couches to my colleagues. It was my four-month-old daughter's first big protest, and a local
Seattle artist made her a little T-shirt with drawing of a baby pacifier and
the words "WTO SUCKS."

I heard speakers from India, the Philippines, Brazil, and Nigeria give
firsthand accounts of natural resources and communities sacrificed to the
goal of increased and unfettered trade. I got to walk the downtown streets
the day before the big protest day and felt the peaceful, hopeful energy of
the crowd. The people there were smart and dedicated, spending their days

learning about issues of sustainability and justice—by and large good people. There were so many of us that we felt change was truly within our reach.

On the day of the big planned march, rumors spread about police hostility toward the protesters, and I decided to stay home with my baby girl. We watched the coverage on my mother's little television, and I got regular frontline updates from my colleagues via their cell phones. It was surreal to see tens of thousands of people from all over the world marching past the department store where I bought my prom shoes in high school and the monorail stop where I used to disembark with kids I babysat twenty years earlier.

Watching the events unfold on TV was disturbing. The newscasters didn't offer substantive background about the WTO. They didn't note how amazing it was that nearly one hundred thousand people were paying enough attention to the WTO to know what a problem it was and that they had left their jobs and homes to voice peaceful opposition. Instead they showed one clip over and over again all day: a couple of young troublemakers smashing storefront windows in downtown Seattle.[117] I was fuming. If they wanted to show faces of the real WTO critics there, why not interview those speakers from other countries who came to tell their stories? Or Public Citizen's Lori Wallach, who was also there? Lori knows the provisions of the WTO so well that during her lectures, she sometimes invites audience members to yell out some topic, almost like a game show—Health care! Banking regulations! Small fisherfolk!—and she explains exactly how the WTO will affect, and undermine, those sectors. I don't think she has ever been stumped.

And if the news wanted to show violence to keep up those ratings, there's plenty of violence caused by the system that the WTO supports! They could have run clips of workers in garment factories being made to work so fast they lost fingers in the machines, or of miners in the Congo being beaten for inadequate results after an endless day's work. Instead the media grossly misrepresented the day's events, trivialized the serious concerns that the citizens voiced, and compounded our society's ignorance of global issues.

Although the inappropriately named "Battle of Seattle" was the biggest WTO protest in the United States to date, such protests are much more common in other countries. In 2001 in India, for example, more than a million farmers protested against the WTO's plan to force India to give equal preference to food grown by megacorporations in other countries and that grown by small-scale Indian farmers.[118] The local farmers feared that the flood of imported food would lead to lower food prices, since corporations can leverage economies of scale. They argued that this would decimate the livelihood of millions of Indians—many of whom were already living on the brink of starvation—and lock the country into a relationship of dependence, when they were perfectly capable of growing food for themselves. Buying foodstuff from overseas would also drain resources to the megacorporations' home countries, whereas buying from local farmers would keep more money in their community, contributing to a stronger, more resilient local economy.

Unfortunately the Indian farmers were not successful in protecting themselves from the flood of imports priced below market. Many of their worst fears were realized. But they keep fighting because their lives depend on it. In 2005, the Indian Coordination Committee of Farmers Movements, a coalition of farmers from around the country, wrote a letter to the prime minister summarizing their demands in the face of the emergency: "The dumping of these agricultural commodities led to depression in the domestic farmgate prices, which led to a deep agrarian crisis and caused increased cases of farmers' suicides . . . We believe that the very structure of WTO rules therefore distorts trade against small farmers, against food sovereignty and against trade justice. That is why we gave a call for the removal of agriculture from WTO . . . Agriculture in India is not an industry. It is the main source of livelihood for 70% of the population of the country. We therefore demand from the Indian government to quit from WTO. We also demand that agriculture should be out of WTO." [119] As I finalize this book in late 2009, farmers throughout India are continuing to fight with increasing desperation to protect their livelihoods and save their economy from being the latest casualty of the WTO.

Huge protests have also occurred against the WTO in Latin America, Europe, and elsewhere in Asia. In 2003, more than 150,000 human rights, agriculture, environmental, and labor advocates descended on Cancún, Mexico, where the WTO was holding a major international meeting. [120] The activists came from literally all over the world to insert their voices into the conversation. Many were desperate. The head of South Korea's Federation of Farmers and Fishermen, Lee Kyung Hae, was so determined to bring attention to the WTO's devastating impact on Korean farmers that he fatally stabbed himself in protest. A fellow South Korean farmers' advocate, Song Nan Sou explained, "His death is not a personal accident but reflects the desperate fighting of 3.5 million Korean farmers." [121]

In the United States, in a land of endless choice and immediate gratification, most of us can't imagine what living on the edge really means. For us, a bad day is having the FedEx delivery delayed or the Internet connection disrupted. But in the rest of the world, millions of miners, farmers, and factory workers literally live on the very edge of survival. These are the people whom trade policies should be designed to benefit the most, yet they are the ones paying the heaviest price for WTO policies. And their voices go unheard by the WTO, which is infamous for being unwelcoming of public participation. It is no wonder these people are increasingly desperate.

In June 2009, the Trade Reform, Accountability, Development and Employment (TRADE) Act was reintroduced into the U.S. Congress with widespread support from both House Democrats and a diverse coalition of labor, consumer, environmental, family farm, and faith-based groups. According to Public Citizen's Global Trade Watch division, the TRADE Act sets out what a good trade agreement must and must not include. Better yet, it requires reviews of the WTO and existing trade agreements, including NAFTA (the North American Free Trade Agreement), on economic, environmental, social, and human rights grounds and requires the president to submit plans to Congress to remedy the problems. It would also hold future trade agreements to the same higher standards.[122] Passing this law would be a huge step forward for environmental and labor rights as well as for improving the United States' relationships with our trading partners. To help turn this bill into law, please visit www.citizen.org/trade/tradeact.

My Revelation in Haiti

Can't these institutions change? Why don't they embrace higher environmental and labor standards, or pursue a development and trade model that promotes equity and environmental conservation?

Over the years, I have come to realize that it is not the institutions themselves that are the real problem (although they are certainly problematic: inefficient, undemocratic, and unaccountable). The real problem is the underlying set of values and assumptions and beliefs—the paradigm—on which these institutions are based. Most of the people running these hugely influential institutions actually believe that their prescriptions work and will ultimately improve life for everyone. At worst, they think it is the dose, rather than the prescription, that is the problem, explains Kevin Gallagher, professor of international relations at Tufts University: "They don't think the reforms are wrong, but that they haven't been implemented wholeheartedly enough. If developing country economies adhere to our programs even more, they say, then things will get better."[123]

This really sank in for me during my first trip to Haiti years ago. I had gone to Haiti because heavy-metal-laden ash from the city of Philadelphia's municipal waste incinerator had been exported to Haiti, mislabeled as fertilizer, and dumped in a big open pile on the beach in Gonaïves. This infuriated me. How could a load of waste from the world's richest country just be dumped on the poorest country in the hemisphere and left there? This incident seemed like a metaphor for how the United States had treated Haiti on so many levels for far too long. So I went to Haiti at the invitation of some Haitians who had contacted me seeking to collaborate to make Philadelphia take back its toxic ash. At that point I knew very little about how larger global systems operated—mostly what I knew about was trash.

The first people I met with were the women from the Disney sweatshop, whom I described in the previous chapter. After they had told me about conditions in the factory, some women shared their stories about moving from rural areas in the Haitian countryside to the city in search of these jobs. I asked them why they stayed in the city, living in slums that had little electricity and no running water or sanitation, and working in such obviously unhealthy environments instead of staying in the countryside with more space and cleaner air. The women said the countryside simply couldn't sustain them anymore. Their families had given up farming since they couldn't compete against the omnipresent "Miami rice," as they called the white rice imported from the United States. "Miami rice" was grown on megafarms in the United States (not actually in Miami!) and delivered to Haiti for much less than the price of the more labor-intensive, more nutritious (and according to the Haitians, tastier) local rice strains. Farming, the women said, is dying in Haiti. They had no choice.

Next I visited farmers and former farmers. The one farmer I remember most clearly lowered his voice at one point and explained that Miami rice and the cancellation of the Haitian government's subsidies for farmers was all part of a plan by the World Bank and its ally, the U.S. Agency for International Development (USAID), to drive Haitians off their land and into the city to sew clothes for rich Americans. Fewer farmers. More garment workers. The destruction of farming as a livelihood, he explained, was necessary to push people to the city, so people would be desperate enough to work all day in miserable sweatshops. When he spoke of it, he whispered and his eyes grew extra intense and I wondered if he was jumping to conclusions too fast, perhaps entertaining a conspiracy theory. I mean, really, how could agencies devoted to alleviating poverty want to have Haitians sewing princess nightgowns instead of growing food for their communities? As I said, this was a long time ago, and I was pretty naïve.

On the drive back to Port-au-Prince, I watched the Haitian countryside roll past, my head pressed against the glass of the van window. As harsh as eking out a living from that depleted countryside would be, it still seemed vastly preferable to the crowded urban slums.

The next day I went to USAID, a government organization that describes itself as "the principal U.S. agency to extend assistance to countries recovering from disaster, trying to escape poverty, and engaging in democratic reforms." [124] I didn't know much about international development agencies back then, and I eagerly anticipated learning about strategies to restore the rural environment and get those farms back in working order again, to allow those who wanted to farm to be able to earn a sustainable, dignified living while producing food locally. It seemed crazy to me that a once-lush tropical island was abandoning farming and importing food. Local food means less packaging, less transportation, more local jobs, and fresher, healthier food. How could anyone not want that?

The USAID office was in downtown Port-au-Prince. When I went there, it was the first time I had felt air-conditioning, seen men in suits, or been surrounded by white people since arriving in Haiti. For the first time since I had been in the country, I worried my dress and sandals weren't nice enough for the setting.

The USAID representative began explaining his agency's vision for "developing" Haiti. To my utter amazement, he laid out the same plan as the whispering farmer had. But he wasn't saying it while leaning closer, in hushed tones, with wild eyes. He sat up straight and tall and announced that USAID did not feel it was "efficient" for Haitians to produce food. Instead, he felt, they should participate in the global economy, leveraging their best resources, which apparently meant many thousands of people so near starvation that they would be willing to sew *Sleeping Beauty* pajamas from morning to night, endure physical and sexual threats, live in slums, only to be able to feed their kids half a meal a day.

He flat out proclaimed that local food sufficiency was not desirable or needed. He explained that a better concept is "food security," which means that a population didn't need to grow its own food but should instead import food, in this case from the United States. Since U.S. farmers (heavily subsidized, I'd like to point out) can grow rice more "efficiently" than can small Haitian farmers, USAID preferred that the rice from the United States be sent to Haiti and Haitians leave their farms to work in the garment factories—a job that, he felt, was less suited to the U.S. population.

I blurted out that "efficiency" was not the only criteria. A farmer's relationship to the land, healthy and dignified work, a parent's ability to spend

time with his or her kids after school, a community staying intact generation after generation—all these things had value, and a real development
plan would prioritize them. "Well," he said, "if a Haitian really wants to
farm, there is room for a handful of them to grow things like organic man-
goes for the high-end export market." I almost fell off my chair. I realized
that the ideas that the Haitian farmer had shared were no conspiracy theory.
A conspiracy requires some attempt at secrecy. But here was USAID just
laying out its grand plan for the people of Haiti—not as self-determinate
people, but as a market for our surplus rice and a supplier of cheap seamstresses, with an occasional organic mango for sale at Dean & DeLuca. It
wasn't a secret plan; it was a plan they openly admitted and justified.

In early 2008, a front page article in the *New York Times* reminded me
of that eye-opening visit to Haiti. The USAID plan has been effective: by
2008 Haiti was importing 80 percent of its rice. This made it very vulnerable to fluctuations in global rice supply and price. The combination of rising fuel costs, a severe drought, and in some places the diversion of water
to more lucrative crops had lowered worldwide rice production. As a result,
global rice prices tripled over a few months in early 2008, leaving thousands of Haitians simply unable to afford this staple food. The newspaper
ran haunting pictures of Haitians who had resorted to eating dirt pies, held
together with bits of lard or butter, in order to have some substance in their
stomachs.[125]

I thought of that USAID man and burned with anger. Had his agency
devoted its resources to supporting farmers in developing sustainable farming practices, rather than investing in infrastructure and polices favoring
garment factories and export processing, a drought in Australia would not
have made people starve in Haiti, literally a half a planet away. And this, in
a nutshell, is the legacy of the global trade and "development" institutions.

The Local Alternative

Once again, at this stage in the Story of Stuff, we're running into limits. A
major limit comes with the increasing scarcity of fossil fuels and the mandate to cut carbon emissions, both of which will hobble the whole system of
global logistics, transport, and freight that is currently in place. Another
limit comes as the developing countries get fed up with providing the
resources and cheap labor that support our bloated consumer lifestyle,
while they struggle to meet basic human needs. Increasingly, they're reject-
ing this imposed division of labor and demanding to be able to chart their
own development paths.

Perhaps the highest profile example of a country refusing to play by IFI rules was the case of the so-called Water Wars in Bolivia. The World Bank and IMF require borrowing countries to open their markets to foreign companies and privatize state-owned enterprises, including utilities. Bolivia complied and in 1999 privatized the water service in its third largest city, Cochabamba, entering into a 40 year contract with an international consortium of corporations led by U.S.-based Bechtel. Because privatization of utilities often results in extreme rate hikes and decreased services for the poor, citizens of Cochabamba worried what this would mean for their access to water. They had ample cause for concern, as it turned out.

By 2000, water rates had increased up to 200%. In a city with a minimum wage of less than $100 a month, many people were paying a quarter of their monthly income on water. Even rain that fell into the residents' rainwater harvesting systems was considered the private property of Bechtel. Peasants who needed the water for irrigation, low income residents, students, workers and many others joined widespread protests demanding the removal of the foreign lead consortium. At first, the government refused, worried about the signal that such a move would send foreign investors, but when the public protests escalated, eventually resulting in 175 injuries, 2 people being blinded, and a police shooting of an unarmed 17 year old caught on film, it relented, revoking the contract and returning water management to the public utility which promised to manage water as a social good, not a commodity.[126]

I'd also say that even here in the land of Wal-Mart and Amazon, consumers are getting tired of the frenetic pace of things. In a sense it is impressive that companies can now make, design, ship, and sell a T-shirt in a couple of weeks, when it used to take months. But to what end? Trendy clothes and gadgets don't actually make life better. In fact, virtually everyone I know is tired and just longs to slow down. At a parent meeting at my daughter's school recently, the meeting facilitator asked, "Who here is not in a rush most of the time?" Not one person raised their hand.

Fortunately, there are ways to do things better, and people are working on all fronts, from increasing transparency in the supply chain (like Dara O'Rourke's wonderful GoodGuide), to protesting and withdrawing investments from the busted system dictated by the WTO, IMF, and World Bank, to reducing the size of supply chains by promoting "local economies."

Maybe you've heard about the local food movement, with restaurants and markets touting the low number of miles that food had to travel there and people calling themselves "locavores." Alisa Smith and J. B. MacKinnon, authors of *Plenty: Eating Locally on the 100 Mile Diet*, point out that a local diet is about "getting to know the seasons (and) understanding where our food comes from, and at what risk to our health and to the environment." [127] More and more American consumers are choosing to support local farmers and food suppliers because the food is fresher, healthier, and tastier.

Many of them also realize they're supporting the wealth and sustainability of their own communities, so there's a moral, even patriotic implication to their choices. And a social one. Bill McKibben, one of today's great environmental writers, applauds farmers markets in his book *Deep Economy*. They are the fastest-growing part of the U.S. food industry, he writes, not just because they provide good, fresh, delicious food. It is also because they are more fun. They rebuild community and the social fabric that has been so eroded by the hectic globalized economy. McKibben claims that on average, people have ten times more social interactions at a farmers market than a grocery store. [128] I believe it! In Berkeley, my local farmers market is a few blocks away. It's small, with a modest selection, with all local and organic food. I like going there. I invariably run into neighbors. It feels so, well, European—the idea of a leisurely walk to a market, putting my fresh vegetables and bread in my cloth bag, chatting with friends, and strolling home. It adds to, rather than undermines, the quality of my day. I can't say the same about a trip to one of those gigantic megastores.

There's a modest but growing movement to support local producers of Stuff other than food, too. In the United States, a nationally active group called the Business Alliance for Local Living Economies (BALLE) unites businesses working to promote local economies and community self-reliance: not just a local food system, but local energy (think solar cells and wind turbines), local clothing manufacturing, and green buildings from local materials. [129] In this model, a global economy still exists, but as a network of locally sustainable economies that trade in products they can't produce themselves. Trade—national or international—isn't the goal, but a means to promote well-being, good jobs, a healthy environment.

Judy Wicks, one of the founders of the local food movement and of BALLE, even makes a connection between local self-reliance and security: "Wars are often fought over access to basic needs like energy, food, and water. Helping every region achieve food security, energy security, and water security builds the foundation for world peace. Self-reliant societies are less likely to start wars than those dependent on long-distance shipments of oil, water or food." [130]

Internationally, there's a growing group of more than one hundred communities that have declared themselves "Transition Towns"—many in Great Britain but a handful in the United States (including Boulder County,

Colorado; Sandpoint, Idaho; and Berea, Kentucky) and elsewhere—that are working toward reducing energy consumption and increasing local energy production, food self-reliance, and industrial ecology, in which the waste of one factory or business is used as the raw materials of the next. According to the official guide to Transition Towns, one of the central ideas is that locally reliant life without fossil fuel dependence will be more enjoyable and fulfilling: "The coming post-cheap oil era [can be viewed] as an opportunity rather than a threat, and [we can] design the future low carbon age to be thriving, resilient and abundant—somewhere much better to live than our current alienated consumer culture based on greed, war and the myth of perpetual growth."[131]

Clearly, both good sense and ecological limits necessitate a shift toward local distribution systems and local economies. Buying, selling, transporting, and sharing Stuff locally as much as possible will help conserve resources and build community—two things we desperately need to prioritize.

That said, there is a dilemma when we consider the system at the global level. For centuries there's been a global division of labor in which some countries specialize in providing resources and labor, while other countries specialize in consuming those resources and the goods of that labor. This was true as far back as colonial Europe's heyday, and it's still true now. One-third of U.S. imports come from poorer nations, a number that includes things we extract or grow or assemble there.[132] Globally, many millions of workers labor in export industries. In the average U.S. home, the majority of our toys, clothes, electronics, and household appliances come from massive factories all over China. I remember when my daughter was just learning her letters. She was playing in her room and came downstairs to ask me, "Momma, what does C-H-I-N-A spell?" "China," I told her (she knew what the word meant—she had friends from there). "So," she asked next, "why is it written on everything?"

So, while moving to more localized economies is a good thing, we have to deal with the legacy of several hundred years of this colonial-style division of labor. It simply isn't fair for us to suddenly say, "OK, we changed our mind. We're pulling out of the globalized Stuff distribution system. Good luck. *Ciao.*"

At the heart of a true solution is solidarity, which writer Barbara Ehrenreich elegantly defines as "love between people who may never meet each other, but share a vision of justice and democracy and are willing to support each other in the struggle to achieve it."[133] International solidarity mandates that while we begin to extract ourselves from the destructive side of the global economy and invest in rebuilding healthy local economies, we also support the workers and communities in developing countries as they transition into (or sometimes, return to) local sustainability themselves. And we must have patience for the fact that their transition into a development model that works for them on their terms, may take more time than our transition. And since unequal consumption of global resources (like water and medicines and fossil fuels) is also limiting their options, we in the regions of the world that have been consuming more than our fair share will need to use less, figure out a way to repay our debts for having used more until now, and share equitably in the future.

CHAPTER 4

CONSUMPTION

So here we are. All sorts of Stuff is lining the real or virtual shelves of stores, ready to slip into our shopping carts or be assembled and shipped according to our desires. *Enter the consumer.* Stage left, stage right, storming stores and online shopping portals, armed with credit cards and freshly cashed paychecks. This stage of the game is What It's All For—at least that's what we're told. For a moment, as the almighty consumer makes her selection from a long menu of choices, the entire world revolves around her. She experiences a surge of power as she trades her hard-earned money for a piece of Stuff and becomes its owner, either meeting a need, indulging a whim, shifting a bad mood—or maybe all three at once. "When things get tough, the tough go shopping," as the bumper stickers used to say.

Lots of our favorite characters and cultural icons surround themselves with signature cool Stuff. Where would 007 be without his latest gadget, his perfectly tailored suit, or his (insert your favorite model of future car here)? What would the Oscars be without the gowns? How could we love Carrie Bradshaw without her outrageous brimmed hats and designer shades and glossy shopping bags full of ruffled dresses and sky-high heels? Would we recognize Holly Golightly without her infatuation with Tiffany's? We're attached to these characters' possessions and obsessions as much as to their personalities; it's all part of our national mythology. It only makes sense that we'd get attached to our own Stuff.

Before I go any further, I want to say that I'm not against *all* consumption. One irate viewer of *The Story of Stuff* film e-mailed me and said, "If you're against consumption, where did you get that shirt you're wearing?"

Duh. Of course everyone needs to consume to live. We need food to eat, a roof over our head, medicine when we're sick, and clothes to keep us warm and dry. And beyond those survival needs, there's a level of additional consumption that makes life sweeter. I enjoy listening to music, sharing a bottle of wine with friends, and occasionally donning a nice new dress as much as the next person.

What I question is not consumption in the abstract but *consumerism* and *overconsumption*. While consumption means acquiring and using goods and services to meet one's needs, consumerism is the particular relationship to consumption in which we seek to meet our emotional and social needs through shopping, and we define and demonstrate our self-worth through the Stuff we own. And overconsumption is when we take far more resources than we need and than the planet can sustain, as is the case in most of the United States as well as a growing number of other countries.

Consumerism is about excess, about losing sight of what's important in the quest for Stuff. Do you remember Jdimytai Damour? In November 2008, on Black Friday, the biggest shopping day of the year, the holiday shopping season kicked off. Across the country, people left their Thanksgiving dinners early to sleep in their cars in store parking lots hours before scheduled store openings, which in many places were moved up to 5:00 a.m. Shoppers began gathering in the parking lot of a Wal-Mart in Valley Stream, New York, at 9:00 p.m. on Thanksgiving evening. By 5:00 a.m., when the store was scheduled to open, a crowd of more than two thousand people had gathered. When the doors opened, a thirty-four-year-old temporary worker from Haiti named Jdimytai Damour—his friends called him Jimbo—was overwhelmed by the surging crowd. He was knocked down, and witnesses said people just walked over his body to get to the holiday bargains. Emergency medical technicians who arrived to help were also jostled and stepped on by the shoppers. Damour was pronounced dead just after 6:00 a.m. He died of asphyxiation; he was trampled to death.[1] An employee in the electronics department, who was in the store during the stampede, reportedly commented, "It was crazy . . . The deals weren't even that good."[2]

And this took place in a recession year, against a background of growing economic insecurity, rising gas prices, mounting consumer debt, collapsing mortgages, and increasing unemployment. Retailers had been worried that Black Friday revenues would suffer. Instead, Damour suffered the ultimate loss, and America kept on shopping. We are a society of consumers, we're told. We shrug and nod and accept this as a fundamental truth. It's just human nature, is more or less what we tell ourselves.

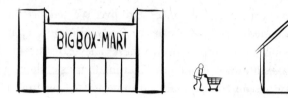

And boy do we shop. Globally, personal consumption expenditures (the amount spent on goods and services at the household level) topped $24 trillion in 2005,[3] up from $4.8 trillion (in 1995 dollars) in 1960.[4] In 2004–05, Americans spent two-thirds of our $11 trillion economy on consumer goods, with more paid for shoes, jewelry, and watches ($100 billion combined) than for higher education ($99 billion).[5] According to the United Nations, in 2003 people worldwide spent $18 billion on cosmetics, while reproductive health care for all women would have come to $12 billion. While eliminating hunger and malnutrition would have cost $19 billion, people spent $17 billion on pet food in the United States and Europe combined. And our tab for ocean cruises came to $14 billion, although it would have cost just $10 billion to provide clean drinking water for everyone.[6] In 2000, teenagers alone (twelve to nineteen years old) spent $115 billion; the same group controlled $169 billion in 2004.[7] The hundred-acre Mall of America—the size of seven Yankee Stadiums—is one of the top visitor attractions in the United States.[8] The average American has 6.5 credit cards.[9] The average U.S. supermarket contains thirty thousand items.[10] As of 2003, the United States had more private cars than licensed drivers.[11]

In the average middle- to upper-middle-class American's 2,000-some-square-foot home,[12] you'll find: several couches and beds, numerous chairs, tables, and rugs, at least two TVs, at least one computer, printer, and stereo, and countless books, magazines, photos, and CDs (although these last, like vinyl and tapes before them, are a dying species now, destined for the dump); in the kitchen there will be an oven, a stove, a refrigerator, a freezer, a microwave, a coffeemaker, a blender, a toaster, a food processor, and endless utensils, dishes, storage containers, glassware, and linens (or at least paper napkins); in the bathroom, a hairdryer, a razor, combs and brushes, a scale, towels, medicines and ointments, and bottles and tubes of personal care products galore; in the closets, dresses, sweaters, T-shirts, suits, pants, coats, hats, boots, and shoes and everything in between. (In 2002, the average American acquired fifty-two additional pieces of clothing, while the average household was throwing away 1.3 pounds of textiles every week.[13]) The average house also contains a washer and dryer, bicycles, skis, other sporting equipment, luggage, garden tools, jewelry, knickknacks, and drawer upon drawer of crap both relatively useful (like staplers, Scotch tape, aluminum foil, candles, and pens) and entirely pointless (like novelty key chains, gift wrap, expired gift cards, and retired cell phones). We've got so much Stuff that, according to builders, families often buy a home with a three-car garage so that one-third of that space can be dedicated to storage.[14]

Even so, our homes are overflowing, inspiring a massive increase in personal self-storage facilities. Between 1985 and 2008, the self-storage industry in the United States grew three times faster than the population, with per-capita square feet of storage space increasing 633 percent.[15] And somehow despite this amazing abundance, we find ourselves drawn into stores like moths to flames, on the quest for yet more.

The Sanctity of Shopping

Shopping is a nearly sacred rite in the United States—in fact, in the wake of the 9/11 tragedy, President George W. Bush included shopping in the daily activities that he said were the "ultimate repudiation of terrorism."[16] When our country was in shock and no one was quite sure what would happen next, Bush told us to hang our "America is open for business" signs in the windows and keep shopping.

Not to buy means to fail our workers and stifle the economy, say most economists and politicians; shopping is our duty. Those who dare challenge the ethic of consumerism have been declared unpatriotic or just plain loony. After The Story of Stuff film was highlighted in the *New York Times* in early 2009 for how many teachers were using it in classrooms to spark discussion about consumerism and environmental issues, conservative commentators accused me of threatening the American way of life, terrorizing children, and called me "Marx in a ponytail." When Colin Beavan, aka No Impact Man, got press for the year-long project in which he reduced his New York City family's consumption to a bare minimum, he received hate mail, including an anonymous death threat! Henry David Thoreau, who in the mid-1800s wrote of living simply and in harmony with nature in *Walden,* was variously described by critics as "unmanly,"[17] "very wicked and heathenish."[18] and an "unsocial being, a troglodyte of sorts."[19]

Even many of the nonprofits and advocacy groups that work on issues related to consumption don't question it on a fundamental level. There are many excellent groups that focus on the *quality* of the goods we consume— fighting for fair trade chocolate over slavery chocolate, for example, or organic cotton clothing over conventional toxic cotton or PVC-free kids toys. But few look at the issue of *quantity* and ask that tough question: aren't we consuming too much? *That's* the question that gets to the heart of the system. I am learning it is not a popular question.

Once upon a time the factors that contributed to our national economic growth included a broader set of activities, especially in extraction of natural resources and production of goods. After World War II, however, the focus shifted to consumption. In the 1950s, the chairman of President Eisenhower's Council of Economic Advisors stated, "The American economy's ultimate purpose is to produce more consumer goods."[20] Really? Rather than to provide health care, safe communities, solid education for our youngsters, or a good quality of life, the main purpose of our economy is to produce Stuff? By the 1970s, consumption had taken a lead role both culturally and economically. Most of us alive today have been raised on the assumption that a consumption-driven economy is inevitable, sensible, and good. We are supposed to participate in this economic model without question. Nevertheless, it's been questioned and continues to be, by a growing number of people. Myself definitely included.

In the same holiday season as Damour's tragic death, the credit card Discover launched a new ad campaign. On top of the serene soundtrack of a simple tune being plucked out on a guitar, the voiceover says: *"We are a nation of consumers. And there's nothing wrong with that. After all, there's a lot of cool stuff out there. The trouble is, there's so much cool stuff, it's easy to get a little carried away. If that happens, this material world of ours can stop being wonderful and start getting stressful. But what if a credit card company recognized that? What if they admitted there was a time to spend and a time to save? . . . We could have less debt and more fun. And this material world could get a whole lot brighter.*[21]

A credit card company challenging consumerism—I'd be thrilled if it weren't so obvious a ploy to win more customers during a time when people were anxious about spending and debt. But what really intrigues me about this commercial is the image sequence at the end: a father and son in the middle of a vast green field, then a couple with a dog on a wide-open beach, then a couple flirting on a park bench, and finally, a gaggle of giggling girlfriends pressing into the back of a cab together. What this tells me is that Discover Card, on some level, is perfectly aware of the actual truth: that it's not Stuff (even "cool Stuff") that makes us happy. It's time with our families, partners, and friends and the experience of the beautiful natural world that makes us happy.

Unhappy People

Consider that Americans reported the highest levels of contentment and happiness in 1957—that is, it was in that year that the highest number of us (about 35 percent) described ourselves as "very happy," a level we've never reached since.[22] Even though we're making more money and buying more Stuff today than we did fifty years ago, we're no happier. To be clear: it's not that none of this new money and Stuff has made us happier—some has— but the extra happiness has been canceled out by greater misery on other fronts. When a person is hungry, cold, in need of shelter or some other basic material necessity, then of course more Stuff will make him or her happier. But once people's basic needs are met (which happens, according to Worldwatch Institute's *State of the World 2004* report, when people earn and consume about thirteen thousand dollars per year, as a global average),[23] the marginal increase in happiness we get from further Stuff actually decreases.[24] In other words, our first and second pair of shoes provide more happiness than our fourteenth and fifteenth pairs. One hundred dollars buys a lot more happiness in the life of a woman living in Smokey Mountain in the Philippines, a community quite literally situated on top of a dump, than it does in mine.

The beautiful women in the magazine and hundreds of other attractive faces flashing their perfect teeth from commercials and advertisements try to persuade us otherwise. They promise we'll get a new dose of happiness when we acquire that new thing, even if it is only a tiny bit different than the one we already have. Yet when we get that thing, if it even gives us a brief buzz, the good feeling fades fast. It turns out more Stuff doesn't make us happier, especially when we factor in the extra time we have to work to pay for it and maintain it, even the time we spend just looking for it in our Stuff-filled drawers and cupboards and homes.

Meanwhile, increased unhappiness results from our deteriorating social relationships. Relationships with family, peers, colleagues, neighbors, and community members have proven over and over to be the biggest determining factor in our happiness, once our basic needs are met.[25] Yet because we're working more than ever before to afford and maintain all this Stuff, we're spending more time alone and less time with family, with friends, with neighbors.

We're also spending less time on civic engagement and community building. In *Bowling Alone,* Harvard professor Robert Putnam chronicles the decline in participation in social and civic groups, ranging from bowling leagues to parent-teacher associations to political organizations.[26] We end up with a situation in which we have fewer friends, fewer supportive neighbors, less robust communities, and near total apathy about our role within a democratic political system.

As a result, our communities can't provide the things they used to. One-quarter of Americans now say they have no one in their lives with whom they can discuss personal trouble; that number has doubled since 1985, when far fewer people reported being socially isolated.[27] Alongside emotional support, logistical support has dried up too: if you need child care, help moving, a ride to the airport, food delivered to your door when you're sick, someone to bring in the mail or walk the dog or water your plants when you travel, or a group with whom to play a game of basketball, softball, or poker, you're likely out of luck. Increasingly we're all too busy and/or too isolated for these things. Since we still need all these things, the market has filled the void. We can now hire someone to watch our pets, coach us through a rough breakup, or move our Stuff. We pay for child care and activities to entertain our kids. We can even buy computer games that simulate sports with live opponents. This is commodification at work: the process of turning things that were once public amenities, neighborly activities, or the role of friends into privately purchasable Stuff or services—i.e., commodities.

Systems thinkers often talk about negative feedback loops—problems that cause an effect that adds to the original problem. For instance, when global temperatures rise, ice caps melt, decreasing the planet's ability to reflect sunlight off that bright snow, so global temperatures rise further. The same thing is happening with our melting communities. We have to work harder to pay for all the services that neighbors, friends, and public agencies used to provide, so we're even more harried and less able to contribute to the community. It's a downward spiral.

Almost every indicator we can find to measure our progress as a society shows that despite continued economic growth over the past several decades, things have gotten worse for us. In the United States, obesity is at record levels, with fully a third of adults over the age of twenty and nearly 20 percent of children between the ages of six and eleven considered obese.[28] A 2007 report revealed a 15 percent rise in teen suicides between 2003 and 2004, the largest increase over a single year's time in fifteen years.[29] In 2005 we had ten times as much clinical depression as in 1945. The use of antidepressants tripled between 1994 and 2004.[30] As many as 40 million Americans are now allergic to their own homes—to the chemicals in paints, cleaning products, treated wood, wallpaper, and plastics. We average 20 percent less sleep at night than we got in 1900.[31] Americans work more hours than people in almost any other industrialized country.[32] The debts of individual consumers have been growing at twice the rate of incomes.[33] According to the U.S. Census Bureau, in 2005 Americans carried approximately $832 billion in credit card debt, a number that is expected to balloon to $1.091 trillion by 2010. This works out to approximately $5,000 in credit card debt per cardholder (projected at nearly $6,200 by 2010).[34] Despite the spending beyond our means, our country still faces devastating levels of income inequity, poverty, homelessness, hunger, and the lack of health insurance.

According to Knox College professor of psychology Tim Kasser, who has written extensively about materialism, it's not just that money can't buy us love and Stuff doesn't make us happy. According to comprehensive studies of people of all different age groups, class backgrounds, and nationalities, *materialism actually makes us unhappy*. In Kasser's surveys, people were identified as having materialist values when they agreed to a number of statements along the lines of "I want a high status job that pays well," "I want to be famous," "It's important to have a lot of expensive possessions," and "I want people to comment on how attractive I look." According to Kasser, "The studies document that strong materialistic values are associated with a pervasive undermining of people's well-being, from low life satisfaction and happiness, to depression and anxiety, to physical problems such as headaches and to personality disorders, narcissism, and antisocial behavior."[35] And Kasser goes even further to document how these afflictions (low satisfaction, physical and mental health problems, and antisocial tendencies) then fuel more consumption.[36] We fall back on the conventional "wisdom" that a little shopping therapy is just what we need to lift our spirits. And so it becomes a vicious cycle.

Unhappy Nation

Even though we're consuming way more resources like energy, paper, and minerals and more manufactured Stuff than most other countries, the United States scores lower on many indices of well-being. The United Nations Development Programme's Human Poverty Index—which examines factors like poverty, longevity, social inclusion—lists the United States last among industrial counties.[37] Another measure, the Happy Planet Index, looks at how happy a country is (measured by a combination of life expectancy and life satisfaction) compared with how many resources it uses: basically it is a measure of how well a country converts resources into well-being. Out of 143 countries evaluated in the 2009 Happy Planet Index, the United States rates a dismal 114th. Scoring above us are those Scandinavian countries, of course, as well as every European country except Luxembourg and all of Latin America, the Caribbean, and pretty much every other region except Africa. Of the 28 countries that ranked lower than the United States, 25 are in Africa. Even war-torn Congo comes in a couple of spots ahead of the United States.[38] The country with the highest score in the 2009 index is Costa Rica, which, by the way, abolished its military back in 1949, freeing up all those funds to divert to education, culture, and other investments that contribute to a long, healthy, and meaningful life. In contrast, the United States has the biggest military budget in the world, spending $607 billion, or 42 percent of global arms spending.[39] We could buy a lot of well-being with that kind of money, by spending it on items like health care, education, clean energy, and efficient mass transit.

The New Economics Foundation, the think tank that produces the annual Happy Planet Index, explains that "it is possible to live long, happy lives with a much smaller ecological footprint than found in the highest-consuming nations. For example, people in the Netherlands live on average over a year longer than people in the USA, and have similar levels of life satisfaction—and yet their per-capita ecological footprint is less than half the size (4.4 global hectares compared with 9.4 global hectares). This means that the Netherlands is over twice as ecologically efficient at achieving good lives. More dramatic is the difference between Costa Rica and the USA. Costa Ricans also live slightly longer than Americans, and report much higher levels of life satisfaction, and yet have a footprint which is less than a *quarter* the size."[40] I find this data reassuring, because it means our poor score isn't set in stone; we've been investing our resources in the wrong place, but that's something we can change.

Unhappy Planet

While excessive shopping, acquiring, and consuming make us unhappy and anxious as individuals (assuming our basic needs are already met) and societies, they make for an extremely unhappy planet as well. The Global Footprint Network (GFN) calculates the Ecological Footprint of various countries and of the earth as a whole. It arrives at the Footprint by calculating the use of both natural resources and ecosystem services like climate moderation and water cycles and then figuring out how much land would be needed to support this use. Globally, GFN reports that we now consume the resources produced by the equivalent of 1.4 earths per year.[41] That is 40 percent more earths than we have! It now takes the earth one year and five months (or very nearly five) to regenerate what we use in a year. How is that possible? Well, the planet produces a certain amount of natural resources each year; we're not only using all of them, but we're also dipping into the store of resources that have been accumulating since the earth began—but they won't last forever. I was in a meeting recently in which people were debating if the number of earths' worth of productive capacity we use annually is actually 1.4 or 1.6. Does the discrepancy even matter, people? Anything over 1.0 is a major problem, especially with population continuing to increase exponentially. This hard truth has inspired the term "one planet living," referring to the goal of redesigning our economies and societies to live well within the ecological limits of our one planet.

While the highest rates of consumption have historically happened in wealthy regions like the United States and Europe, most developing countries now have a rising "consumer class" that is increasingly adopting the same patterns of hyperconsumption. India's consumer class alone is thought to include more than 1 million households. The global consumer class in 2002 included 1.7 billion people, a number that is expected to rise to 2 billion by 2015—with almost half the increase occurring in developing countries.[42]

What would it look like if everyone on the planet consumed at U.S. rates? And what about at the rates of certain other countries in both the so-called developed and developing worlds? Here's a list of how many planets' worth of biocapacity we would need if we globalized the consumption patterns in nine different countries:

United States: 5.4
Canada: 4.2
United Kingdom: 3.1
Germany: 2.5
Italy: 2.2
South Africa: 1.4
Argentina: 1.2
Costa Rica: 1.1
India: 0.4

Global Footprint Network has also identified the day each year in which we go into "overshoot"—the point after which we are consuming more than the earth is able to regenerate in that year. The first year in which we used more than the planet could sustain was 1986, but just by a smidgen. Earth Overshoot Day that year was December 31. Less than a decade later, in 1995, the day we reached the limit had moved up a month, to November

21. Another decade brought it up another month: in 2005, it fell on October 2.[43] So humanity is consuming more than the planet can regenerate each year. At the same time, millions of people actually need to consume more to meet even basic needs: food, shelter, heath, education (that's an issue I'll discuss more fully later in this chapter). This is not a good trajectory. In fact, in the most literal meaning of the term, it's unsustainable.

We need to chart a different course. Let's start by challenging the fundamental assumption that producing and consuming Stuff is the central purpose and engine of our economy. We need to understand that the drive to overconsume is neither human nature nor a birthright. We need to object when we are identified as "a nation of consumers"; individually and collectively, we are so much more than consumers, and those other parts of ourselves have been relegated to subordinate roles for too long. To help us see a way out of this consumer mania, it helps to understand just how deliber-

---

THRIFT THROUGH THE AGES

I'm certainly not the first to have argued for restraint in our resource consumption, even long before we were so seriously butting up against the planet's limits. Consider for a moment these examples of how our revered sources of wisdom in cultures around the world, from ancient to contemporary, renounce materialism and embrace sufficiency as the right way to live.

Buddhist: "Whoever in this world overcomes his selfish cravings, his sorrows fall away from him, like drops of water from a lotus flower." (Dhammapada, 336)

Christian: "What shall it profit a man if he shall gain the whole world and lose his own soul?" (Mark 8:36)

Confucian: "Excess and deficiency are equally at fault." (Confucius, XI.15)

Hindu: "That person who lives completely free from desires, without longing . . . attains peace." (Bhagavad Gita, II.71)

Khalil Gibran: "The lust for comfort murders the passion of the soul, and then walks grinning in the funeral." (The Prophet)

Islamic: "The best kind of wealth is to give up inordinate desires." (Imam Ali A.S.)

Jewish: "Give me neither poverty nor riches." (Proverbs 30:8)

Liberation Theology: "The poverty of the poor is not a call to generous relief action, but a demand that we go and build a different social order." (Gustavo Gutiérrez)

Native American: "Miserable as we seem in thy eyes, we consider ourselves . . . much happier than thou, in this that we are very content with the little that we have." (Traditional)

Shaker: "Tis a gift to be simple." (Elder Joseph Brackett)

Taoist: "He who knows he has enough is rich." (*Tao Te Ching*)

Thoreau: "A man is rich in proportion to the number of things which he can afford to let alone." (*Walden*)

---

ately the culture and structures promoting consumerism have been engineered over the last century.

The Construction of a Consumer Nation

A century ago, the economic, political, and social life of the United States was not so single-mindedly focused on consumerism. Yes, people bought things, but that was balanced more evenly with other activities and goals. What caused the shift to overconsumption?

As Oberlin College professor David Orr writes, "The emergence of the consumer society was neither inevitable nor accidental. Rather, it resulted from the convergence of four forces: a body of ideas saying that the earth is ours for the taking; the rise of modern capitalism; technological cleverness; and the extraordinary bounty of North America, where the model of mass consumption first took root. More directly, our consumptive behavior is the result of seductive advertising, entrapment by easy credit, ignorance about the hazardous content of much of what we consume, the breakdown of community, a disregard for the future, political corruption and the atrophy of alternative means by which we might provision ourselves."[44]

In other words, in the United States in particular, there were a lot of resources to take, we thought it was our right to take them, and we figured out slick new ways to do so. As capitalism (see the introduction for more on capitalism), with its incessant need for profit, developed into the dominant economic model, a culture of consumerism became necessary to support it.

Time Versus Stuff

With the "technological cleverness" of the Industrial Revolution—the shift from hand-crafted goods to assembly-line mass production, powered by steam engines—industrialized countries became much more efficient at producing Stuff. In 1913, it took a worker 12.5 hours to make an automobile chassis; by 1914 it took 1.5 hours.[45] The cost of producing one megabit of computing power in 1970 was about twenty thousand dollars; by 2001, the cost had sunk to two cents.[46]

With this huge increase in productivity, industrialized societies faced a choice: keep producing roughly the same amount of Stuff as before and work far less, or keep working the same number of hours as before, while continuing to produce as much as possible. As Juliet Schor explains in *The Overworked American,* after World War II, political and economic leaders—economists, business executives, and even labor union representatives—chose the latter: to keep churning out the "goods," keep working full time, keep up the frenzied pace of an ever-expanding economy.[47]

Faced with the same decision, Europe veered towards the first option, prioritizing social and individual health and well-being over hyperconsumption. There were a number of historical and cultural factors that led to Europe and the United States charting such different paths. In Europe, governments were generally more socially focused (or people focused) than business focused. European trade unions, political parties, and other civic groups—influenced by their wartime experience and a more socially oriented culture—were similarly focused on public benefits rather than pure business interests. Remember this was the postwar era: much of Europe was decimated and needed to take care of its people (and by the way, Big Business—including IBM, GM, Kodak, DuPont, GE, and Shell[48]—had aligned itself with the Nazis, so it was a bit discredited at this point). Meanwhile, in the United States, factories were producing at an all-time high, generating employment and boosting national morale such that few wanted to question this economic model. Slogans like "Better dead than red" and McCarthy-era persecution further discouraged voicing alternative viewpoints on the economy.

If you've visited friends in Europe, I'm sure you've noticed that they have smaller homes, refrigerators, and cars. They use mass transit far more than we do. They have those well-designed folding racks that hang over doors and radiators to air-dry their clothes. They have fewer, smaller TVs that air fewer commercials. Their food is fresher, more local, less packaged, often bought from a shopkeeper with whom they share a conversation, both because they know him and because they aren't in such a darn rush. Paying for a university education and health care is not a major source of stress, as it is in the United States. Most European countries have a smaller environmental footprint and a higher quality of life, too.

Are they sad to live in smaller quarters, drive smaller cars, and be surrounded by less Stuff? According to all the data on national happiness, clearly not. With a less consumption-focused society, accumulating more, bigger, newer Stuff isn't the be-all and end-all. For example, instead of watching hours of TV alone in their big houses among all their possessions, in Europe people spend more time hanging out in public places and socializing with friends and neighbors.[49] When I visited Turkey last year for a meeting and a screening of *The Story of Stuff*, I spent many hours sitting in sidewalk cafés with my new Turkish friends. We had long, spirited, and often loud conversations, filling a whole row of tables, with people coming and going, dropping in to join us. I commented on how unfortunate it is that we don't have a café culture in the United States, where we can linger and discuss politics and art and love and plans to make the world a better

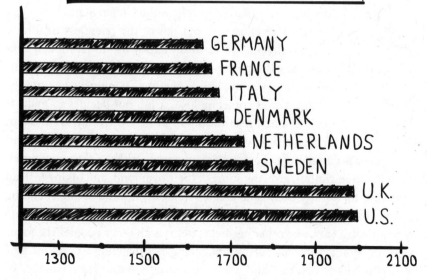

Source: R. Layard, Happiness: Lessons from a New Science (2006).

place. My Turkish friends were surprised and wanted to know why we don't. I realized that it's because in the United States, we're too busy, too stressed to sit around and just converse. Maybe as college students we hung out and talked in cafés, but we seldom do as adults. And in those rare instances when we do meet friends at a café, we increasingly have to talk really quietly or all the people plugged into laptops will glare at us.

Indeed, Americans now work harder than the citizens of nearly any other industrialized country.[50] We're caught in what I call the work-watch-spend treadmill: exhausting ourselves at work, then decompressing in front of the TV, which blares commercials telling us we need to go shopping, which we do, only to find we need to work even harder to pay for it all, and so the cycle continues. And what do we have to show for it? Monster houses, bigger cars, and a growing lack of physical, mental, and environmental health (not to mention a ton of trash and CO_2).

As a result, nearly everyone reports an increasing sense of anxiety. I was recently at a public lecture on food issues. One of the speakers was Mollie Katzen, author of our college kitchen bible, the *Moosewood Cookbook*. She explained that she's been writing recipes and sharing cooking advice for more than twenty five years, and she has witnessed a huge change in our relationship to food preparation. Years ago, she said, she received fascinating questions about what to do with particular spices or unusual vegetables. Nowadays, she said, the most frequent request she gets is for quick and easy meals that require few ingredients and take as little time as possible. That's what we get—stress and fast food—in return for working like dogs?

A growing movement of people in the United States and internationally have chosen to opt out of the relentless treadmill. This approach—known variously as downshifting, enough-ism, or voluntary simplicity—involves embracing a shift toward working and spending less. Sometimes it happens voluntarily, other times after someone loses a job but decides to make it the start of a new relationship to work. Downshifters choose to prioritize leisure, community building, self-development, and health over accumulating more Stuff. Some make slight adjustments such as buying used clothes, growing some of their own food, and biking instead of driving to work. Others take greater steps, such as adjusting spending patterns to live well on far less money so they can work part-time. Some share housing, cars, and other big-ticket items with other people. The focus is not on doing without, but on enhancing nonmaterial aspects of their lives, which they believe—and evidence supports—are greater sources of happiness and security anyway. As Duane Elgin, author of *Voluntary Sim-*

plicity, explains, "The objective is not dogmatically to live with less, but it is a more demanding intention of living with balance in order to find a life of greater purpose, fulfillment and satisfaction."[51]

Downshifters are sometimes criticized for lacking awareness about the role of privilege in their big life change: they tend to have more education (often at the graduate level), connections, and confidence in their ability to navigate the system, all of which sets them apart from the poor, who *involuntarily* live with less. After "escaping" the system, many downshifters fail to engage politically. I would argue, as Professor Michael Maniates does in *Confronting Consumption*, that a portion of the hours downshifters win from working fewer hours should be dedicated to the "collective struggle aimed at transforming institutions that drive consumerism and overconsumption."[52] Some of the policy battles to be fought in the name of creating a wholly downshifted society (and thus, one that has a smaller environmental footprint and, as important, is happier) include benefits for part-time work, limits on extremely high compensation of corporate leaders (with the money saved going to increases in low-end wages), a shorter work week, and reinvestment in the social commons: parks, libraries, public transportation, and other public facilities that can provide people access to things they need without having to buy each and every one.

Regardless of the critique, downshifters help prove that there's a functional, enjoyable alternative to a fifty-hour-plus workweek, second and third jobs, etc. Overworking didn't emerge inevitably from the genetic makeup or innate desire of Americans. Instead, the overwork-overspend model was the result of conscious decisions made by our government, business, and even some labor leaders. The good news, as downshifters illustrate on an individual level, is that these decisions can be unmade as well.

Forging a Consumer Class

So once the system to make more Stuff was set in place, the dilemma then became how to sell enough of that Stuff to keep the machine running. When this humongous increase in the capacity to produce consumer goods first occurred, most people had neither the expendable income nor the desire to orient their lives around accumulating ever more Stuff.

Henry Ford, best known for his perfection and standardization of the assembly line, came up with an answer. He knew that his company's success depended not only on continuing to produce reliable products as quickly and cheaply as possible, but also in helping to create a consumer class, made up of the broader public, that could actually buy the cars. Ford's theories of mass production have been so influential that they are widely referred to as Fordism, but what many people don't realize is that the assembly line piece of it is only half of the story. As much as it involved increasing mass production, Fordism was equally concerned with facilitating mass consumption because, as Ford realized, producers can't keep churning out all this Stuff unless someone is going to buy it.

In 1914, Ford took the unprecedented step of voluntarily doubling his workers' salaries to five dollars a day (equivalent to just over one hundred dollars a day in 2008 dollars). He also decreased the workday from nine to eight hours. His reward: lower worker turnover, the ability to run three shifts a day instead of two, and greater car sales as the workers themselves joined his customer base. Other companies watching this process soon followed Ford's lead, and the foundation for mass consumerism was set.[53]

With Fordism set into motion, people had the means to buy Stuff, but not yet the inclination. Shortly after the end of World War II, retailing analyst Victor Lebow described what was needed to keep the people consuming and factories producing: "Our enormously productive economy . . . demands that we make consumption our way of life, that we convert the buying and use of goods into rituals, that we seek our spiritual satisfaction, our ego satisfaction, in consumption . . . we need things consumed, burned up, replaced and discarded at an ever-accelerating rate."[54]

In order to achieve this vision, industry executives and their minions developed an array of strategies:

- transitioning from local stores to ubiquitous shopping malls to the big-boxes and Internet retailers of today, which I described in chapter 3 on distribution;
- making it possible for customers to buy now and pay later (plus interest) with the invention and heavy promotion of credit and credit cards;
- systematizing and normalizing the concepts of planned and perceived obsolescence (which I describe below);
- removing self-reliant and/or community-based ways to fulfill basic needs, as for example with the deliberate destruction of light rail systems by the major car manufacturers;
- the intentional merging of identity and status with consumption (i.e., that you are what you buy);
- and the crown jewel, *advertising*.

There are whole books written about each of these tools, so I'm going to review just the two most insidious of them here.

Two Tricks of the Trade

1. Planned Obsolescence

As the production of Stuff ratcheted up, one of the first messages broadcast to consumers was that it was better to have more than one of most things. A second (and then third, fourth, and fifth) bathing suit, when the previous norm for most women had been to make do just fine with one. A second car. And finally a second home, with a whole other set of contents to fill it up, so ultimately you had at least two of everything.

But even so, producers of Stuff realized that there was an eventual limit to how much people could consume. At some point, everyone would have enough shoes and toasters and cars. At some point, there would be total saturation. And if the factories were going to keep churning out Stuff once consumers were Stuff saturated, then there'd be a glut. And a glut would be very bad for business indeed.

So the architects of the system came up with a strategy to keep consumers buying: planned obsolescence. Another name for planned obsolescence is "designed for the dump." Brooks Stevens, an American industrial designer who is widely credited with popularizing the term in the 1950s, defined it as "instilling in the buyer the desire to own something a little newer, a little better, a little sooner than is necessary." [55]

In planned obsolescence, products are intended to be thrown away as quickly as possible and then replaced. (That's called "shortening the replacement cycle.") Now, this is different from true technological obsolescence, in which some actual advance in technology renders the previous version obsolete—like telephones replacing the telegraph. The instances when new technology honestly surpasses the old are rarer than we're led to believe. Today's cell phones, for example, which have an average life span of only about a year, are pretty much never technologically obsolete when we throw them away and replace them with new ones. That's planned obsolescence at work.

The idea of planned obsolescence gained currency in the 1920s and 30s as government and businesspeople realized that our industries were making more Stuff than people cared to, or could afford to, buy. In 1932, a real estate broker named Bernard London who wanted to play his part in stimulating the economy distributed his now infamous pamphlet called *Ending the Depression through Planned Obsolescence*. In it London argued for creating a government agency tasked with assigning death dates to specific consumer products, at which time consumers would be required to turn the Stuff in for replacements, even if they still worked fine. This system, London explained, would keep our factories humming along.[56]

Some obsolescence was planned to be not just *soon* but *instant*—with the advent of disposable goods. The first breakthroughs in this arena were diapers and sanitary pads, and it's pretty obvious why these particular items caught on. But soon we were sold on disposable cooking pans that don't need to be washed and disposable barbeques that don't need to be lugged home from the park. Now we have disposable cameras, mops, rain ponchos, razors, dishes, cutlery, and toilet brushes (flushable, even!).

Then there are other things that aren't advertised as disposable but are treated as such in practice. For instance, appliances and electronics break so routinely these days, and it's become such a hassle to get these items repaired, and new ones are so cheap because of externalized costs, that we just replace them. "We'll just get another one," we sigh. I grew up with the same telephone, refrigerator, and kitchen clock, none of which were replaced by my mother for years and years until the fridge finally broke and she gave up the old rotary phone in order to get an answering machine when her kids all went off to college. (She still has the clock.)

Consumers are not just resigned to the practically disposable nature of this Stuff; we've come to accept it. In fact, we barely notice it anymore. That widespread social acceptance of ever quicker obsolescence is key to the success of the system. There were a number of things that had to happen in order for us to become so amenable to it. First, the cost of getting something repaired needs to be close to, or even greater than, the replacement cost, urging us to toss the broken one. Replacement parts and servicing need to be hard to access, which anyone who has called a customer service line recently can verify. Current products must be incompatible with new upgrades or accessories. And the way Stuff looks has to keep changing, providing an incentive to toss an older model, even if it is still working just fine.

This last quality is what's known as "perceived obsolescence." In this case the item isn't broken, nor is it really obsolete at all; we just perceive it as such. Some people call this "obsolescence of desirability" or "psychological obsolescence." This is where taste and fashion come in to play. The ever-shifting hem lengths of women's skirts and dresses; the chunky heels that are in fashion one season only to be replaced by skinny stilettos the next; the width of men's ties; this year's hot color for cell phones, iPods, toasters, blenders, couches, even kitchen cabinets: this is all perceived obsolescence at work. It's not, as I say in *The Story of Stuff* video, that there's a raging debate among podiatrists as to whether fat heels or skinny heels provide better orthopedic support. Those twenty-six distinct fashion seasons rushing in and out of stores, which I described in the previous chapter—that's all part of the strategy of perceived obsolescence. Retailers and producers want you to believe that you can't wear the same color or cut from one week to the next and that you'll be less cool, less savvy, and less desirable if you do.

Now, not every lousy thing that industry has done was intentional and manipulative, but this one was. Corporate decision makers, industrial designers, economic planners, and advertising men actively, strategically promoted planned obsolescence as a way to keep the engine of the economy running. In his 1960 book *The Waste Makers* (one of my all time favorite reads), social critic Vance Packard documents the early debates about planned obsolescence in consumer products in the 1950s and 60s. While some individuals opposed the idea, worrying that it was unethical and jeopardized their professional credibility, others recognized it as a way to ensure never-ending markets for all the Stuff they designed, produced, and advertised—and they embraced it wholeheartedly. Packard cites Brooks Stevens, who shamelessly explained, "We make good products, we induce people to buy them, and then the next year we deliberately introduce something else that will make those products old-fashioned, out of date, obsolete . . . It isn't organized waste. It's a sound contribution to the American economy."[57]

The strategy has worked beyond the wildest dreams of the people who instituted it. Planned obsolescence continues to dominate and define consumer culture today, and we dispose of (often perfectly good) products at an ever-increasing rate. In the service of perceived obsolescence in particular, there's a whole industry hard at work spending billions of dollars each year to manipulate us into buying something new, better, different, and more "us." That industry is known as . . . advertising.

2. Advertising

Advertising is like a constant background hum in our lives. The average American spends a total of one year of his/her life watching advertisements,[58] while the regular American child sees 110 TV commercials a day.[59] By the time she is twenty, the average American has been exposed to nearly a million advertising messages. According to the Center for a New American Dream, brand loyalties are established in children as early as age two, and by the time they get to school, they can identify literally hundreds of logos.[60]

Two-thirds of our newspaper space and 40 percent of our mail is unsolicited advertising.[61] In 2002, global spending on advertising reached

$446 billion, an almost ninefold increase since 1950.[62] In 2005, in the United States alone, $276 billion was spent on ads.[63] China, meanwhile, spent $12 billion in 2006 and is projected to reach $18 billion by 2011, which will make it the third-largest advertising market in the world.[64] In 2007—the year before they requested massive government bailouts to keep them from going bankrupt—the big three automakers in the United States spent over $7.2 billion on ads: General Motors spent more than $3 billion, Ford spend more than $2.5 billion, and Chrysler spent $1.7 billion.[65] In 2008, Apple spent $486 million on advertising.[66] These staggering sums provide no service to humanity at all.

While advertising has been with us for generations, its sophistication and scale have made it an entirely different animal than in its earliest days. In the beginning, advertisements were mainly used to announce goods in stock ("Just imported!" "Available now!") and didn't necessarily even name specific brands. By the time I was a kid, in the late 1960s and early 1970s, advertising had become a robust industry, but still nothing like it is today.

Today, advertisers enlist psychologists, neuroscientists, even trendy consumers themselves to figure out how to best reach and influence more shoppers. Their main intent is to make us feel bad about what we have or what we lack, and to make us want to purchase some specific thing to make us feel better.

The ads I remember from my youth focused on why a particular product was better than its competitors: for example, one dish soap had special ingredients that made your glasses sparkle or removed the soap scum from your plates. Or this laundry detergent would prevent you from having embarrassing ring-around-the-collar. In that era, we bought Stuff because we were told it would perform some function we needed or wanted.

But these days, with literally hundreds of brands of soap and shoes and just about everything, there's no way that brands can even hope to distinguish themselves with actual information on their product alone. So today's ads often don't even bother with describing the product, but instead associate it with an image, a lifestyle, a social status. Rather than describe qualities or ingredients, we see advertisements showing the kind of people who use this product. The implication is that if we want to be like those people (thin, happy, loved, surrounded by other beautiful people, etc.), we need that product. A current ad for a television actually states, "Change your TV, change your life."[67]

In addition to getting more sophisticated, ads are also more intrusive.

They seem to be everywhere these days, even places that, one would hope, would be off-limits to commercial messages. When I was leaving the hospital with my newborn daughter, a nurse handed me a package of "educational" materials, which turned out to include credit card applications and advertisements for baby products. When I walked across the border from Pakistan to India, the archway under which I entered the country had painted across the top "Welcome to India—Drink Pepsi."

An innovative company called the Hanger Network developed clothes hangers covered with cardboard on which advertisements are printed. It distributes these free to dry cleaners around the country. Hanger Network says their hangers are even better than direct mail: for starters, dry-cleaning customers tend to be in higher income brackets, so are great advertising targets. Second, most people put dry-cleaned clothes directly into their closets on those hangers rather than throw them away, as they increasingly do immediately with junk mail before even opening it. So they wind up looking at those ads every time they open their closet, for weeks or even months, making them "an ongoing billboard in (their) bedroom."[68] Yuck. Who wants a billboard in their bedroom?

There seems to be no limit to how far advertisers will go. Some corporations have even paid people hundreds or thousands of dollars to have brand logos tattooed onto their bodies. In 2005, Kari Smith, a mother in Utah, sold the space on her forehead on eBay to raise funds to pay for private school tuition for her son, who was struggling in the local public school. A Canadian online gambling company paid Smith $10,000 so it could tattoo its website address onto her forehead.[69]

Then there are the sneaky ads that many people don't even think of as ads. Rampant product placement is all over TV and movies (an Apple laptop on the desk or a can of Pepsi on the counter). Or Tiger Woods and those Nike products . . . is that cap Super Glued to his head or something? Does his contract forbid him from ever being Swooshless in public?

Worst of all, advertisers have identified children as the final frontier in target audiences. Advertisers have not only succeeded at getting kids to influence their parents' purchasing, but also at influencing kids' own not insignificant spending. Of course they are simultaneously creating the next generation of brand-loyal customers. Tragically, many cash-strapped boards of education are inviting advertisers right into the schools. So now we have corporate logos on sports uniforms, educational posters, and book covers. The math curriculum comes complete with product placement (12 M&M's + 24 M&M's = how many M&M's?); there are brand names on cafeteria menus. Channel One, which at its high point in 2002 was viewed daily by 10 million teens (ages eleven to eighteen) in 320,000 classrooms[70] provides programs with "educational content," news, and commercials. To its captive audience of kids in classrooms (and on school buses via similar BusRadio programs), Channel One ads promoted violent and/or sexually provocative movies and TV shows, online social networking sites, the U.S. Army/Navy/Marine Corps, and, before opponents prevailed in 2007, junk food.[71]

I had read about the relentless advertising to children, but I didn't really get how well coordinated it was until I had my own daughter. Advertisers defend their actions by claiming it's the *parents'* responsibility to protect their kids from excessive marketing. But, in my experience, despite my best efforts, it's been impossible to keep ads from influencing her. I find that the hardest advertising to resist is the kind that appears in different settings, across a variety of platforms. Dora the Explorer, whom my daughter actually resembled when she was younger, was my biggest nemesis. Dora popped up everywhere—on TV, toothbrushes, shampoo, backpacks, electronic games, pencil sets, underwear, bikes, sweatshirts, birthday party goodie bags, pillowcases, beach pails, ice cream, and even breakfast cereal. I noticed that my daughter, who was about three years old at the time, would respond to Dora as if she were seeing a friend. "There's Dora!" she would squeal in the toothpaste aisle of the supermarket (which is not usually a place that generates excitement among preschoolers). Buying that toothpaste became like bringing a friend home. And who doesn't want another friend?

Free to Be You and Me

The success of fashion (that most visible form of perceived obsolescence) and brand marketing (how companies and their advertisers sell us on the lifestyle image of a product as opposed to its inherent qualities) are related to some pretty fundamental ideas we hold about ourselves as citizens of the U.S. of A. We pride ourselves on being individuals: rugged individuals, pioneers, the first man on the moon; quirky individuals, someone with a strong individual style or mark. We also cherish the idea of our boundless freedom. Our country was built on ideas of liberty from persecution and the freedom to be individuals. And last but certainly not least, there's the sacred American Dream, the self-made man, the rags-to-riches success story. We love the idea that our wide-open, bountiful country allows the least among us to achieve tremendous status, if we just work enough for it.

Or shop enough for it. The engineers of consumerism have played into these values that we hold dear in a big way. They took these sources of national pride and twisted them into reasons to buy Stuff. And then at some point it was like the transitive property kicked in: all we have to do now in order to achieve or display our individuality, or to express our freedom, or to go from the pauper to the prince, is shop. How on earth did they accomplish that, and what does that mean for us as people, exactly?

Today the pressure to buy more, newer, fancier Stuff has everything to do with the pressure to express our identity and status. In *The Bridge at the End of the World*, Gus Speth writes, "Psychologists see people as hardwired to find security by both 'sticking out' and 'fitting in.' Consumption serves both goals; the culture of capitalism and commercialism emphasizes both 'sticking out' and 'fitting in' through possessions and their display." [72]

That's why we tend to spend more extravagantly on Stuff that is visible compared to Stuff we consume in private. Economist Juliet Schor has identified the house, car, and wardrobe as the "visible triangle." We spend less on Stuff others don't see. For example, the popularity of health clubs, Schor says, contributed to the creation of designer underwear. And women spend far more on lipstick—which is applied and worn in public—than on facial cleanser, which seldom leaves the bathroom. [73]

This phenomenon is based in large part on social comparisons. Schor, along with other economists, has documented how our sense of wealth and material well-being is relative; that is, it has to do with how much Stuff we have compared to other people. So, if we're hanging around a bunch of ostentatious spenders, we feel poor. If we're hanging around with people who are lower than us on the economic ladder, we feel rich. The saying "keeping up with the Joneses," inspired by a comic strip from the early twentieth century, refers to our tendency to compare our material well-being with our neighbors'. Back then, we were most likely to compare our living room furniture with that of our neighbors and families, because there weren't other people around to be our yardsticks. But that all changed with television.

In 1950, only 5 percent of U.S. households had televisions. A decade later, 95 percent of U.S. households had them. [74] On average, American homes now have more television sets than people. In 2008, the average American watched an all-time high of about five hours of TV a day, or 151 hours a month, up 3.6 percent from the 145 or so hours Americans reportedly watched the previous year. [75] In *The Overspent American*, Juliet Schor explains the link between TV viewing and consumer spending and debt; each additional five hours of television watched per week led to an additional thousand dollars of spending per year. [76]

Each of us in the United States is bombarded with up to three thousand commercial messages a day, including TV ads, billboards, product place-ments, packaging, and more—but it's not just the actual commercials, it's the images promoted in shows and movies too, big time. On TV shows, people are disproportionately rich, thin, and fashionable. So all of a sudden, rather than comparing ourselves to the Joneses in the house next door, we are comparing ourselves to millionaires and celebrities. That's why the more television people watch, the more they overestimate how wealthy everyone else is, making them feel poorer by comparison.[77] What peer pressure! Not only do my clothes and house and car have to be on par with my colleagues and the other parents at my kid's school, but now also with the lavish lifestyles of Jennifer Aniston and Beyoncé. Juliet Schor calls this phenomenon the "vertical expansion of our reference group."[78]

As soon as I read about that concept in Schor's *The Overspent American,* I remembered countless times when I had fallen into that trap myself. For many years, my work required a lot of international travel. I noticed that wearing the exact same outfit could make me feel stylish and good in Dhaka but shabby and outdated in Paris. I live in Berkeley where, fortu-nately, there's not a lot of fashion pressure. I wear my flip-flops or clogs most days and am just fine, reassured by the fact that a good number of the people I pass are wearing the same. But for years, every time I'd go to Man-hattan, I'd see women with gorgeous designer shoes everywhere. I'd just *have* to buy a new pair of shoes even though—believe me—I really do not need any more shoes. It was irresistible. They have such good shoes there and they are for sale on almost every corner. Then I read Schor's book. In my experience, a powerful way to free oneself from an unhealthy dynamic is simply to name it. Now when I am in Manhattan and I get that rush of need, I can call it out: "There's that vertical expansion of my reference group thing again; just gotta hang on until I get home," and I can walk right past those shoe stores.

To my mind, my ability to see the peer pressure exerted by an unrealistic reference group like that and refuse to yield to it is real freedom. I consider myself freer for being able not to bow to the pressure. But the economic system, on the other hand, wants me to associate my personal freedom with consumption.

Our obsession with individual rights got off track in this country. Put-ting aside the hugely significant issues of the native Americans and African slaves whose rights were obliterated, the United States was built upon the promise of the unassailability of individual rights. But I am pretty sure those early patriots meant *political rights,* not consuming rights. I am not saying consumers should have no choice in what we buy, but freedom in the marketplace is simply not the most important freedom.

Consumer Choice

Currently we have this great illusion of choice in this country—but it is almost entirely limited to the consumer realm. Walk into any supermarket these days, and what do we see: choice, or actually, the *appearance* of choice. Thousands of products. Producers gladly offer different hair conditioners for dry, limp, color-treated, or healthy hair, but can I find one that is free of toxic chemicals? I can pick between a variety of pajamas for my daughter or furniture for my living room, but I can't pick any that aren't treated with toxic flame retardants, because such treatment is still required by law. If I want a cup of coffee, I may choose between grande, venti, single, double, tall, short, skim, soy, decaf, etc. But the meaningful decisions about coffee have to do with where and how the coffee was grown, transported, processed, and sold—everything from farm and labor conditions to international trade agreements—not the decisions offered at the counter.

In 2002, a few thousand people in Berkeley, California, signed a petition to put a measure on the ballot that would have required all coffee sold in Berkeley to be Fair Trade certified, organic, and shade grown—all things that have enormous positive environmental and social benefits for the coffee growers and the environment. While the ballot didn't pass, it was exciting: *that* is the kind of discussion we should have about coffee specifically as well as our consumer choices in general. The bill garnered intense opposition from many who insisted that they had the right to drink whatever they want (including a cheaper and more destructive product). Some in the business community also opposed the proposal. John DeClercq, the chair of the Berkeley Chamber of Commerce, said, "It's an improper restriction on business . . . anti-free choice. If coffee can be restricted, do we have politically correct chocolate, beef, vegetables? There's just no end to it."[79]

The voice of the consumer, stoked by the crafty engineers of our consumerist economy, demands unlimited choice in coffees, anytime, anywhere, and claims that anything else operates against freedom. But isn't that a fairly childish notion of freedom? In his book *Consumed: How Markets Corrupt Children, Infantilize Adults, and Swallow Citizens Whole,* Benjamin Barber very convincingly argues that consumerism effectively keeps adults in a childlike mental state where it's always OK to demand "Gimme that!" Consumerism privileges impulse over deliberation; instant gratification over long-term satisfaction; narcissism over sociability; entitlement over responsibility; and the now over the past and future.[80]

If we are going to be adults about the issue of coffee (or any consumer product), we need to recognize that we have responsibilities as well as rights. We know that the world is complex and interconnected and that each act (and purchase) has consequences. Coming at it from this angle, it makes sense to prefer coffee that doesn't deplete the soil or move more pesticides into our water, air, or bodies. We recognize that Joe Coffee-Grower is a person just like me or you and has just as great a right to a

---

WHO'S REALLY DRIVING?

Is consumer demand really the key force that causes Stuff to be made and sold? A lot of people believe that, and I guess it makes them feel good about themselves, thinking they're holding all that power. But I've got to beg to differ. As just one example . . .

I mentioned above how right after giving birth to my baby daughter, a nurse gave me a packet of "educational" materials, which turned out to be credit card applications, coupons, and advertisements. That wasn't all they gave me. The other "welcome new mommy" goodies included a one-pound can of Enfamil-brand baby formula, disposable diapers, and a diaper bag. Guess what the diaper bag was made of? Easy-to-clean, entirely-toxic PVC. I flipped out. The hospital was allowing corporations to distribute hazardous schlock to new mothers and their precious infants?

I wrote a letter to the editor of the local paper about what a moral outrage this was, how corporations overstepped all ethical boundaries. The story promptly got picked up and became front-page news. As a result, I received a bunch of letters from mothers, some of whom were grateful and others of whom objected to what I'd said.

I still have one of the letters I received, along with my response, which I'm excerpting here:

Dear Ms. Leonard,

Congratulations on the birth of your baby! Now stop spoiling it for the rest of us. I am referring, of course, to the article . . . concerning your displeasure at receiving a free diaper bag with samples, etc., from your maternity hospital . . . You voiced the notion that "rampant commercialism . . . has affected the hospital-patient relationship." Good Lord, woman, of course it has! We do, after all, live in a consumer-driven society, or weren't you aware . . . We, the consumer, control the manufacturers. It is never them controlling us, and it never has been. Don't like the free coupons? Toss 'em! Ha ha, that's money that they've spent to no avail! . . . Get it now?

Most of us in this world are not the stupid, biddable sheep you seem to think we are . . . Everyone has a mind of their own. I certainly hope you weren't being so patronizing to the "poorer mothers" on purpose—I can assure you that most of them aren't likely to run out and buy formula just because they now have a coupon for it! The vast majority of women giving birth in today's maternity hospitals are simply not as gullible as you think.

And that includes me. Little Toby is now four months old, and I use his free Enfamil diaper bag every day. To date, I have received innumerable coupons and freebies from manufacturers and formula companies, and it's been a blast getting free stuff.

Yours sincerely,

(it was signed but I'm withholding the name in this book)

Dear Ms. ———,

Thank you for your recent letter with congratulations on the birth of my baby. I, too, congratulate you on the recent birth of your son Toby and I wish him a healthy future . . .

I do, however, disagree . . . with the claim that "We, the consumer, control the manufacturers. It is never them controlling us, and it never has been." Corporations around the world make decisions based on a number of factors. Profit, not consumer demand, is the primary driving force. Every day corporations take actions that are not only *not* demanded by consumers, but which are against consumers' best interests . . . For example, let's consider the diaper bag produced by the Enfamil infant formula company and given to you by the hospital. Your letter states that you use this bag every day. If it is the same Enfamil bag that I received (a green one decorated with Peter Rabbit), it is made of polyvinyl chloride plastic or PVC.

PVC's entire lifecycle, from production through use and disposal, has severe environmental and public health impacts. Most notably, the production and disposal of PVC is closely linked to the creation of dioxin, the most toxic man-made substance known to science . . . Since dioxin concentrates in fat, and breast milk contains high amounts of fat, women's breast milk around the world is now contaminated with this highly toxic chemical which is known to cause cancer and disrupt hormonal systems. Every time I breastfeed my baby, I think of the corporations that knowingly create and release dioxin into our environment . . . Enfamil is fully aware of the controversy around PVC . . . The representative with whom I spoke was aware of the concerns and was knowledgeable about the details . . . The irony is that an infant formula company is a culprit in making our breast milk less safe.

Will you continue to use your Enfamil diaper bag knowing that it may leach chemicals that threaten Toby's reproductive and hormonal systems, neurological development, and may cause cancer? . . . Do you really believe that the production and distribution of a diaper bag made from a dangerous and unnecessary plastic—which will obviously be around small children—is consumer driven? Do you believe it is appropriate for a hospital nursery to distribute a PVC diaper bag without even warning of the dangers? . . .

> Again, best wishes for a healthy future for your son.
> Sincerely,
> Ann Leonard

My point then, as now, is that what is best for the corporation is not always best for the consumer. The choices that are offered to us may be touted as "consumer driven" but often are actually corporation driven, which is to say profit driven.

---

decent, family-supporting wage and a healthy work environment. We might even grasp the notion that supporting the prosperity and self-sufficiency of coffee-growing communities around the world contributes to our national security. From a childish point of view, I want the best, cheapest, fastest coffee. From an adult point of view, I want coffee that makes the world safe, healthy, and just.

Being a powerful, free individual actually means being able to demand an economic system that respects, rather than exploits, workers and the environment, not being able to choose between an infinite number of coffee flavors and styles. Barber writes in *Consumed*, "We are seduced into thinking that the right to choose from a menu is the essence of liberty, but with respect to relevant outcomes the real power, and hence the real freedom, is in the determination of what is on the menu. The powerful are those who set the agenda, not those who choose from the alternatives it offers."[81] And the places where we enact our real freedoms to define what's on the menu and set the agenda—those places are our town halls and community meetings, the offices of elected officials, the op-ed pages of newspapers, and sometimes simply the streets—not the aisles of shopping markets or the counters of coffee shops.

Consumer Self, Citizen Self

I can't tell you how many times I've been speaking to a community group or at a college and been asked by audience members, "OK, so what SHOULD I buy?"

I've come to believe that each of us has two parts of our identity: a consumer self and a citizen or community self. In American society today, the consumer part of our self is spoken to, validated, nurtured from Day One. From the moment we are born, we are bombarded with messages that reinforce our role as consumers. We're experts in consuming; we know where and how and when to get the best deals. We know how long we have to wait until the shirt we want goes on the sale rack. We know how to navigate the Internet to get what we want the very next day.

Our consumer self is so overdeveloped that it has drowned out all our other identities. What should be our core identities—as parents, students, neighbors, professionals, voters, etc.—are smothered underneath it. Most of us lack a basic understanding of how to utilize the citizen muscle.

The hyperdevelopment of our consumer self and the atrophying of our citizen self isn't natural; social scientists, historians, child development experts, academics, and many others see it as a result of nearly a century of consumerist conditioning. Survey after survey has shown an increasing commercialization of our culture and a simultaneous decrease in investment in civic literacy and engagement. The Intercollegiate Studies Institute annually tests the civic knowledge of Americans. Its 2008 report found that not only can fewer than half of us in the United States name all three branches of government, which is a pretty fundamental foundation on which to understand our governance system, but that the more TV—even news!—we watch, the lower our civic literacy.[82]

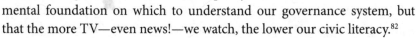

CITIZEN MUSCLE   CONSUMER MUSCLE

"It is not that Americans do not accept the Constitution, indeed they love it," write law professor Eric Lane and journalist Michael Oreskes in their 2007 book *The Genius of America—How the Constitution Saved Our Country and Why It Can Again,* "but . . . they no longer have any idea of its contents or its context. For them, Government has become a place to seek a product and they grow angry at government when it does not deliver."[83] Some see the government solely as a service provider; others see it as an obstacle to individual success. Either way, the fundamental sense is of gov-

.ernment being external to or separate from us. What happened to the idea that government, and governance more generally, is something we can, indeed must participate in? Remember "government of the people, by the people, for the people"? That's us—the people! But we're letting all that drift away because we're busy watching TV or shopping at the mall.

The result: two-year-olds can articulate brand preferences and teenagers spend more time in shopping malls than reading or exercising, while about half of adults don't bother to vote regularly in public elections [84] and fewer than 15 percent have ever been to a public meeting.[85]

Of all the worrisome trends and data on the state of the planet—and there are many—the one that I am most worried and sad about is the withering away of this community/citizen self because that is what we most need right now. Given how constantly we're bombarded with messages that reinforce us as consumers, it's understandable that we get stuck there. It's familiar, and that's comforting. We know what is expected of us, we know the rules, and we know the system.

A Buddhist teacher I know named Dr. Rita Lustgarten cautioned me about the lure of familiarity. She explained that repeated experiences bring with them a reassuring sensation, which we can easily mistake as being a good thing, when it is just the familiarity that feels attractive. Familiarity can feel like an old friend. That is why we repeat all kinds of patterns in our lives that aren't always good for us. In other words, as my friend Peter Fox says, "Sometimes we're in a rut so deep, we think it's a groove." A familiar dead end is often more appealing than an unknown open road.

Conscious Consuming

Trying to consume our way out of the mess we're in is a familiar dead end. Many people believe or hope that if we just buy greener, if we buy this instead of that, everything will be OK. Sorry to be a buzzkill here, but we need way more than that. This is why I am uninspired by all the hype about the latest "green" product line or the "green shopping guides" that seem to be springing up all over the place.

Skeptics call this concept "greensumption," while advocates call it "conscious consuming." It's about bringing a new level of awareness to your consumption. In practice, it means giving preference to products that are the least toxic, least exploitative, and least polluting—and steering clear of products linked to environmental, health, or social injustices.

Don't get me wrong: of course when we do shop, we should buy the least toxic, least exploitative, least harmful product available—and thanks to the GoodGuide we can better and more quickly assess which products those are. But conscious consumption is not the same thing as citizen engagement. Being an informed and engaged consumer is not a substitute for being an informed and engaged citizen. The "what should I buy differently" response to the critically serious environmental and social mess we're facing now worries me because it shows how much our citizen or community self has become dormant. What we really need is a revitalization of that citizen self.

Three Reasons to Reactivate Your Inner Citizen

1. Participating in strong, vibrant communities makes us happier and healthier.

There's lots of evidence that the single biggest contribution to our happiness is the quality of our social relationships.[86] People with strong social ties tend to live longer and be healthier. Strong communities also have less crime and survive disasters better because neighbors watch out for one another and are more likely to raise a voice when they see a potential problem.

As just one example: the environmentalist filmmaker Judith Helfand is making a film about a massive heat wave in Chicago in 1995 that killed about six hundred people.[87] She explains that the greatest common denominator among the victims was that they were socially isolated. They didn't have friends or family or trusted neighbors to notice they hadn't been out of their house lately, or to check that their air conditioners were working well.[88] In fact, three-quarters of all Americans don't know their neighbors.[89] Judith argues that the best way to prevent deaths from future heat waves is not the policy of handing out discount air conditioner coupons, but providing community-building activities that strengthen social ties through-out the year.

2. A vibrant community lifestyle, as opposed to a strong individualist lifestyle, lessens our toll on the planet.

Having stronger local communities means we buy less Stuff, use less energy, consume fewer resources because we can share things and help one another. The more resources we can get locally—from vegetables to borrowed hand tools—the less energy is spent transporting this Stuff all over the planet. Some great examples of this idea being put into practice are the success of farmers markets across the country, or the Tool Lending Library in the Berkeley Public Library system: anyone with a library card can borrow hammers, drills, ladders—for free!

3. Reinvigorating that citizen muscle will rebuild public participation in politics and generate real collective solutions to the considerable problems we're facing on this planet.

This point is really important. When we allow the consumer part of our-selves to dominate, our thinking about anything—from which product to buy to attitudes about recycling or global warming—skews toward favoring ourselves as individuals (or families), rather than as part of the larger com-munity. Then the option that seems best is always the fastest, cheapest, easi-est, and safest for me and my family. But when we act from our community or citizen selves, we can think more broadly. We consider the impacts of our actions (i.e., how will this purchase or this action influence the broader environment, workers, the climate, communities?) and, importantly, we can broaden our thinking about strategies to make change. We can go beyond that limiting arena of consumer action, which is what we really need to do, since the solutions we need simply aren't for sale in the store! So, instead of "What can I, as an individual consumer, do?" we can ask, "What can we, as a community, as citizens, do to fix this problem once and for all?"

And you know what is good about that? Joining up with others around a shared goal is fun! It makes us happy. Richard Layard, economist and pio-neer in the field of happiness studies, says that "the greatest happiness comes from absorbing yourself in some goal outside yourself."[90] How for-tunate that the very thing that will solve challenges like universal health care, poverty, climate chaos, and water scarcity turns out to be the thing that makes us most happy! Imagine the positive feedback loop: if we spend less time watching TV and shopping, and more time building community and engaging in civil society, then our community and our world become better, more fulfilling, more fun, so we want to engage with them more. Who wants to watch five hours of TV a day when we could instead be gathered around a big dinner table with neighbors and friends?

Equalizing Consumption

So. A big part of the solution is for people like you and me to step off the work-watch-spend treadmill and consume less Stuff. But an important thing to keep in mind is that many people, all over the world, need to consume quite a bit more. That's because there are massive differences in the levels of consumption around the world. While it's true that most Americans are experiencing material wealth unimaginable just a couple of generations ago, that's not true of all people even in this country, let alone in other parts of world, where many, many people are unable to meet their basic human needs.

According to the *State of the World 2004* report, calculations of overall global growth in consumption mask massive disparities. The 12 percent of the world living in North America and Western Europe accounts for 60 percent of global personal consumption expenditures,[91] while the one-third of the world's population that lives in South Asia and sub-Saharan

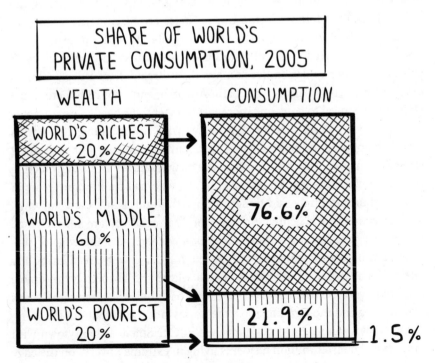

SHARE OF WORLD'S
PRIVATE CONSUMPTION, 2005

WEALTH   CONSUMPTION

WORLD'S RICHEST 20%

WORLD'S MIDDLE 60%

WORLD'S POOREST 20%

76.6%

21.9%

1.5%

Source: World Bank Development Indicators, 2008.

Africa accounts for only 3.2 percent.[92] Globally, the 20 percent of the world that lives in the highest-income countries accounts for 86 percent of total private consumption expenditures—the poorest 20 percent a minuscule 1.3 percent.[93] More specifically:

- The richest fifth of the global population consumes 45 percent of all meat and fish; the poorest fifth 5 percent
- The richest fifth consumes 58 percent of energy generated globally; the poorest fifth less than 4 percent
- The richest fifth has 74 percent of all telephone lines; the poorest fifth 1.5 percent
- The richest fifth consumes 84 percent of all paper; the poorest fifth 1.1 percent
- The richest fifth owns 87 percent of the world's vehicle fleet; the poorest fifth less than 1 percent [94]

For the first time in history more than 1 billion people on our planet—one-sixth of the total population—are living in serious hunger, eating fewer than 1,800 calories a day. This milestone was reached in June 2009 and means that 100 million more people are going hungry in 2009 than in the previous year.[95] While we in the United States are reaching never-before-attained levels of wealth-related diseases like obesity and a return of gout (caused by high-fat foods and traditionally associated with aristocracy),[96] half the world's population lives on less than three dollars a day.[97] Clearly, many people across Africa, Asia, Latin America, and even right here in the United States need to consume more just to meet their needs.

Sometimes I think that for those of us who count among the world's haves (as opposed to the have-nots), our comfort dulls our imagination. It is hard to imagine what it means to really be without. At an all-day meeting last year, I turned to the woman next to me, who had spent many years in Haiti, and unthinkingly said to her, "I hope this ends soon. I am starving." She turned to me and gently reminded me, "My dear, you are *not* starving." When we're not starving, when we're not anywhere near the edge of survival, it is hard to imagine what it is like for those who are. During my international travels, I've had moments where the absolutely miserable truth of poverty shook me, but then I went back home where, in the chaos of parenting and modern life, most memories fade. Most, but not all.

One that I will never forget happened in Cité Soleil, a shantytown with more than a quarter million residents living in extreme poverty on the edge of Port-au-Prince, the capital of Haiti. Their single-room homes are made of scraps of metal or plastic and often contain not even one piece of furniture on the dirt floor. There are open ditches of rotting trash and sewage forming a network throughout the slum. There are no stores, no place to get clean water, almost no electricity. Few residents live past the age of fifty.

On the material side, it's as bad as it gets. For someone like me, who can mistake a mild stomach grumbling for being starving, visiting Cité Soleil is a profound event, one that is not easily forgotten. I remember one woman in particular whose situation brought home for me just what desperate poverty means. She held a young child, probably about seven or eight months old, in her arms. His forehead had been badly burned—from falling into a cooking fire, she explained. As I walked through the area— gathering the expected level of attention—she held him out to me, pleading for help. There was something bluish black smeared all over his forehead, which had combined with the infection to create a clearly serious problem. I asked what the blue color was, hoping it was some kind of iodine that would help fight the infection. No such luck. The mother had been desperate to put something sterile on the wound but had no access to antibiotics, gauze, or even clean water. So she broke open a ballpoint pen she found and, thinking that the ink inside was the only thing she could access that had not been contaminated by the filth around her, she smeared it over her baby's forehead. I emptied my wallet for her, probably doubling her annual income on the spot, and left feeling entirely inadequate in my response.

You don't have to travel that far, however, to meet people who need more Stuff. Even here in the United States there is inequity—just look at any major city. Until the embarrassing economic crisis in 2008–09, our economic planners loved to tell their success story, evidenced by the increased total wealth generated in this country each year. But that number wasn't telling the whole story at all: while the rich have been getting richer, the poor have been getting poorer. In his 1999 book *Luxury Fever*, Robert Frank calculated that the top 1 percent of earners had captured 70 percent of the earnings growth from the mid-1970s through the mid-1990s.[98] The cycle just perpetuates itself as the superrich, constantly depicted in the news, the movies, and TV shows, keep setting a new bar of consumption for the rest of us to aspire to.

It's just not going to work. There isn't enough for everyone to consume at this high bar. And if we were to make the selfish and immoral choice of going any farther down that path, then we would have to build bigger walls and fences and hunker down, because it would get ugly. As an official of the U.N. World Food Programme said, "A hungry world is a dangerous world.

Without food, people have only three options: They riot, they emigrate or they die. None of these are acceptable options."[99]

Consumption, Climate, and Equity

We're hearing a lot these days about how much we urgently need to reduce CO_2 emissions to stabilize the climate. CO_2 is produced at every stage of the Story of Stuff, from drilling for oil to running factories to shipping our Stuff all over the planet. Stuff is the common denominator here. The more Stuff we consume, the more CO_2 we'll keep pumping out. Here's the dilemma: levels of CO_2 are already over the threshold beyond which catastrophic climate change will occur, as determined by top scientists, yet a lot of people need to increase their consumption in order to meet even basic human needs.

This dilemma is proving to be a huge obstacle in international negotiations around climate solutions. The rich, overconsuming countries say they won't commit to significant CO_2 reductions unless everyone else does—especially India and China, which are fast approaching the top of the CO_2 emitters list, but with far larger populations than ours (and thus much lower per-capita emissions).

Developing countries resent the notion of limits being placed on their industrial activities and economic growth when historically they have contributed far less to the ecological crisis than the rich countries. A Brazilian diplomat at the 1997 Kyoto climate conference explained the climate negotiations from a developing country's perspective: "They invite you in, only for coffee after the dinner. Then they ask you to share the check, even though you didn't get to eat."[100]

A first-ever analysis and comparison of the carbon footprints of different countries was created by researchers at the Norwegian University of Science and Technology and the Center for International Climate and Environment Research-Oslo. Not surprisingly, it shows that the higher a country's per-capita consumption expenditures are, the bigger its carbon footprint. The national average per-capita footprints varied from 1 ton of carbon dioxide equivalents per year in African countries such as Malawi and Mozambique to roughly 30 tons per year in industrialized countries such as the United States and Luxembourg. The study also found that in poorer countries, food and services are a bigger contributor to the carbon footprint, while mobility—transportation—and the consumption of manufactured goods result in the greatest greenhouse gas emissions in rich countries.[101]

One of the key innovations of the study is that it assigns the global carbon footprint from imports to the country that imports the goods—not the country that manufactures the goods. This approach is really important because globalized production chains allow companies to outsource the manufacturing of carbon-intensive products, thus hiding the real carbon costs of imported goods. What we need to avoid is a scenario in which countries with tight carbon emission limits can simply outsource the production of Stuff they consume to countries where the emission limits are not so restrictive.

Redistribution and Reverence

Around the world, current consumption patterns are destroying remaining environmental resources and the services that the earth provides and exacerbating inequalities. The crises of poverty, inequality, and the environment are all related—and they are all related to consumption. It is simply not an option for those of us in the wealthy countries to refuse to reevaluate our consumption patterns: the planet is in crisis, we're not sharing fairly, and it's not even making us happy.

Here's an alternative scenario: we realize that things have got to change, because the previous scenario isn't the world we want. We need to make room at the table for those who don't yet have a seat. According to Duane Elgin, author of *Voluntary Simplicity,* "If the human family sets a goal for itself of achieving a moderate standard of living for everyone, computer projections suggest that the world could reach a sustainable level of economic activity that is roughly 'equivalent in material comforts to the average level in Europe.'" [102] Now, that doesn't sound half bad to me; in fact, it sounds like the way to go.

I like Alan Durning's poetic vision of what the above level of consumption could look like: "Accepting and living by sufficiency rather than excess offers a return to what is, culturally speaking, the human home: to the ancient order of family, community, good work, and good life; to a reverence for skill, creativity, and creation; to a daily cadence slow enough to let us watch the sunset and stroll by the water's edge; to communities worth spending a lifetime in; and to local places pregnant with the memories of generations." [103]

All we have to do is rethink and redesign how we're living in order to produce and consume less Stuff, to better share the resources and Stuff we do have among us, and—the topic of the next chapter—to throw a whole lot less of those precious resources away.

CHAPTER 5

DISPOSAL

A funny thing happens to most of our Stuff almost immediately after we buy it. What we paid for in the store and brought home was a treasure, a *prize*—a shiny toy, a stylish T-shirt, the latest model cell phone or laptop or camera. But once it belongs to us and takes up space inside our home, the Stuff starts losing value. "Our houses are basically garbage processing centers," comedian Jerry Seinfeld riffed during a 2008 tour.[1] As soon as Stuff enters our homes, it begins the transformation. We get something and it starts out prominently displayed, then gets moved into a cupboard or onto a shelf, then stuffed in a closet, then thrown in a box in the garage and held there until it becomes garbage. The words "garage" and "garbage" must be related, Seinfeld points out, because pretty much everything that enters the first becomes the second.

But in all seriousness, economists have a real term for this transformation: "depreciation." Now, it's true that not every last thing we can buy depreciates: certain luxury items like fine art, antiques and collectibles, jewelry and well-crafted rugs are bought by the small percentage of people who can afford them with the expectation that these things will increase in value over time. But all the ordinary things that fill up our homes and our lives—this Stuff loses value like an inflatable PVC pool float loses air.

For example, it's commonly said that your car loses more of its value the day you drive it off the lot than on any other day (barring a day of catastrophic collision). In that very instant, just minutes from the moment in which you bought it, your car is worth about 10 percent less than the price you paid[2]—even though it's still got that new car smell (which is often the toxic additives in the PVC off-gassing, may I remind you) and there's not a scratch on it!

The words "prize," "praise," "price," "appreciate," and "depreciate" are all related—they come from the same Latin root word *pretium,* meaning "value." So how and why exactly does a shiny new thing go from a prize that we praise, appreciate, and pay a high price for to something that suddenly and steadily depreciates in value? As comedian George Carlin put it, "Have you noticed that their stuff is shit and your shit is stuff?"[3] The value or lack of value that we assign to things is really arbitrary.

Accountants use complex calculations to determine how the value of objects (or money, or business entities, or even whole countries) is reduced over time, usually related to usage, wear and tear, decay, technological obsolescence, inadequacy, or perceived inadequacy caused by shifting fashions. But I think there's more going on here than what accountants tell us things ought to be worth—it's the same system-wide message we looked at last chapter that influences our opinions about our Stuff. This message tells us our Stuff is no longer good enough for us and fuels our desire for more. And when our Stuff is no longer good enough, it's like a magic wand is waved over it: Poof! Our Stuff is transformed into waste.

There's an exercise I often do with kids when I'm speaking at a school. I take an empty soda can and I set it on a desk. "Can someone tell me what this is?" I ask them. "It's a can!" they always yell out. Then I hold up a little trash bin. "What about this?" "That's trash," they say. I show them what's inside the bin: an empty soda can. In the bin, it's trash. I take it out and place it next to the first one. "What about now?" "It's a can." The point, of course, is that there's no difference between the can on the desk and the can in the bin. Waste is defined by where something is, not what it is. It's about context, not content.

This is the same argument made by Dr. Paul Connett, a chemistry professor at St. Lawrence University, whose fascination with waste may even surpass my own. Over the last twenty-five years, Connett has given more than 1,200 presentations on waste to students, urban planners, community residents, policy makers, and anyone else who will listen.[4] In his presentations, Connett sometimes picks up a garbage can and pulls out its contents for people to consider. He holds up paper, a glass bottle, a pen out of ink, a plastic bag, maybe a banana peel, and asks that each of them be identified. "Is anything in here called *waste*? No—these are all *resources* in the wrong place. 'Waste' is a verb, not a noun. Waste is what we do by mixing them together . . . Separated, they are resources; mixed together, we waste them."

I agree with Connett in all cases except for those items designed so poorly or made from ingredients so toxic that they should never have been produced, sold, or bought in the first place, like a PVC shower curtain or a PVC anything. Or a disposable plug-in air freshener. Or a flushable single-use toilet bowl brush. Or a Hummer private vehicle. Or those rigid plastic cases that hold new electronic gadgets hostage inside. Or just about anything in the SkyMall catalog. In my opinion (and actually, in Connett's as well) all these things *are* a waste—of materials, of energy, and of the human ingenuity spent designing and marketing this junk instead of spent figuring out how to meet people's actual needs in healthy ways.

It's in communities that own the least amount of Stuff that you really see just how subjective that line is between waste and resources. I learned of this subjectivity especially clearly in South Asia, where I spent three years in the mid-1990s. There, broken, outdated, or empty objects were and are understood as potentially useful materials rather than items destined for a trash can. You've heard that expression "Necessity is the mother of all invention"? How about: Poverty is the mother of recognition of trash as containing valuable resources? Not so catchy, I know, but it really is true.

In Dhaka, Bangladesh, I lived in a house with a half-dozen Bangladeshis. Having a westerner live with them was a novelty, and they had fixed up a clean and sparsely furnished bedroom especially nicely for my arrival. As I unpacked my Stuff (some clothes and personal "care" products like my Pantene Pro-V—this was pre-GoodGuide, and I didn't know about the nasty chemical ingredients), I noticed there was no garbage can in my room. So on my first trip to the market, I bought a simple little trash can. But soon I discovered that the "away" of my throwing things away had a different meaning than back in the States. What I threw into the trash resurfaced around the neighborhood, put back to use. I noticed my light blue flowered deodorant container on a neighbor's living room shelf, now a vase filled with flowers. I saw my empty Pantene conditioner bottle again in the form of a toy: someone had stuck small rods through it and attached wheels, and a neighbor boy pulled it around on a string as a toy car.

Back in the United States (and in other wasteful, wealthy countries) we need to overcome the social stigma of reuse. What if "secondhand," "used" or "preowned" signified an attractive, desirable option for everyone, rather than a poverty-driven necessity? Throughout our country's history, when times have been tough—either on the individual or national level—our response has been to waste less, share more, and hold on to our Stuff longer. The economic downturn that began in 2008 again inspired many to rethink frugality and thrift. Waste haulers across the country are reporting a decrease in waste put out at the curb as well as a change in content: less packaging and fewer single-use disposable items as people are buying less overall and switching to money-saving and waste-reducing alternatives.[5] Some recyclers are noticing an increase in bulk food containers as families are opting to stay home and cook real food, rather than eat out or buy pre-processed food.[6]

However, there's a whole industry known as "waste management" that relies on a rigid understanding of waste. And since they're making a bundle on it, to the tune of $50 billion a year,[7] they'd prefer not to have us questioning their definition. To them, waste is unquestionably waste, and the more that's produced for them to "manage," the merrier they are.

This industry divides waste into several different categories based on the source of the waste, what it's made of, and how it needs to be handled. The main categories are: industrial waste, municipal waste, and construction and demolition waste. There's also medical waste and electronic waste, which are often handled separately because of specific hazardous components in each. Here's a rundown on these categories:

Industrial Waste

Industrial waste includes all the leftovers from the extraction and production processes I described in previous chapters—the result of making everything from paper, steel, and plastics, to clothes, glassware, ceramics, electronics, and processed food, to pharmaceuticals and pesticides. It is generated by mines, factories, sweatshops, paper mills—"from fabricating, synthesizing, modeling, molding, extruding, welding, forging, distilling, purifying, refining, and otherwise concocting the finished and semifinished materials of our manufactured world," says the sustainable business guru and author Joel Makower.[8] The hundreds of hazardous materials used in those processes—cleaners and solvents, paints and inks, and pesticides and chemical additives—are in there too. Ray Anderson, the CEO of the carpet manufacturer Interface and a sustainable business pioneer, says that a full 97 percent of all the energy and material that goes into manufacturing products is wasted: "We are operating an industrial system that is, in fact, first and foremost a waste-making machine."[9]

Industries (everything from manufacturers of paper, steel, glass, and concrete to food processing, textiles, plastics, and chemical manufacturing, to water treatment) do waste prolifically, generating 7.6 billion tons a year, according to the U.S. Environmental Protection Agency,[10] but as much as 13 billion tons according to other sources![11] And both these figures omit agricultural waste, which runs in the additional billions of tons, as well as greenhouse gas emissions and air and water pollution, which could very reasonably be counted as well.[12] Yet because the industrial waste is created and disposed of where most of us never see it (unless we work in the industry or have the misfortune of living alongside a factory or disposal site), it's easy to forget it exists. Out of sight, off-site, out of mind.

To help bring this issue to light, Joel Makower has charted our Gross National Trash:

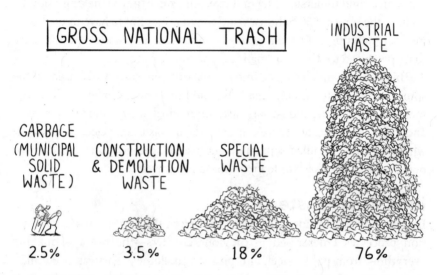

Source: J. Makower, 2009. Note: "Special waste" was defined under the U.S. Resource Conservation and Recovery Act of 1976 and refers to waste from mining, fuel production, and metals processing. In other words, it's more industrial waste.

As Makower writes:

> It's only a matter of time before the story of Gross National Trash gets told and the public recognizes that for every pound of trash that ends up in municipal landfills, at least 40 more pounds are created upstream by industrial processes—and that a lot of this waste is far more dangerous to environmental and human health than our newspapers and grass clippings.* At that point, the locus of concern could

---

* While Makower now estimates that forty times more waste is created upstream than by households, previous estimates have been much higher. The seventy-times figure used in *The Story of Stuff* film came from Brenda Platt, a waste analyst with the Washington, D.C., based Institute for Local Self-Reliance. Her report (with co-author Neil Seldman) *Wasting and Recycling in the United States 2000* stated that "for every ton of municipal discards wasted, about 71 tons of manufacturing, mining, oil and gas exploration, agricultural, coal combustion, and other discards are produced." Platt based this calculation on data in the Office of Technology Assessment report *Managing Industrial Solid Wastes from Manu-*

shift away from beverage containers, grocery bags, and the other mundane leftovers of daily life to what happens behind the scenes— the production, crating, storing, and shipping of the goods we buy and use.[13]

 While still the exception, many industries are getting serious about reducing their waste, showing others that doing so is both possible and economical. Some have done so because they realize that waste is made of materials they paid good money for and there are bigger profits to be made, both in buying less replacement material and in paying less for waste disposal. Some are reducing their waste because their directors honestly care about the planet. Some are doing it because it's good PR. And on some level, it's not important which motivation fuels them as long as the result is a serious reduction in waste and environmental impact. Of course, still others are just pretending to reduce their waste or are hyping marginal reductions to make their businesses look better—a practice called greenwashing. This false advertising is a huge problem. It undermines the credibility of those in the business world who are making good-faith efforts, and it diverts attention and delays governmental action to force higher standards across the board, which is still the most effective way to get businesses to address their massive environmental impact.

My hero in industrial waste reduction is the previously mentioned CEO of Interface, Ray Anderson. Interface is the largest producer of commercial floor covering in the world, supplying about 40 percent of all the floor tiles used in commercial buildings globally.[14] In 1994, Anderson had what he himself calls a revelation, when he realized that the planet was in deep trouble—not to mention his grandchildren—and that his beloved company was contributing to the problem. Anderson now believes that virgin materials must be switched for recycled materials; that the linear system of "take-make-waste" must shift to a cyclical "closed-loop" process (in which materials are infinitely reused or repurposed so that waste is eliminated); that power from fossil fuels must be replaced by renewable energy; that wasteful processes must become waste free; and that labor productivity

---

facturing, Mining, Oil and Gas Production, and Utility Coal Combustion (OTA-BP-O-82), February 1992, pp. 7, 10. Either way, the point is that there's a whole lot more waste being made beyond the Stuff we haul to our curbs each week, so if we really want to make a dent in our waste production, we need to be looking upstream to where the bulk of it is generated.

must be replaced by resource productivity.[15] That right there is the next industrial revolution—at least the materials part of it—in a nutshell.

Anderson's complete overhaul of Interface proved that the shift of a billion-dollar petroleum-based industry toward environmental sustainability is feasible: since the adoption of its zero-impact goals in 1995, the firm's use of fossil fuels and water, its greenhouse gas emissions, and waste generation has fallen drastically, while sales have increased by two-thirds and profits have doubled. Interface has diverted 148 million pounds (74,000 tons) of used carpets away from landfills, while more than 25 percent of its materials are renewable and recycled, a ratio Anderson says is growing rapidly. The $400 million Interface saved in costs avoided through the pursuit of zero waste has paid for all the costs of transforming its practices and facilities.[16] Anderson notes that the company's "products are the best they have ever been, because sustainable design has provided an unexpected wellspring of innovation, people are galvanized around a shared higher purpose, better people are applying, the best people are staying and working with a purpose, [and] the goodwill in the marketplace generated by our focus on sustainability far exceeds that which any amount of advertising or marketing expenditure could have generated." The Interface example, he says, clearly "dispels the myth of the false choice between the environment and the economy . . . if we, a petro-intensive company, can do it, anybody can. And if anybody can, it follows that everybody can."[17]

Green business experts often note that there are some potential silver linings to the huge scale of many companies today. For one thing, if a company with multiple suppliers all over the world demands greener standards—for example by banning packaging made of PVC—there can be a ripple effect throughout its supply chain, spreading the positive change as suppliers hustle to comply with the new requirements. Green business advocates also point out that bigger companies can leverage their economies of scale to finance environmental improvements as Nike, Whole Foods, and even Wal-Mart have done. What doesn't get addressed by these arguments, though, is that the foundation of those businesses is still about making and selling more Stuff—which relies on the trashing of existing Stuff to make room for it.

So what excites me most about Interface is how they're experimenting with shifting that fundamental paradigm that sees business's role only as producing and selling ever more Stuff. Listen up, business-minded folks, because this is a hugely important innovation.

Interface was built on a conventional retail model: customers buy carpet. When it wears out, they pull it up, chuck it (so it ends up in the landfill or incinerator), and come buy new carpet. Ray Anderson was concerned that so much used and discarded carpet was going to the landfill each year. He also realized that most wear and tear generally only happened on about 20 percent of a carpeted area, yet the whole thing was being ripped out and thrown away. He figured out two things: (1) if carpets were designed to be modular (made of interchangeable tiles), just the worn part could be replaced; and (2) commercial carpet users only wanted the services provided by a carpet (e.g., noise reduction or attractive interior spaces) but actually had no need to own the floor covering outright. Thus, his business started selling carpet "tiles" and experimenting with leasing carpet, in the same way the copier company owns the copy machine and provides service to users who simply lease the machines.[18]

In 1995, Interface developed the Evergreen Lease program, which aimed to sell a floor covering service rather than an actual carpet. Rather than make a costly onetime purchase of carpet, businesses could pay a monthly lease fee for the service of having a floor covering, complete with the repairs and upkeep needed. And when the carpeting really was at the end of its life, the office didn't have to figure out what to do with a few tons of spent carpet—Interface would come reclaim and recycle it, closing the loop.[19]

It's a brilliant idea. It has huge environmental and economic advantages. This is the kind of change that moves from the realm of tinkering to transformation. But it hasn't caught on (yet). It turns out that there's a whole slew of accounting procedures and tax laws, institutional barriers, and subsides for virgin material (especially oil) that make it really hard to apply the leasing model. But Anderson isn't giving up on the idea. He is confident that its time will come, as the price of oil and other virgin materials increases.[20]

Imagine if Wal-Mart owned the DVD player that you leased from them. After all, we don't need to actually own a DVD player; we just want to be able to watch DVDs. When the player broke, Wal-Mart would take it back to repair it. They would have a financial incentive to design products to be modular, repairable, and upgradable rather than 100 percent disposable. Imagine how this shift would impact the contents of the trash that we set out on the curb every week.

Municipal Solid Waste (MSW)

In today's world, especially in the United States, we throw a ton of Stuff away. Out it goes—when we don't know how to repair it, when we want to make room for new Stuff, or because we're sick of the old Stuff. Sometimes we throw something out thinking it will be easier to replace later than to store it until we need it again. Sometimes we even consider throwing things away a cathartic activity and congratulate ourselves on a productive day of getting Stuff out of the house.

Everything we commonly think of as garbage—from packaging and yard waste to broken Stuff, rotten food, or recyclables; everything we put in the bins that we set out on the curb—collectively makes up what's known as the municipal solid waste stream, or MSW. All those nasty ingredients we examined in chapter 2 on production that end up in consumer goods, from mercury and lead to flame retardants and pesticides, and more than eighty thousand other chemicals—they're in this stream now, too.

Some people in the recycling and reuse industry point out that "municipal solid waste" is a term that has outlived its usefulness and is actually an obstacle to getting people to think differently about the valuable materials they throw away. Dan Knapp, co-founder of Urban Ore, the premier reuse center in Berkeley, California, has long advocated using an alternative concept: "MSD," or "municipal supply of discards." Knapp explains that MSD "doesn't carry the negative connotation of worthless crap that 'waste' does."[21] I like Knapp's idea; just because someone has discarded something doesn't mean it has no value. Nonetheless, I have used "MSW" here, since I draw largely on U.S. Environmental Protection Agency and industry data, which still uses that term.

In 1960, we made 88 million tons of MSW in the United States—that's 2.68 pounds per person, per day. In 1980, it had risen to 3.66 pounds each. By 1999, at which time recycling was a household word, we were at 4.55 pounds, just below our current rates.[22] According to the EPA, Americans made 254 million tons of municipal solid waste in 2007. That comes out to 4.6 pounds per person per day![23] Compare that to your average Canadian (1.79 pounds per day), Norwegian (2.30), Japanese (2.58), or Australian (2.70). In China, the number is just 0.70 pounds per day.[24]

PER CAPITA GARBAGE PRODUCTION

AVERAGE POUNDS PER PERSON PER DAY

U.S.A.	AUSTRALIA	JAPAN	CANADA	CHINA
4.6	2.70	2.58	1.79	.70

Source: Based on data from The UN Statistics Division, Statistics Canada, and Index Mundi. See note 24 for this chapter.

So what exactly is in our municipal waste? In the United States, here's what the breakdown looks like:

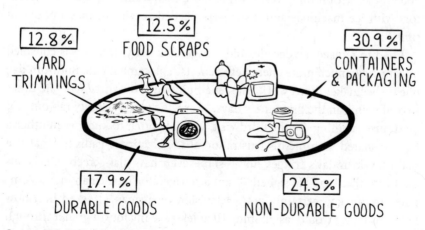

U.S. HOUSEHOLD GARBAGE (MUNICIPAL SOLID WASTE)

12.8% YARD TRIMMINGS

12.5% FOOD SCRAPS

30.9% CONTAINERS & PACKAGING

17.9% DURABLE GOODS

24.5% NON-DURABLE GOODS

Source: U.S. Environmental Protection Agency, 2007.

According to the EPA, nearly three-quarters of the weight of municipal solid waste is products—things that were designed, produced (usually from a combination of materials), and sold—including containers and packaging, nondurable goods (generally defined as having an intended lifetime of less than three years), and durable goods.[25] This percentage of products in the mix is the most important shift, historically speaking, in garbage. One hundred years ago, even sixty years ago, most municipal waste took the form of coal ashes (from heating and cooking) and food scraps. In fact, the number of products in the MSW stream has increased more than tenfold over the course of the twentieth century, from 92 to 1,242 pounds of product waste per person per year.[26]

The explosion of manufactured products in the trash will hardly come as a surprise to most people who live in the United States. Consumer goods are so plentiful and relatively cheap that it honestly is easier and cheaper just to replace Stuff than to repair it. We all have dozens of examples of this fact. When my VCR (remember those?) broke, it cost $50 just to have a repair guy look at it, while a new one that played DVDs as well only cost $39. The zipper on my fleece jacket broke. It cost $35 to have a new one sewn in, for which I could have easily bought a replacement jacket. The earphones for the little $4.99 radio I got at RadioShack broke. Big surprise, eh? No problem, I thought. I can just replace them with something from my drawer of parts salvaged from other broken electronics. No such luck. The whole radio was in one piece, connected without screws or snaps, so if any one part broke—the dial, the case, even the ear bud—it couldn't be replaced or repaired. According to *Consumer Reports,* at least a fifth of the appliances (dishwashers, washing machines, gas ranges) sold between 2003 and 2006 broke within three years, while more than a third of those refrigerators with ice machines and dispensers needed service in that amount of time.[27]

I had to replace my decades-old refrigerator last year and was consoled only by how much more energy efficient its replacement was. But from day one the icemaker didn't work. The repair guy came out three separate times to deal with it in the first ninety days, after which the warranty ran out and he stopped coming. By the third visit, we had gotten to know each other a bit. He shared with me his frustration at the electronic gadgetry that is a mainstay in today's fridges now—some even have flat-screen televisions built into the door. He sighed: "I am a refrigerator repairman, not a computer technician, certainly not a television repairman." I asked him how long this fridge would last, hoping I'd at least see my fourth grader through college before having to replace it again. "They used to last twenty, thirty

years," he said, "but nowadays you're lucky to get five out of them." I asked him why that was. He pulled his head out of the freezer, paused, looked at me, and said, "Ya know, it's funny. It's kinda like they want you to buy a new one faster."

That's the norm in the United States today. Since not many people are involved in making this Stuff anymore, few people know how to repair any of it, even the repair guys! The combination of our inability to repair things plus the ease of replacing them makes us mistake a lot of perfectly good Stuff for waste. Elsewhere in the world there are definitely places where repair is still the default response. My Bangladeshi friends keep their clothes for a long time and update the cut as fashion dictates, since most of them know how to sew, and there are also inexpensive seamstresses in every neighborhood. When furniture upholstery fades or tears, the fabric—rather than the whole chair or couch—is replaced. All over India, there are small shopkeepers, sometimes just sitting on a blanket on the sidewalk, who expertly repair clothes and shoes and electronics. In India, I ripped a pair of blue jeans across the knee. I took them to a tailor whose shop was an elevated cement platform, about one square meter, on a side street in Calcutta. All day he sat there cross-legged, mending people's clothes and sharing tea with his neighboring shopkeepers and customers. I was amazed when I went to pick up my jeans hours later; he had actually woven the fabric back together, not just patched it. On further trips to India from the United States, I learned to take a whole suitcase of worn shoes, broken cameras, and other electronic gadgets since I knew someone there could repair them. Here in the States, they would have been trash.

There are signs that repairs will make a comeback in the United States. The economic meltdown in 2008 coincided with the first increase in consumer electronics service centers in fourteen years, and the first increase in appliance service centers since 2002, according to the Professional Service Association, which collects yearly data on appliance and consumer electronics service centers.[28] Shoe repair shops are also experiencing a boom after a long decline. During the Great Depression, there were about 120,000 shoe repair shops in the United States. Today there are only 7,000[29]; however, many of these are reporting a 50 percent increase in business since the economic meltdown started in 2008. In 2009, Rhonda Jensen, owner of Reuter's shoe repair shop in Topeka, Kansas, reported an increase from about thirty-five repairs each day to fifty. "When the economy gets bad, people get their shoes fixed, so we're seeing a great influx of people. Maybe rather than throwing that shoe away they get it fixed."[30]

Packaging

The largest and perhaps most annoying category of products we're wasting in the United States is containers and packaging. Maybe you're even surprised that this Stuff fits under the header of "products," but it does, because it was designed by someone and produced for this purpose. You may not be going out of your way to buy it (what you generally want is the peanut butter inside the jar, or the MP3 player, not its plastic case, or the shaving foam, not its metal canister), but companies designed and produced it because they thought it would entice us—sometimes overtly, sometimes subliminally—to buy whatever is inside. Of course in the case of some foods or delicate items, packaging plays a role in keeping it fresh or intact, but even then, attracting potential customers is still a primary goal of packaging designers.

In *The Waste Makers,* Vance Packard cites some marketing psychologists justifying a belt sold inside packaging: "'normally a woman will not be attracted by a belt hanging from a rack . . . It is limp, unstimulating, and undesirable. To the normal, healthy, energetic woman a hanging belt is not a symbol of virility or quality. It cannot possibly be associated with her man' . . . On the other hand, 'a belt that is encased in a psychologically potent package' has favorable symbolism and 'is naturally assigned the role of symbolizing respect, affection, and even great love.'"[31]

Particularly pernicious examples of packaging are the flimsy plastic bags given out by stores in which to carry Stuff home, and single-serving beverage containers. With the former, government regulation is increasing: in San Francisco, Los Angeles, China, and South Africa there are outright bans—at least on the thinnest, least durable bags—and in Ireland, Italy, Belgium, and Taiwan, there's a tax on plastic bags.[32] Within six months of the Irish tax on plastic bags in 2002, their use declined by 90 percent. The BBC reported that in the three months after the ban was introduced, shops handed out just more than 23 million plastic bags—about 277 million fewer than normal.[33]

As for beverage containers, we have a ways to go. Each day in the United States, we use more than 150 billion single-use containers for beverages, plus another 320 million takeout cups.[34] Disposable (or "one-way") beverage bottles are a relatively new phenomenon in this country. For decades, we drank from refillable glass bottles, which were often washed and refilled locally, a process that conserved materials and energy and resulted in jobs. In 1960, one-way containers only accounted for 6 percent of packaged soft drinks in the United States. By 1970, the number had risen to 47 percent. Today less than 1 percent of packaged soft drinks is in refillable bottles.[35] Other than in Berkeley, the bubble where I live and where walking around with a disposable plastic water bottle is as shameful as donning a fur coat, use of disposables keeps rising. Industry analysts expect U.S. demand for single-serving beverage containers to keep increasing by 2.4 percent a year, to 272 billion units in 2012.[36]

The simple bottle bill has been proven over and over to be a uniquely effective regulatory tool for reducing bottle waste and encouraging refillable bottles and recycling while also conserving raw materials, saving energy, and creating local jobs. Bottle bill laws require a small—usually 5 or 10 cent—deposit per container (beverage bottles or cans, usually), which is repaid to the customer when the empty bottle is returned. Despite massive industry opposition, bottle bills are now in place in eleven states in the United States, plus eight Canadian provinces and a number of other countries (including Denmark, Germany, the Netherlands, and Sweden).[37] In 2009, Representative Ed Markey of Massachusetts introduced the Bottle Recycling Climate Protection Act of 2009 to Congress. The bill, H.R. 2046, would require a deposit on all beverages in standard containers up to a gallon. Deposits that aren't collected will fund government programs to reduce greenhouse gas generation.[38]

Because bottle bills are so effective, every time an attempt is made to introduce or expand a bottle bill, the beverage industries go ballistic opposing it—to the tune of $14 million in campaign contributions aimed at defeating a national bottle bill between 1989 and 1994.[39] The opponents argue that deposits are inefficient and old-fashioned, that reusing bottles threatens public health, that deposits simply duplicate what recycling already achieves, and that it constitutes a regressive tax that will hurt local businesses, leading to job losses. Their arguments are bogus. Really, it's about money: it's the beverage industries that will bear the costs of collecting and refilling bottles. The Container Recycling Institute, which tracks bottle bill progress, says, "The most outspoken opponents to bottle bills are almost exclusively the big-name beverage producers. The Coca-Cola Company, PepsiCo, Anheuser-Busch, and their bottlers and distributers fight deposit laws at every turn. Retail grocers and liquor storeowners also oppose deposit laws, and in recent years, waste haulers and owners of materials recovery facilities who want the revenue from valuable aluminum cans have joined the opposition."[40] These are the very same companies that boast in their commercials and public relations materials that they support recycling! Sure, they love recycling, as long as there are no bottle bills requiring it.

In 1953, a number of companies involved in making and selling disposable beverage containers created a front group that they maintain to this day, called Keep America Beautiful (KAB). Since the beginning, KAB has worked diligently to ensure that waste was seen as a problem solved by improved individual responsibility, not stricter regulations or bottle bills; it even coined the term "litterbug" to identify the culprit. By spreading slogans like "People start pollution, people can stop it," KAB effectively shifted attention away from those who design, produce, market, and profit from all those one-way bottles and cans.[41] In 1971, KAB created an infamous ad campaign featuring the "crying Indian" (played by actor Iron Eyes Cody, who was, in fact, not a native American at all, but of Italian descent),[42] about which writer Ted Williams wrote, "It's the single most obnoxious commercial ever produced . . . the ultimate exploitation of Native Americans: First we kicked them off their land, then we trashed it, and now we've got them whoring for the trashmakers."[43] More recently, in mid-2009, KAB made an unsuccessful attempt to buy out the National Recycling Coalition (NRC), the largest national coalition of serious recyclers and recycling advocates in the United States. NRC members protested loudly, saying that the KAB "is dominated by contributing commercial interests, most of whom are unwilling or unable to address the systemic changes needed to improve recycling."[44] Among the NRC members' chief complaints is that KAB resists legislative or regulatory approaches, advocating only for voluntary industry initiatives that clearly are just not working.

Packaging Done Better

So far, the most serious effort to reduce packaging waste has been undertaken in Germany. In 1991, the German government adopted a packaging ordinance, the foundation of which is the belief that the companies that design, produce, use, and profit from packaging should be held financially responsible for it—an idea known as extended producer responsibility.[45] What a concept!

The ordinance requires companies to pay according to both the volume and type of packaging they use, which gives them incentive not just to reduce packaging, but also to use safer materials. A full 72 percent of bottles are required to be refillable![46] To simplify the logistics of meeting the requirements, some companies got together and set up the Duales System Deutschland (DSD). Companies pay DSD based on their packaging use, and the money is used to collect the packaging waste and safely reuse, recycle, or dispose of it. DSD is commonly called the Green Dot program because participating companies put a green dot on their packages, indicating their participation in the program.[47] It looks kind of like the yin-yang symbol, which somehow seems fitting.

Prior to the ordinance, packaging waste in Germany was increasing at 2 to 4 percent each year. Then, between 1991 and 1995, their packaging waste decreased by a total of 14 percent, while during the same period packaging waste in the United States increased 13 percent. After the impressive initial reductions, the rate of further reductions slowed. Subsequently the program focused on developing efficient collection, recovery, and recycling industries, enabling recovery rates of between 60 percent and more than 90 percent for glass, paper, cardboard, packaging waste, metals, and biowaste by 2001.[48]

Germany's system isn't perfect. At the beginning, the government had to subsidize it since the infrastructure wasn't in place to make it work smoothly. Their definition of recycling is also so broad that it is not limited to recycling a material for the same use: the majority of plastics are not mechanically recycled back into plastics but processed into synthetic crude oils and chemicals or used as a reducing agent in steel production. Inexcusably, some burning of packaging waste is allowed under the definition of "recovery" in the ordinance.[49] There have been scandals in which piles of Green Dot waste have been found in dumps in developing countries, including by me. Those are all problems, yes. But at least the German government has taken a stand declaring that producers are responsible and is tackling the problem, unlike in the United States, where we're drowning ever deeper in packaging. The German model inspired the European Union to adopt a Europe-wide directive on packaging and packaging waste in 1994.[50] Again, it's not perfect, but at least the governments are trying something to reduce packaging and are moving in the right direction, albeit slowly. And the progress that has been achieved with both these directives is evidence that the incredible amount of packaging waste in the United States is absolutely not inevitable.

Taking Out the Trash: Whose Job Is It Anyway?

In fact, that solution for packaging waste is the best solution for all forms of product waste. You see, we have a big problem when it comes to our municipal trash. The term "municipal" means that it falls within the jurisdiction of local government. Garbage management first became a function of local government (instead of individuals) between 1910 and 1930, after it became clear that there were enough people concentrated in urban settings that their sewage, rotting food scraps, and the wastes from their animals were becoming a public health hazard; the problem needed a uniform, centralized solution to protect the health and even the lives of residents.[51] But today, our local governments are overwhelmed with the scope of the garbage problem. The Product Policy Institute (PPI) notes that local governments (funded by our tax dollars) are essentially "shouldering the burden of cleaning up after producers and consumers of wasteful products . . . providing welfare for waste."[52]

Based on analysis of more than forty years of data on waste disposal, the nonprofit Product Policy Institute concluded that municipalities have only truly been successful at effectively minimizing one kind of waste: yard trimmings! That said, municipal recovery of food scraps (aka composting) was only started a few years ago—and it looks like it will be equally successful.[53] However, what municipalities have been overwhelmed by is the rising tide of products, including recyclables. (I'll go into more depth about the complexities of recycling later in this chapter.)

The recommendation of the Product Policy Institute—with which I strongly agree—is that municipal waste departments handle the kinds of waste they were originally created to handle: biowastes and biodegradable materials. Everything else should fall under extended producer responsibility, or EPR, which means that the company that makes the product or packaging must deal with it (with required preference for recycling or reusing it) at the end of its lifecycle. As PPI states, "The rationale for placing responsibility on producers is that they make design and marketing decisions and therefore have the greatest ability to reduce the environmental impact of their products."[54] Also, let's not forget—it's their business: they profit from making and selling all those products. EPR only makes sense, right?

In the absence of extended producer responsibility systems, municipal waste departments—paid for by us, let me remind you once again—are left trying to figure out how to collect, transport, and safely dispose of every product that comes through the system. I constantly meet recycling champions who are dedicated and earnest and who agonize over how to increase recycling rates. But I have to ask: why all this effort to keep cleaning up after corporations that aren't cleaning up after themselves?

It reminds me of an insight I had about being a mom. One day I was walking around my house in frustration, picking up my kid's shoes and schoolbooks and musical instruments and art projects that were scattered all over the house. Why did I always have to pick up after her? In a thundering clap of clarity, I realized why: because I am always picking up after her! Holding her accountable may be more work up front but is better for both of us. Similarly, citizens don't have to be running around picking up after and reinforcing the bad behavior of companies who persist in making poorly designed, excessively packaged toxic junk that breaks too easily and is hard to recycle. If the companies which design and produce this Stuff were held responsible, they'd be making better, longer-lasting, and less-toxic Stuff in the first place. In this scenario, municipalities would be left dealing only with wastes that are compostable and biodegradable. Of course, we still need effective recycling and reuse infrastructure for existing and even future discards; with EPR, the product manufacturers will pay both for this recycling system and for the shift toward more easily recyclable product designs. In this way, EPR is not an alternative to recycling, but an essential complement. With these pieces in places, we'll have taken a major step toward both corporate accountability and zero waste.

Construction and Demolition Waste (or C&D)

This waste stream is considered a subset of MSW but takes up so much landfill space that it often gets addressed as a separate category. C&D waste includes concrete, wood, gypsum drywall, metal, bricks, glass, plastic, and building components such as doors, windows, old bathtubs, pipes, and more. This is the Stuff you get when you do a remodeling project or tear down an old house. If you have ever done either, you know that the easiest way to get rid of an unwanted wall, room, or entire building is just to demolish it. But smashed up and mixed together, you've got a big dusty pile of waste. Separately, what you've got are reusable construction materials.

The Construction Materials Recycling Association estimates that more than 325 million tons of C&D waste are produced in the United States each year.[55] Much of that contains good Stuff that could be recovered and reused, which would reduce not only waste but also the pressure to go cut down more trees and mine more metals.

 Fortunately, increasing costs of and restrictions on landfilling this Stuff, plus a desire to avoid waste and create jobs, have encouraged dozens of new businesses devoted to recovering these valuable resources. While salvaging fireplace mantels, doors, windows, and other parts, especially woodwork and metalwork, from old buildings has been happening as long as buildings have existed, more recently, an entire green industry—called deconstruction—has blossomed. Deconstruction is like construction in reverse; it is the careful dismantling of buildings in a way that recovers the components, rather than simply trashes and clears them. From Berkeley to the Bronx, deconstruction companies are salvaging and reselling components from old buildings, keeping materials out of landfills, avoiding virgin extraction and energy-intensive production, and simultaneously creating good local jobs that can't be outsourced.

Not far from my home in Berkeley, a pioneer in this arena since 1980, Urban Ore, has been recovering valuable materials from the waste stream and selling them for reuse. I got my bathroom sink, my office desk, a replacement panel for my garage light fixture, and the metal poles that hold up my previously collapsing backyard fence from there—all used, otherwise headed for the dump, and costing a fraction of new ones. Urban Ore favors reuse over recycling because reuse conserves not just the material in an item but also the embedded energy and craft that went into making it. And when they sell a brass faucet or an old Arts and Crafts style door for reuse, they make far more money than they would have if they sold the same piece of metal or wood for its market value for recycling. Across the top of each of sales receipt from Urban Ore is printed "Ending the Age of Waste."

On the other side of the country, in the South Bronx, a neighborhood plagued by high unemployment, piles of waste materials all over the place, environmental degradation, and devastating rates of asthma, cancer, and other environmentally related diseases, a cooperatively run business called ReBuilders Source was launched in the spring of 2008. They are diverting much of the estimated 2,000 tons of C&D waste that arrive at waste transfer stations in the South Bronx on a daily basis and reselling it at their 18,000-square-foot retail warehouse. Their mission statement proclaims:

"We work to create living wage jobs by recycling and reusing building materials. We work to create alternatives to landfills. We stand for equal opportunity, and economic and environmental justice."[56] The reason this is such a great model is that ReBuilders Source sees the connection between environmental, economic, and justice issues and is tackling them all at once.

Medical Waste

This stream gets a lot of attention, and often more than it merits: there's actually a major gap between the real and perceived threat. People tend to freak out about waste from medical facilities, fearing it may spread AIDS or other viruses. In reality, the bulk of the waste coming out of a medical facility is the same as waste coming out of a hotel, restaurant, or office, because hospitals serve all those functions. It is not unlike other municipal waste.

A small portion of medical waste is hazardous or potentially hazardous and definitely does require special treatment; this kind of medical waste includes sharps (needles), some pharmaceutical wastes, some low-level radioactive wastes from specialty clinics, and any waste that may have come in contact with a sick patient and thus has the potential to infect others.

Glenn McRae, founder of CGH Environmental Strategies, who has championed safe management of wastes in health care since 1990 and who has personally sorted through waste at hospitals around the world, says, "Very little is actually hazardous, and, depending on the type of hospital, no more than 5–10 percent is potentially infectious if it is carefully segregated."[57]

That means an effective segregation system is all that's needed to keep this slim 5 to 10 percent of potentially hazardous waste separated from a clinic's office paper, equipment packaging, leftover food, etc. Combine that with a systematic replacement of all the disposables (dishes, gowns, sheets, and equipment) with reusable Stuff, and a hospital can seriously reduce its waste disposal needs and costs. Beth Israel Medical Center in New York City has saved more than $600,000 a year through improved segregation and waste reduction efforts.[58]

And what about the potentially infectious 5 to 10 percent, the legitimate red bag waste? The best, most cost-effective solution is known as autoclaving, which means high temperature steam sterilization in a machine that is basically a big dishwasher. This is a much safer alternative than incineration, though many hospitals turn to that in their desire to destroy pathogens. The catch is that incineration burns not only the germs or viruses but also the material on which they're hanging out, which is usually plastic.

And burning that plastic creates toxic air emissions, which in turn causes diseases like asthma, neurological and reproductive problems, and cancer.[59] Medical waste incineration is so polluting that activist friends of mine in India wanted to hang a banner on a cancer specialist hospital with a belching incinerator in New Delhi to proclaim: "CANCER: caused AND cured here."

An international coalition of health care professionals, environmental health advocates, and community members called Health Care Without Harm partners with hospitals to reduce waste, eliminate the use of supertoxins like mercury and PVC, and replace incineration with safer and less expensive alternatives. See www.noharm.org for more information.

Electronic Waste

Electronic waste, or e-waste, comprises all the cell phones, computers, TVs, DVD players, electronic toys, appliances, remote controls, etc. that we throw out. The fastest growing, and most toxic, of today's garbage, e-waste is increasing three times faster than other municipal waste and is packed with hazardous metals and chemicals.[60] According to the Electronics Take-Back Coalition, the five most common sources and reasons for e-waste are:

1. Cell phone upgrades: Mobile phone service providers notoriously give free or cheap phones with new or renewed contracts. And since most of the phones are engineered to break after a couple years, it seems ridiculous to turn down their offer for a sparkly new model with all the latest bells and whistles and risk having the old one break midcontract, when replacement phones are much pricier. Out goes the old one!

2. Digital TV conversion: In the largest government-planned obsolescence ever, 2009 witnessed the end of analog TV broadcasts, which were replaced with digital. This rendered millions of perfectly fine televisions useless without a special converter box.[61] For many people, the hassle of getting the converter inspired them to get the new flat-screen or HDTV they'd been coveting. Out with the old TVs—which each contain about 4 to 7 pounds of lead![62] Amazingly, only six states currently ban dumping these toxic-laden things in landfills: California, Maine, Massachusetts, Minnesota, New Hampshire, and Rhode Island. Another six states (Oregon, New York, Connecticut, New Jersey, Illinois, and North Carolina) agreed to bans that will come into effect between 2010 and 2012—not soon enough to stop the toxic tsunami of 2009.[63]

3. Software upgrades: Often new software can't run on older machines because they lack the memory or processing speed. Out with the old, perfectly functional computers! For example, when Microsoft released its Vista operating system, it caused a spike in the e-waste stream.[64] The tight mix of plastics, metals, and glass in computers makes them really hard to recycle.

4. Can't change the battery: Sometimes it is so hard to access and replace batteries in products that people just replace the whole product. When my daughter was younger, she loved a Sesame Street book that included a phone on which she could call the book's characters and hear recorded messages. When the battery ran out, I had to pay more than the book originally cost for a replacement battery at RadioShack. Apple's iPods pose the most infamous battery challenges; unless you're an electronics whiz, you can't change the battery yourself but must return it to Apple for a new one, which requires paying a fee and deleting anything stored on the device. With the price of iPods declining, why bother? Out with the old!

5. Disposable printers: Printers are so cheap, sometimes they're even free with the purchase of a new computer. They're often less expensive than a cartridge of replacement ink! Even reaching a real human on the manufacturer's customer service line to ask about a malfunction can be more of a hassle than just getting a new one. Out once again with the old!

"Let's just get a new one" has become the default response when electronics or appliances break or need some kind of replacement part. As a result, about 400 million electronic products are chucked in the United States each year. In 2005—the most recent year for which we have data—it amounted to 4 billion pounds of e-waste, much of which was still functioning![65] And this Stuff is highly toxic: today's electronics contain mercury, lead, cadmium, arsenic, beryllium, and brominated flame retardants, among other nasties. Yet rather than segregating and handling it carefully and responsibly, as is necessary with this level of hazard, in the United States we still dump 85 percent of our e-waste in landfills[66] or, even worse, burn it in incinerators.

In 2009, I visited a huge e-waste recycling facility in Roseville, California. The first room looked like a Costco store, with floor-to-ceiling shelving lining the walls, but rather than being filled with products to be sold, the shelves were filled with products waiting to be destroyed. There were pallets full of printers, piles of TVs, and pallet-sized cardboard boxes (called gaylords) full of cell phones and MP3 players and BlackBerries. Staring into one of these gaylords full of BlackBerries, I realized that many still had the protective plastic film that's on the screen when you buy it. "They're new," our guides explained.

Every product in the place was there to be dismantled. Some were smashed first by hand, by workers with mallets and hammers on an assembly line. I watched as a series of identical printers went by, each adorned with one of the blue tags that you have to pull off before use: all new. Smash, smash, smash! I asked one guide what percent of products coming in here were brand new. "About half," she replied. I was aghast. What kind of economic system makes it more sensible to destroy perfectly good electronics rather than sell or share them? Why not put them on Craigslist? Or in the parking lot out front, labeled with "Free" signs? Our very forthcoming guide Renee explained: "The companies don't want this Stuff coming back to them through their warranty programs and then have to be responsible for it. It's easier for them to just destroy it." And then there's all the Stuff that's not new but still perfectly functional. What a waste!

The products travel along a series of conveyer belts, past other workers who pop them open to remove the batteries to dispose of them separately, as the hazardous waste they are. This step isn't actually required by law but is vital to keeping the hazardous chemicals in the batteries out of the shreds of material on the backend, some of which will be landfilled or incinerated. It's one of the ways the Roseville facility distinguishes itself as one of the best e-waste processors out there.

After battery removal, the Stuff moves along more conveyer belts to the grinders, which sit in the middle of the compound. The gigantic grinding machines occupy an enclosed two-story building the size of an urban townhouse. I saw a TV as big as my couch move into their vicious metal chompers, which are constantly monitored for jams or explosions.

After being chewed and spit out by the grinders, the shreds of Stuff are carried on still more conveyor belts through a maze of moving platforms and magnets and screens, like a giant's Erector Set. These sort the debris into segregated gaylords. The plastics fall in one place, too mixed for any options besides landfill or incineration. The precious metals—the prize at the end of the process, the only recovered resource worth any real money—fall into yet another box. These metals are then sent by train three thousand miles to the Noranda copper smelter in Quebec, Canada, where they are smelted and prepared for use in other products. The copper is shipped to China, where it is used to make a printer or computer or cell phone that just might end up back here again. The whole process is beyond shocking; if I hadn't witnessed it with my own eyes—especially the fact that half the Stuff was brand new—I'd never believe it. It's like the plot of some dystopian sci-fi movie in which an evil mastermind sets up a global system specifically designed to trash resources.

In the United States some e-waste also gets sent to U.S. prisons for recycling. From 2003 to 2005, prisoners processed more than 120 million pounds of e-waste, in processes plagued with health and safety violations—often no protective gear was provided, although smashing the electronics released lead, cadmium, and other hazards.[67] Federal Prison Industries (aka UNICOR), which manages prison e-waste processing, is now the focus of a Department of Justice investigation for the toxic exposures prisoners suffer. While the investigation is ongoing, an interim report conducted by NIOSH (National Institute for Occupational Safety and Health) for the investigation confirmed that e-waste recycling had been taking place without adequate worker health and safety protection.[68] Meanwhile, the practice continues.[69]

Although about 12.5 percent of e-waste in the United States is supposedly collected for some form of "recycling" either by facilities like the one in Roseville or by prison labor, investigations by the Basel Action Network (BAN) have revealed that about 80 percent of that amount is actually exported overseas to developing countries, where much is simply dumped.[70] Some is processed in the most horrific manner one can imagine: whole families, wearing zero protective gear, smashing open computers to recover the minute amounts of precious metals, burning the PVC off wires to get the copper, and soaking components in acid baths before pouring the bathwater into rivers. This is a toxic nightmare of gigantic proportions. You'll hear people argue that e-waste recycling provides these struggling communities with jobs, but as Jim Puckett, executive director of BAN, says, offering people this kind of work is offering them a "choice between poison and poverty."[71] And actually, since they don't make more than pennies, they wind up with both.

In early 2009, Dell announced that it will no longer export any nonworking electronic product from developed nations to developing nations for recycling, reuse, repair, or disposal. "Even though U.S. laws don't restrict most exports, Dell has decided to go well beyond these inadequate regulations," Puckett said. "Dell deserves high marks for leading the way as a responsible corporate citizen with their new e-waste export policy."[72]

As meticulous as the Roseville facility tries to be, e-waste is much too massive an issue, with far too many hazardous implications, for that model. The most effective place to solve the e-waste problem is upstream, where decisions about design and ingredients are made. Producers of computers and other electronics could introduce vast improvements to make electronics more durable, less hazardous, and easier to upgrade and repair. (And, as a last option, to recycle.) Some companies are starting to move in the right direction: Dell, HP, and Apple all now have take-back programs that allow customers to return old computers when buying new ones—but they only instituted these programs after concerned consumers and citizens mounted major campaigns, in some cases years long. This issue is too serious and urgent to wait for these companies to come around on their own. We need laws to force responsibility on producers by mandating take-back and recyclability.

Fortunately, this is starting to happen. At the time of writing this book, nineteen U.S. states (California, Maine, Maryland, Washington, Connecticut, Minnesota, Oregon, Texas, North Carolina, New Jersey, Oklahoma, Virginia, West Virginia, Missouri, Hawaii, Rhode Island, Illinois, Michigan, and Indiana, in chronological order by adoption date)—and New York City—have passed legislation requiring e-waste recycling. Even better, all of these laws except the one in California use a producer responsibility approach, meaning the companies that made the computers pay for the recycling.[73] This is a great incentive for the producers to think hard about ways to eliminate toxics and design for repair and recycling, since they have to bear the cost of dealing with the Stuff eventually. If you live in any other U.S. state, contact the Electronics TakeBack Coalition to learn how to get e-waste recycling laws in your state.

Another positive development is the expansion of the e-Stewards program, a third-party certification program that checks out electronics recyclers and certifies those that meet strict environmental and social justice standards. Facilities certified as e-Stewards commit to recycling e-waste (using a process similar to the one I witnessed at the Roseville facility) at sites here in the United States and do not send any toxic e-waste to landfills, incinerators, prisons, or developing countries.[74] Find an e-Steward certified responsible recycler near you at www.e-stewards.org.

The Away Myth

So here are all these huge piles of waste from various sources. Where does it all go? You probably already know this, but if not, here's the big revelation:

for the great majority of these billions of tons of Stuff, there is no "away." Period. We do one of two things with most of our waste: we bury it, or we burn it. Yes, some of it gets recycled, which is as close to "away" as it gets—I'll talk about that later on. But there's another important aspect of "away": too often, because we don't want to deal with the hassle and the pollution associated with the bury or burn methods (or for that matter, the recycling) here in the United States, boatloads of our American waste are sent to other regions of the world, often under the guise of being recycled there. Not only is it unethical and immoral to dump our often toxics-contaminated wastes on other communities—it turns out we can't escape the health and environmental consequences anyway, which drift back to us via the air, the water, and the bodies of the creatures we eat.

Away by Burial

In the most common scenario for disposal—for 64.5 percent of municipal solid waste in the United States,[75] we dig a big hole in the ground and fill it up with garbage. This is commonly known as a dump, but since open-air dumps developed an image problem (and a rodent problem), some engineers figured out that they could upgrade the hole with a liner and systems to collect the liquid runoff (leachate) and then call it a "sanitary landfill." That term always reminds me of what green-collar jobs advocate Van Jones says about so-called clean coal: "It represents a breakthrough in the marketing of coal, not in the actual technology."[76] "Sanitary landfill" sounds much better than "dump," but they are still just holes in the ground full of garbage that stinks and leaks and that could have been prevented, reused, or recycled instead.

The purpose of a landfill is to bury the trash in such a way that it will be isolated from groundwater, will be kept dry, and will not come in contact with air. If these conditions are achieved (which happens, basically, never), the trash doesn't decompose much, which is the point. That's the "sanitary" part. Your typical landfill takes up at least several hundred acres of land, of which maybe a third is dedicated to the actual landfill.[77] (The enormous and now-closed Fresh Kills landfill on New York's Staten Island was 2,200 acres.[78]) The remaining land is used for supporting services: runoff collection ponds, leachate collection ponds, drop-off stations, truck parking, and fifty- to hundred-foot buffer areas.[79]

So here are the problems with landfills:

1. All Landfills Leak

No matter how well engineered the landfills are, liquid ends up inside the chambers. Rain seeps in and mixes with the liquid from within the garbage (rotting food waste, nail polish remover, spoiled milk, the last bit of Windex in the bottle, etc.). It trickles through the dry trash and picks up contaminants (like the heavy metals in printing ink, paints, household and garden pesticides, oven cleaner, drain un-cloggers—you name it) and turns into a disgusting witches' brew. This liquid, called leachate, can seep directly into the ground, contaminating surface water, underground water supplies, and anything else in its path. Contamination of underground water is worse than other kinds of water pollution because we can't see it so have a hard time tracking it. We can never properly clean it up and we are likely to need it more with increasing climate change. We shouldn't contaminate rivers either, but at least they regularly flush with fresh water. Underground aquifers, which contain one hundred times the volume of fresh water found in all the rivers and other water bodies on the earth's surface, take thousands of years to do the same.[80]

To prevent this, engineers have designed collection systems—networks of pipes at the lowest part of the landfill—in an attempt to divert and collect the leachate, which then gets treated as wastewater (not unproblematic itself). But the liquid can only be collected if it doesn't escape through the liners first, and the problem is that there are lots of things in the garbage that can puncture or erode those liners. Also, the collection pipes can get clogged or broken by the weight of all that garbage. Leachate can also overflow from the top, like an overfilled bathtub. In fact, even the EPA admits that landfill liners inevitably leak, despite the claims of landfill operators to the contrary.[81]

2. Landfills Are *Always* Toxic

In the United States our laws distinguish between hazardous and nonhazardous waste, which is more of a legal differentiation than a reality.[82] Landfills for hazardous waste are more strictly regulated and engineered than those limited to municipal solid waste. Unfortunately, even though it's considered nonhazardous, municipal solid waste contains a lot of dangerous chemicals—not just from the batteries and paint cans and electronics stuck in there by folks who just don't care enough to separate them out, but also from Stuff not yet banned from regular household trash, like flame-retardant-treated fabrics, PVC-coated cables, lead-painted toys, household cleaners, nail polish remover, etc. Even seemingly benign plastics contain toxic heavy metals as stabilizers. Researchers have found that leachate from municipal waste landfills is just as toxic as that from hazardous waste landfills. In fact, 20 percent of the top-priority contaminated sites awaiting cleanup under our national Superfund program are former municipal landfills.[83]

3. Landfills Foul the Air and Contribute to Climate Chaos

Pollution comes out of landfills in the form of nasty gases, too. You see, when the organic material (banana peels, yard waste, soggy pizza boxes, wilted salad, etc.) in landfills rots, it releases methane gas, a powerful greenhouse gas that, although it disperses faster, is over twenty times more damaging than the more famous carbon dioxide.[84] The odorless and explosive methane can also travel underground into the basements of nearby buildings, which can be a real bummer when someone lights a match down there.

Methane gas is what is known as a volatile organic compound, or VOC. There are also nonmethane VOCs released from dumps—fumes from things like paint, paint thinners, cleaning supplies, glues, solvents, pesticides, and some building materials. Routine VOC emissions are one reason that living near landfills is dangerous. Common symptoms from exposure to concentrated VOCs include headaches, drowsiness, eye irritation, rashes, and respiratory and sinus problems. Many studies have documented increases in cancer (especially leukemia and bladder cancer) and other health problems in communities adjacent to landfills.[85]

Waste industry representatives often promote the concept of burning landfill gas as a renewable energy source, which would make landfills eligible for massive governmental subsidies, or carbon-offsetting credits, and grant them some invaluable public relations. They argue that the gas is going to be produced anyway, and burning it to create energy is better than just letting it seep into the atmosphere. The catch is that landfill gas is dirty gas; it contains methane as well as other nasty VOCs and potential contaminants that can form supertoxic dioxin when burned. Burning landfill gas to produce energy is far more polluting than burning natural gas. Nevertheless, the landfill lobby succeeded in having it included in the renewable energy standard in the 2009 Waxman-Markey climate bill, as well as in the Senate's renewable energy standard.[86]

Composting
The main source of methane is rotting organics, which are also the source of most of the liquid, aside from rain, that becomes leachate. By simply keeping all organics out of landfills, we could virtually eliminate the methane released from them, significantly reduce leachate, and keep our climate cooler. In many cities, organics—food scraps, yard trimmings, soiled paper—make up a third or more of the municipal waste.[87] That means that just by keeping organics out of the trash, we can cut our municipal

waste by a third! The best way to do this is to mandate wet-dry separation of garbage at the source—i.e., in our kitchens and everywhere we eat—and then dispose of food remains by composting. This also keeps recyclables from getting gunked up with yesterday's meals, keeps the organics from getting contaminated with the toxics in consumer products, and creates a valuable additive for soil.

I think composting suffers from an image problem. Mention composting—or worse, worm bins—to most people, and they imagine quaint farmers or hippie throwbacks. But actually, composting is a simple thing we can each do to get our own household's materials flows in better balance. It isn't a big political statement. It is a smart, easy, responsible thing to do. Plus, it makes your garden bloom. If you eat, compost. Simple.

Where I live, in the San Francisco Bay Area, we have curbside collection of organics. Every resident gets a little green bin to keep in our kitchen for food scraps. We dump it into a bigger green bin with our yard trimmings and this gets emptied weekly, along with the recycling and the (shrinking amount of) garbage. In the first large-scale urban food scrap composting program in the country, San Francisco's residents, restaurants, and other businesses send more than 400 tons of food scraps and other compostable material to be composted rather than landfilled *each day*.[88]

If your city doesn't have a municipal composting program, don't worry. Organic waste can also be composted at the household or neighborhood level. I like decentralized backyard or neighborhood composting best anyway, because then we're not using trucks to haul around this material that is mostly water. There are lots of easy systems for backyard composting. I have four tidy little black bins outside my back door full of worms that chomp up all my food trimmings, table scraps, yard waste, and soiled paper and turn it into a rich, effective fertilizer. When I visited my friend Jim Puckett in his tiny apartment in Amsterdam, he had an attractive wooden box just inside the front door. It looks like a regular bench but you can lift the seat and see the worms inside doing their thing to last night's dinner.

Of course, you don't need fancy compost bins to get started. I've seen neighborhood composting programs in New Delhi, India, and Quezon City in the Philippines that use old fifty-five-gallon barrels or just long ditches filled with worms into which residents dump their organic waste. In developing countries, composting is even easier since generally their waste contains an even higher portion of organics than in heavily industrialized, consumer-maniac countries, with all our disposable Stuff. From Cairo to

Calcutta, community organizations and sometimes forward-thinking municipal officials are setting up composting programs.

While backyard (or garage, laundry room, or front hallway) or neighborhood composting happens at the level of individual households and communities, there are lots of ways government can support it. Where I live, the government waste agency—the Alameda County Waste Management Authority—subsidizes compost bins for residents. These high-end backyard composters or worm bins regularly cost about one hundred dollars if bought in a store. The Waste Management Authority buys them in bulk at a discounted rate, subsidizes part of the remaining cost, and sells them to the public for about forty dollars each. They don't mind subsidizing the cost because they save so much more money by not having to pick up all that heavy organic waste. Since beginning the program in 1991 (and through July 2009) they have sold more than 72,000 compost and worm bins, which, they estimate, have diverted more than 110,000 tons of organic waste from landfills.[89]

Government can also get involved in bigger ways. In 1999, the European Union passed a landfill directive that required a steady reduction of organic waste sent to landfills over the next twenty years. In 1998, Nova Scotia, Canada, adopted a complete ban on landfilling or incinerating organics, which spurred the development of an impressive composting infrastructure.[90] So far, twenty-one states in the United States have banned landfilling of yard waste,[91] which is a good start because once yard waste composting systems are set up, it's not hard to add kitchen and restaurant scraps too. Any method of composting is less expensive and much smarter than building sanitary landfills or high-tech incinerators.

4. Landfills Waste Resources

How are resources wasted? Let me count the ways. For starters, there's the hundreds and thousands of acres of perfectly good land taken up with landfills. It's true that once landfills are filled up, they're usually covered with dirt and then replanted. After that many of them are turned into parks, parking lots, or shopping malls. But these are ill-fated. Trash settles over time, making the ground unstable, so structures built on top of them often shift and sink. As for the parks, they attract children—and having our kids running around on top of a garbage heap leaching VOCs is just a bad idea.

As Peter Montague, director of the Environmental Research Foundation, explains, "The moment human efforts cease, nature takes over and disintegration begins: nature has many agents that work to dismantle a landfill: small mammals (mice, moles, voles, woodchucks, prairie dogs, etc.), birds, insects, reptiles, amphibians, worms, bacteria, the roots of trees, bushes, and shrubs, plus wind, rain, lightning, freeze-thaw cycles, and soil erosion—all combine to take apart even the most carefully engineered landfill. Eventually a landfill's contents disperse into the local environment and then move outward from there, often into local water supplies. It may take a decade or it may take 50 years or more before a landfill spills its contents, but nature doesn't care. Nature's got all the time in the world. Sooner or later wastes buried in a shallow hole in the ground will escape and disperse." [92]

But the main waste of resources is the garbage itself. Consider the life-cycle of Stuff as laid out in these pages—behind every piece of garbage is a long history, of extraction in mines, harvesting in forests or fields, production in factories, and extensive ferrying along supply chains. How ridiculous is it to lock up all those resources underground after spending all that effort to extract and make and distribute them in the first place! I've said it before, and I'll say it again: the amount of resources on this planet is finite. We're running out of them. Locking them up underground is just plain stupid.

Away by Fire

Incinerators are big machines that burn waste. Back in 1885, when the first one in the country was built on Governors Island in New York, it seemed like a good way to get rid of potato peels, chicken bones, and fabric scraps. Even then there were much better ways of dealing with those much more benign materials (compost, papermaking, soapmaking, etc.), but today we have no excuse: fire is *not* an appropriate method of trying to make garbage go "away," especially since today's trash contains Stuff like cell phones, VCRs, paint cans, PVC, and batteries.

There are many scientists, recyclers, activists, municipal officials, and others who are working against incinerators. You could fill a library with their reports as to why incineration is the wrong way to go. Here are my top ten reasons:

1. Incinerators Pollute

Incinerators liberate the toxics contained in products into the air. We breathe that air. Those airborne poisons can also easily drop into water. We drink that water and use it to irrigate our food. The poisons in the air also land on farms, fields, and the sea, moving up the food chain into the fish,

meat, and dairy that we eventually eat. Even worse, burning trash creates new toxins that weren't in the original waste. That is because the actual process of combustion takes apart and recombines chemicals into new supertoxins. Some of these combustion by-products are the most toxic man-made industrial pollutants known, like dioxin, for which incinerators are among the top sources globally.[93] For example, if anything containing chlorine—clothes, paper, flooring, PVC, cleaning products—is burned, dioxin is created. Older and badly operated incinerators release toxins into both the air and into ash, while more advanced plants release toxins into the ash. In both cases, the toxins include chemicals known to cause cancer, birth defects, damage to organs—especially the lungs and eyes—and endocrinological, neurological, circulatory, and reproductive problems.[94] Meanwhile many of the toxins haven't even been tested for health impacts.

2. Incinerators Don't Eliminate the Need for Landfills

Incinerator pushers love to claim they make waste disappear, even bragging about their 99 percent destruction removal efficiency (DRE), which implies that 99 percent of the waste actually does disappear. But that's not quite true: the waste is just converted to air pollution and ash. And guess what? That ash still needs to be landfilled. In general, for every 3 tons of waste one shoves into an incinerator, we get 1 ton of ash that requires landfilling.[95] Waste isn't destroyed in incinerators; its appearance just changes. Instead of a truckload of trash, we wind up with a slightly smaller pile of ash, plus pollution in the air, our lungs, and our food supplies.

Incinerator ash is more toxic than the original waste because the heavy metals (which are elements and can't be destroyed) become concentrated. There are two kinds of ash: fly ash, which comes up the smokestack, and bottom ash, which piles up at the base of the combustion chamber. Fly ash is generally smaller in volume but way more toxic than bottom ash. In any case, some incinerator operators merge the two before they get landfilled.

And here's the kicker: the more effective the filter atop the smokestack is, the more toxic its ash. (Think about it: a bad filter is letting more bad Stuff escape, while a good filter catches it, meaning it's caught in the ash.) You hear a lot about advances in filter technology, as if that's going to solve everything. But filters don't get rid of the toxins, they just put them in a different place—it's like the shell game in which the pea keeps getting secretly moved from under one shell to another.

3. Incinerators Violate the Principles of Environmental Justice

Incinerators fall into the category of dirty industrial development that I described in chapter 2 on production. Dirty development follows the path of least resistance, seeking out those communities that developers perceive to lack the economic, educational, or political resources to resist. That means incinerators get built in low-income communities and communities of color, forcing a disproportionate share of the resulting toxic pollution on the people who live there. Plus, not only does an incinerator create pollution directly from its smokestack, it also means heavy traffic from exhaust-spewing trucks that deliver and sometimes drop stinky, hazardous garbage.

4. Incinerators Are So 1980s

Is there *any* fashion from the 80s that is really worthy of a comeback? I don't happen to think so, but definitely not incinerators. In the 1980s, proposals for municipal trash incinerators were all the rage in the United States. Ellen and Paul Connett, editors of the *Waste Not* newsletter, which tracked municipal waste incinerators for years, estimate that more than four hundred incinerators were proposed during the 1980s as their proponents went from community to community, touting the environmental benefits of burning trash and promising a techno-fix to the growing problem of waste.[96] Most of these planned incinerators were stopped by informed organized community resistance. Those that were built were plagued with technical and financial problems, not to mention those billowing plumes of really noxious smoke and the inevitable ash.

Following these fiascos, the incinerator industry came to a virtual standstill in the United States for nearly twenty years, with no incinerator larger than those that burn 2,000 tons per day built since 1992.[97] Meanwhile, the incinerator industry focused its attention overseas, on countries that were just getting on the disposables-consumption bandwagon. To the industry's surprise, people there didn't want them either! GAIA, the Global Alliance for Incinerator Alternatives, boasts nearly one thousand members in eighty-one countries who share information and strategies and collaborate to stop incineration and promote sustainable solutions.[98]

When the incinerator industry realized the strength of the global resistance movement, they started putting fancy new names on slightly updated technology. The word "incineration" is hardly seen in today's promotional material; instead these new facilities are called plasma arc, pyrolysis, gasification, and waste-to-energy plants. GAIA calls them "incinerators in disguise."[99] Don't be fooled by the fancy packaging: they are still gigantic, expensive machines that burn garbage (aka resources) and that produce hazardous air pollution and ash.

5. Waste-to-Energy Plants Should Be Called Waste *of* Energy

The latest fashion among incinerator proponents is to call them waste-to-energy plants, promising to burn up all that stinky garbage and turn it into energy, even claiming that garbage is renewable energy and these monstrosities should get renewable energy credits! Since we have too much garbage and not enough energy, that sure sounds appealing. But here's the deal: first off, the little bit of energy recovered from burning trash is a very dirty energy, releasing far more greenhouse gases than burning natural gas, oil, or even coal. According to the U.S. Environmental Protection Agency, waste incinerators produce 1,355 grams of CO_2 per kilowatt hour; coal produces 1,020, oil 758, and natural gas 515.[100]

Second, let's step back and look at the grand scheme of things for a moment. When you burn something, the most energy you can recover is a fraction of the energy value (the "calories") of the actual material; you can't recover any of the energy investments of that thing's entire lifecycle. When we burn Stuff, it means we have to go back and extract, mine, grow, harvest, process, finish, and transport new Stuff to replace it. Doing all that takes waaaaay more energy than the smidgen that can be recovered from burning it. If the ultimate goal is to conserve energy, we could "produce" far more energy by reusing and recycling Stuff than we ever could by burning it.

6. Incinerators Drain the Local Economy and Create Few Jobs

Capital costs for building incinerators in industrialized countries often run to $500 million—a 2009 proposal for one in Maryland came to $527 million.[101] Meanwhile, their counterparts in developing countries generally cost between $13,000 and $700,000, which tells us something about double standards[102]; most of the incinerators built in poorer countries would never meet the standards set by U.S. or European health and safety laws, as inadequate as those laws still are. Either way, a lot of money gets spent, much of it on high-tech equipment manufactured overseas, and engineers and consultants who obviously aren't needed after the facility is finished. Once built, incinerators are capital- and machine-intensive, not labor-intensive, offering only a few lousy jobs and even fewer specialized jobs. In contrast, recycling and zero waste programs offer a huge number of jobs—jobs that are safer, cleaner, and greener. For every dollar invested in recycling and zero waste programs, we get ten times as many jobs as in incineration—local, respectable jobs that conserve resources and build community.[103]

7. Incinerators Are the Most Costly Waste Management Option

Any solution to our waste problem is going to cost money, but we should invest in methods and facilities that are actually moving us in the right direction. Incinerators are enormously expensive, by far the most expensive waste disposal option available, short of sending the Stuff to the moon (which some people have considered!). In contrast to the more than $500 million that the above-mentioned Maryland incinerator would have cost, a new state-of-the-art materials reclamation center not far from me in Northern California—the Davis Street Transfer Center, the West Coast's most advanced facility of its kind—cost just over $9 million. While the Maryland incinerator would expect to burn 2,000 tons of trash per day, Davis Street handles 4,000 tons of materials per day, of which currently 40 percent is recycled. Davis Street provides 250 people with unionized jobs; the incinerator might hope to provide about 30 full-time positions.[104] You do the math.

The cost differential is even more stark in developing countries where recycling and composting are less mechanized and therefore more labor intensive. GAIA has calculated that decentralized low-tech composting in countries in the Global South can have equipment costs 75 times lower than incinerator investment costs.[105] Even the World Bank admits that capital and operating costs for incinerators are at least twice that for landfills, even though it continues to fund incinerators in developing countries.[106] The only communities that should even be thinking of incinerators are those with money to burn. By which I mean: none.

8. Incinerators Actually Encourage Waste

Incinerators are waste addicts. They work better when they are run continuously, so they need a constant supply of waste. Incinerator companies often try to include in their contract clauses that allow them to import waste from other locations if the local waste generation falls below a certain point. How regressive is that? We should be making commitments to reduce waste, not to perpetuate it!

Also, it turns out that the trash that is most easily burned is the most preventable waste (like single-use disposable Stuff and packaging) and most recyclable waste (like paper). That means incinerators directly compete with efforts to reduce or recycle materials. In many cities, incinerator owners have pushed local governments to take steps to ban informal recyclers, in order to ensure they have enough Stuff to burn.

9. Incinerators Undermine Creative, Real Solutions

If your city invests hundreds of millions of dollars to build one of these things, and then you come along with an ingenious idea for reducing waste at its source—forget about it! Relying on an incinerator to solve the garbage challenge signifies a real failure of imagination. It is for those who go along with impulsive temporary fixes, rather than those who can hold the long-term view and consider the broader system that created the problem in the first place. What decisions were made at the production, distribution, consumption, and disposal points that resulted in this waste? How can we go back and make different decisions to design the waste out of the system? Preventing a problem upstream is always far preferable—and more economical—than just focusing on a quick solution.

10. Incinerators Just Don't Make Sense

I've met many an engineer who strives to convince me that his latest bells and whistles incinerator is really different: that it really *does* solve the dioxin issue; that it really *does* recover energy, etc. Dr. Paul Connett, who has testified at hundreds of hearings on incineration, has a mantra: "Even if you could make them safe, you could never make them sensible." [107] It just doesn't make sense to invest hundreds of millions of dollars developing machines designed to destroy resources. It is not an investment in the right direction.

Toxics Use Reduction in Massachusetts

Municipal leaders, community residents, and businesses will often focus on the question of what's to be done with the hazardous waste that's being produced. If both burying and burning are off the table, what's the alternative? In fact, a real solution requires shifting our attention upstream, to stopping the flow of waste at its source. This may seem counterintuitive if you're looking at a discharge pipe pouring muck into a river, but it's the best strategy for long-term change.

Here's an analogy I often use: Suppose you come home from a vacation to find that you left your kitchen faucet running. The sink has overflowed and water covers the kitchen floor, the dining room floor, and most of the living room. It's a mess. Where do you start: mopping up the lovely oriental carpets or turning off the tap? It's a no-brainer, right? In the context of hazardous waste, turning off the tap translates to reducing the amount of toxic chemicals used in production.

An impressive example of how this can work is Massachusetts' Toxics Use Reduction Act (TURA), which was passed in 1989. The law included ambitious waste reduction goals, requiring Massachusetts companies to track their chemical use and release and to develop plans detailing how the company would reduce toxics by changing the materials or processes they used. In 1990, TURA established the Toxics Use Reduction Institute (TURI) at the University of Massachusetts Lowell to help companies and communities research toxic chemicals, figure out innovative and cost-effective alternatives, and provide a range of technical assistance with toxics use reduction and energy and water efficiency.[108]

It worked. As just one example, the lighting company Lightolier reduced its VOC emissions by 95 percent, its toxics use by 58 percent, and its electricity and natural gas use by 19 and 30 percent respectively. In the process, it saved millions of dollars in operating costs.[109] Statewide, TURI's work has led to a reduction in industries' toxic chemical use by 41 percent, toxic chemical waste by 65 percent, and emissions by an impressive 91 percent. Manufacturers participating in the program recently reported $4.5 million in annual operating cost savings.[110]

Those are impressive numbers—I give them to every public official considering incineration or landfilling of hazardous waste. With such proven viability, TURI-style options should be exhausted before even considering any other approach. TURI has proven that industries can cut their waste by more than half and their emissions more than 90 percent.

Although TURI's work focuses on Massachusetts, its resources and tools are available online for anyone, anywhere. For those working to clean up industries, finding TURI is like hitting the jackpot. No longer can polluting industries get away with saying they'd love to change, but there just aren't alternatives. TURI's CleanerSolutions database offers options including "find a cleaner" and "replace a solvent." Its online Pollution Prevention Gems (P2gems.org) has reams of information on reducing toxics in specific sectors, industrial processes, and products, for everything from bleaching and metal finishing to printing and wood finishing.

The bad news is that, as this book was going to press, funding for TURI was in jeopardy. In spite of its phenomenal success in reducing toxic chemical use, it may fall victim to budget cuts in the state of Massachusetts. Environmental health advocates are fighting back, pointing out that the program pays for itself, as industries' fees cover the costs of administering TURI, not to mention that preventing hazardous waste in the first place is far more economical than cleaning it up later. For updates, visit TURI at www.turi.org.

Over the Sea and Far Away . . .

In twenty years of working on waste, I've seen a lot of attempts by companies in our country to get rid of our trash—especially our most troublesome toxic trash—by shipping it somewhere else in the world. But guess what? The problems don't go away. May I repeat: there is no "away." Here are some of the most tragic stories I collected while tracking the trafficking of waste around the globe.

To Bangladesh

In late 1991, four South Carolina–based companies secretly mixed 1,000 tons of hazardous waste containing high amounts of lead and cadmium into a shipment of fertilizer that the Bangladesh government had purchased with a loan from the Asian Development Bank. This was discovered by U.S. environmental authorities at the local and state level during a random inspection of the Stoller Chemical facility (which produced the fertilizer). They found that Stoller had mixed in an unapproved material with levels of lead and cadmium beyond the legal limits, and they alerted criminal investigators at the Environmental Protection Agency. At that time, I was in close touch with EPA officials who tracked the international waste trade, and one of them told me about it.

Unfortunately, the EPA didn't learn of the illegal export until the contaminated fertilizer had already reached Bangladesh. By U.S. law, the companies would have been able to export this kind of toxic waste only after first obtaining written permission from the importing country.[111] In this case they'd ignored that step, so the shipment was illegal. The companies were fined for the procedural violation, but neither the United States nor the Bangladeshi government was interested in taking action to recall the waste.

I headed straight to Bangladesh. My goal was to find out what had happened to the fertilizer and, if it had already been used on farms, to collect soil samples as evidence to force both governments to clean it up. First, I visited the U.S. embassy in the capital city of Dhaka. I hoped the embassy would express some concern, or perhaps embarrassment, over the export of the contaminated fertilizer. On the contrary, the embassy staff person kept repeating, "It is not our responsibility. The shipment was a private transaction between private companies and we do not get involved in private business transactions." Sure, U.S. embassies stay out of U.S. business activities overseas, just like those relentless Bangladeshi mosquitoes stayed out of my face.

A representative of a local environmental organization in Bangladesh was far more helpful, accompanying me by bus and then bicycle rickshaw to a small town in the countryside where the contaminated fertilizer was rumored to still be for sale. Stepping off the bus, it was hard for me to imagine why any farmer felt the need to add fertilizer in this environment; everywhere I looked, the rice paddies were the most luscious vibrant green I had ever seen.

But sure enough, at the local agricultural supply shop, I found one last bag of the crap still for sale, months after both the United States and Bangladeshi governments had been informed of the contamination. I couldn't leave it in the shop for some unsuspecting farmer to pick up, so I bought that last bag for the equivalent of four dollars and carried it along on our journey. I also got the names of the local farmers who had bought some. One of those farms was my next stop.

The Bangladeshi farmer welcomed us into his modest home for tea. The walls were made of earth and the roof from thatched grass. After we introduced ourselves and explained our purpose, he enthusiastically led us to the fields to take soil samples. I was confused about why the farmer kept smiling as my translator friend explained that the fertilizer on his fields contained toxic waste illegally sent from the United States. But then she translated what he was saying: "Now that your government knows where the toxic fertilizer has been used, they will come and clean it up so we will be safe." Standing there, I was overwhelmed with sadness and shame. "No," I explained, remembering my meeting with the U.S. embassy staff person, "I don't think they will come." But I promised him that I'd deliver his cleanup request to my government and I'd use the evidence from this case to support the call for an end to global waste trafficking. Saying that to this farmer, whom I had just informed that he had put toxic waste all over his fields, made me feel like such a schmuck. What good did it do him to know that the evidence from his field would be used to strengthen a United Nations convention on waste trafficking? Of all my times traipsing around the world investigating toxic waste, that moment was the lowest.

I returned to the capital city of Dhaka with a heavy heart and a heavy bag of fertilizer. I didn't know what to do with either. After musing on it for some days, I came up with a plan. U.S. embassies are considered U.S. soil overseas. U.S. hazardous waste law requires prior written permission to export this type of hazardous waste to another country. Although the original exporter had violated this law, I doubted the U.S. embassy would repeat the mistake, especially if they knew I was watching. So I decided to return the contaminated fertilizer to the U.S. embassy, knowing that the staff would be unable to simply throw it in the garbage.

I wrapped up the fertilizer in a nice package, addressed to the staff person I had previously met with, and dropped it off at the embassy's front desk with a little note informing him that I was returning this U.S. waste to U.S. soil, from which re-export was illegal. Although the embassy never did formally contact me, someone in the State Department anonymously sent me a copy of a telex message sent from the Dhaka embassy to their State Department offices in Washington, complaining about the waste, wondering what to do with it, and bemoaning my meddling. They concluded that they suspected they had "not seen the last of Leonard."

To South Africa

One of the worst cases of international waste trafficking I've ever worked on was in a small, heavily industrialized town called Cato Ridge in South Africa. There, a British-owned South African company called Thor Chemicals was importing mercury waste from the United States and Europe, supposedly for reprocessing. The British parent company, Thor Chemical Holdings, had previously operated a mercury processing plant in the United Kingdom, which it closed in 1987 in the face of increasing controversy and potential government action based on excessive mercury levels in the air and in the workers. Thor relocated its mercury processing operation to South Africa in 1988.[112]

Thor Chemicals in Cato Ridge was a very busy plant, importing thousands of tons of mercury during the 1990s. Two of the biggest exporters were the U.S. companies American Cyanamid in New Jersey and Borden Chemical in Louisiana. Although there were mercury-processing plants in the United States, none of them would accept mercury waste with as high a level of organic contamination as that which American Cyanamid and Borden Chemical produced. So Thor Chemicals willingly took it off their hands, for a fee of more than a thousand dollars per ton.[113]

Thor's operations in South Africa were even worse than in England. Within a year of starting operations, the local water board found high levels of mercury pollution in a nearby river. In 1989, a U.S. journalist from the *St. Louis Post-Dispatch* named Bill Lambrecht became interested in the case. He visited Cato Ridge to test the waters himself. Lambrecht found mercury levels in the Mngeweni River behind the plant of 1.5 million parts per billion, 1,500 times higher than the U.S. level for toxicity.[114] The Mngeweni flows into the Umgeni River, which continues through populated areas, irrigates agricultural and cattle grazing lands, is used for washing and playing, and feeds into the drinking supply of the big coastal city of Durban. As far as forty miles downstream, near Durban, mercury levels were found to be 20 times the U.S. limit.[115]

Thor's workers began immediately complaining of a metal taste in their mouths, black fingernails, skin problems, dizziness, and other signs of mercury poisoning. At one point, nearly one-third of the workers were found to have mercury poisoning. Thor documents, leaked to the South African organization Earthlife Africa, revealed that some workers had mercury concentrations in their urine hundreds of times higher than limits set by the World Health Organization. In 1992, three workers fell into mercury-induced comas and eventually died. The situation garnered international attention when Nelson Mandela visited one sick worker's bedside in 1993.[116]

Local environmentalists in South Africa, including Earthlife Africa and the Environmental Justice Networking Forum, joined forces with Greenpeace International to publicize and stop this disaster. Protests and letter writing campaigns were organized to pressure the waste exporters and Thor in both the United Kingdom and South Africa. In the mid-1990s, the South African government ordered the closure of the plant. However, a massive amount of mercury waste was left at the site.

I visited Cato Ridge in 1996 to work with local activists concerned about the potential incineration of this toxic waste. My host, the indomitable Durban-based environmental justice activist Bobby Peek, pulled over his car and led me on a trail that allowed us to get right alongside the factory fence. With no workers on site, not even a security guard, it was easy to get unobstructed views. We saw holding ponds of mercury waste—like uncovered swimming pools—sure to overflow in the heavy rains, as well as storage sheds, which, Peek said, contained even more barrels of waste. There was so much untreated mercury on the site that local environmentalists suspected that Thor may never have intended to process the waste at all. Even worse, we followed a drainage stream out of the factory to the spot where it joined the larger river. The mercury discharge from the plant was so heavy that actual streaks of silver lined the drainage ditch, reminding me of the mercury balls from broken glass thermometers that my mother warned me not to touch as a child.

It wasn't until 2003 that Thor—now renamed Guernica Chemicals—finally agreed to contribute 24 million rand ($2.5 million at the time of writing) toward cleaning up the plant. This was less than half the estimated costs to clean up about 8,000 tons of mercury waste left on site.[117]

As I write this, cleanup still hasn't happened. Meanwhile, mercury contamination continues to be a problem beyond the factory fence. In October 2008, the South African Medical Research Council released its report detailing extreme mercury levels in community residents near a local dam, Inanda, whose lake is Durban's main drinking water source. It also reported that 50 percent of the fish sampled from the Umgeni River, downstream from the Thor plant, had mercury levels above the safe eating limits recommended by the World Health Organization.[118]

Some of the workers have taken legal action against Thor in search of both compensation and justice. In 1994 and again in 1998, a number of injured workers, plus representatives of three workers who had died, took legal action in the United Kingdom against Thor's British parent company, Thor Chemical Holdings (TCH). The workers claimed that the parent company was negligent in designing and overseeing such a clearly unsafe facility and was responsible for the illnesses and death of the workers. In both cases, TCH attempted to wriggle out of the legal action, initially trying in vain to have the case moved to South African courts, where it presumably could have more influence over the outcome. In both cases, TCH ended up settling out of court; in 1997, it paid 1.3 million British pounds (more than $2 million), and in 2003 it paid another 240,000 British pounds (more than $300,000 at then current exchange rates).[119]

To Haiti

I have a small jar of grey powder on my desk. It usually goes unnoticed amidst the piles of paper, but every now and then someone asks about it. It's from Haiti. Actually, it's from Philly. It's Philadelphia's municipal incinerator ash that I got in Haiti. "Huh?" you might say. It's a jar of the most famous incinerator ash in the world.

You see, for years the city of Philadelphia had burned its trash in a municipal waste incinerator. Like many incinerators, its operators didn't have a solid plan for disposing of the mounds of ash it churned out, which they just piled ever higher in an adjacent lot. In 1986, the city hired Joseph Paolino & Sons and paid them $6 million to get rid of the ash. Paolino & Sons turned around and hired another company, Amalgamated Shipping, which owned a cargo ship named the *Khian Sea*. Amalgamated loaded 14,000 tons of the ash onto the *Khian Sea*, which headed for a dump site in the Caribbean.[120]

At the time, I worked with Greenpeace's Toxic Trade Team, which tracked international shipments of waste, alerting target governments about the hazardous contents. Thanks largely to our warnings, the ship was turned away by the Bahamas, Bermuda, the Dominican Republic, Honduras, Guinea-Bissau, and the Netherlands Antilles. (In gratitude, some very nice bottles of rum were sent from several of these embassies to our Washington, D.C., Greenpeace offices.) The *Khian Sea* continued to sail the region in search of a dump site.

In December 1987, the *Khian Sea* arrived in Gonaïves, a tiny, dusty, and very poor port town in Haiti. It had in hand a permit signed by the Haitian government to import "fertilizer." Anxious to be finished with its nightmare voyage, the crew began unloading the ash onto the beach immediately. But when Greenpeace alerted the Haitian government to the real contents of the cargo, government officials ordered the ash reloaded and removed. The crew stopped unloading but left 4,000 tons of ash on the open beach and took off.

The remaining 10,000 tons was definitely the best-traveled pile of ash ever. The voyage ultimately lasted for twenty-seven months, visiting every continent except Antarctica. Our Greenpeace team continued to track the *Khian Sea*, warning each country it approached. During the saga, the ship got a paint job and changed its name from the *Khian Sea* to the *Felicia*, then to the *Pelicano*, but it couldn't shake us. At one point in its journey, the ship returned to Philadelphia in defeat, hoping to return the ash to the original contractor, Paolino & Sons. But Paolino & Sons refused to let the ship dock at its pier in Philly. By strange coincidence, the pier caught on fire that very night and was destroyed, preventing the ship from docking. Finally, in November 1988 the ship appeared in Singapore with its cargo holds empty. The captain refused to disclose where the ash had been dumped. Eventually an enterprising lawyer, Howard Stewart, from the Environmental Crimes division of the Department of Justice tracked down photos surreptitiously taken by one of the sailors that showed the ash being dumped overboard into the ocean, which is a violation of international law.[121]

Meanwhile, the other 4,000 tons remained uncovered on the beach in Gonaïves, decreasing in size as more and more of it was blown away or washed into the sea each rainy season. I visited Haiti three times while the ash sat on the beach. I was amazed how widely known the ash was; wherever I went in Haiti, if I introduced myself as a person working on waste, immediately each person would ask if I had seen the ash in Gonaïves. I asked my Haitian friends why—with the many problems that Haiti was facing, including much more immediate health threats—the ash had gained so much attention. My friends told me that Haitians have long felt "dumped upon" by the United States, and the actual ash dumping was widely perceived as the epitome of that careless attitude. What is more symbolic than the richest country in the hemisphere dumping its waste on the poorest and then turning a deaf ear to all pleas for help? So Haitians were especially committed to sending the ash home. It was a matter not just of environmental health, but of dignity and justice.

Frustrated with the lack of responsibility taken by either Philadelphia or the U.S. Environmental Protection Agency, some Haitians living in the United States approached Greenpeace seeking assistance. In alliance with them, my Greenpeace colleague Kenny Bruno and I reached out to members of Philadelphia's faith-based communities, especially the Quakers, and launched Project Return to Sender. We demanded that Philadelphia take responsibility for the ash in Gonaïves and dispose of it in a regulated landfill in this country. For more than ten years we hounded the mayors of Philadelphia, organized citizens to speak up at city hall meetings, and met with Haitians here and in Haiti. In response, successive city administrations kept changing the official party line. Sometimes they said Philadelphia bore no responsibility, other times they said they would take the ash back but had no money to help pay. Mayor Edward Rendell and most city council members turned a deaf ear, saying it just wasn't their problem.

So finally we decided to make it their problem.

In the mid to late 1990s, Project Return to Sender organized a number of creative actions to get the attention of political leaders in Philadelphia and Washington. The mayor of Philadelphia and the EPA administrator received hundreds of envelopes from individual Haitians, each containing a pinch of the ash and marked "WARNING: contains toxic ash mislabeled as fertilizer, RETURN TO SENDER." American students across the country sent valentines to the mayor, encouraging him to "have a heart, clean up Philadelphia's ash." Philadelphia residents attended city council meetings to demand the city take responsibility for its waste. In a wonderful demonstration of solidarity, a group of Philadelphians even went from Philly to Haiti to visit the ash and to protest in front of the U.S. embassy there.

For months, the mayor's office faxed me a daily schedule of the mayor's events. (It was easily available upon request—a policy that may have since been revisited.) We ensured that groups of students, Quakers, or Haitians greeted him at each event with a gigantic banner: "MAYOR RENDELL: Do the right thing, bring the ash home." At the airport, celebrating a new direct flight to the Netherlands, there we were. At a gala at a museum, guests in tuxedos and evening gowns all passed the banner on the way from their limos to the entrance.

One morning, going over the fax of Mayor Rendell's appearances, I was delighted to see that that very evening he'd be in D.C., where I was. The city of Philadelphia was hosting an event at a big hotel on Capitol Hill. My friends Dana Clark and Heidi Quante and I got dressed up and headed there. It's a funny thing to put on high heels in an effort to get toxic ash cleaned up. We lingered at the entrance to the gigantic ballroom where the party was held, listening to the band and waiting for the right moment to make our move. Mayor Rendell, his wife, and some other local politicos were at the door greeting each person as they entered. As soon as the news cameras turned to Mayor Rendell, my friends and I went through the line. When I got to the mayor, I told him about the toxic ash left on the beach. I held his hand so tightly he couldn't get away, while Heidi pinned a bright red badge on his lapel that said: "Mayor Rendell, do the right thing, BRING THE ASH HOME." He brushed me aside, only to find the next young woman in line demand the same thing. And the next. Finally he said, "OK, I'll give fifty thousand dollars and not a penny more."

Fifty thousand dollars was only a fraction of the $600,000 estimated for the cleanup, but we nonetheless felt like celebrating. So we joined the party. Amazingly, no one kicked us out. We strolled around the ballroom, handing out flyers and explaining the situation to people who asked us about our big red badges. One gentleman from my hometown of Seattle was especially interested and asked us lots of questions. Shortly thereafter, the music stopped and the mayor took the stage, welcoming people and extolling the virtues of Philadelphia, the City of Brotherly Love. To our surprise, the guy from Seattle began yelling, "Bring the ash home!" We joined him and kept it up until the security guards made it known we had overstayed our welcome.

Through a series of complicated negotiations, a deal was finally reached to bring the ash back to the United States. On April 5, 2000, what was left of the ash was loaded onto a ship and removed from Gonaïves. Today there's a big billboard in its place that reads "Toxic Dumping in Haiti: Never Again."

No Away In Sight

After years of traveling around investigating international waste dumping and meeting the people whose communities had been dumped on, my conviction was unshakable. It is simply wrong for the world's richest countries to dump hazardous waste on the world's poorest ones. Period. I remember talking to a U.S. congressional representative who told me I should find a compromise position. Like what? It is OK to dump on adults, but not kids? Or on Asians, but not Africans? No way. If it is too hazardous for my child, it is too hazardous for any child, anywhere.

 Outraged by international waste trade scandals around the world, many countries have signed on to a United Nations convention called the Basel Convention on the Control of Transboundary Movements of Hazardous Wastes and Their Disposal. The Basel Convention was adopted on March 22, 1989, and went into force on May 5, 1992. In its first iteration, the convention regulated, rather than banned, waste exports from wealthy countries to poorer ones.[122] Around the world, human rights activists, environmentalists, and representatives of developing countries (i.e., the targets of waste traffickers) condemned the convention for "legalizing toxic waste." Fortunately, the treaty was updated with a provision *banning* waste exports from the worlds' richest countries (primarily OECD members) to less wealthy ones (non-OECD countries), effective January 1, 1998.[123] The United States is the only industrialized country in the world that hasn't yet ratified the Basel Convention.

While Basel is a tremendous victory, the battle is not yet over. Some countries and business associations continue to argue for exemptions from the ban for certain waste streams. An NGO watchdog group, the Basel Action Network, monitors the Basel Convention and publishes a list of entities working to undermine the ban. Whole countries are on the list: Australia, Canada, New Zealand, and the United States, and so are a number of trade associations: the International Council on Mining and Metals, the International Chamber of Commerce, and the United Nations Center for Trade and Development. To get involved and keep waste from being dumped on unsuspecting communities worldwide, visit the Basel Action Network at www.ban.org.

And Then There's Recycling

Recycling is amazing in its ability to stir people—some people are inspired by it, many proud of it, others bored, cynical, or even angered by it. I've gone through all those stages; in fact, I go through most of those stages on a daily basis.

Like many people, my earliest relationship with environmental causes was through recycling—starting in childhood. This was in the day prior to curbside recycling programs, so my mother had us kids collect our newspapers, bottles, and cans, pile them into the station wagon, and drive them up to the collection center at the local grocery store parking lot. I remember the heavy bundles and the rainbow paintings on the side of the storage sheds. I recall feeling good putting the bottles in the correct color-coded bins. I am not alone in having experienced that; around the world, many people recognize the good feeling that they get from recycling.

The feel-good aspect is at the heart of much of the debate about recycling. Is recycling a con that keeps us deluded into feeling like we're helping the planet while leaving industry free to keep churning out ever more badly designed toxic Stuff? Heather Rogers, author of a book about garbage called *Gone Tomorrow,* writes that "industry accepted recycling in lieu of more radical changes like bans on certain materials and individual processes, production controls, minimum standards for product durability, and higher standards for resource extraction." [124]

Or is recycling a good first step into broader awareness and activism on sustainability issues; a gateway experience to get people interested and then guide them along to taking more strategic and effective action? Neil Seldman, president of the Institute for Local Self-Reliance, who has chronicled recycling in the United States for three decades, says that recycling has the power to transform industry: "It may have to do with one of society's most mundane problems, garbage, or discarded materials, but its implications go to the heart of our industrial system." [125]

Actually, I believe it's both. Recycling can lull us into believing we have done our part while nothing, really, has changed. *And* recycling can play an important role in the transformation to a more sustainable and more just economy.

The Good

In 2007—the most recent year for which data is available—people in the United States generated 254 million tons of trash, of which 85 million tons—or about a third—was recycled.[126]

The environmental benefits are obvious. Recycling keeps materials in use, thus reducing the demand for extracting and producing new materials and avoiding—or more likely delaying—the point at which the materials become waste. Reducing harvesting, mining, and hauling resources, as well as the production of new Stuff, can reduce energy use and greenhouse gas emissions. The Environmental Protection Agency estimates that even our meager 33.4 percent recycling rate in the United States results in an annual benefit of 193 million metric tons of CO_2 reduction, which is equivalent to removing 35 million passenger vehicles from the road.[127]

And those CO_2 reductions are just the start. Recycling also creates more jobs—and better ones—than other waste management options. The Institute for Local Self-Reliance, a Washington, D.C., think tank specializing in waste and economic development, estimates that for every one hundred jobs created in recycling, just ten were lost in waste hauling.[128]

The Questionable

However, considering that it would be possible to make 100 percent of our Stuff so that it could be easily and safely reused, recycled, or composted, 33 percent is a pretty lame recycling rate. It's especially alarming when we look at the data for waste generation. Yes, recycling is increasing, but so is total waste produced on both a national and per-capita level.

Our goal should not be to *recycle more,* but to *waste less.* Focusing on the wrong end of the question can point our efforts in the wrong direction. For example, I heard about a recycling contest in which a number of U.S. colleges participated to see who could collect the most plastic bottles to recycle. At one school, kids went to Costco and bought bulk boxes of single-serving water bottles in order to win. The same nutty dynamic is happening anywhere people are measuring progress by an increase in recycling rather than a decrease in waste.

At a recycling conference I attended recently, I learned about Recycle-Bank, a program that weighs residents' recycling bins at the curb and awards people points for heavier bins. That means the neighbor who buys cases of single-serving bottled water gets points over the one who installed a filter and drinks tap water in reusable containers! But wait, there's more. Guess what you get for those points? More Stuff! Residents cash in those points for goods at partner retailers including Target, IKEA, Foot Locker, and Bed Bath & Beyond. Who invented these programs—Keep America Beautiful?

Programs like this give recycling a bad name, by encouraging more consumption and more waste. They allow producers to escape responsibility for their wasteful packaging and, perversely, subsidize the generation of disposable Stuff. And perhaps worse of all, programs like this claim to be making real change.

The Ugly

Despite its rainbow-bright image, recycling is often a dirty process. If Stuff contains toxic components, then recycling perpetuates them, exposing recycling workers and yet another round of consumers and community residents to potential health threats. Even if the material isn't toxic, large-scale municipal recycling requires trucks and factories that use a lot of energy and create more waste. Just because it's called recycling doesn't mean it's green. As currently practiced, recycling is largely controlled by huge waste hauling companies like Waste Management, Inc., which operates facilities for both recycling and wasting (and whose profit is far higher for the wasting part).

BIOPLASTICS: AN OXYMORON OR A SIGN OF HOPE?

Currently most plastics are made from petroleum and a host of chemicals, many toxic. We have to figure out how to meet our needs using materials that are renewable, safe, and ecologically sound. So what about bioplastics?

There are two generations of contemporary bioplastics (I am not counting some of the early plastics that were made from plant material, like cellophane, which was originally made from cellulose from wood pulp). The first generation was what I call the Total Scam Round of Biodegradable Plastics and the second generation is what I call the Jury's Still Out Round of Biodegradable Plastics.

Round One: By the late 1980s, garbage was on the alarmed American public's radar screen. In response, Mobil Chemical Company, producer of Hefty brand plastic garbage bags, mixed cornstarch with petroleum plastic and declared its bags "biodegradable." Mobil's spokespeople actually admitted this was just a PR stunt, not any kind of substantive claim regarding biodegradability.[129]

Environmental groups, scientists, and even some state governments were outraged by Mobil's absurd claim. Within a couple years, lawsuits filed by seven states, as well as an agreement with the Federal Trade Commission (FTC), forced Mobil to drop its "biodegradable" label.[130]

Round Two: Today, many companies make and use plastics that are produced 100 percent from plants—corn, potatoes, agricultural waste. These bioplastics are being used in food packaging, water bottles, and even computers, cell phones, and some car parts. Are these new bioplastics truly sustainable? Or do they just reinforce our disposability culture and infrastructure?

Unfortunately, right now the crops that make up today's bioplastics are mostly grown in huge centralized farms, with heavy inputs of pesticides and fossil fuels, using genetically modified organisms and poorly paid farmworkers. Some of them use food-grade crops that could be used, duh, for food, rather than the single-serving containers for which much bioplastic is utilized.

And even though they are technically compostable, that's only in large-scale composting operations that reach the desired conditions for them to degrade. As an experiment, I put a bioplastic cup and some cutlery in my backyard bin four years ago and none have even the slightest hole in them yet. Bioplastics often end up in the regular trash or mucking up recycling programs since they have very different properties from other plastic containers and have to be sorted out before recycling.

The jury is still out on whether bioplastics could be made in a truly sustainable way that supports a reduction in packaging and avoids single-use packaging completely; that supports small farmers and farmworkers; that adheres to the principles of green chemistry; and that avoids fossil fuel use. There's a great group called the Sustainable Biomaterials Collaborative that's working on this very issue.

Also, much of our waste collected for recycling is exported overseas, especially to Asia, where environmental and worker safety laws are weaker and less well enforced. I've tracked plastic waste, used car batteries, e-waste, and other toxic-containing components of our municipal waste to Bangladesh, India, China, Indonesia, and other places. I've snuck into facilities (in various disguises!) to get a firsthand look at what happens to our waste overseas. The awful conditions I witnessed are not what conscientious individuals in the United States have in mind when they diligently wash out their plastic bottles or return their used car batteries.

Another complaint about recycling is that it often isn't even recycling but is actually something called downcycling. True recycling achieves a circular closed loop production process (a bottle into a bottle into a bottle), while downcycling just makes Stuff into a lower-grade material and a secondary product (a plastic jug into carpet backing). At best, downcycling reduces the need for virgin ingredients for the secondary item, but it never reduces the resources needed to make a replacement for the original item. In fact, by being able to advertise a product as "recyclable," the demand for that first item may actually rise, which, ironically, is more of a resource drain.

The classic example of this is plastic—where the industry cleverly appropriated the popular "chasing arrows" recycling logo and added to it the numbers 1 to 9 to indicate the grade of plastic. As Heather Rogers points out in *Gone Tomorrow,* this "misleadingly telegraphed to the voting consumer that these containers were recyclable and perhaps had even been manufactured with reprocessed materials." [131] For the record, it is extremely difficult to actually recycle plastics; almost always, they are downcycled. If you're curious, ask your local recycler what it is doing with those bottles it picks up—are they being made into new bottles or shipped off to China, where they're turned into some secondary product?

Dr. Paul Connett says that "recycling is an admission of defeat; an admission that we were not clever enough or didn't care enough to design it to be more durable, to repair it, or to avoid using it in the first place." [132] It's not that recycling itself is bad, but our overemphasis on it is a problem. There is a reason recycling comes third in the eco mantra "Reduce, reuse, recycle." Recycling is the *last* thing we should do with our Stuff, not the first. As a last resort, recycling is better than landfill or incineration *for sure.* And hats off to those dedicated people who have built and voraciously defended the recycling infrastructure that does exist in this country. Let's use that infrastructure when our backs are against the wall, when we're out of better options and have to chuck something.

Unfortunately though, recycling is most often not seen as a last resort, but as the primary environmental duty of an engaged citizen. It's the number-one way people demonstrate their environmental commitment. In fact, more people recycle than vote regularly in this country! I can't tell you how many times, when I get asked what I do for a living, people respond with a proud, "Oh, I recycle!" And while it's good that they do, there must be greater awareness of the limitations of recycling, as well as widespread understanding of the other things that must happen to solve our problems with waste.

It is this aspect of recycling that most irritates those with a broader systemic understanding of the problems and broader vision for change. Recycling is easy: it can be done without ever raising questions about the inherent problems with current systems of production and consumption, about the long-term sustainability of a growth-obsessed economic model or about equitable distribution of the planet's resources. Clearly, sorting used bottles and papers into a blue bin is not going to fundamentally change, or even challenge, the massive negative impacts of the way we extract, make, distribute, use, and share or don't share all the Stuff in our lives. In fact, because it makes us feel good, because it makes us feel like we're doing something useful, the worry is that recycling may actually bolster those very patterns of production and consumption that are trashing the planet and distract us from working for deeper change.

Recycling Done Right

But does all this mean we should abandon recycling? No way!

I think the way to go is to look at our waste and figure out who is responsible for what.

It seems to me that green waste—yard trimmings, leaves, and food scraps—fall into the category of our personal individual responsibility. We ate the food and planted the tree, or at least enjoyed its shade. It's not too much to expect us, then, to manage this green waste responsibly, just as we manage other aspects of our homes. This could mean composting it ourselves or lobbying to institute a municipal composting program, paid for by taxpayer dollars.

Then there's all the other Stuff in the garbage: the Stuff that is the product of intentional choices in design and manufacturing, choices that were outside our reach of immediate influence.

This Stuff falls under someone's responsibility—the people who designed, produced, and profited from it. If you, Mr. Ketchup Producer, switch from a recyclable glass bottle to a squeezable one made of multiple plastic resins bonded together that can never be separated for recycling, you need to figure out how to deal with that at the end of its life. If you, Ms. Printer Producer, decide to make toner cartridges that are impossible to open and refill and so must be thrown out while still perfectly functional, then you deal with it. That is your choice, not mine.

The official term for the "you made it, you deal with it" approach—of which I am a huge fan—is "extended producer responsibility" (EPR), which holds the producers of goods responsible for their entire lifecycle. This encourages producers to make improvements upstream, in the design and production phases, to avoid getting stuck with a pile of poorly designed, toxic-containing, nonupgradable junk. As I've previously mentioned, there are already strong government-mandated models of EPR in place, notably Germany's Green Dot system and the European Union's WEEE (waste electrical and electronic equipment) directive, that illustrate how entirely feasible this approach is.

Zero Waste

True recycling and EPR are both elements of the broader Zero Waste plan. Zero Waste includes, but goes well beyond, recycling. Zero Waste advocates look at the broader system in which waste is created, from extraction to production all the way through consumption and disposal. In this way, Zero Waste is a philosophy, a strategy, and a set of practical tools.

The cool thing about Zero Waste is that it breaks free from the self-defeating "what can we do with all this waste?" paradigm. Zero Waste challenges the very acceptability and inevitability of waste. It seeks to eliminate waste, not manage it. That's why Zero Waste advocates can't stand the term "waste management." Their efforts don't focus on better waste management, but on moving closer to zero waste. Unrealistic? Maybe so, but it's the right goal to have. Just like factories have a zero defects goal and airlines have a zero accident goal. They aren't there yet, but they are really clear about where they are heading. Can you imagine United Airlines saying "Zero accidents . . . or darn close?" No way; I'm aiming for zero.

For a long time, when I would test the phrase "zero waste" in random conversations (with my dentist, the guy at the bus stop, the woman next to me on the plane), I'd get blank stares. For most people, "zero" and "waste" just didn't fit together. It didn't compute. We've all been taught that waste is inevitable, the price of progress. I still get odd stares on a regular basis, but I am happy to report that the term is catching on. *Newsweek* magazine's 2008 Earth Day issue included Zero Waste on its list of "10 fixes for the planet." The *Newsweek* article said, in essence, that recycling paper, plastic, and aluminum is a start, but oh so twentieth century.[133] Jeffrey Hollender, executive chairperson of Seventh Generation, which makes nontoxic, recycled paper towels and other products, says, "Zero Waste is the mother of environmental no-brainers."[134]

That the concept is seeping into common vocabulary and the media is nice, but I'm really more interested in it seeping into practice. That too is happening. There is no one place that has it down pat, but there are lots of places that have, as we say, pieces of Zero. These pieces look different in different places because Zero Waste isn't a cookie-cutter model, but a set of approaches designed to meet the needs of each place it is implemented.

The international organization GAIA (Global Alliance for Incinerator Alternatives) lays out nine core components of Zero Waste programs, which can be tailored and added to for different settings, from schools to neighborhoods to whole states or countries:

1. Reducing consumption and discards
2. Reusing discards
3. Extended producer responsibility
4. Comprehensive recycling
5. Comprehensive composting or biodigestion of organic materials
6. Citizen participation
7. A ban on waste incineration
8. Improving product design upstream to eliminate toxics and instead design for durability and repair
9. Effective policies, regulations, incentives, and financing structures to support these systems [135]

That covers it: you've got the upstream waste prevention and the corporate responsibility, the downstream waste reuse, composting and recycling, and the active, informed public and responsive government to create and implement the policies needed to make it all work. To get to Zero, we need this whole-systems approach.

GAIA notes that "a Zero Waste approach is one of the fastest, cheapest and most effective strategies to protect the climate." In its 2008 report *Stop Trashing the Climate*, GAIA explains that significantly decreasing the waste disposed of in landfills and incinerators will reduce greenhouse gas emissions the equivalent of closing one-fifth of U.S. coal-fired power plants.[136]

Already there are many cities around the world that have adopted Zero Waste policies, goals, or actual plans: Buenos Aires and Rosario, Argentina; Canberra, Australia; Oakland, Santa Cruz, and San Francisco, California; Kovalam, India. In New Zealand, 71 percent of local authorities have passed a resolution to head for zero waste, and the government runs a national benchmarking system to track their progress called "Milestones on the Zero Waste Journey."[137]

In the United States, San Francisco was the first city to adopt a serious Zero Waste plan and to move aggressively toward zero. San Francisco committed to diverting 75 percent of its municipal waste from disposal by 2010 and reaching zero by 2020. San Francisco mayor Gavin Newsom acknowledged the roles of "producer and consumer responsibility to prevent waste and take full advantage of our nation-leading recycling and composting programs." [138] San Francisco currently has the strongest recycling and composting laws in the United States for households and businesses and, is now diverting 72 percent of its waste—the highest rate in the country. [139]

On the other side of the world, the coastal town of Kovalam in South India is also aggressively working toward Zero Waste. Kovalam transformed in one generation from a quiet fishing town to a crowded holiday destination. The explosion of Western tourists led to an explosion of waste, or "dumping tourist syndrome" as my friend there, Shibu Nair, calls it. The beach, the roads, and makeshift dumps in the area overflow with empty bottles for shampoo, sunscreen, lotion, and increasingly, for water. Concerned, the local tourism department proposed building an incinerator in 2000. Local activists organized an international e-mail campaign, in which potential visitors from all over the world wrote to the tourism department, saying they wouldn't come to a beach anywhere near an incinerator. The tourism ministry turned to a local environmental group, and Zero Waste Kovalam was born. [140]

The Zero Waste Kovalam activists looked for opportunities to design waste out of the system. They set up stations for people to refill water bottles with boiled and filtered water, rather than buy new bottles. They set up worker cooperatives that trained local unemployed people to make reusable cloth bags from leftovers from the tailor shops, thus eliminating the formerly ubiquitous plastic bags.

The founder of Zero Waste Kovalam, Jayakumar Chelaton, is proud of how the issue of waste connected to bigger issues like governance, environmental health, and economic justice in Kovalam. The Zero Waste philosophy for him "is about relationships. It is about people and communities and how we want to live together." [141]

And that's exactly why I became so passionate about waste some twenty years ago. I understood waste was connected to everything else in our world. Unraveling the story of waste is what led me to the Story of Stuff.

EPILOGUE
WRITING THE NEW STORY

When (if) people stop to think about it, we all worry at some level about the sacrifices that will be necessary to rewrite the Story of Stuff. We worry about big things like jobs lost in Stuff-producing factories, and we worry about little things like the lack of convenience when disposable bottles and cans disappear. Some worry that switching away from the growth-driven model of economic progress and redirecting our priorities away from amassing ever more Stuff will lower the quality of life, perhaps lead us back to living like cavemen.

I want to start by challenging the fear of sacrifice and describing one version of what life can look like when we focus on the quality of our life, rather than the quantity of our Stuff. This is not some pie-in-the-sky scenario of how the eco-perfect person would live if she spent less time on the work-watch-spend treadmill; this is my actual lifestyle, right now.

I've mentioned that I live in a tight community in downtown Berkeley, which can be considered a type of co-housing. It isn't a hippie commune; we don't swap partners; our children are perfectly clear on who their parents are. It's really just a bunch of good friends who chose to live near one another—really near, like next door. We chose to relocate from various parts of the country to live in community with each other. We find life easier and more rewarding because we focus more on building community than on buying Stuff. We share a big yard; we often eat meals together; but each family has its own self-contained home into which we can retreat when we want to be alone. Some of us even watch TV, but usually together, so even that is a community activity.

We share Stuff all the time. As the older children in the community outgrow their toys, books, and clothes, the younger children inherit them. Once, after my daughter begged me to let her try skiing, I sent an e-mail out to my community members asking for advice on where I should take her and what I'd need for the trip (not being a skier myself). When I got home from work the next day, there were three bags full of children's ski equipment and clothes waiting for me on the front step. And that's not unusual. Before buying some specialty tool that I need, I check to see if anyone else in the community already has one.

We share advice. We coach each other when making difficult decisions in our personal or professional lives. I have had the best course in parenting one could ever possibly buy, in that I've had five sets of parents to watch as role models—this, of course, has been free. We swap services. Someone who can bake makes almost all the birthday cakes while another who is handy with a wrench helps us all with plumbing emergencies. We organize carpools. We trade off watching the kids or taking them on outings to provide one another with downtime. We host parties together, sharing the costs of setup and all pitching in to clean things up the next day.

When I got really sick (in the last weeks before the manuscript for this book was due) with a 102 degree fever, one person drove me to the doctor while another one stepped in to watch my kid and a third brought me flowers. And you can be sure that I'll return those favors the next time someone else in the community gets sick. Not out of obligation, but out of the pleasure of sharing.

Because we share and borrow many of the things we need, we are able to consume less Stuff. Because we provide one another with services like baby-sitting, repairing, and listening, we pay less for services than others do. We turn to each other first, before relying on the commercial marketplace. My point is we're living the same lifestyle as someone who's paying for those goods and services. In all these ways, we're not sacrificing; we're sharing.

And while there are material benefits to our sharing (saving money and creating less waste, because we consume less), the real benefit goes far beyond these. Rather than keep strict tabs on how many hours or how much Stuff we give one another, we cultivate a culture of reciprocity. In his book *Bowling Alone*, Robert Putnam explains that "networks of community engagement foster sturdy norms of reciprocity: I'll do this for you now, in the expectation that you (or perhaps someone else) will return the favor." [1]

Putnam talks about two kinds of reciprocity: specific, in which you actually measure and negotiate individual trades ("I'll pick up both kids from school on Monday, you do it on Tuesday") and the more valuable norm of generalized reciprocity ("I'll do this for you without expecting anything specific back, confident that someone else will do something for me down the road"). A society based on generalized reciprocity is more efficient than one that negotiates every interaction. It provides greater security and is more fun. "Trustworthiness lubricates social life," Putnam says.[2] We've got one another's backs. I know that I always have someone to call if I get a flat tire, if I need emergency childcare, if I'm hungry and too tired to cook. Sometimes I visualize this social fabric as an actual fabric that surrounds me and would catch me if I fall, as it has done metaphorically over the years.

Individual Response

So that's my community-rich lifestyle. Without feeling any deprivation, we save money and resources and have more fun. However, let me be crystal clear: our community is not perfect and even if it were, living with a more community-focused life alone will not solve the world's pressing environmental and social problems. If we want all six and a half billion humans on this earth plus future generations to have enough food in their bellies, fresh water to drink, and medicine when they're sick, individual lifestyle shifts like mine won't cut it. In fact, here in the United States we live inside a system so thoroughly based on fossil fuels, carbon emissions, toxic chemicals and wasted resources that no matter how much we scale back our consumption, we still can't achieve a truly sustainable lifestyle—one within the earth's capacity. That's what Colin Beavan, aka No Impact Man, found when he spent one year with his family in Manhattan living as low-impact as possible: no trash, no elevators, no subway, no products in packaging, no plastics, no air-conditioning, no TV, and no food from farther than 250 miles away. While he achieved the lowest impact of anyone I've heard of in an industrialized country, Beavan learned that in a metropolitan U.S. city today, it's just impossible to achieve a sustainable life. The only way to do it would be to disengage completely from modern life and, as Beavan says, "it shouldn't be that way."[3]

The shift we need to make in order to live within the planet's limits is big. It requires our government, banks, labor unions, media, cultural trendsetters, schools, and corporations and business owners to get on board. Creating change this big requires that we move way beyond the simple lifestyle changes promoted as solutions through an endless parade of lists and books on "ten easy things that you can do to save the planet." Michael Maniates, a professor of political science and environmental science at Allegheny College and an expert on consumption issues, says that the fundamental flaw of the "ten easy things" approach is that it implies: (1) our greatest source of power as individuals is in our role as consumers; (2) we humans, by nature, aren't interested in or willing to do anything that isn't easy; and (3) change will only happen if we convince every single person on the planet to join us. Let's get real. It's simply not possible to get 100 percent agreement from nearly 7 billion people on any issue, and our ecological systems are on such overload, that we simply don't have time to try. Imagine if we had had to wait for 100 percent consensus before getting women the vote or ending slavery: we'd still be waiting.

Not to mention that individual responsibility to save the planet can be a big drag. Let's face it: you will become wildly unpopular if you become the disposable cup police and the PVC alarmist and the Debbie Downer about the toxins in cosmetics. People will stop inviting you to their parties if you insist on resorting their recycling for them (trust me, they will). Keeping track of all the corporations you want to avoid because of their poor labor policies or their environmental impacts will cause you no end of anxiety and stress. There's too much wrong with the system for even the most obsessive-compulsive among us to get every action and every choice just right. And because that scenario is so overwhelming, the individual-responsibility model of change risks causing people to freak out, throw their hands up in despair, and sink back into overconsumptive, wasteful lifestyles. People are busy enough already: rather than offering an over-whelming range of green lifestyle choices, we need meaningful opportunities to make big choices (for example on policy) that make big differences.

In a 2007 op-ed piece in the *Washington Post,* Maniates lamented, "Never has so little been asked of so many at such a critical moment. The hard facts are these: If we sum up the easy, cost-effective eco-efficiency measures we should all embrace, the best we get is a slowing of the growth of environmental damage . . . Obsessing over recycling and installing a few special lightbulbs won't cut it. We need to be looking at fundamental change in our energy, transportation and agricultural systems rather than technological tweaking on the margins, and this means changes and costs that our current and would-be leaders seem afraid to discuss . . . To stop at 'easy' is to say that the best we can do is accept an uninspired politics of guilt around a parade of uncoordinated individual action. What of the power and exhilaration that comes from working with others toward bold possibilities for the future?"[4]

No doubt about it: humanity needs to undertake the much bigger and harder task of changing the way the system works. That way everyone, even those individuals too busy or too tired or too clueless to care, can still end up making low-impact choices—because that's the new default option. With a solution of proper scope, the influence we have as consumers only gets asserted *after* the system has been fundamentally changed to serve sustainability and fairness—so there are entirely different choices about how to spend our money. First and foremost, the influence we have as individuals comes from our role as informed, engaged citizens: citizens who participate actively in communities and the broader political arena. And in that arena, there are an almost infinite number of policies, laws, systems, and innovations we can work toward that really would make a difference.

Many people have written into the Story of Stuff Project saying they want to make change but don't know what to do since they are only one person. But here's the thing: I'm only one person too; we're each just one person. By joining together, we can accomplish goals well beyond our reach as individuals. That's why hooking up with an organization, a campaign, or a group of like-minded friends and neighbors working toward a shared goal is an essential first step.

In terms of focusing our political engagement, one of the great things about such an all-pervasive system-level problem is that there are so many places to intervene. To figure out where to plug in, I recommend that you take an inventory of your interests, passions, and skills and then look out in the world and see which organizations are a good match. If toxics in consumer products worry you, join or form a national campaign for chemical policy reform like the Safer States coalition in the Unites States. If healthy food systems are your passion, you might get involved with community-supported agriculture (CSA). My daughter's school is a drop off site for a local organic farm's CSA. Would that work where you live? If you're sick of hearing your friends in Europe talk about their month-long vacations and leisure time, get involved in a national campaign for a shorter workweek and mandatory vacation law. A great place to find organizations in your region or interest area is a huge online database called WiserEarth, created by the sustainable business guru Paul Hawken. WiserEarth includes about a million organizations working for environmental and social justice and can be searched by topic and geographic region, so it's easy to find like-minded people with whom to collaborate. There's so much work to be done in overhauling our current systems that it doesn't really matter which issue you choose; what matters is that the work is done towards the broader goal of a sustainable and just world for everyone.

Paradigm Shifts

Drawing from conversations with dozens of colleagues and experts in economics, natural resources, industrial production, cultural issues, corporate accountability, and community organizing, I've compiled a list of four major shifts that would lay the groundwork for creating an ecologically compatible life on earth—life with greater happiness, greater equity and, for many of us, less polluting, wasteful, cluttering Stuff.

1. Redefine Progress

We pay attention to what we measure. Establishing a system of measurement helps us clarify our goals and mark our progress toward them. Currently, the main measure of how well a country is doing is the gross domestic product (GDP). As I've discussed, GDP doesn't distinguish between economic activities that make life better (like an investment in public transportation) and those that make it worse (like building a big new belching incinerator). And it fully ignores activities that make life sweeter but that don't involve money transactions, like planting a vegetable garden or helping a neighbor. We need a new metric that matches the new paradigm, measuring the things that actually promote well-being: the health of the people and environment, happiness, kindness, equity, positive social relations, education, clean energy, civic engagement. These, not economic metrics alone, are a measure of how well we're doing.

Alternatives to the GDP include the Index of Sustainable Economic Welfare, developed in the late 1980s, which evolved into the Genuine Progress Indicator (GPI). This measure evaluates a number of factors beyond traditional economic activity, including pollution, resource depletion, amount of leisure time, and income distribution, although some have critiqued it for operating from within the same fundamental pro-growth paradigm as the GDP.[5] The United Nations' Human Development Index also looks at broader development goals, beyond economic growth. Then there's the previously mentioned Happy Planet Index, combining environmental impact with human well-being to measure the environmental efficiency with which, country by country, people live long and happy lives.

How do we actually promote adoption of a different metric as an official macroeconomic welfare indicator at the international, national, and local levels? John Talberth, a senior economist at the Center for Sustainable Economy who worked on the GPI, says that community-based sustainability planning processes provide fertile ground: community leaders often need help defining key environmental, economic, and social objectives and measuring progress toward those objectives.[6] Many organizations, including the Center for Sustainable Economy and Earth Economics, track public planning processes and legislation that promotes sustainability. To find out more, visit www.sustainable-economy.org and www.eartheconomics.org.

Of course, we're not measuring for measurement's sake. The new indica-

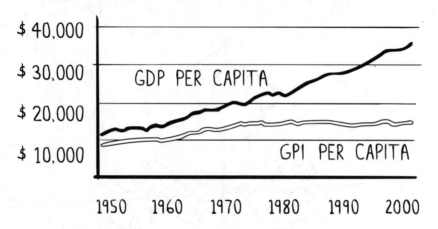

Source: Redefining Progress, 2007.

tors must inform and evaluate a comprehensive set of goals, policies, and systems that prioritize the well-being of people and the planet.

2. Do Away with War

In 2008 governments around the world spent a record amount of money on upgrading armed forces—and that amount continues to increase. They spent $1.46 trillion in 2008, which is 4 percent more than in 2007 and 45 percent more than a decade ago. The United States continues to be the largest arms spender, followed by China.[7] The nonprofit National Priorities Project (NPP), which maintains an ongoing tally of the costs of war, calculates that as of July 2009, U.S. spending since 2001 on the wars in Iraq and Afghanistan has topped $915 billion.[8]

In our work for clean renewable energy and carbon reduction, public transportation, nontoxic alternatives in industrial production, cleanup of polluted sites—as well as health care for all, excellent public schools, and just about any social good—how often do we hear that our suggestions are nice but are too expensive? That there just isn't the money to pay for the changes we seek? It is infuriating to hear this while we're hemorrhaging billions for needless wars that destroy lives and communities and devastate the environment. And don't forget, many of our wars are fought primarily to maintain access to oil, a substance from which we absolutely need to be weaning ourselves! Imagine how we could have built the electric grid that

would enable decentralized renewable energy generation, or the high-speed train network which would replace millions of individual cars—not to mention how many lives we could have saved—had we invested the war money in real solutions instead. As mentioned earlier, the top ranking on the Happy Planet Index is Costa Rica, which abolished its military in 1949 and redirected those funds to social goals.[9]

In my home state of California, we have a severe financial crisis. Our news is filled with stories about additional teachers being laid off, libraries and state parks being closed, and cuts in health care for poor children. The NPP calculates that taxpayers in California have paid about $115 billion for the wars in Iraq and Afghanistan since 2001.[10] For the same amount of money, we could have had:

47,712,271 people with health care for one year, or
206,545,462 homes with renewable electricity for one year, or
346,992 affordable housing units, or
1,664,958 elementary school teachers for one year, or
2,070,973 public safety officers for one year, or
1,464,132 port container inspectors for one year.[11]

Enough of letting our leaders cut vital public services or deny funding for transitioning our economy toward sustainability, claiming there's no money. There is money, plenty of it, being wasted on wars around the world. It's our right and responsibility as citizens to make sure that our government's spending is consistent with our values. Funding wars while cutting schools and health clinics and other vital social needs doesn't work for me and I hope it doesn't work for you.

3. Internalize Externalities

As you've seen throughout this book, many costs of making, transporting, and disposing of all the Stuff in our lives are basically ignored by businesses, which set artificially low prices to attract consumers. Yet those "externalized costs" are piling up—stress, disease, and other public health crises, environmental impacts, social erosion, and damage to future generations—while none of these are reflected in the price tags on Stuff. The *New York Times* recently ran a front page story about indigenous communities around the world that are threatened with actual extinction because of climate-related changes in the natural systems on which their survival depends. The Kamayurá tribe in the Amazon depends on fish for survival, but as water warms and disappears, fish populations have collapsed. Dr. Thomas Thornton of the Environmental Change Institute at the University of Oxford was quoted as saying, "They didn't cause the problem, and their lifestyle is being threatened by pollution from industrial nations." [12] The extinction of whole cultures is among the most serious hidden costs of polluting industries I can imagine.

Many economists still argue that the miraculous hand of the free market will adjust prices and influence supply and demand such that everything will stay in some "optimal" balance. But optimal for whom? The failure to account for externalized costs encourages excessive consumption and unfairly leaves others to pay the real cost of our systems of production and consumption, while business owners earn illegitimately high profits since they aren't paying the full expenses of their operations. That's a market failure if ever there was one.

Paul Hawken notes, "Instead of markets giving proper information, everything else is giving us proper information: our air sheds and watersheds, our soil and riparian systems, our bodies and health, our society, inner cities and rural counties, the breakdown of stability worldwide and the outbreak of conflicts based on environmental shortages. All these are providing the information that our prices should be giving us but don't." [13]

Calculating costs for social and ecological losses ranges from straightforward to impossible. How do you adjust the price of a laptop to reflect the cancer and neurological damage in workers, the loss of habitat for gorillas in the Congo's coltan reserves, and the contamination of soil and ground-water after the computer gets trashed? Prices go way up, that's for sure.

The price of gasoline, for example, was about three dollars per gallon in the United States in 2007, which reportedly reflected the costs of discovering the oil, pumping it to the surface, refining it into gasoline, and delivering the gas to service stations. It did not include the cost of providing tax subsidies to the oil companies, building public infrastructure to facilitate their operations, health care in communities where the oil is drilled or processed, or, of course, the significant costs associated with climate change. It also excluded the enormous costs of maintaining a military presence in the oil-producing regions of the Middle East to secure our access to that oil. A study by the International Center for Technology Assessment found these costs would total nearly twelve dollars per gallon of gasoline—bringing the total to fifteen dollars per gallon.[14]

Economist Dave Batker adds that while internalizing externalities is necessary, it's not the whole solution: "Rather than figure out the economic cost of poisoning a child with mercury and adding that to the bill for your coal-fired electricity, the companies should have to stop emitting mercury, period. Let's ban these toxic products and processes outright. For those costs that don't threaten to push us across a critical ecological threshold or damage people's rights to life and health, internalizing those costs into the price of the product corrects for market failures."[15]

4. Value Time over Stuff

There's ample evidence now that working too much leads to greater stress, social isolation, overconsumption, health problems, and even climate change. Reducing work hours is good for people and the planet. As economist Juliet Schor explains, "The key to achieving a more sustainable path for consumption is to translate productivity growth into shorter hours of work instead of more income."[16] A study by the Center for a New American Dream found between one-fifth and one-third of people want to trade income for time.[17] They're exhausted by the work-watch-spend treadmill and realize that the benefits of reduced stress and more time with friends and family will actually contribute more to their happiness than a marginal pay increase with which to buy more Stuff.

But what will happen if we all work less and shop less? Won't the economy collapse, since it's currently disproportionately driven by consumer spending? Yes, if it happened overnight. But don't worry; that's not likely. Working less and buying less need to be phased in gradually and simultaneously to make the transition as smooth as possible. We can do it. We've got massive productivity in this country. The key is that the consumer demand side and the labor market side both shift down in tandem. As Schor says, "Depending on how the policy aspects of the transition are managed, it can expand employment opportunities by reducing the average number of hours worked in every job."[18] We need gradual, structural changes to enable people to reduce their work without being penalized. Some policies that would advance this are a mandatory vacation law, career options that allow for career advancement without full-time work, and the development of job-sharing programs. Many European countries have such structures. In the Netherlands and Denmark, for example, up to 40 percent of the population works part-time, protected by nondiscrimination laws.[19] Another way to decrease work hours is to increase vacation. Only 14 percent of Americans get a vacation of two weeks or longer, and unlike 127 other countries, we don't currently have a law requiring paid vacation.[20]

Perhaps the single most effective tool for facilitating a reduction in working hours is the separation of benefits (especially health care) from full-time work. Currently, many people who would like to work less can't, for fear of losing health benefits. The best way to accomplish this would be by implementing a national universal health care program that ensures quality health care to everyone who needs it, regardless of their employment status. Pending that, a short-term transitional proposal is to have employers pay for health care costs by the hour, or by a percentage of salary, rather than by the number of employees. When organizations pay for health care by employee, they have built-in incentive to hire one overworked employee rather than two healthier part-time workers. The interesting thing is that, absent a systems view, most environmentalists wouldn't identify health care reform as a top priority. Yet it turns out that obtaining a national health care program would be a significant step toward reducing our overall environmental impact—because, again, if people don't need to work full-time to get health benefits, many will choose to work fewer hours and earn less and will therefore buy and trash less Stuff and have more time to engage in community and civic activities that help the planet.

New World Vision

We know what the world of today looks like: climate chaos, toxic chemicals in every body on the planet including newborn babies, growing social inequity, disappearing forests and fresh water, increasing social isolation and decreasing happiness. So how might the future look after we make the necessary shifts? Here's one scenario, inspired by my dreams and informed by the projections of various scientists and economists.[21] Of course our society's new vision will be collaboratively developed and may diverge from this one, but the important thing is to keep in clear sight a vision of what we are fighting *for,* because the things we are fighting *against* are all around us:

It's 2030. There is the sound of laughter and birdsong here in the city. Children everywhere are playing in the streets, just out of the line of vision of grown-ups hanging laundry to dry in the breeze and tending to the vegetable gardens planted in former lots and lawns. The high-density housing is built with community life in mind: bicycle paths, shaded gathering places, fruit and vegetable stands, and cozy cafés fill the streets.

The air is clean nowadays, for two main reasons. The first is that personal cars have almost totally disappeared, while the punctual public transit system now serves every corner of the city, powered on clean, renewable energy. The second is that polluting industries have become extinct, driven out by the one-two-three punch of high taxes on carbon, waste, and pollutants; the high price of virgin raw materials; and government incentives for clean industries.

Because of the strict ban of toxic chemicals, on top of the costs of repairing their past damages to public health and the environment, industries can no longer afford to use hazardous chemicals in products. Green chemists and biomimicry experts have stepped in to provide nontoxic alternatives for everything from parabens and phthalates in cosmetics to fire retardants in furniture to PVC in toys. Inefficient and toxic buildings have been retrofitted and people are no longer allergic to their homes and offices.

We are well under way with the conversion to an ecologically compatible economy. Governments around the world have collaboratively instated a team of biologists, climatologists, and ecologists to work out what levels of consumption and emission are sustainable within the earth's limits and in keeping with social equity. We don't use natural resources faster than they can be replenished by the planet; we distribute those precious resources fairly and sensibly; and we are near our target of zero waste. There is no such thing as extraneous packaging now, eliminating a gigantic portion of the former waste stream. We generate organic wastes at levels at which they can be composted, returning their valuable nutrients to the soil.

Designers, engineers, and technology types constantly invent and improve on ways to do more with the resources we already have. Businesspeople cooperate to maximize resource efficiency and minimize waste, and "industrial ecology," in which the waste of one factory is used as the raw materials of the next, is widespread. An increasing number of businesses are worker owned, and in those that aren't, union membership is welcome.

We have a different relationship with Stuff. Because externalized costs have been internalized at every stage from extraction of natural resource to product distribution, Stuff is much more expensive. We have realized that much of the Stuff we used to buy just wasn't worth it—neither in terms of its impact on the planet or the amount of our own time we devoted to paying for and maintaining it. There are other things we'd rather devote our time to now. Most communities have vibrant local economies with a healthy margin of goods, especially food, textiles, and energy, sourced from local production. Disposable goods are extremely expensive and rare. Products are built to last, and many of them are leased with service agreements, rather than purchased by consumers. At the end of their useful lives, products are taken back by the companies that made them and repaired or disassembled for parts.

This means that maintenance, repair, and disassembly—as opposed to production—are much more important sources of employment than before. So are science and technology. Without as much economic growth as before, we can't maintain full employment—but nobody's complaining. Instead, people work part-time with full benefits, often with an ownership stake in the business.

Resource use is taxed, allowing for basic-needs-based levels of use with minimal or no taxes, but placing higher taxes on higher-volume use. This raises the price of those resources and encourages people and industries to use them efficiently and sparingly. To tackle the staggering inequality of wealth we inherited from the old growth-based system, we are gradually redistributing resources by setting upper limits for income inequality. Hard work and extra contributions are still rewarded, but not as extremely as before. (In the U.S. corporate sector back in the early twenty-first century, executive pay was as much as five hundred times the lowest salary.) We have lowered the range to a factor of fifty, so if the lowest salary in a company is $20,000, the highest is $1,000,000. Plans are in place to close the gap even further in the coming years. One measure of progress widely used is the Happy Planet Index, which reflects how efficiently we use natural resources to achieve well-being.

The whole pace of life is more relaxed: "slow and low(-impact)" is the new mantra. Incomes are lower but we are rich in something that many of us had never experienced before: time. There is far more leisure time. Levels of obesity, depression, suicide, and cancer are down. Library and civic memberships are up, as are basketball, soccer, and bocce clubs. While people spend less time working and watching TV alone, they spend far more time engaged in civic activities. People are voting in record numbers, as well as volunteering and campaigning for the things they care about. Citizens, not big corporations, have the greatest influence. Now that government is accessible, inviting, and responsive, there are nearly infinite possibilities for ways to make life even better. A sense of optimism and hope prevails.

Change And Hope

System change is inevitable. The question is not *if* we will change, but *how*. Will we be forward thinking enough to change by design, or will we wait until we're forced to change by default? If we change by design, it's going to require hard work, some hardship, but more gain. If we dig our heels in and maintain, as George Bush the First said (or Dick Cheney, it's attributed to both), that the American way of life is not negotiable, and we refuse to budge on our resource use as though we had a second planet on reserve, then there's going to be a lot more violence, suffering, and injustice than need be. Even in that scenario, change is still going to happen. Faced with serious, life-threatening resource scarcity as the planet runs out of things like clean water, productive farmland, and fossil fuels, the people around the world with the least access—those with no water, no fish, no shelter—will eventually not tolerate the vast inequity in resource use. When this happens, we will hit not only physical limits of the planet's capacity, but also social and moral limits. At that point, change will be forced upon us.

People ask me all the time how I remain hopeful, given the seeming intractability of the dysfunctional take-make-waste system and the grimness of statistics regarding climate chaos and the loss of natural resources. The thing is, I really believe there's hope for us yet. My unshakable optimism stems both from the knowledge that alternatives systems exist and the belief that if enough people want change, together we can chart a very different path. Four-fifths of Americans favor mandatory controls on greenhouse gases; nine-tenths of us want higher fuel efficiency standards; and three-quarters want cleaner energy, even if they have to pay a little more for it.[22] More Americans are relearning how to live within their means and save for the future—since 2008 the personal savings rate has been climbing for the first time in nearly a decade.[23] More of our voting-age population turned out for the federal elections of 2008 (nearly 57 percent) than in any year since 1968.[24] These are good signs. Eco-visionary Paul Hawken recently said, "If you look at the science about what is happening on earth and aren't pessimistic, you don't understand data. But if you meet the people who are working to restore this earth and the lives of the poor, and you aren't optimistic, you haven't got a pulse."[25]

I constantly meet with people from all over the planet who are working to restore the biosphere and promote social equity. Their very existence, alongside the practical solutions they are nurturing and implementing, is a powerful antidote to despair and hopelessness. They reinforce my confidence in our ability to realize an alternative world. How can we give up when we know that it is totally feasible to meet our energy needs through conservation and renewables, to make our Stuff without toxics and waste, and to replace the culture of consumerism with one of community and civic engagement?

In mid-2009, I had to travel to England for a family gathering. While there, a friend took me on a weeklong tour of rural Wales. Though my impressions were formed in just seven days, we covered much of the small country in that time, and I was impressed by what I saw, or actually, what I didn't see. And yes, Wales is a small and relatively homogenous country. But that doesn't mean we can't learn from its successes, in the same way we can learn from all the Latin American and Asian countries that rank higher than us on the Happy Planet Index.

There were two things in particular I was shocked not to see in Wales. First, I saw almost no advertising, and not a single billboard. We went from town to town without seeing any blaring signs telling us to buy something. I felt like I'd gone back in time one hundred years. Being free of the constant assault of ads was such a relief. It was like experiencing silence again after growing accustomed to the jackhammers of a never-ending construction project. All week I saw only one mall and two big-box stores along the highway; the stores in the towns were mostly small and locally owned, selling a mix of imported and local products, thus keeping more money in the community. It made me realize yet again how commercially saturated our landscapes are in the United States and I wondered how that relentless assault affects us all on a daily basis.

Second, I noticed the absence of something even more important: homeless people. I didn't see a single homeless person, shanty, or slum. No trashed neighborhoods. No piles of garbage in the neighborhoods deemed unimportant by municipal officials. The homes we passed were modest compared to U.S. McMansions but were in good shape and well maintained. I asked my guide, local waste expert Alan Watson, where the poor people lived, and he looked at me quizzically. "We have a strong social safety net here, so we don't have a lot of poor people like you do."

Finally, in a far-off field, I saw a bunch of small structures that looked almost like shanties from a distance. "Aha!" I declared. "So that is where your poor people live." "No," my host explained, "those are camper vans in a caravan park on holiday." Oh.

Each time we got out of the car, Watson had to remind me that I didn't need to lock the doors, even though it was packed to the gills with our camping gear—and the laptop with my book manuscript. He told me that his family seldom locks their house door. "Nothing bad will happen," he promised. And he was right.

I thought about my daughter and how different it would be to grow up in a world with that atmosphere: *nothing bad will happen.* To the best of our ability, we should be able to make that promise to our children and to future generations. If that means rewriting the Story of Stuff—which I firmly believe it does—then let's get to it.

APPENDIX 1
EXAMPLES OF PROMISING POLICIES, REFORMS, AND LAWS

While each community and country requires a custom approach, there is a delicious smorgasbord of possible policies, regulations, laws, and programs that can improve humanity's well-being and the state of the planet.

Some of these are already under way and just need to be scaled up. Some could be implemented right away, some over the short term, some more gradually. Some are straightforward; others are going to take some serious thought and planning in order to be implemented compassionately and justly.

This is not a comprehensive list, just a few of the possibilities I'm most excited about, presented in an order that matches up with the five stages in the Story of Stuff.

Extraction

1. Strengthen and implement government-led international agreements and monitoring systems (not voluntary industry-led codes of conduct) on environmental sustainability and human rights issues for all mining operations—gold, diamonds, coal, coltan, everything. The Kimberley Process needs to be strengthened and enforced to be effective, and additional systems are needed to cover other types of mining. Many organizations are working on reforming mining practices; check out Earthworks in the United States, Minerals Policy Institute in Australia, and Mines, Minerals and People in India.

2. Stop logging in the planet's endangered remaining forests, from Canada's boreal forest to Indonesia's rainforest. Enact and enforce strict environmental and human rights standards for logging in other forests, prioritizing the protection of natural forests required to restore climate stability. Strengthen the Forest Stewardship Council certification program so it ensures protection of endangered forests, the rights of forest-dwelling peoples, and ecological values of the forests.

3. To reduce greenhouse gas emissions to the level needed to stabilize the climate, we simply must wean ourselves from fossil fuels and massively reduce carbon emissions. As activists from Ecuador to Nigeria to Appalachia, we need to say, "Keep the oil in the soil, keep the coal in the hole." Policies that promote this path could include:

- Redirecting government subsidies for extractive energy industries toward the development of clean, renewable energy options.
- Redirecting subsidies for gas guzzler vehicles and highways toward promoting public transportation and zoning laws that discourage sprawl and create sidewalks, bike lanes, and public transportation, so people can reach the places they need to go without driving.
- Establishing strict guidelines on fuel efficiency for cars and energy efficiency for buildings. Fuel efficiency and energy standards should be set and enforced by the government and should be based on sound science, free from industry influence. The Obama administration has recently announced a goal of an average of 35.5 miles per gallon for U.S. vehicles by 2016. Considering that some current cars get more than 50 mpg, with the technology available to achieve even higher fuel efficiency, why stop at a measly 35.5 mpg? Likewise, buildings can be required to be vastly more energy efficient, saving energy on both cooling and heating.
- In the United States, upgrading the obsolete General Mining Act of 1872 to protect water sources, require reclamation, and deny mining claims that conflict with the protection of other resources. The Washington, D.C.–based environmental organization Earthworks coordinates a campaign to overhaul this ancient law as well as address other environmental and social issues related to mining in the United States and internationally.
- Banning mountaintop removal mining, in which entire mountaintops are blown up to access the coal inside. To see what this looks like and to get involved, visit www.ilovemountains.org.
- Ceasing development of Canada's tar sands. Tar sands consist of heavy crude oil mixed with sand, clay, and bitumen. Extracting the oil entails burning natural gas to generate enough heat and steam to melt it out of the sand and uses up to five barrels of water for each barrel of oil produced. Rainforest Action Network (RAN) says that tar sands oil is the worst type for the climate, producing three times the greenhouse gas emissions of conventionally produced oil because of the energy required to extract and process it. RAN is organizing to redi-

rect the $70 to $100 billion the United States plans to invest in tar sands infrastructure into research and development of sustainable energy alternatives such as electric vehicles, plug-in hybrids, and solar and wind energy.

Production

1. Reform chemicals policy, focusing on prevention rather than futile attempts to regulate hazardous chemicals after they've dispersed into our products, environment, and bodies. Ban the supertoxic chemicals, including chemicals that build up in our bodies (known as persistent bioaccumulative toxins, or PBTs) and toxic metals like lead and mercury. We in the United States have an opportunity to help pass the Kid-Safe Chemicals Act, the first effort to protect the public health through comprehensive chemical policy reform in more than thirty years. Sign up to join the campaign at www.saferchemicals.org.

2. Strengthen unions by protecting the right to organize and choosing unionized businesses for everything from clothing to hotels. Support worker cooperatives too; co-ops build democratic engagement and ensure that profits are kept in the local economy and shared more fairly.

3. Tax pollution at levels high enough to make investments in prevention vastly cheaper. Because the amount of carbon in the atmosphere has reached such crisis levels and we must reduce it to 350 ppm (see www. 350 .org for more information), taxes aren't enough for this particular pollutant. For carbon, we have to go to the main source of the problems—the biggest CO_2 point emitters—and force them to change their energy consumption systems, sometimes quite radically. Many of the suggestions under the extraction section, above, will help achieve this.

Distribution

1. Ensure that sustainability and equity are the top goals of all trade agreements. In the United States, support the Trade Reform, Accountability, Development and Employment Act of 2009 (the TRADE Act, H.R. 3012), which would significantly improve destructive trade policies like those of NAFTA and the WTO. To learn more and get involved, visit www.citizen.org/trade/tradeact/.

2. Give preference to locally made products with tools like a gradual tariff on goods that is based on how far they've traveled. Support local business and locally made products to reduce transportation and support local economies. The goal is not to prohibit all long-distance trade but to increasingly strengthen local production and distribution to create self-

reliant communities while also securing a just transition in those communities with export-dependent economies. For those products that are shipped long distances, prioritize rail transport over the more polluting planes and trucks.

3. Promote transparency and democracy in supply chains so everyone—workers, host communities, customers, and businesses along the chain—have access to information and a voice in decision making. Laws to support this would require that companies disclose all their suppliers (as both Dell and Hewlett-Packard now do), ensure worker rights and environmental sustainability along their supply chain, and make this information available to the public.

Consumption

1. Decommercialize our culture. Reclaim our mental and physical landscape from commercial advertisers. Ban billboards and other intrusive advertising. Prohibit commercial advertising to children and in public places. Get commercial advertising out of textbooks, classrooms, and all educational facilities. The Campaign for a Commercial-Free Childhood conducts research and advocates for protective policies; to get involved visit www.commercialexploitation.org. Commercial Alert (www.commercialalert.org) runs numerous campaigns to decommercialize our schools, media, and communities.

2. Ensure public investment in commons like libraries, athletic facilities, and parks so that residents can meet their needs and enjoy leisure time without buying Stuff. Attend city council meetings to voice your opinion about budget priorities, or better yet, run for office yourself!

3. Adopt a progressive tax on resource consumption, allowing free use for basic needs while taxing higher-quantity use. For example, water to drink is free; water to wash your SUV or water your desert lawn is really expensive. A vibrant and often-heated discussion is happening on the international level as to what constitutes basic needs.

Disposal

1. Adopt extended producer responsibility (EPR) laws that hold producers responsible for the end-of-life management of their products, motivating better design at the front end and decreasing waste at the back end. Examples of EPR already in action include bottle bills, Germany's Green Dot program, and the computer take-back legislation in many U.S. states. To learn how to promote EPR in your community, visit www.product action.org, www.productpolicy.org, and www.productstewardship.us.

2. Implement significant taxes to discourage wasteful packaging and products, such as single-use beverage containers and disposable plastic bags. Ban outright those materials that are inherently toxic, such as consumer products containing mercury or PVC. Germany's Green Dot program, national bottle bills, and disposable bag taxes and bans in numerous countries demonstrate the waste reduction potential of these tools.

3. Develop a national composting infrastructure to ensure that organic waste is kept out of landfills and that composting biomaterials moves from ideal to reality. This should include support for decentralized (backyard or community level) composting where possible, supplemented by municipal composting operations.

4. Prohibit all waste incineration. It's simply not needed; technically viable and less polluting nonincineration alternatives exist for medical, municipal, and hazardous wastes. Instead, adopt a zero waste goal and invest in waste prevention, reuse, and recycling programs that conserve resources, reduce greenhouse gas emissions, and create jobs. Prohibit all scams aiming to give renewable energy credits or carbon offset credits to waste incinerators and landfill gas burning! To get involved, contact the Global Alliance for Incinerator Alternatives at www.no-burn.org.

5. For municipal wastes, implement pay-as-you-throw systems at the local level in which households and businesses pay more for waste disposal the more they throw away. For hazardous wastes, focus on prevention, as the wonderful Toxics Use Reduction Institute (www.turi.org) has demonstrated is possible.

Other Good Ideas

Taxes and Banking

1. Tax resource use rather than labor; this motivates employers to conserve resources and hire more people.
2. Eliminate government subsidies for environmentally destructive activities and products, from mining to SUVs.
3. Cancel debts for poor countries, many of which were obtained under corrupt conditions to build projects benefiting the donor country.

Corporate Accountability

1. End the guarantees of limited liability for corporate wrongdoing and constitutional protections of corporations as individuals that are currently conferred upon them, via their corporate charters, under U.S. corporate law.

2. Institute limits on executive salaries and raise minimum wages to reduce the obscene gap between rich and poor in the United States. A good start would be immediately restricting the compensation of top earners to one to two hundred times as much as the company's lowest-paid employee (still far higher than in other countries), with progressive restrictions each year to further shrink the income gap to a much healthier and fair ratio.

3. Strengthen corporate accountability domestically and internationally by improving rules on transparency and public involvement in decision making. In the United States, protect the Alien Tort Claims Act (ATCA) which allows foreign nationals to bring legal cases against U.S. companies for human rights or environmental abuses they cause beyond U.S. borders. Business organizations that advocate for corporate rights and free trade, including the National Foreign Trade Council and USA* Engage, are lobbying the U.S. government to weaken or repeal ATCA. To support this important law, contact the Center for Constitutional Rights (www.ccrjustice.org), EarthRights International (www.earthrights.org), and Human Rights Watch (www.hrw.org).

International Cooperation and Solidarity

1. Be a part of the solution, not the problem. Insist that the U.S. Government cooperate in international environmental fora and agreements. Across the board, from the Basel Convention, which deals with international waste trafficking, to the critically important UN climate convention, the U.S. delegation routinely blocks progress toward binding environmental agreements. In order to achieve real solutions to our global environmental threats and to begin a new era of U.S. environmental leadership and cooperation after years of embarrassing obstructionism, our government simply must start enthusiastically promoting environmental solutions in international settings. There's no time to stall—especially on the climate front. Write to your elected representatives urging strong action to reduce carbon emissions. Then, since the climate crisis calls for more than letter writing, visit www.350.org, www.1Sky.org, and Climate Justice Now (www.climate-justice-now.org) for further action ideas.

2. Join international solidarity campaigns led by communities, trade unions, and environmentalists who ask for support in their work against corporations engaged in destructive extraction, production, or disposal practices, especially when those corporations are from our home countries. Such campaigns—like sanctions against apartheid in South Africa

and the Burmese junta or the International Campaign for Justice in Bhopal—are a vital tool for promoting corporate accountability, improving industrial operations, increasing local involvement in decision making, supporting broader eco-social improvement, and strengthening international solidarity.

APPENDIX 2
RECOMMENDED INDIVIDUAL ACTIONS

I always resist offering ten easy things individuals can do that will save the planet, because as I've explained, there are no ten easy things that will save the planet. I'm not saying that we shouldn't bother with being responsible and smart in our actions at the individual and household level. There are things we can do to lessen environmental health impacts on our families and workers. These actions can also reduce our ecological footprint a bit. So, yes, we should engage in these actions, as long as we don't let them either lull us into a false sense of accomplishment or let the effort of maintaining this constant, uptight, rigorous green screen on our lifestyle exhaust us. In other words, as long as taking these actions doesn't stand in the way of your engaging in the broader political arena for real change, knock yourself out.

There's an abundance of guides on how to live a greener life. This book is not one of them. Yet, since so many Story of Stuff viewers have asked for specific suggestions, I'll share what I do. This isn't a comprehensive list, and it's not in any particular order, but it's a good place to start and includes suggestions for additional resources.

AT HOME
1. Avoid products that leach toxics into our food, bodies, or homes. If you're not sure if a product contains these hazardous chemicals, call the customer service number on the package. If they can't confirm it's toxic free, don't buy it. Check GoodGuide.com for information on the toxic chemicals present in thousands of specific products. And if you want to study the latest science on these toxic chemicals, check out the invaluable resources at Environmental Health News: www.environmental healthnews.org.

Some prime offenders:

- Teflon nonstick pans: the nonstick Stuff is polytetrafluoroethylene which, when heated—as pans often are—releases toxic gasses linked to cancer, organ failure, reproductive damage, and other harmful health effects.
- PVC toys, PVC shower curtains, PVC food wrap, PVC anything—PVC is the most hazardous plastic at all stages of its lifecycle: production, use, and disposal. Don't bring it into your home. To learn more about PVC, visit www.besafenet.com/pvc/.
- Mattresses, pillows, couches, or other furniture treated with polybrominated diphenyl ethers (PBDE), a supertoxic chemical linked to liver, thyroid, and neurodevelopmental toxicity. If the label says "treated for flame resistance," beware. To learn more about flame retardants, see www.cleanproduction.org and www.greenscience policy.org. The Washington Toxics Coalition's Green Guide on PBDEs explains how to avoid toxic flame retardants in consumer products and is available online at www.watoxics.org/files/GreenProduct Guide.pdf.

2. Reduce your waste. Even though household waste is a fraction of the volume of industrial waste, it's a no-brainer to do what we can to reduce it. It's easy, it conserves resources, and each bag of trash prevented from being dumped in a landfill or, even worse, burned in an incinerator, is a good thing. Here are some places to start:

- Avoid single-use bottles, plastic bags, coffee cups, cans: these items, designed to be used for seconds, are grossly wasteful and easy to virtually eliminate with a modicum of advance planning. Don't beat yourself up when you are in a jam and have to use one, but try to make it the exception.
- Compost: Get a separate bin in your kitchen for food scraps and compost these in a municipal composting program or use any number of home composting techniques. It's easy, it keeps organics out of the landfill, it prevents your kitchen garbage bag from stinking, and it provides a great natural fertilizer for soil (thus avoiding nasty chemical fertilizers) for gardens and house plants. There are many composting guides for rural, suburban, and urban settings available online. I personally prefer composting with worms—see www.worm woman.com to learn how.

3. Go organic in your food, your garden, your cleaning products. Pesticides and toxic chemicals have no place in our food, our yards, and our homes. Remember, pesticides are designed to kill; that's what they are for. They're linked to a wide range of health problems from cancer to neurological and reproductive problems, and they're building up in our environment and bodies. Avoid chlorine bleach and use nontoxic cleaners. The fancy-packaged ones cost more, and cheap and easy substitutes can be made from inexpensive ingredients like vinegar, baking soda, and lemon juice. How hard is that? If you don't know how to make homemade nontoxic cleaners, ask your grandma or visit one of the many websites with recipes. My favorite is Women's Voices for the Earth: www.womenand environment.org/campaignsandprograms/SafeCleaning/recipes.

4. Power down: Drive less. Fly less. Get a clothesline. Get a bike. Turn down the heat and put on a sweater. Do a home energy audit to find energy leaks and fix them. No explanation needed here, I hope.

5. Unplug your TV: Why sit and stare at a box beaming messages indoctrinating us into consumer culture for hours a day when there are so many more enjoyable alternatives available? I realized this a few years ago, when at the end of TV Turnoff Week (a national program in which kids pledge to resist TV for a week), my daughter turned to me and said, "I had so much fun this week. I wish every week was TV Turnoff Week." And so it was.

6. Invest in the economy you want: When you're shopping, investing, choosing a bank, paying someone who helped you around the house—really doing anything with your money—think about whether your hard-earned dollars are supporting the kind of economy you want or the one you want to escape from. Buying locally produced, union made, or fair trade certified are all good things to consider. And remember, buying secondhand, or not buying at all, is often the best option.

At School, Work, Church

Of course, all those individual and householder action ideas apply to any setting in which you spend part of your days, such as school, work, or church. In these places, you have the automatic benefit of already being part of a group, which means your potential influence and impact is magnitudes greater. Some additional ideas for greening these settings are:

- Get your institution to adopt a sustainability policy that confirms its commitment to environmental and social sustainability. Ensure the policy is visibly supported. Include it in outreach material, orientation packets for new students, new members, or new hires, and other publications so that it becomes part of the institution's culture. Then, reach out to other organizations in your sector and invite them to join you. For guidance in working with K–12 schools, contact the Green Schools Initiative at greenschools.net; for working with faith-based institutions, contact GreenFaith at www.greenfaith.org.

- Leverage your procurement dollars. Universities, businesses, and organizations of all sorts generally buy more Stuff than individuals do, so they can demand more of their suppliers. Requiring printers to use recycled paper, caterers to serve organic food, suppliers to minimize packaging, or janitorial services to avoid toxic cleansers can help, slowly, shift these business sectors to better practices.

Why do any or all of these things, even when we know they aren't enough to turn things around? The value of individual action includes:

- It demonstrates potential and alternative ways to live. Each time we visibly choose quality of life over quantity of Stuff, each time we ignore those consumer messages telling us we must have the latest gadget, we demonstrate the possibility of another way. I have solar panels on my roof. After reducing my energy use with things like using a clothesline and installing insulated curtains, the panels produce enough power for my whole house and enough extra to power the small used electric vehicle that gets my daughter and me around town. I know that the cost of solar panels and a solar-powered electric vehicle are beyond the reach of many. And I know that, really, they don't make a difference in my country's massive CO_2 emissions. But every time someone stops me to ask me about the car, and I tell them that I don't have to go to gas stations anymore, it spreads a sense of possibility. It's chipping away at the myth that our current industrial model is inevitable.
- Conscious consuming includes buying the least toxic, least exploitative products available or sometimes not buying something at all. Avoiding toxic-containing consumer products reduces exposure to toxics for ourselves and our families and, if it gets enough traction, sends messages upstream to producers to phase toxics out, thus benefiting workers, host communities, and the broader environment. Buying locally keeps your money in the local economy, supports local jobs, and reduces miles traveled for your Stuff—all good for the planet and communities.

- The individual actions we take to reduce our impact help us find the flaws in our system that need to be changed. I think of them as metal detectors leading us straight to what's wrong. Where the onus is on us individuals to do the right thing, these are the places in the system that need to be changed. Why does taking public transportation cost more than the bridge toll if I drive to San Francisco? Systems flaw! Clearly we need to increase public investment and subsidies to expand mass transit. Why do I have to study GoodGuide for hours to figure out which shampoo, sunscreen, and lotions don't have carcinogens and reproductive toxics? Systems flaw! Instead, let's ban toxics in body care products so that everyone knows they are buying toxic free without investing hours of research.

- Integrity: I believe that people are good. We want to do the right thing; we care about the planet, our global neighbors, and our grandchildren. It doesn't feel good to know that so many of our daily choices erode the planet's health, perpetuate inequality, and are downright toxic. Making these small choices to lessen our impact helps bring greater integrity to our values and our actions, which in turn makes us feel better about ourselves. If these small steps are lulling us into inaction in the larger picture, that's obviously not beneficial, but if we can harness that greater sense of personal integrity and that newly freed time to making real change, that is certainly a good thing.

APPENDIX 3
SAMPLE LETTER TO PVC RETAILERS, MANUFACTURERS, AND LOBBYISTS

Even with the best of intentions, I find that PVC (polyvinyl chloride) plastic still sneaks its way into my house occasionally. Whether it is in kids' toys received as gifts from well-meaning relatives to that horrible child-sized Barbie pink raincoat that was left at our home to products in which I didn't recognize the PVC until I opened the package and smelled that telltale smell, there it is. Sometimes PVC is in the product and sometimes it is the packaging. The problem with PVC is that once we have it, we're stuck. We can't give it to a thrift store, where someone who may be unaware of its hazards would bring it home, potentially exposing her family. We can't throw it away, since PVC releases toxics when landfilled or, worse, incinerated. So what to do? I stick this junk in an envelope or box and send it back to the retailer, the producer, or, in cases in which I can't identify either, the Vinyl Institute, which is the PVC industry's lobby group in Washington, D.C., along with an explanation and a request to stop selling, making, and advocating for the poison plastic. If I am returning a product I purchased, I always ask for a refund and donate the money to an organization working to ban PVC. If you want more information on identifying PVC in consumer products and joining campaigns to get rid of this poison plastic, please visit www.besafenet.com/pvc.

Here's a letter that you're welcome to adapt for your own use. Share it with friends. Perhaps if stores get enough of this back in the mail, they'll join the many retailers and producers who have agreed to stop using and selling PVC.

The Vinyl Institute's address is: Vinyl Institute, 1737 King Street, Suite 390, Alexandria, VA, 22314 USA.

Dear [Producer, Store, Vinyl Institute],

Enclosed is a [raincoat, handbag, rubber duck, binder, shower curtain, etc.] that I am returning to you because it contains polyvinyl chloride, or PVC. PVC does not contribute to a healthy household or a healthy planet. In fact, PVC is *the most hazardous plastic* at all stages of its life-cycle, from production through use and disposal. I encourage you to stop [making/selling/promoting] PVC and to instead opt for materials that are safer for workers, communities, consumers, and the planet.

Production: PVC production is especially hazardous for workers and communities where plants are located. PVC production requires vinyl chloride monomer (VCM), a dangerous explosive, and creates toxic waste, notably ethylene dichloride (EDC) tars—two things no neighborhood wants. Wastes from PVC production have been proven to contain the powerful carcinogen dioxin, which then is spread to wherever the waste is buried or burned. In addition to the inherent hazards of PVC, its production requires even more toxic chemical additives to prepare the PVC for different uses: plasticizers (such as phthalates) are added to make it soft and pliable, heavy metals (such as lead and cadmium) are added as stabilizers, and fungicides are added to stop fungi from eating the other additives.

Use: The chemical additives added to PVC are not bound to the plastic so they leach out or evaporate over time. That is why PVC items often reek of a "new car smell" and lead dust has been often found on PVC window frames and mini-blinds. The most common plasticizer used in PVC is DEHP, a suspected carcinogen and endocrine disruptor that is now showing up in human and wildlife bodies tested all over the planet. If we bring this Stuff into our homes, schools, and workplaces, we end up with these toxics in our bodies.

Disposal: Whenever PVC is burned, dioxins and acidic gases are released. This happens when discarded PVC ends up in an open burn pile or a waste incinerator. It also happens when buildings catch on fire, since PVC is widely used in building materials. When PVC is dumped in a landfill, the additives leach into the environment, and it is also at risk of burning since landfill fires are common.

PVC recycling is not a solution. PVC recycling is technically difficult, not economically feasible, and polluting, releasing a range of toxics into the air. Even more basic, though, recycling a hazard perpetuates a hazard. Faced with such a uniquely hazardous material, a better response is to reduce its circulation rather than to figure out how to use it yet again.

The good news about PVC is that it isn't necessary. Alternative materials are available, including many safer materials that PVC has displaced over recent years: glass, cotton, metal, paper, ceramics, leather, and wood as well as less hazardous plastics. Many companies around the world, including Nike, IKEA, Sony, the Body Shop, a dozen automobile makers, and even Wal-Mart, have taken steps to reduce or fully eliminate PVC in their products.

Knowing how hazardous PVC is, and knowing that alternatives exist, why are you continuing to [use/sell/promote] this material? If all those companies can take a stand on the side of community, worker, and environmental health, you can too.

Please write back to me to clarify [company name here]'s position regarding PVC. Specifically, I would like to know if you have a plan, with a timetable, to phase out PVC from your operations.

I look forward to hearing from you.

> Sincerely,
> [Your name here]

ENDNOTES

Introduction

1. "Recycle City: Materials Recovery Center," U.S. Environmental Protection Agency (epa.gov/recyclecity/print/recovery.htm).
2. Ken Stier, "Fresh Kills: Redeveloping one of the biggest landfills in the world," *Waste Management World,* December 2007 (waste-management-world.com/display_article/ 314941/123/ARCHI/none/none/1/Fresh-Kills/).
3. "Earth at a glance," Ecology Global Network (ecology.com/features/earthataglance/ youarehere.html).
4. Astronomy: Measuring the Circumference of the Earth," Schlumberger Excellence in Educational Development (seed.slb.com/v2/FAQView.cfm?ID=1105).
5. "Earth at a glance."
6. CO2 Now website: co2now.org/.
7. "Body Burden—The Pollution in Newborns: A benchmark investigation of industrial chemicals, pollutants and pesticides in umbilical cord blood," executive summary, Environmental Working Group, 2005 (ewg.org/reports/bodyburden2execsumm .php).
8. *Fourth Global Environmental Outlook—Environment for Development,* summary, United Nations Environment Programme, 2007 (unep.org/geo/geo4/media/fact_ sheets/Fact_Sheet_3_Air.pdf).
9. "Ten Facts About Water Scarcity," World Health Organization (who.int/features/fact files/water/en/index.html).
10. "Income Inequality," UC Atlas of Global Inequality (ucatlas.ucsc.edu/income .php).
11. Tim Jackson, "What Politicians Dare Not Say," *New Scientist,* October 18, 2008, p. 43.
12. "More than five times" the CO2 emissions as the 2050 goal is based on the mandate from top scientists for an 80 percent reduction in CO2 emissions by 2050. For an explanation of that target, see "Global Warming Crossroads: Choosing the Sensible Path to a Clean Energy Economy," Union of Concerned Scientists, May 2009 (ucsusa.org/ global_warming/solutions/big_picture_solutions/global_warming_crossroads.html).
13. Joseph Guth, "Law for the Ecological Age," *Vermont Journal of Environmental Law,* vol. 9, no. 3, 2007–2008 (vjel.org/journal.php?vol=2007–2008).
14. Thom Hartmann, *The Last Hours of Ancient Sunlight* (New York: Three Rivers Press, 2004), pp. 14–15.
15. Personal correspondence with Dave Batker, May 2009.
16. Bill McKibben, *Deep Economy* (New York: Henry Holt & Company, 2007), pp. 203–4.
17. "More than Half the World Lives on Less than $2 a Day," Population Reference Bureau (prb.org/Journalists/PressReleases/2005/MoreThanHalftheWorldLivesonLess Than2aDayAugust2005.aspx), citing data from the World Bank's *World Development Report 2000/2001.*
18. James Gustave Speth, *The Bridge at the Edge of the World: Capitalism, the Environment, and Crossing from Crisis to Sustainability* (New Haven: Yale University Press, 2008), pp. 7–9.
19. Interview with Michael Cohen, July 2009.

20. James Pethokoukis, "McCain or Obama: Who's Pro-Growth?" *US News & World Report,* June 2, 2008 (usnews.com/blogs/capital-commerce/2008/06/02/mccain-or -obama-whos-pro-growth.html).

21. Donella Meadows, *The Global Citizen* (Washington, D.C.: Island Press, 1991), p. 4.

22. Donella Meadows, "Places to Intervene in a System," *Whole Earth Review,* Winter 1997 (wholeearth.com/issue/2091/article/27/places.to.intervene.in.a.system).

23. Ibid.

24. Interview with Jeffrey Morris, May 2009.

A Word About Words

1. Thomas Princen, Michael Maniates, and Ken Conca, *Confronting Consumption* (Boston: MIT Press, 2002), pp. 45–50.

2. James Gustave Speth, *The Bridge at the Edge of the World: Capitalism, the Environment, and Crossing from Crisis to Sustainability* (New Haven: Yale University Press, 2008), pp. 170.

3. Speth, *The Bridge at the End of the World,* p. 62.

4. Herman E. Daly and Joshua Farley, *Ecological Economics* (Washington D.C.: Island Press, 2003), p. 433.

5. N. Senanayake and L. Karalliedde, "Neurotoxic effects of organophosphorus insecticides," *New England Journal of Medicine,* March 26, 1987, pp. 761–63.

6. Ken Geiser, *Materials Matter* (Boston: MIT Press, 2001), p. 22.

7. *Report of the World Commission on Environment and Development,* UN World Commission on Environment and Development, 1987 (worldinbalance.net/pdf/1987 –brundtland.pdf).

8. Robert Gilman's definition of sustainability is widely quoted, by organizations such as the Environmental Protection Agency (yosemite.epa.gov/R10/OI.NSF/5d8e61924 8fe0bd88825650f00710fbc/7dc483330319d2d888256fc4007842da!OpenDocument) and the Center for World Leadership (earthleaders.org/sii/goal).

9. Center for Sustainable Communities, quoted in Sustainable Sonoma County's "Key Concepts: Defining Sustainability" (sustainablesonoma.org/keyconcepts/sustainability .html).

Chapter 1: Extraction

1. Paul Hawken and Amory L. Hunter, *Natural Capitalism* (New York: Little Brown & Co., 1999), p. 50.

2. Washington State official website: wa.gov/esd/lmea/sprepts/indprof/forestry.htm.

3. Bill Chameides, "Pulse of the Planet: U.S. Whiffs on Climate Change While Rain Forests Burn," *The Huffington Post,* July 14, 2008 (huffingtonpost.com/bill-chameides/ pulse-of-the-planet-us-wh_b_112588.html).

4. Charles Czarnowski, Jason Bailey, and Sharon Bal, "Curare and a Canadian Connection," *Canadian Family Physician,* vol. 53, no. 9, September 2007, pp. 1531–32 (pubmedcentral.nih.gov/articlerender.fcgi?artid=2234642).

5. Peter Rillero, "Tropical Rainforest Education" (ericdigests.org/2000–1/tropical .html).

6. Ibid.

7. "Cancer Cured by the Rosy Periwinkle," The Living Rainforest (livingrainforest.org/ about-rainforests/anti-cancer-rosy-periwinkle).

8. Ibid.

9. "Rainforest Facts," Raintree (rain-tree.com/facts.htm). Raintree is an informational

website founded by Leslie Taylor, author of *The Healing Power of Rainforest Herbs* (Square Garden City Park One Publishers, 2005) and founder of the company Raintree Nutrition, which markets rainforest botanicals.

10. Ibid.

11. *Global Diversity Outlook,* Secretariat of the Convention on Biological Diversity, United Nations Environment Programme, 2001, p. 93 (cbd.int/gbo1/gbo-pdf .shtml).

12. "About Rainforests," Rainforest Action Network (ran.org/new/kidscorner/about_rainforests/forests_of_the_world_map/').

13. Don E. Wilson and DeeAnn M. Reeder (eds.), *Mammal Species of the World: A Taxonomic and Geographic Reference,* 3rd. ed. (Baltimore: Johns Hopkins University Press, 2005); Available online from Bucknell University's Mammal Species of the World database (bucknell.edu/msw3/browse.asp?id=14000691).

14. "Promoting Climate-Smart agriculture" Food and Agriculture Organization of the United Nations (fao.org/forestry/28811/en/).

15. Condition and Trends Working Group of the Millennium Ecosystem Assessment, *Ecosystems and Human Well-Being: Current States and Trends,* vol. 1 (Washington, D.C.: Island Press, 2005), p. 2.

16. "The Economics of Ecosystems and Biodiversity," European Commission (ec.europa .eu/environment/nature/biodiversity/economics/).

17. Richard Black, "Nature Loss 'Dwarfs Bank Crisis,'" BBC News, October 10, 2008 (news.bbc.co.uk/2/hi/science/nature/7662565.stm).

18. "Deforestation and net forest area change," Food and Agriculture Organization of the United Nations (fao.org/forestry/30515/en/).

19. *State of the World's Forests 2007,* Food and Agriculture Organization of the United Nations (fao.org/docrep/009/a0773e/a0773e00.htm).

20. "Old Growth," Rainforest Action Network (ran.org/what_we_do/old_growth/about_the_campaign/).

21. *State of the World's Forests 2007.*

22. Allen Hershkowitz, *Bronx Ecology* (Washington, D.C.: Island Press, 2002), p. 75.

23. Stephen Leahy, "Biofuels Boom Spurring Deforestation," Inter Press Service, March 21, 2007 (ipsnews.net/news.asp?idnews=37035).

24. Jack Kerouac, *The Dharma Bums* (New York: Viking Press, 1958; Penguin Books, 1976), pp. 225–26.

25. John Muir, *My First Summer in the Sierra* (Boston: Houghton Mifflin, 1911; Sierra Club Books, 1988).

26. "Forestry; Wood; Pulp and Paper: ILO Concerns," International Labour Organization (ilo.org/public/english/dialogue/sector/sectors/forest/concerns.htm).

27. Leahy, "Biofuels Boom Spurring Deforestation."

28. "Common and Uncommon Paper Products," TAPPI (tappi.org/paperu/all_about_paper/products.htm). TAPPI is the leading technical association for the worldwide pulp, paper, and converting industry.

29. "Facts About Paper," Printers National Environmental Assistance Center (pneac.org/ sheets/all/paper.cfm).

30. "Environmental Trends and Climate Impacts: Findings from the U.S. Book Industry," Book Industry Study Group and Green Press Initiative (ecolibris.net/book_industry _footprint.asp).

31. "Forest Products Consumption and Its Environmental Impact" Sierra Club (sierra club.org/sustainable_consumption/factsheets/forestproducts_factsheet.asp).

32. "Good Stuff? Paper," Worldwatch Institute (worldwatch.org/node/1497).
33. "What are some ways to save paper at the office?" *E/The Environmental Magazine,* October 18, 2004 (enn.com/top_stories/article/186).
34. "Recycling Facts and Figures," Wisconsin Department of Natural Resources, 2002 (dnr.state.wi.us/org/aw/wm/publications/).
35. International Institute for Environment and Development, *A Changing Future for Paper: An Independent Study on the Sustainability of the Pulp and Paper Industry* (Geneva: World Business Council for Sustainable Development, 1996), p. 4 (wbcsd .org/web/publications/paper-future.pdf).
36. Environmental Paper Network website: environmentalpaper.org.
37. "ForestEthics Junk Mail Campaign," fact sheet, Forest Ethics (forestethics.org/down loads/dnm_factsheet.pdf).
38. Ibid.
39. "Recycle City: Materials Recovery Center," U.S. Environmental Protection Agency (epa.gov/recyclecity/print/recovery.htm).
40. *FCS-US: Leading Forest Conservation and Market Transformation,* Forest Steward- ship Council (fscus.org/images/documents/FSC_prospectus.pdf).
41. Personal communication with Todd Paglia, November 2008.
42. "What Percentage of the Human Body is Water?" *The Boston Globe,* November 2, 1998 (boston.com/globe/search/stories/health/how_and_why/011298.htm).
43. Personal communication with Pat Costner, August 2009.
44. "Fascinating Water Facts," Agua Solutions (aguasolutions.com/facts.html).
45. John Vidal, "UK gives £50m to Bangladesh climate change fund," *The Guardian* [UK], September 8, 2008 (guardian.co.uk/world/2008/sep/08/bangladesh.climat echange).
46. Seth H. Frisbie, Erika J. Mitchell, Lawrence J. Mastera, et al., "Public Health Strategies for Western Bangladesh That Address Arsenic, Manganese, Uranium, and Other Toxic Elements in Drinking Water," *Environmental Health Perspectives,* vol. 117, no. 3, March 2009 (ehponline.org/docs/2008/11886/abstract.html).
47. Amie Cooper, "The Lawn Goodbye," *Dwell Magazine,* February 26, 2009 (dwell.com/ articles/the-lawn-goodbye.html).
48. "Cleaner Air: Gas Mower Pollution Facts," People Powered Machines (people poweredmachines.com/faq-environment.htm).
49. Cooper, "The Lawn Goodbye."
50. Rebecca Lindsey, "Looking for Lawns," *NASA Earth Observatory,* November 8, 2005 (earthobservatory.nasa.gov/Features/Lawn/printall.php).
51. "Productgallery: Paper," Water Footprint Network (waterfootprint.org/?page=files/ productgallery&product=paper).
52. "Productgallery: Cotton" Water Footprint Network (waterfootprint.org/?page=files/ productgallery&product=cotton).
53. "Productgallery: Coffee" Water Footprint Network (waterfootprint.org/?page=files/ productgallery&product=coffee).
54. "Siemens Offers Tips for Manufacturers to Reduce Their Water Footprint," PRNews- wire/Reuters, August 17, 2009 (reuters.com/article/pressRelease/idUS142222+17 -Aug-2009+PRN20090817).
55. "Where Is Earth's Water Located?" U.S. Geological Survey (ga.water.usgs.gov/edu/ earthwherewater.html).
56. Ibid.
57. Ger Bergkamp and Claudia W. Sadoff, "Water in a Sustainable Economy," *State of the World 2008* (Washington, D.C.: The Worldwatch Institute, 2009), p. 107.

58. Ibid., p. 108.
59. World Health Organization and UNICEF, *Water for Life: Making It Happen* (Geneva: WHO Press, 2005), p. 5.
60. "Human Appropriation of the World's Fresh Water Supply," University of Michigan Global Change Program (globalchange.umich.edu/globalchange2/current/lectures/freshwater_supply/freshwater.html).
61. Bergkamp and Sadoff, "Water in a Sustainable Economy," p. 108.
62. Maude Barlow, "A UN Convention on the Right to Water—An Idea Whose Time Has Come," Blue Planet Project, November 2006 (blueplanetproject.net/documents/UN_convention_MB_Dec06.pdf).
63. "Running Dry," *The Economist,* August 21, 2008. The quote "water is the oil of the 21st century" was from Andrew Liveris, the chief executive of Dow Chemical Company.
64. "The Soft Path for Water," Pacific Institute (pacinst.org/topics/water_and_sustainability/soft_path/index.htm).
65. "'Virtual Water' Innovator Awarded 2008 Stockholm Water Prize," Stockholm International Water Institute (siwi.org/sa/node.asp?node=25).
66. Quote appears on the Water Footprint website: waterfootprint.org/?page=files/home.
67. Bergkamp and Sadoff, "Water in a Sustainable Economy," p. 114.
68. "Dublin Statements and Principles," Global Water Partnership (gwpforum.org/servlet/PSP?iNodeID=1345).
69. Ray Anderson, "The business logic of sustainability," TED talk filmed February 2009, posted May 2009 (ted.com/talks/ray_anderson_on_the_business_logic_of_sustainability.html).
70. *Dirty Metals: Mining, Communities, and the Environment,* Earthworks and Oxfam America, 2004, p. 4 (nodirtygold.org/pubs/DirtyMetals.pdf).
71. "Bingham Canyon Mine," Wikipedia (wikipedia.org/wiki/Bingham_Canyon_Mine).
72. *Rich Lands Poor People: Is Sustainable Mining Possible?* Centre for Science and the Environment, 2008, p. 1 (cseindia.org/programme/industry/pdf/miningpub.pdf).
73. *Dirty Metals: Mining, Communities and the Environment,* p. 4.
74. Ibid.
75. Ibid.
76. "Mining: Safety and Health," International Labour Organization (ilo.org/public/english/dialogue/sector/sectors/mining/safety.htm).
77. "Mineworkers Rights," GRAVIS (gravis.org.in/content/view/26/46/).
78. "1872 Mining Law," Earthworks (earthworksaction.org/1872.cfm).
79. Ken Geiser, *Materials Matter* (Boston: MIT Press, 2001), p. 170.
80. Ibid.
81. "H.R. 699: Hardrock Mining and Reclamation Act of 2009," Congressional Research Service summary, GovTrack (govtrack.us/congress/bill.xpd?bill=h111-699&tab=summary).
82. Radhika Sarin, *No Dirty Gold: Consumer education and action for mining reform* (Washington, D.C.: Earthworks, 2005), pp. 305–6.
83. "Why a Campaign Focused on Gold?" No Dirty Gold (nodirtygold.org/about_us.cfm).
84. "Poisoned Waters," No Dirty Gold (nodirtygold.org/poisoned_waters.cfm).
85. "Cyanide process," *Encyclopaedia Britannica* (britannica.com/EBchecked/topic/147730/cyanide-process).
86. "The Gold Discovery That Changed the World: Coloma, California, 1848," Coloma Valley website, adapted from *Discover Coloma: A Teacher's Guide,* by Alan Beilharz (coloma.com/gold/).

87. Pratap Chatterjee, *Gold, Greed and Genocide* (Berkeley, Calif.: Project Underground, 1998).

88. "NIH Mercury Abatement Program," National Institutes of Health, Office of Research Facilities (orf.od.nih.gov/Environmental+Protection/Mercury+Free/).

89. Rebecca Solnit, "Winged Mercury and the Golden Calf," *Orion*, September/October 2006 (orionmagazine.org/index.php/articles/article/176/).

90. "The Golden Rules," No Dirty Gold (nodirtygold.org/goldenrules.cfm).

91. "Combating Conflict Diamonds," Global Witness (globalwitness.org/pages/en/conflict_diamonds.html).

92. "Leaders of diamond-fuelled terror campaign convicted by Sierra Leone's Special Court," press release from Global Witness, February 26, 2009 (globalwitness.org/media_library_detail.php/723/en/leaders_of_diamond_fuelled_terror_campaign_convicted_by_sierra_leones_special_court).

93. Ibid.

94. Ibid.

95. "The Kimberley Process," Global Witness (globalwitness.org/pages/en/the_kimberley_process.html).

96. "Conflict Diamonds: Sanctions and War," United Nations (un.org/peace/africa/Diamond.html).

97. *Loupe Holes: Illicit Diamonds in the Kimberley Process,* Partnership Africa Canada and Global Witness, November 2008, p. 1 (globalwitness.org/media_library_detail.php/674/en/loupe_holes_illicit_diamonds_in_the_kimberley_proc).

98. "Tantalum," *Encyclopaedia Britannica* (britannica.com/EBchecked/topic/582754/tantalum). The entry states: "Tantalum was discovered (1802) by the Swedish chemist Anders Gustaf Ekeberg and named after the mythological character Tantalus because of the tantalizing problem of dissolving the oxide in acids."

99. "Congo's Tragedy: The war the world forgot," *The Independent* [UK], May 5, 2006 (independent.co.uk/news/world/africa/congos-tragedy-the-war-the-world-forgot-476929.html).

100. Ibid.

101. Ibid.

102. Ibid.

103. *Faced with a Gun, What Can you Do? War and the Militarisation of Mining in Eastern Congo,* Global Witness, July 2009. Tables with statistics on the mineral exports from 2007 and the first half of 2008 can be found on p. 90 (globalwitness.org/media_library_detail.php/786/en/global_witness_report_faced_with_a_gun_what_can_yo).

104. "Congo's Tragedy: The war the world forgot."

105. Jack Ewing, "Blood on Your Phone? Unlikely It's 'Conflict Coltan,'" *Der Speigel Online International,* November 18, 2008 (spiegel.de/international/world/0,1518,591097,00.html).

106. Larry Greenemeier, "Trashed Tech: Where Do Old Cell Phones, TVs and PCs Go to Die?" *Scientific American,* November 29, 2007 (scientificamerican.com/article.cfm?id=trash-tech-pc-tv-waste).

107. American Chemical Society, *Chemistry in the Community,* 5th ed. (New York: W. H. Freeman, 2006), p. 176.

108. Ibid.

109. "The Next 10 Years are Critical—The World Energy Outlook Makes the Case for Stepping up Co-operation with China and India to Address Global Energy Challenges," press release from the International Energy Agency, November 7, 2007 (iea.org/press/pressdetail.asp?PRESS_REL_ID=239).

110. Steve Connor, "Warning: Oil supplies are running out fast," *The Independent* [UK], August 3, 2009 (independent.co.uk/news/science/warning-oil-supplies-are-running-out-fast%C2%AD1766585.html).

111. Ibid.

112. Ibid.

113. Lou Dematteis and Kayna Szymczak, *Crude Reflections: Oil, Ruin, and Resistance in the Amazon Rainforest* (San Francisco: City Lights Publishers, 2008), pp. 6–18.

114. "Carbon plan in Ecuador would leave jungle oil reserves untapped," *Yale Environment 360*, Yale School of Forestry and Environmental Studies (e360.yale.edu/content/digest.msp?id=1897).

115. Haroon Siddique, "Pay-to-protect plan for Ecuador's rainforest on the brink," *The Guardian* [UK], October 9, 2008 (guardian.co.uk/environment/2008/oct/09/endangeredhabitats.endangeredspecies).

116. Ibid.

117. Jess Smee, "Oil or Trees? Germany Takes Lead in Saving Ecuador's Rainforest," Sustainable Development Media Think Tank, June 24, 2009 (sustainabilitank.info/2009/06/24/will-germany-go-for-the-oil-of-ecuador-or-for-the-trees-as-credits-for-its-own-pollution-who-are-the-future-good-samaritans/).

118. "The Ogoni Bill of Rights," Movement for the Survival of the Ogoni People, October 1990 (mosop.org/ogoni_bill_of_rights.html).

119. Andrew Walker, "Fresh start for Nigerian oil activists?" BBC News, August 11, 2008 (news.bbc.co.uk/2/hi/africa/7509220.stm).

120. "Shell in Nigeria: What Are the Issues?" Essential Action (essentialaction.org/shell/issues.html).

121. Andy Rowell, "Secret papers 'show how Shell targeted Nigeria oil protests,'" *The Independent* [UK], June 14, 2009 (independent.co.uk/news/world/americas/secret-papers-show-how-shell-targeted-nigeria-oil-protests-1704812.html).

122. "Ken Saro-Wiwa's closing statement to the Nigerian military-appointed special tribunal," *Southern Africa Report*, vol. 11, no. 2, January 1996 (africafiles.org/article.asp?ID=3906). The following is the full text of Ken's final statement:

We all stand before history. I am a man of peace, of ideas. Appalled by the denigrating poverty of my people who live on a richly endowed land, distressed by their political marginalization and economic strangulation, angered by the devastation of their land, their ultimate heritage, anxious to preserve their right to life and to a decent living, and determined to usher to this country as a whole a fair and just democratic system which protects everyone and every ethnic group and gives us all a valid claim to human civilization, I have devoted my intellectual and material resources, my very life, to a cause in which I have total belief and from which I cannot be blackmailed or intimidated. I have no doubt at all about the ultimate success of my cause, no matter the trials and tribulations which I and those who believe with me may encounter on our journey. Nor imprisonment nor death can stop our ultimate victory.

I repeat that we all stand before history. I and my colleagues are not the only ones on trial.

Shell is here on trial and it is as well that it is represented by counsel said to be holding a watching brief. The Company has, indeed, ducked this particular trial, but its day will surely come and the lessons learnt here may prove useful to it for there is no doubt in my mind that the ecological war that the Company has waged in the Delta will be called to question sooner than later and the crimes of that war be duly punished. The crime of the Company's dirty wars against the Ogoni people will also be punished.

On trial also is the Nigerian nation, its present rulers and those who assist them. Any nation which can do to the weak and disadvantaged what the Nigerian nation has done to the Ogoni, loses a claim to independence and to freedom from outside influence. I am not one of those who shy away from protesting injustice and oppression, arguing that they are expected in a military regime. The military do not act alone. They are supported by a gaggle of politicians, lawyers, judges, academics and businessmen, all of them hiding under the claim that they are only doing their duty, men and women too afraid to wash their pants of urine. We all stand on trial, my lord, for by our actions we have denigrated our Country and jeopardized the future of our children. As we subscribe to the sub-normal and accept double standards, as we lie and cheat openly, as we protect injustice and oppression, we empty our classrooms, denigrate our hospitals, fill our stomachs with hunger and elect to make ourselves the slaves of those who ascribe to higher standards, pursue the truth, and honour justice, freedom, and hard work. I predict that the scene here will be played and replayed by generations yet unborn. Some have already cast themselves in the role of villains, some are tragic victims, some still have a chance to redeem themselves. The choice is for each individual.

I predict that the denouement of the riddle of the Niger delta will soon come. The agenda is being set at this trial. Whether the peaceful ways I have favoured will prevail depends on what the oppressor decides, what signals it sends out to the waiting public. In my innocence of the false charges I face Here, in my utter conviction, I call upon the Ogoni people, the peoples of the Niger delta, and the oppressed ethnic minorities of Nigeria to stand up now and fight fearlessly and peacefully for their rights. History is on their side. God is on their side. For the Holy Quran says in Sura 42, verse 41: "*All those that fight when oppressed incur no guilt, but Allah shall punish the oppressor.*" Come the day.

123. Stephen Kretzmann, "Shell's Settlement Doesn't Hide Unsettling Reality in Nigeria," *The Huffington Post,* June 10, 2009 (huffingtonpost.com/stephen-kretzmann/shells-settlement-doesnt_b_213352.html).

124. "The Case Against Shell," Center for Constitutional Rights and EarthRights International (wiwavshell.org/the-case-against-shell/).

125. Jad Mouawad, "Shell to Pay $15.5 Million to Settle Nigerian Case," *The New York Times,* June 8, 2009 (nytimes.com/2009/06/09/business/global/09shell.html?_r=1&ref=global).

126. Shai Oster, "Shell to Start Talks with Nigeria," *The Wall Street Journal,* May 31, 2005, page A7.

127. "The Ogoni Issue," Shell Oil (shell.com/home/content/nigeria/about_shell/issues/ogoni/ogoni.html).

128. *Oil for Nothing: Multinational Corporations, Environmental Destruction, Death and Impunity in the Niger Delta,* a U.S. nongovernmental delegation trip report, September 6–20, 1999, p. 18 (essentialaction.org/shell/Final_Report.pdf).

129. "Bowoto v. Chevron Case Overview," Earth Rights International (earthrights.org/site_blurbs/bowoto_v_chevrontexaco_case_overview.html).

130. David Morris and Irshad Ahmed, *The Carbohydrate Economy: Making Chemicals and Industrial Materials from Plant Matter* (Washington, D.C.: Institute for Local Self-Reliance, 1992). This and many other titles about alternatives to petroleum are listed on the website of the Institute for Local Self-Reliance at ilsr.org/pubs/pubscarbo.html.

131. Sustainable Biomaterials Collaborative website: sustainablebiomaterials.org.

132. "Electricity Overview," based on data from the International Energy Agency (IEA),

Key World Energy Statistics 2008, Pew Center on Global Climate Change (pew climate.org/technology/overview/electricity).

133. Shaila Dewan, "T.V.A. to Pay $43 Million on Projects in Spill Area," *The New York Times,* September 14, 2009 (nytimes.com/2009/09/15/us/15ash.html).

134. Jeff Goodell, *Big Coal: The Dirty Secret Behind America's Energy Future* (New York: Houghton Mifflin Harcourt, 2006), p. 146.

135. Ibid., p. 10.

136. Ibid., p. xx.

137. "National Memorial for the Mountains," iLoveMountains.org (ilovemountains.org/memorial).

138. Deborah Bräutigam, *Taxation and Governance in Africa,* American Enterprise Institute for Public Policy Research, April 2008 (aei.org/outlook/27798).

139. *United Nations Declaration on the Rights of Indigenous Peoples,* adopted by the General Assembly September 13, 2007 (un.org/esa/socdev/unpfii/en/declaration.html).

140. "Sustainable Development and Indigenous Peoples," International Work Group for Indigenous Affairs (iwgia.org/sw219.asp).

141. "Extractive Industries," issue brief, World Bank Group (ifc.org/ifcext/media.nsf/AttachmentsByTitle/AM08_Extractive_Industries/$FILE/AM08_Extractive_Industries_IssueBrief.pdf).

142. "Environmental and Social Policies," Bank Information Center (bicusa.org/EN/Issue.Background.4.aspx).

143. Extractive Industries Transparency Initiative (eiti.org/ru/node/614).

144. "Anti World Bank, IMF Activists Say," Agence France-Presse, March 14, 2000 (global policy.org/component/content/article/209/43161.html).

145. "World Bank Bonds Boycott," Center for Economic Justice (econjustice.net/wbbb/).

146. Jared Diamond, "What's Your Consumption Factor?" *The New York Times,* January 2, 2008 (nytimes.com/2008/01/02/opinion/02diamond.html).

147. "The State of Consumption Today," Worldwatch Institute (worldwatch.org/node/810).

148. "Earth Overshoot Day," Global Footprint Network (footprintnetwork.org/en/index.php/GFN/page/earth_overshoot_day/). For much more detailed information on the resource use of individual countries, see the *Living Planet Report 2008,* coauthored by the World Wildlife Fund and the Global Footprint Network (footprintnetwork.org/en/index.php/GFN/page/national_assessments/).

149. One Planet Living website: oneplanetliving.org/index.html.

150. Ibid.

151. Hawken and Hunter, *Natural Capitalism,* p. 8.

152. "1994 Declaration of the·Factor 10 Club" Factor 10 Institute (techfak.uni-bielefeld.de/~walter/f10/declaration94.html).

Chapter 2: Production

1. Many references, including: Our Stolen Future (Ourstolenfuture.org); *State of the World 2006,* Worldwatch Institute; Nancy Evans, ed., *State of the Evidence 2006,* executive summary, Breast Cancer Fund, p. 4 (breastcancerfund.org/atf/cf/%7BDE 68F7B2–5F6A-4B57–9794-AFE5D27A3CFF%7D/State%20of%20the%20Evidence% 202006.pdf); Gay Daly, "Bad Chemistry," *OnEarth,* Winter 2006 (nrdc.org/onearth/06win/chem1.asp).

2. "Of the more than 80,000 chemicals in commerce, only a small percentage of them have ever been screened for even one potential health effect, such as cancer, reproductive toxicity, developmental toxicity, or impacts on the immune system. Among

the approximately 15,000 tested, few have been studied enough to correctly estimate potential risks from exposure. Even when testing is done, each chemical is tested individually rather than in the combinations that one is exposed to in the real world. In reality, no one is ever exposed to a single chemical, but to a chemical soup, the ingredients of which may interact to cause unpredictable health effects." From "Chemical Body Burden," Coming Clean (chemicalbodyburden.org/whatisbb.htm).

3. Theo Colburn, John Peter Myers, and Dianne Dumanoski, *Our Stolen Future: Are We Threatening Our Fertility, Intelligence, and Survival?* (New York: Plume Books, 1997). See the Our Stolen Future website for chapter synopses (ourstolenfuture.org/Basics/chapters.htm) and recent news about chemical exposures (ourstolenfuture.org/New/recentimportant.htm).

4. Fred Pearce, *Confessions of an Eco-Sinner: Tracking Down the Sources of My Stuff* (Boston: Beacon Press, 2008), p. 89.

5. A. K. Chapagain, A. Y. Hoekstra, H. H. G. Savenije, and R. Gautam, "The water footprint of cotton consumption," *Ecological Economics*, vol. 60, no. 1, November 1, 2006, pp. 201–2 (waterfootprint.org/Reports/Report18.pdf).

6. Ibid., p. 187.

7. Ibid., p. 195.

8. Ibid., p. 186.

9. Ibid., p. 187.

10. Pearce, *Confessions of an Eco-Sinner*, pp. 111–12.

11. Ibid., p. 90.

12. Worldwatch Institute, *State of the World 2004* (New York: W. W. Norton & Company, 2004), p. 162.

13. "Problems with conventional cotton production," Pesticide Action Network North America (panna.org/Node/570).

14. Ibid.

15. Pearce, *Confessions of an Eco-Sinner*, p. 114.

16. Charles Benbrook, *Pest Management at the Crossroads* (Yonkers, N.Y.: Consumer's Union, 1996), p. 2.

17. "Problems with conventional cotton production."

18. Ibid.

19. Ibid.

20. Billie J. Collier, Martin Bide, and Phyllis Tortora, *Understanding Textiles* (Upper Saddle River, N.J.: Prentice Hall, 2008), p. 11.

21. Ibid., pp. 20–27.

22. Michael Lackman, "Care What You Wear: Facts on Cotton and Clothing Production," Organic Consumers Association, June 29, 2007 (organicconsumers.org/articles/article_6347.cfm).

23. Michael Lackman, "Permanent Press: Facts behind the fabrics,"OrganicClothing .blogs.com, January 3, 2009 (organicclothing.blogs.com/my_weblog/2009/01/permanent-press-facts-behind-the-fabrics.html).

24. "Formaldehyde," U.S. Environmental Protection Agency (epa.gov/iaq/formalde .html#Health Effects).

25. Lackman, "Care What You Wear."

26. Chapagain, Hoekstra, Savenije, and Gautam, "The water footprint of cotton consumption," p. 202.

27. Pearce, *Confessions of an Eco-Sinner*, p. 104.

28. "Haitian Garment Factory Conditions," *Campaign for Labor Rights Newsletter*, July 8, 1997 (hartford-hwp.com/archives/43a/136.html).

29. Personal correspondence with Yannick Etienne, August 2009.

30. "Lawmakers Vote to Increase Minimum Wage for Haitians," Caribarena, August 5, 2009 (caribarena.com/caribbean/haiti/haiti-lawmakers-vote-to-increase-minimum -wage-for-haitians.html).

31. Pearce, *Confessions of an Eco-Sinner,* p. 91.

32. "The Footprint Chronicles: Tracking the Environmental and Social Impact of Patagonia Clothing and Apparel," Patagonia (patagonia.com/web/us/footprint/index .jsp).

33. Susan Kinsella, "The History of Paper," *Resource Recycling,* June 1990 (conservatree .org/learn/Papermaking/History.shtml).

34. Ibid.

35. "Environmentally Sound Paper Overview: Environmental Issues. Part III—Making Paper: Content," Conservatree (conservatree.org/learn/Essential%20Issues/EIPaper Content.shtml).

36. "Book Sector," Green Press Initiative (greenpressinitiative.org/about/bookSector .htm).

37. "The Trees of Central Park," Central Park Conservancy (centralparknyc.org/site/ PageNavigator/virtualpark_cptreedbase).

38. "Impacts on Climate," Green Press Initiative (greenpressinitiative.org/impacts/ climateimpacts.htm).

39. "Paper Making and Recycling," U.S. Environmental Protection Agency (epa.gov/ waste/conserve/materials/paper/basics/papermaking.htm).

40. *Comparison of Kraft, Sulfite, and BCTMP Manufacturing Technologies for Paper,* white paper, Environmental Defense Fund, December 19, 1995 (edf.org/documents/ 1632_WP12.pdf).

41. Carola Hanisch, "Finished in 15 Minutes: Paper Industry Global View," *Clariant,* February 1999 (emt-india.com/process/pulp_paper/pdf/Paper_industry_globalview .pdf).

42. *Pulp and Paper Chemicals: Industry Forecasts for 2011 and 2016,* Freedonia Group, February 2008 (reuters.com/article/pressRelease/idUS68793+23-Jan-2008+BW2008 0123).

43. Jeffrey Hollender, "Putting the Breast Cancer/Chlorine Connection on Paper," *The Non-Toxic Times,* July 2004 (consumerhealthreviews.com/articles/WomansHealth/ BreastCancerChlorine.htm).

44. *Draft Dioxin Reassessment: Draft Exposure and Human Health Reassessment of 2,3,7,8-Tetrachlorodibenzo-p-Dioxin (TCDD) and Related Compounds,* U.S. Environmental Protection Agency, 2003 (cfpub.epa.gov/ncea/cfm/part1and2.cfm?ActType =default) ; "Dioxin," U.S. Environmental Protection Agency, National Center for Environmental Assessment (cfpub.epa.gov/ncea/CFM/nceaQFind.cfm?keyword =Dioxin); "Polychlorinated Dibenzo-*para*-Dioxins and Polychlorinated Dibenzofurans," *IARC Monographs on the Evaluation of Carcinogenic Risks to Humans,* vol. 69, August 12, 1997; J. Raloff, "Dioxin confirmed as a human carcinogen," *Science News,* May 15, 1999, pp. 3–9 (monographs.iarc.fr/ENG/Monographs/vol69/volume69.pdf).

45. *The American People's Dioxin Report,* Center for Health Environment and Justice (mindfully.org/Pesticide/Dioxin-Report-CEHJ.htm).

46. "Chlorine Free Processing," Conservatree (conservatree.org/paper/PaperTypes/ CFDisc.shtml).

47. "Getting Mercury Out of Paper Production," Natural Resources Defense Council (nrdc.org/cities/living/mercury.asp).

48. Michelle Carstensen and David Morris, *Biochemicals for the Printing Industry,* Insti-

tute for Local Self-Reliance; available for purchase at ilsr.org or online at pneac.org/
sheets/all/Biochemicals_for_the_Printing_Industry.pdf.

49. Ibid., p. 5.
50. Ibid., p. 4.
51. Elizabeth Grossman, *High Tech Trash* (Washington, D.C.: Island Press, 2006), p. 5.
52. Ibid., p. 78.
53. Michael Dell, speech given at the Gartner Symposium/ITxpo, October 2002, quoted
    in *Clean Up Your Computer,* a Catholic Agency for Overseas Development report
    (cafod.org.uk/var/storage/original/application/phpYyhizc.pdf).
54. Grossman, *High Tech Trash,* p. 5.
55. Interview with Ted Smith, June 2009.
56. Andrew S. Grove, *Only the Paranoid Survive* (New York: Doubleday Business, 1996).
57. *Trade and Development Report, 2002,* UN Conference on Trade and Development,
    p. vii (unctad.org/en/docs/tdr2002overview_en.pdf).
58. Grossman, *High Tech Trash,* p. 4.
59. Ibid., p. 37.
60. Ibid., p. 36.
61. Ibid., pp. 37–38.
62. Ibid., p. 59.
63. Interview with Ted Smith, June 2009.
64. Alexandra McPherson, Beverley Thorpe, and Ann Blake, *Brominated Flame Retar-
    dants in Dust on Computers: The Case for Safer Chemicals and Better Computer
    Design,* Clean Production Action, June 2004, p. 5 (cleanproduction.org/library/
    BFR%20Dust%20on%20Computers.pdf).
65. Ibid., p. 24.
66. Ibid., pp. 30–32.
67. Grossman, *High Tech Trash,* p. 42.
68. Eric Williams, Robert Ayers, and Miriam Heller, "The 1.7 Kilogram Microchip: En-
    ergy and Material Use in the Production of Semiconductor Devices," *Environmental
    Science and Technology Vol. 36,* no. 24, 2002, p. 5509.
69. Peter Singer, "The Greening of the Semi-Conductor Industry," *Semiconductor Inter-
    national,* December 1, 2007 (semiconductor.net/article/205812-The_Greening_of_
    the_Semiconductor_Industry.php).
70. Ibid.
71. Grossman, *High Tech Trash,* pp. 42–43.
72. Ibid., p. 41.
73. Michiel van Dijk and Irene Schipper, *Dell: CSR Company Profile,* SOMO, the Centre
    for Research on Multinational Corporations, May 2007, p. 19 (somo.nl/publications
    -en/Publication_1956).
74. Interview with Dara O'Rourke, June 2009.
75. "Environmental Responsibility," Dell (content.dell.com/us/en/corp/dell-earth.aspx).
76. "Soesterberg Principles Electronic Sustainability Commitment," Clean Production
    Action (cleanproduction.org/Electronics.Green.php).
77. "Life Cycle Studies: Aluminum Cans," *World Watch,* vol. 19, no. 3,May/June 2006
    (worldwatch.org/node/4062).
78. Alan Thein Durning and John C. Ryan, *Stuff: The Secret Lives of Everyday Things*
    (Washington, D.C.: World Future Society, 1998), pp. 62–63.
79. Pearce, *Confessions of an Eco-Sinner,* p. 146.
80. Durning and Ryan, *Stuff,* p. 63.
81. Pearce, *Confessions of an Eco-Sinner,* p. 148.

82. Durning and Ryan, *Stuff*, pp. 63–64.
83. Personal communication with Juan Rosario, July 2009.
84. "Life Cycle Studies: Aluminum Cans."
85. Jennifer Gitliz, *The Role of the Consumer in Reducing Primary Aluminum Demand*, a report by the Container Recycling Institute for the International Strategic Round-table on the Aluminum Industry, São Luís, Brazil, October 16–18, 2003, p. 2.
86. Pearce, *Confessions of an Eco-Sinner*, p. 149.
87. Gitliz, *The Role of the Consumer in Reducing Primary Aluminum Demand*, p. 4.
88. Ibid.
89. "The Aluminum Can's Dirty Little Secret: On-going Environmental Harm Outpaces the Metal's 'Green' Benefits," press release from the Container Recycling Institute and International Rivers Network, May 17, 2006 (container-recycling.org/media/news release/aluminum/2006-5-AlumDirty.htm).
90. "Calculating the Aluminum Can Recycling Rate," Container Recycling Institute (container-recycling.org/facts/aluminum/data/UBCcalculate.htm).
91. Gitliz, *The Role of the Consumer in Reducing Primary Aluminum Demand*, p. 18.
92. Ibid., p. 13.
93. Ibid., p. 14.
94. Elizabeth Royte, *Garbageland: On the Secret Trail of Trash* (New York: Little, Brown & Co., 2005), p. 155.
95. "Life Cycle Studies: Aluminum Cans."
96. Ibid.
97. Michael Belliveau and Stephen Lester, *PVC—Bad News Comes in Threes: The Poison Plastic, Health Hazards and the Looming Waste Crisis*, The Environmental Health Strategy Center and the Center for Health, Environment and Justice, 2004, pp. 16–18 (chej.org/BESAFE/pvc/pvcreports.htm).
98. Ibid., p. 18.
99. Ibid., pp. 19–20.
100. Stephen Lester, Michael Schade, and Caitlin Weigand, "Volatile Vinyl: the New Shower Curtain's Chemical Smell," Center for Health, Environment and Justice, June 12, 2008 (cela.ca/publications/volatile-vinyl-new-shower-curtains-chemical -smell-0).
101. Belliveau and Lester, "PVC," pp. 1, 35.
102. Ibid., p. 2.
103. Ibid., p. 13.
104. Ibid., p. 21.
105. Beverley Thorpe, "Closing the Product Loop: How Europe Is Grappling with Waste," Clean Production Action, February 11, 2003 (ecologycenter.org/recycling/beyond 50percent/closingtheloop.ppt).
106. "PVC Governmental Policies Around the World," Center for Health, Environment and Justice (besafenet.com/pvc/government.htm).
107. Ibid.
108. Payal Sampat and Gary Gardner, *Mind Over Matter: Recasting the Role of Materials in Our Lives*, Worldwatch Institute, December 1998 (worldwatch.org/node/846).
109. Personal correspondence with Ted Schettler, July 2009.
110. "Lead, Cadmium, and Other Harmful Chemicals Found in Popular Children's Toys," press release from the Washington Toxics Coalition, December 12, 2007 (watoxics .org/pressroom/press-releases/popular-holiday-toys-contaminated-with-high-levels -of-toxic-chemicals/).
111. David Duncan, *Experimental Man* (Hoboken, N.J.: John Wiley & Sons, 2009), p. 159.

112. Michael Hawthorne, "Pregnant women get new mercury warning," *Chicago Tribune,* February 7, 2004 (ewg.org/node/22671).

113. Duncan, *Experimental Man,* p. 129.

114. "Mercury in the Environment," U.S. Geological Survey (usgs.gov/themes/fact sheet/146–00/).

115. Duncan, *Experimental Man,* p. 159.

116. "Historic Treaty to Tackle Toxic Heavy Metal Mercury Gets Green Light," press release from the United Nations Environment Programme, February 20, 2009 (unep .org/Documents.Multilingual/Default.asp?DocumentID=562&ArticleID=6090&l=en/).

117. Ibid.

118. Ibid.

119. Stacy Malkan, *Not Just a Pretty Face: The Ugly Side of the Beauty Industry* (Gabriola Island, B.C.: New Society Publishers, 2007), p. 2.

120. Ibid., p. 54, citing the research of the Environmental Working Group that resulted in the Skin Deep database, a review of more than 150,000 personal care products. Ingredients evaluated by Skin Deep come from the following sources: product labels; industry ingredient listings; assessments of the personal care product industry's internal safety panel, the Cosmetic Ingredient Review; fifty data sources on the toxicity, regulatory status, and study availability of chemicals in personal care products; and ingredients entered into the database by manufacturers and individual users (cos meticsdatabase.com/about.php).

121. Jane S. Fisher, "Environmental anti-androgens and male reproductive health: Focus on phthalates and testicular dysgenesis syndrome," white paper for the University of London School of Pharmacy, Department of Toxicology, 2004 (reproduction-online .org/cgi/content/full/127/3/305).

122. Malkan, *Not Just a Pretty Face,* p. 26, citing Jane Houlihan, Charlotte Brody, and Bryony Schwan, *Not Too Pretty: Pthalates, Beauty Products and the FDA,* Environmental Working Group, Coming Clean, and Healthcare Without Harm, July 8, 2002 (ewg.org/reports/nottoopretty).

123. "A Poison Kiss: The Problem of Lead in Lipstick," The Campaign for Safe Cosmetics, October 2007 (safecosmetics.org/article.php?id=327).

124. "No More Toxic Tub," The Campaign for Safe Cosmetics, March 2009 (safecosmetics .org/article.php?id=414).

125. Malkan, *Not Just a Pretty Face,* p. 60.

126. Ibid., pp. 65–68.

127. Ibid., p. 70.

128. "Statement of Jane Houlihan on Cosmetics Safety. Discussion Draft of the 'Food and Drug Administration Globalization Act' Legislation: Device and Cosmetic Safety Before the Subcommittee on Health of the Committee on Energy and Commerce United States House of Representatives, May 2008," Environmental Working Group (ewg.org/node/26545).

129. Skin Deep cosmetics safety database (cosmeticsdatabase.com). See note 120.

130. Barry Commoner's foreword to Ken Geiser, *Materials Matter* (Boston: MIT Press, 2001), p. x.

131. "Chemical Body Burden," Coming Clean (chemicalbodyburden.org/).

132. "The Foundation for Global Action on Persistent Organic Pollutants: A United States Perspective," U.S. Environmental Protection Agency, March 2002 (scribd.com/ doc/1799026/Environmental-Protection-Agency-POPsa).

133. David Santillo, Iryna Labunska, Helen Davidson, et al., *Consuming Chemicals— Hazardous chemicals in house dust as an indicator of chemical exposure in the home,*

Greenpeace Research Laboratories (greenpeace.org/international/press/reports/consuming-chemicals-hazardou).

134. "Body Burden: The Pollution in Newborns," Environmental Working Group, July 14, 2005 (ewg.org/reports/bodyburden2/execsumm.php).

135. Sonya Lunder and Renee Sharp, *Mother's Milk: Record Levels of Toxic Fire Retardants Found in American Mothers' Breast Milk,* Environmental Working Group, September 2003, pp. 15–17 (ewg.org/reports/mothersmilk/).

136. Ibid., p. 17.

137. Ibid., p. 5.

138. Joene Hendry, "Being Breast-fed May Lower Breast Cancer Risk," *Reuters Health,* May 9, 2008 (breastcancer.org/risk/new_research/20080509.jsp).

139. Lunder and Sharp, *Mother's Milk,* p. 33.

140. "What is REACH?" EUROPA-Environment (ec.europa.eu/environment/chemicals/reach/reach_intro.htm).

141. "Why We Need the Kid-Safe Chemicals Act," Environmental Working Group (ewg.org/kid-safe-chemicals-act-blog/kid-safe-chemicals-act/).

142. "Lautenberg, Solis, Waxman Introduce Legislation to Protect Americans from Hazardous Chemicals in Consumer Products—'Kid Safe Chemical Act' Would Ensure All Chemicals Used in Every Day Products, Including Those Used in Baby Bottles and Children's Toys, Are Proven Safe," press release from the office of Senator Frank R. Lautenberg, May 20, 2008 (lautenberg.senate.gov/newsroom/record.cfm?id=298072).

143. "Landmark Chemical Reform Introduced in Congress," press release from the Environmental Working Group, May 20, 2008 (ewg.org/node/26571).

144. "More than a Paycheck," Sweet Honey in the Rock (youtube.com/watch?v=UzlEGxiHpEU).

145. Personal correspondence with Peter Orris, July 2009.

146. "Occupational Cancer," National Institute for Occupational Safety and Health (cdc.gov/niosh/topics/cancer/).

147. Ibid.

148. "Environmental Justice," U.S. Environmental Protection Agency (epa.gov/oecaerth/basics/ejbackground.html).

149. Benjamin F. Chavis, Jr., and Charles Lee, *Toxic Wastes and Race in the United States: A National Report on the Racial and Socio-Economic Characteristics of Communities with Hazardous Waste Sites,* United Church of Christ, 1987, p. xiv (ucc.org/about-us/archives/pdfs/toxwrace87.pdf).

150. Temma Kaplan, *Crazy for Democracy: Women in Grassroots Movements* (New York: Routledge, 1997), p. 69.

151. "Environmental Justice," U.S. Environmental Protection Agency (epa.gov/compliance/environmentaljustice/index.html).

152. Robert D. Bullard, Paul Mohai, Robin Saha, and Beverly Wright, *Toxic Wastes and Race at Twenty: 1987–2007,* United Church of Christ, March 2007, p. xii (ucc.org/justice/pdfs/toxic20.pdf).

153. Steve Lerner, "Fenceline and Disease Cluster Communities: Living in the Shadow of Heavily-Polluting Facilities," Collaborative on Health and the Environment, October 1, 2006 (healthandenvironment.org/articles/homepage/751).

154. Mick Brown, "Bhopal gas disaster's legacy lives on 25 years later," Telegraph.co.uk, August 6, 2009 (telegraph.co.uk/news/worldnews/asia/india/5978266/Bhopal-gas-disasters-legacy-lives-on-25-years-later.html); Helene Vosters, "Bhopal Survivors Confront Dow," CorpWatch, May 15, 2003 (corpwatch.org/article.php?id=6748).

155. "What Happened in Bhopal?" The Bhopal Medical Appeal (bhopal.org/index .php?id=22).

156. Researchers found heavy concentrations of carcinogenic chemicals and heavy metals like mercury. Mercury was found at between 20,000 to 6 million times the expected levels, and elemental mercury was discovered to be widely distributed across the plant premises. Twelve volatile organic compounds, most greatly exceeding EPA standard limits, were found to have seeped and continue to seep into the water supplies of an estimated twenty thousand people in the local area. Three water wells in this community, northeast of the factory, were discovered to have the most severe contamination. Other wells, though not as severely contaminated, also showed elevated levels of toxic chemicals. I. Labunska, A. Stephenson, K. Brigden, et al., "Toxic contaminants at the former Union Carbide factory site, Bhopal, India: 15 years after the Bhopal accident," Greenpeace Research Laboratories, April 1999.

157. Srishti, *Surviving Bhopal 2002: Toxic Present, Toxic Future,* Fact Finding Mission on Bhopal, January 2002 (bhopal.net/oldsite/documentlibrary/survivingbhopal 2002.doc).

158. "What Happened in Bhopal?"

159. Rashida Bee and Champa Devi Shukla, Goldman Prize 2004 acceptance speech (goldmanprize.org/node/83).

160. "Padyatra/Dharna/Hungerstrike 2008 Demands," International Campaign for Justice in Bhopal (bhopal.net/march/padyatra2008_demands.html).

161. Ann Larabee, *Decade of Disaster* (Chicago: University of Illinois Press, 2000), p. 136.

162. Kim Fortun, *Advocacy after Bhopal: Environmentalism, Disaster, New Global Orders* (Chicago: University of Chicago Press, 2001), p. 58.

163. Ibid.

164. "Responsible Care," American Chemistry Council (americanchemistry.com/s_respon siblecare/sec.asp?CID=1298&DID=4841).

165. *Trust Us, Don't Track Us: An Investigation of the Chemical Industry's Responsible Care Program,* U.S. Public Interest Research Group Education Fund, January 28, 1998 (static.uspirg.org/usp.asp?id2=6997&id3=USPIRG&).

166. "What is the Toxics Release Inventory (TRI) Program," U.S. Environmental Protection Agency (epa.gov/TRI/triprogram/whatis.htm).

167. "2007 TRI Public Data Release," U.S. Environmental Protection Agency (epa.gov/ TRI/tridata/tri07/index.htm).

168. "Pollution Report Card for Zip Code 94709, Alameda County," Scorecard.org (score card.org/community/index.tcl?zip_code=94709&set_community_zipcode_cookie _p=t&x=0&y=0).

169. Ibid.

170. "Limitations of EPA's Exposure Estimates," Scorecard.org (scorecard.org/env -releases/def/tri_ei_risk_methods.html).

171. "What You Need to Know About Mercury in Fish and Shellfish: 2004 EPA and FDA Advice for: Women Who Might Become Pregnant, Women Who Are Pregnant, Nursing Mothers, Young Children," press release from the U.S. Food and Drug Administration, March 2004 (fda.gov/Food/FoodSafety/Product-SpecificInformation/ Seafood /FoodbornePathogensContaminants/Methylmercury/ucm115662.htm).

172. Ricardo Alonso-Zaldivar, "FDA Moves to Advise Pregnant Women to Consume More Mercury-Laced Seafood," Associated Press, December 15, 2008 (ewg.orgnode/27440).

173. Lyndsey Layton, "FDA Draft Report Urges Consumption of Fish, Despite Mercury Contamination," *The Washington Post,* December 12, 2008 (washingtonpost.com/ wp-dyn/content/article/2008/12/11/AR2008121103394.html).

174. Ibid.

175. Research compiled by Renee Shade, from the official websites of the U.S. Office of Environmental Quality, Department of Health and Human Services, Department of Labor, Department of Commerce, and Environmental Protection Agency.

176. Geiser, *Materials Matter,* p. 140.

177. "Federal Advisory Committee Act: Issues Related to the Independence and Balance of Advisory Committees," U.S. Government Accountability Office, GAO-08–611T, April 2, 2008 (gao.gov/htext/d08611t.html).

178. "FDA Statement on Release of Bisphenol A (BPA) Subcommittee Report," press release by the U.S. Food and Drug Administration, October 28, 2008 (fda.gov/news events/newsroom/pressannouncements/2008/ucm116973.htm).

179. "NTP, FDA at Odds on Bisphenol-A," *Integrity in Science Watch,* Center for Science in the Public Interest, week of September 8, 2008 (cspinet.org/integrity/press/200809081.html).

180. Kirsten Stade, *Twisted Advice: Federal Advisory Committees Are Broken,* Center for Science in the Public Interest, January 2009 (cspinet.org/new/pdf/twisted_advice _final_report.pdf).

181. Ken Geiser, "Comprehensive Chemicals Policies for the Future," Lowell Center for Sustainable Production, University of Massachusetts Lowell, November 2008 (hhh .umn.edu/centers/stpp/pdf/Geiser_Chemicals_Policy_Paper.pdf).

182. M. King Hubbert, "Nuclear Energy and the Fossil Fuels," *Drilling and Production Practice,* American Petroleum Institute, 1956 (energybulletin.net/node/13630).

183. William McDonough quoted in *Sidwell Friends Alumni Magazine,* Spring 2005, p. 9 (sidwell.edu/data/files/news/AlumniMagazine/spring_2005.pdf).

184. "Mobile Industry Unites to Drive Universal Charging Solution for Mobile Phones," press release from the GSMA, February 17, 2009. GSMA (Groupe Special Mobile) is the association of the worldwide mobile communications industry.

185. Ibid.

186. Biomimicry Institute website: biomimicryinstitute.org.

187. Ibid.

188. Janine Benyus, "Janine Benyus shares nature's designs," TED talk filmed February 2005 (ted.com/talks/janine_benyus_shares_nature_s_designs.html).

Chapter 3: Distribution

1. Sarah Anderson, John Cavanagh, and Thea Lee, *Field Guide to the Global Economy,* rev. ed. (New York: New Press, 2005), p. 6.

2. Interview with Dara O'Rourke, April 2009.

3. Ibid.

4. Ibid.

5. Robert Goldman and Stephen Papson, *Nike Culture: the Sign of the Swoosh* (London: Sage Publications Ltd., 1999), p. 168.

6. Interview with Dara O'Rourke, April 2009.

7. Ibid.

8. Ibid.

9. William Greider, "A New Giant Sucking Sound," *The Nation,* December 31, 2001 (thenation.com/doc/20011231/greider).

10. David C. Korten, *When Corporations Rule the World,* 2nd ed. (San Francisco: Berrett-Koehler Publishers, 2001), p. 216.

11. Interview with Dara O'Rourke, April 2009.

12. Gary Fields, *Territories of Profit: Communications, Capitalist Development and the*

Innovative Enterprises of G. F. Swift and Dell Computer (Palo Alto, Calif.: Stanford University Press, 2004), p. 208.

13. Interview with Dara O'Rourke, April 2009.
14. Personal communication with Patrick Bond, professor at the University of KwaZulu-Natal, August 2009.
15. Interview with Dara O'Rourke, April 2009.
16. Ibid.
17. Correspondence with Dara O'Rourke, September 2009.
18. Interview with Dara O'Rourke, April 2009.
19. Ibid.
20. Personal correspondence with Michael Maniates, March 2009.
21. *America's Freight Challenge*, a report by the American Association of State Highway and Transportation Officials (AASHTO) for the National Surface Transportation Policy and Revenue Study Commission, May 2007, p. 25.
22. Ibid.
23. Wayne Ellwood, *The No-Nonsense Guide to Globalization* (London: Verso, 2005), p. 18.
24. "Ship Sulfur Emissions Found to Strongly Impact Worldwide Ocean and Coastal Pollution," *Science Daily*, August 20, 1999, based on research from Carnegie Mellon and Duke universities.
25. Rochester Institute of Technology, "Pollution from Marine Vessels Linked to Heart and Lung Disease," FirstScience News, November 7, 2007 (firstscience.com/home/news/breaking-news-all-topics/pollution-from-marine-vessels-linked-to-heart-and-lung-disease_39078.html).
26. "Commercial Ships Spew Half as Much Particulate Pollution as World's Cars," NASA Earth Observatory, February 26, 2009 (earthobservatory.nasa.gov/Newsroom/view.php?id=37290).
27. "Large Cargo Ships Emit Double Amount of Soot Previously Estimated," *Science Daily*, July 11, 2008 (sciencedaily.com/releases/2008/07/080709103848.htm).
28. John W. Miller, "The Mega Containers Invade," *The Wall Street Journal*, January 26, 2009 (online.wsj.com/article/SB123292489602813689.html).
29. *America's Freight Challenge*, p. 13.
30. *Freight and Intermodal Connectivity in China*, a report sponsored by the U.S. Department of Transportation, Federal Highway Administration, May 2008, pp. 19–23 (international.fhwa.dot.gov/pubs/pl08020/pl08020.pdf).
31. Ibid., p. 23.
32. Ibid., p. 31.
33. *America's Freight Challenge*, pp. 18–19.
34. Ibid., p. 19.
35. Ibid.
36. "Quantification of the Health Impacts and Economic Valuation of Air Pollution from Ports and Goods Movement in California," California Air Resources Board, April 20, 2006 (arb.ca.gov/planning/gmerp/gmerp.htm).
37. David Bensman and Yael Bromberg, "Deregulation has wrecked port trucking system," *The Record*/NorthJersey.com, March 29, 2009.
38. David R. Butcher, "The State of U.S. Rail, Air and Sea Shipping," ThomasNet News, February 3, 2009 (news.thomasnet.com/IMT/archives/2009/02/shipping-carrier-container-trends-challenges-in-us-state-of-industry.html).
39. Helen Lindblom and Christian Stenqvist, "SKF Freight Transports and CO2 Emissions: A study in environmental management accounting," master's thesis, Depart-

ment of Energy and Environment, Chalmers University of Technology, 2007 (chalmers.se/ee/SV/forskning/forskargrupper/miljosystemanalys/publikationer/pdf-filer/2007_2/downloadFile/attachedFile_3_f0/2007–18.pdf).

40. "SmartWay," U.S. Environmental Protection Agency (epa.gov/smartway/basic-infor mation/index.htm).

41. Justin Thomas, "UPS Unveils 'World's Most Efficient Delivery Vehicle,'" TreeHugger, August 10, 2006 (treehugger.com/files/2006/08/ups_unveils_wor_1.php).

42. Michael Graham Richard, "FedEx Converts 92 Delivery Trucks to Diesel Hybrids with Lithium-Ion Batteries," TreeHugger, July 21, 2009 (treehugger.com/files/2009/07/fedex-converts-92-delivery-trucks-to-diesel-electric-hybrids.php).

43. Andrew Posner, "DHL Unveils Guilt-free Shipping," TreeHugger, March 9, 2008 (treehugger.com/files/2008/03/dhl-guiltfree-shipping.php).

44. Mark Bernstein, "Driving the Integrated Global Supply Chain from the Top," *World Trade 100*, September 1, 2005 (worldtrademag.com/Articles/Feature_Article/5a7707 fc6aaf7010VgnVCM100000f932a8c0).

45. Sarah Raper Larenaudie, "Inside the H&M Fashion Machine," *Time*, February 9, 2004 (time.com/time/magazine/article/0,9171,993352,00.html).

46. Ola Kinnander, "H&M Profit Falls 12% as Currencies Aggravate Weak Sales," *The Wall Street Journal*, March 26, 2009 (online.wsj.com/article/SB123807961431048401. html).

47. Larenaudie, "Inside the H&M Fashion Machine."

48. Susanne Göransson, Angelica Jönsson, and Michaela Persson, "Extreme Business Models in the Clothing Industry: A case study of H&M and ZARA," dissertation, Department of Business Studies, Kristianstad University, December 2007, pp. 50–52.

49. Interview with Dara O'Rourke, April 2009.

50. Göransson, Jönsson, and Persson, "Extreme Business Models," p. 55.

51. Interview with Dara O'Rourke, April 2009.

52. Larenaudie, "Inside the H&M Fashion Machine."

53. Keisha Lamothe, "Online retail spending surges in 2006," CNNMoney.com, January 4, 2007 (money.cnn.com/2007/01/04/news/economy/online_sales/?postversion=2007 010410).

54. Stacy Mitchell, *Big-Box Swindle: The True Cost of Mega-Retailers and the Fight for America's Independent Businesses* (Boston: Beacon Press, 2007), p. 12.

55. Speech by Jeff Bezos at MIT, November 25, 2002 (mitworld.mit.edu/video/1/).

56. Ibid.

57. Renee Wilmeth of Google Books and Literary Architects, quoted by Dave Taylor, Ask Dave Taylor (askdavetaylor.com/what_percentage_of_books_printed_end_up _destroyed.html).

58. H. Scott Matthews and Chris T. Hendricks, "Economic and Environmental Implica tions of Online Retailing in the United States," dissertation, Graduate School of Industrial Administration, Carnegie Mellon University, August 2001.

59. "By 2010, more than 50 percent of books sold worldwide will be printed on demand at the point of sale in the form of library-quality paperbacks," predicts Jason Epstein, the former editorial director of Random House and author of *Book Business: Publishing—Past, Present, and Future*, quoted by *Wired* magazine, May 2002 (wired .com/wired/archive/10.05/longbets.html?pg=4).

60. Collin Dunn, "Online Shopping vs. Driving to the Mall: The Greener Way to Buy," TreeHugger, February 13, 2009 (treehugger.com/files/2009/02/online-shopping-vs -driving-mall-greener.php).

61. Freecycle website: freecycle.org.

62. Mitchell, *Big-Box Swindle*, p. 13.
63. Ibid.
64. "Wal-Mart awarding $2B to U.S. hourly employees, report says," Reuters, March 21, 2009 (usatoday.com/money/industries/retail/2009–03–19-walmart-workers_N.htm).
65. Mitchell, *Big-Box Swindle*, p. 13.
66. Ibid., p. 12.
67. Ibid., p. 15.
68. Ibid.
69. Ibid., p. 13.
70. Ibid., p. 14.
71. Sonia Reyes, "Study: Wal-Mart Private Brands Are Catching On," *Brandweek*, August 21, 2006 (brandweek.com/bw/esearch/article_display.jsp?vnu_content_id=1003019846).
72. Mitchell, *Big-Box Swindle*, p. 7.
73. "Where to buy appliances: Big stores aren't necessarily the best," *Consumer Reports*, September 1, 2005.
74. Mitchell, *Big-Box Swindle*, p. xvii.
75. "The Real Facts About Wal-Mart," WakeUpWalMart.com (wakeupwalmart.com/facts/).
76. *Wal-Mart: The High Cost of Low Price*, Robert Greenwald, director, 2005.
77. "The Real Facts About Wal-Mart," citing data from the UFCW analysis of Wal-Mart's health plan, WakeUpWalMart.com, March 2008 (wakeupwalmart.com/facts/).
78. "Disclosures of Employers Whose Workers and Their Dependents Are Using State Health Insurance Programs," Good Jobs First, updated October 26, 2009 (goodjobsfirst.org/corporate_subsidy/hidden_taxpayer_costs.cfm).
79. "How Wal-Mart Has Used Public Money in Your State," Wal-Mart Subsidy Watch (walmartsubsidywatch.org).
80. Mitchell, *Big-Box Swindle*, p. xv.
81. Al Norman, "Barstow, CA., Lawsuit Freezes Wal-Mart Distribution Center Until May," Wal-Mart Watch, January 12, 2009 (walmartwatch.com/battlemart/archives/barstow_ca_lawsuit_freezes_wal_mart_distribution_center_until_may/).
82. Mike Troy, "High-tech DC streamlines supply chain," *DSN Retailing Today*, May 9, 2005 (findarticles.com/p/articles/mi_mOFNP/is_9_44/13734506/ai_n).
83. Norman, "Barstow, CA., Lawsuit Freezes Wal-Mart Distribution Center Until May."
84. Bensman and Bromberg, "Deregulation has wrecked port trucking system."
85. Ibid.
86. Stephanie Rosenbloom and Michael Barbaro, "Green-Light Specials, Now at Wal-Mart," *The New York Times*, January 24, 2009 (nytimes.com/2009/01/25/business/25walmart.html?pagewanted=1&_r=1). Also see the fact sheets that Wal-Mart regularly up-dates on their company website (walmartstores.com/FactsNews/Fact Sheets/#Sustainability).
87. "Zero Waste," Wal-Mart (walmartstores.com/Sustainability/7762.aspx).
88. Mitchell, *Big-Box Swindle*, pp. 3–4.
89. Ibid., pp. 5–6.
90. Ibid.
91. Ibid.
92. *Wal-Mart: The High Cost of Low Price*.
93. Mitchell, *Big-Box Swindle*, p. 40.
94. "The Real Facts About Wal-Mart," WakeUpWalMart (wakeupwalmart.com/facts/),

based on data from the U.S. Department of Labor, Bureau of Labor Statistics (bls.gov/news.release/empsit.t16.htm).

95. "The Real Facts About Wal-Mart," quoting directly from Wal-Mart's "A Manager's Toolbox to Remaining Union Free," pp. 20–21.

96. *Wal-Mart: The High Cost of Low Price.*

97. Ross Perot with Pat Choate, *Save Your Job, Save Our Country* (New York: Hyperion Books, 1993), p. 41.

98. Thomas Friedman, "Mexico feels job-loss pain," *Arizona Daily Star,* April 3, 2004 (azstarnet.com/sn/related/16486).

99. Mitchell, *Big-Box Swindle,* p. xv.

100. Uri Berliner, "Haves and Have-Nots: Income Inequality in America," National Public Radio, February 5, 2007 (npr.org/templates/story/story.php?storyId=7180618).

101. John M. Broder, "California Voters Reject Wal-Mart Initiative," *The New York Times,* April 7, 2004 (nytimes.com/2004/04/07/national/07CND-WALM.html).

102. Ellwood, *The No-Nonsense Guide to Globalization,* pp. 24–27.

103. Ibid.

104. Ibid., pp. 27–34.

105. "World Bank energy complex creates hell on earth for Indian citizens," Probe International, March 1, 1998 (probeinternational.org/export-credit/world-bank-energy-complex-creates-hell-earth-indian-citizens).

106. "About Us," The World Bank (web.worldbank.org/WBSITE/EXTERNAL/EXTABOU TUS/0,,contentMDK:20040565~menuPK:1696892~pagePK:51123644~piPK:32982 9~theSitePK:29708,00.html).

107. Amitayu Sen Gupta, "Debt elief for LDCs: The new Trojan Horse of Neo-Liberalism," International Development Economics Associates (networkideas.org/news/aug2006/ Debt_Relief.pdf).

108. "Status of Kenya's Debt," fact sheet, Jubilee USA (jubileeusa.org/fileadmin/user_up load/Resources/Kenya_2005.pdf), citing Njoki Githethwa, "Government of Kenya should declare official position on debt," press release from the Kenya Debt Relief Network, July 19, 2005 (odiousdebts.org/odiousdebts/index.cfm?DSP=content& ContentID=13408).

109. "How Big is the Debt of Poor Countries?" Jubilee Debt Campaign (jubileedebtcam paign.org.uk/2 How big is the debt of poor countries%3F+2647.twl).

110. Ibid.

111. "World Bank/IMF Questions and Answers," Global Exchange (globalexchange.org/ campaigns/wbimf/faq.html). See also 50 Years Is Enough, a campaign of the U.S. Network for Global Economic Justice (50years.org/issues/).

112. "H.R. 2634: Jubilee Act for Responsible Lending and Expanded Debt Cancellation of 2008," Open Congress (opencongress.org/bill/110-h2634/actions_votes).

113. "Clinton pledges more than $50m in aid for Haiti," Agence France-Presse, April 14, 2009 (google.com/hostednews/afp/article/ALeqM5i0vtqlmpiKI-5VkFrRKXqINsYsJw).

114. "Top Reasons to Oppose the WTO," Global Exchange (globalexchange.org/cam paigns/wto/OpposeWTO.html). See also Ellwood, *The No-Nonsense Guide to Globalization,* p. 34.

115. Ellwood, *The No-Nonsense Guide to Globalization,* pp. 36–37.

116. Amory Starr, *Global Revolt: A guide to the movements against globalization* (London: Zed Books, 2005), p. 30.

117. For images of the 1999 Battle of Seattle, see youtube.com/watch?v=_JXPIBsxdk$; youtube.com/watch?v=YdACqgxRLsQ; video.google.com/videosearch?q=News+W TO+Seattle+1999&hl=en&client=firefox-a&emb=0&aq=f#.

118. "A Million Farmers Protest Against the WTO in India," Karnataka State Farmers' Association, March 21, 2001 (organicconsumers.org/corp/wtoindia.cfm).

119. "Memorandum submitted to the Prime Minister: Keep Agriculture Out of WTO," Members of the Indian Coordination Committee of Farmers Movements, October 2, 2005 (focusweb.org/india/index.php?option=com_content&task=view&id=744&Ite mid=30).

120. "Suicide and protests mar summit," BBC News, September 11, 2003 (news.bbc.co .uk/2/hi/business/3098916.stm).

121. "South Korea Activist Kills Himself, Others Injured in Cancun Protest," Agence France-Presse, September 11, 2003 (commondreams.org/headlines03/0911–06.htm).

122. "TRADE Act Fact Sheet 2009," Public Citizen (citizen.org/trade/tradeact/).

123. Personal correspondence with Kevin Gallagher, August 2009.

124. "This is USAID," USAID (usaid.gov/about_usaid/).

125. Marc Lacey, "Across Globe, Empty Bellies Bring Rising Anger," The New York Times, April 18, 2008 (nytimes.com/2008/04/18/world/americas/18food.html?pagewanted =1&_r=1).

126. Oscar Olivera and Tom Lewi, Cochabamba!: Water War in Bolivia (Boston: South End Press, 2004).

127. "100 Mile Diet: An interview with James and Alisa" (100milediet.org/faqs). Find out more in their book: Alisa Smith and J. B. MacKinnon, Plenty: Eating Locally on the 100 Mile Diet (New York: Three Rivers Press, 2007).

128. Bill McKibben, Deep Economy (New York: Times Books, 2007), p. 128.

129. David Kupfer, "Table for Six Billion, Please: Judy Wicks on her plan to change the world, one restaurant at a time," The Sun Magazine, iss. 392, August 2008 (thesun magazine.org/issues/392/table_for_six_billion).

130. Ibid.

131. Rob Hopkins and Peter Lipman, Who We Are and What We Do, Transition Network, February 1, 2009 (transitionculture.org/wp-content/uploads/who_we_are_high.pdf).

132. Anderson, Cavanagh, and Lee, Field Guide to the Global Economy, p. 52.

133. Barbara Ehrenreich, foreword to Anderson, Cavanagh, and Lee, Field Guide to the Global Economy, p. viii.

Chapter 4: Consumption

1. Robert D. McFadden and Angela Macropoulos, "WalMart Employee Trampled to Death," The New York Times, November 28, 2008 (nytimes.com/2008/11/29/ business/29walmart.html).

2. Ken Belson and Karen Zraick, "Mourning a Good Friend and Trying to Make Sense of a Stampede," The New York Times, November 29, 2008 (nytimes.com/2008/11/30/ nyregion/30walmart.html).

3. Christian Sylt, "Christopher Rodrigues: Visa is far more than just a card, says its Cambridge Blue boss," The Independent [UK], November 6, 2005 (independent .co.uk/news/people/profiles/christopher-rodrigues-visa-is-far-more-than-just-a-card -says-its-cambridge-blue-boss-514061.html).

4. Worldwatch Institute, State of the World 2004: Special Focus—Consumer Society (New York: W. W. Norton & Company, 2004), p. 5.

5. John De Graaf, David Wann, and Thomas H. Naylor, Affluenza: The All-Consuming Epidemic, 2nd ed. (San Francico: Berrett-Koehler Publishers, Inc., 2005), p. 13.

6. Worldwatch Institute, State of the World 2004, p. 10.

7. Benjamin Barber, Consumed: How Markets Corrupt Children, Infantilize Adults, and Swallow Citizens Whole (New York: W.W. Norton & Co., 2008), p. 8.

8. Paul Lomartire, "The Monster That Is the Mall of America," *Chicago Tribune,* May 11, 2003 (chicagotribune.com/travel/midwest/minnesota/chi-071219twincities-monster mall,0,1792859.story).

9. Mellody Hobson, "Mellody's Math: Credit Card Cleanup," ABC News, February 28, 2009 (abcnews.go.com/GMA/FinancialSecurity/story?id=126244&page=1).

10. De Graaf, Wann, and Naylor, *Affluenza,* p. 41.

11. Worldwatch Institute, *State of the World 2004,* p. 4.

12. Margot Adler, "Behind the Ever-Expanding American Dream House," National Public Radio, July 4, 2006 (npr.org/templates/story/story.php?storyId=5525283).

13. Juliet Schor, "Cleaning the Closet," essay in Duane Elgin's *The Voluntary Simplicity Discussion Course* (Portland: Northwest Earth Institute, 2008), p. 35.

14. Michelle Hofmann, "The s-t-r-e-t-c-h Garage," *Los Angeles Times,* October 1, 2006 (articles.latimes.com/2006/oct/01/realestate/re-garages1).

15. *SSA Industry Report and SSA Update for 2009,* Self Storage Association (selfstorage .org/SSA/Home/AM/ContentManagerNet/ContentDisplay.aspx?Section=Home& ContentID=4163).

16. See the transcript of Bush's speech in Atlanta on November 8, 2001; the quote is "People are going about their daily lives, working and shopping and playing, worshipping at churches and synagogues and mosques, going to movies and to baseball games. Life in America is going forward, and as the fourth grader who wrote me knew, that is the ultimate repudiation of terrorism." (archives.cnn.com/2001/US/ 11/08/rec.bush.transcript/).

17. Robert Louis Stevenson, "Henry David Thoreau: His Character and Opinions," *Cornhill Magazine,* June 1880.

18. Edward Wagenknecht, *John Greenleaf Whittier: A Portrait in Paradox* (New York: Oxford University Press, 1967), p. 112.

19. Wynn Yarborough, "Reading of Thoreau's 'Resistance to Civil Government,'" Virginia Commonwealth University, 1995 (vcu.edu/engweb/transcendentalism/authors/ thoreau/critonrcg.html).

20. Eisenhower quoted by Joni Seager in *Earth Follies: Coming to Feminist Terms with the Global Environmental Crisis* (New York: Routledge, 1993), p. 221.

21. "Brighter" by Discover Card (youtube.com/watch?v=LKFZjg4eGMk).

22. Bill McKibben, *Deep Economy* (New York: Henry Holt & Company, 2007), pp. 35–36.

23. Worldwatch Institute, *State of the World 2004,* p. 166. (The thirteen thousand dollars is annual per person income in 1995 dollars or "purchasing parity.")

24. Richard Layard, *Happiness: Lessons from a New Science* (London: Penguin Press, 2005), pp. 29–35.

25. Layard, *Happiness,* pp. 34–35.

26. Robert Putnam, *Bowling Alone* (New York: Simon & Schuster, 2000).

27. Shankar Vedantam, "Social Isolation Growing in U.S., Study Says," *The Washington Post,* June 23, 2006 (washingtonpost.com/wp-dyn/content/article/2006/06/22/AR 2006062201763.html).

28. "Obesity and Overweight Statistics," U.S. Centers for Disease Control and Prevention (cdc.gov/obesity/data/index.html).

29. From the U.S. Centers for Disease Control and Prevention's *Morbidity and Mortality Weekly Report,* reported in *Science Daily,* September 8, 2007 (sciencedaily.com/ releases/2007/09/070907221530.htm).

30. De Graaf, Wann, and Naylor, *Affluenza,* p. 77.

31. Ibid., p. 45

32. McKibben, *Deep Economy,* p. 114.

33. Worldwatch Institute, *State of the World 2004*, p. 112.
34. "Credit Card Debt Statistics," Money-zine.com (money-zine.com/Financial -Planning/Debt-Consolidation/Credit-Card-Debt-Statistics).
35. Tim Kasser, *The High Price of Materialism* (Boston: MIT Press, 2003), p. 22.
36. Ibid., p. 59.
37. Worldwatch Institute, *State of the World 2004*, p. 18.
38. *The Happy Planet Index 2.0: Why good lives don't have to cost the earth,* The New Economics Foundation, 2009, p. 61.
39. Malin Rising, "Global Arms Spending Rises Despite Economic Woes," *The Independent* [UK], June 9, 2009 (independent.co.uk/news/world/politics/global-arms -spending-rises-despite-economic-woes-1700283.html).
40. *The Happy Planet Index 2.0*, p. 5.
41. "Earth Overshoot Day 2009," Global Footprint Network (footprintnetwork.org/en/ index.php/GFN/page/earth_overshoot_day/).
42. Worldwatch Institute, *State of the World 2004*, pp. 6–7.
43. "Earth Overshoot Day 2009."
44. David W. Orr, "The Ecology of Giving and Consuming," in *Consuming Desires: Consumption, Culture and the Pursuit of Happiness,* edited by Roger Rosenblatt (Washington D.C.: Island Press, 1999), p. 141.
45. Worldwatch Institute, *State of the World 2004*, p.12.
46. Ibid.
47. Juliet B. Schor, *The Overworked American: The Unexpected Decline of Leisure* (New York: Basic Books, 1993), p. 77.
48. "Corporate Deals with Nazi Germany," *UE News,* United Electrical, Radio and Machine Workers of America (ranknfile-ue.org/uen_nastybiz.html).
49. Elaine Ganley, "French Spend More Time Sleeping and Eating than Other Nations," *The Huffington Post,* May 4, 2009 (huffingtonpost.com/2009/05/04/french-spend -more-time-ea_n_195548.html).
50. McKibben, *Deep Economy,* p. 114.
51. Duane Elgin, *The Voluntary Simplicity Discussion Course,* p. 15.
52. Thomas Princen, Michael Maniates, and Ken Conca, *Confronting Consumption* (Boston: MIT Press, 2002), p. 216.
53. Michael Burawoy, *Manufacturing Consent: Changes in the Labor Process Under Monopoly Capitalism* (Chicago: University of Chicago Press, 1979), pp. 32–40.
54. Victor Lebow in the *Journal of Retailing,* quoted in Vance Packard, *The Waste Makers* (New York: David McKay, 1960), p. 24.
55. "Industrial Strength Design: How Brooks Stevens Shaped Your World," Milwaukee Art Museum (mam.org/collection/archives/brooks/index.asp).
56. Bernard London, *Ending the Depression Through Planned Obsolescence,* originally published in 1932. Text of this pamphlet is posted at adbusters.org/blogs/blackspot _blog/consumer_society_made_break.htm.
57. Packard, *The Waste Makers,* p. 46.
58. Elgin, *The Voluntary Simplicity Discussion Course,* p. 31.
59. This is based on the widely cited figure of forty thousand TV commercials per year; see "Television Advertising Leads to Unhealthy Habits in Children; Says APA Task Force," press release from the American Psychological Association, February 23, 2004 (apa.org/releases/childrenads.html). Some analysts say fifty thousand; see the excerpt from Nolo Press's *Marketing Without Advertising* (nolo.com/product.cfm/ objectID/5E5BFB9E-A33A-43DB-9D162A6460AA646A/sampleChapter/5/111/277/ #summary).

60. Barber, *Consumed,* p. 29.

61. Elgin, *The Voluntary Simplicity Discussion Course,* p. 30.

62. Worldwatch Institute, *State of the World 2004,* p. 14.

63. Barber, *Consumed,* p. 11.

64. Barber, *Consumed,* p. 13.

65. "Big Three Spent $7.2 Billion on Ads in 2007," Dollars & Sense Blog (dollarsandsense. org/blog/2008/12/big-three-spent-72-billion-on-ads-in.html).

66. "Apple's Advertising Budget: Revealed!" BNET Technology Blog (industry.bnet.com/ technology/1000574/apples-advertising-budget-revealed/).

67. "Sharp will change your life?" Media Mentalism (mediamentalism.com/2008/07/15/ sharp-will-change-your-life/).

68. "Advertisers go after bedroom eyes," *Sustainable Industries Journal,* February 2007.

69. Aaron Falk, "Mom sells face space for tattoo advertisement," *Deseret News,* June 30, 2005 (deseretnews.com/article/1,5143,600145187,00.html).

70. Mya Frazier, "Channel 1: New Owner, Old Issues," Commercial Alert (commercial alert.org/issues/education/channel-one/channel-one-new-owner-old-issues).

71. Ibid. See also obligation.org.

72. James Gustave Speth, *The Bridge at the Edge of the World: Capitalism, the Environment, and Crossing from Crisis to Sustainability* (New Haven: Yale University Press, 2008), p. 159.

73. Juliet B. Schor, *The Overspent American: Why We Want What We Don't Need* (New York: Harper Perennial, 1999), pp. 49–50.

74. Vedantam, "Social Isolation Growing in U.S.," quoting Robert B. Putnam, author of *Bowling Alone* (washingtonpost.com/wp-dyn/content/article/2006/06/22/AR200606 2201763.html).

75. "Average Home Has More TVs than People," *USA Today,* September 21, 2006 (usa today.com/ . . . /television/ . . . /2006-09-21-homes-tv_x.htm).

76. Alana Semuels, "Television viewing at all-time high," *Los Angeles Times,* February 24, 2009 (articles.latimes.com/2009/feb/24/business/fi-tvwatching24).

77. Schor, *The Overspent American,* p. 81.

78. Layard, *Happiness,* p. 89.

79. Schor, *The Overspent American,* pp. 74–79.

80. Sandra Gonzales, "Berkeley to Vote on Politically-Correct Coffee," *San Jose Mercury News,* October 24, 2002 (commondreams.org/headlines02/1024–05.htm).

81. Barber, *Consumed,* pp. 82–88.

82. Ibid., p. 139.

83. "Our Fading Heritage: Americans Fail a Basic Test of Their History and Institutions," Intercollegiate Studies Institute, 2008 (americancivicliteracy.org/2008/summary_ summary.html).

84. Eric Lane and Michael Oreskes, "The Scary Consequences of Our Mindless Indifference to the History of the Constitution," History News Network, October 8, 2007 (hnn.us/articles/43202.html). Lane and Oreskes are authors of *The Genius of America: How the Constitution Saved Our Country—and Why It Can Again* (NY: Bloomsbury USA, 2007).

85. "National Voter Turnout in Federal Elections," Infoplease (infoplease.com/ipa/ A0781453.html).

86. Putnam, *Bowling Alone;* an excerpt published online by the League of Women Voters cites the number of people ever attending a public meeting as 13 percent in 1993 (xroads.virginia.edu/~HYPER/DETOC/putnam1/putnam.htm).

87. Layard, *Happiness,* pp. 8, 63.

88. Jane E. Dematte, "Near-Fatal Heat Stroke During the 1995 Heat Wave in Chicago," *Annals of Internal Medicine*, vol. 129, no. 3, August 1, 1998, pp. 173–81.

89. Personal communication with Judith Helfand, 2009.

90. McKibben, *Deep Economy*, p. 117.

91. Layard, *Happiness*, p. 74.

92. Worldwatch Institute, *State of the World 2004*, p. 5.

93. Ibid., p. 6.

94. "Overview," *Human Development Report 1998*, United Nations Development Programme (hdr.undp.org/en/media/hdr_1998_en_overview.pdf).

95. Ibid.

96. "1.02 Billion People Hungry: One Sixth of Humanity Undernourished, More than Ever Before," *Science Daily*, June 20, 2009 (sciencedaily.com/releases/2009/06/090619121443.htm).

97. Andrew Pollack, "Disease of Rich Extends Its Pain to Middle Class," *The New York Times*, June 12, 2009 (nytimes.com/2009/06/13/health/13gout.html?_r=1&scp=1&sq=disease%20of%20kings&st=cse).

98. "More than Half the World Lives on Less than $2 a Day," Population Reference Bureau (prb.org/Journalists/PressReleases/2005/MoreThanHalftheWorldLivesonLessThan2aDayAugust2005.aspx), citing data from the World Bank's *World Development Report 2000/2001*.

99. Robert Frank, "Market Failures," *Boston Review*, Summer 1999 (bostonreview.net/BR24.3/frank.html) and in *Luxury Fever*, New York: Free Press, 1999.

100. World Resources Institute, quoting Josette Sheera, executive director of the World Food Programme (earthtrends.wri.org/updates/node/349).

101. William Greider, "One World of Consumers," in *Consuming Desires*, p. 27.

102. Carbon Footprint of Nations website, Norwegian University of Science and Technology: carbonfootprintofnations.com.

103. Elgin, *The Voluntary Simplicity Discussion Course*, p. 16.

104. Alan Durning, *How Much Is Enough? The Consumer Society and the Future of the Earth* (Washington, D.C.: Worldwatch Institute, 1992), p. 150.

Chapter 5: Disposal

1. Jerry Seinfeld live on tour, 2008. (My friend, Andre Carothers, was in attendance and reported this to me.)

2. The automotive information website Edmunds.com states, "A car loses roughly a quarter of its value the moment it leaves the dealer's lot" (edmunds.com/reviews/list/top10/122630/article.html), but 10 percent is the figure usually referred to as "common knowledge."

3. "George Carlin Talks About 'Stuff'" (youtube.com/watch?v=MvgN5gCuLac).

4. Personal correspondence with Paul Connett, June 2008.

5. "The Impact of the Economic Downturn on Solid Waste Services," Solid Waste Association of North America (swanacal-leg.org/downloads/SWANA%20LTF%20white%20paper%20on%20letterhead.pdf).

6. Maria Elena Baca, "One Silver Lining of the Economic Downturn," Star Tribune, August 2, 2009 (startribune.com/local/north/52269857.html).

7. "U.S. Waste Management Industry Overview," Themedica, February 23, 2009 (themedica.com/articles/2009/02/us-waste-management-industry-o.html).

8. Joel Makower, "Industrial Strength Solution," *Mother Jones*, May/June 2009 (motherjones.com/environment/2009/05/industrial-strength-solution).

9. Ray Anderson, *Confessions of a Radical Industrialist* (New York: St. Martin's Press, 2009), pp. 64–65.

10. "Non-Hazardous Waste," U.S. Environmental Protection Agency (epa.gov/epawaste/ nonhaz/).

11. Joel Makower, "Calculating the Gross National Trash," March 17, 2009 (readjoel .com/joel_makower/2009/03/calculating-the-gross-national-trash.html).

12. Makower, "Industrial Strength Solution."

13. Ibid.

14. "A Natural Step Network Case Study: Interface, Atlanta, Georgia," The Natural Step (naturalstep.org/en/usa/interface-atlanta-georgia-usa).

15. Ray Anderson, "The business logic of sustainability," TED talk filmed February 2009, posted May 2009 (ted.com/talks/ray_anderson_on_the_business_logic_of_sustain ability.html).

16. Ibid.

17. Ibid.

18. Charles Fishman, "Sustainable Growth—Interface, Inc." *Fast Company,* December 18, 2007 (fastcompany.com/magazine/14/sustaing.html).

19. Kate Fletcher, *Sustainable Fashion and Textiles* (London: Earthscan, 2008), p. 158.

20. Personal correspondence with Ray Anderson, August 2009.

21. Personal communication with Dan Knapp, August 2009.

22. *Municipal Solid Waste in the United States 2007 Facts and Figures,* U.S. Environmental Protection Agency, November 2008, p. 3 (epa.gov/waste/nonhaz/municipal/pubs/ msw07-rpt.pdf).

23. Ibid.

24. Research by Renee Shade based on data from Statistics Canada (40.statcan.gc.ca), the United Nations Statistics Division (unstats.un.org/unsd/environment/wastetreat ment.ht), Index Mundi (indexmundi.com/), and the U.S. Passport Service Guide figures on China's population (us-passport-service-guide.com/china-population.html).

25. The figure that "75% of municipal solid waste is products" is calculated by weight. This comes from a U.S. Environmental Protection Agency data series going back to 1960, called *Characterization of Municipal Solid Waste* (epa.gov/osw//nonhaz/ municipal/msw99.htm).

26. Helen Spiegelman and Bill Sheehan, *Unintended Consequences: Municipal Solid Waste Management and the Throwaway Society,* Product Policy Institute, 2005, p. 8.

27. Julie Scelfo, "Appliance Anxiety: Replace It or Fix It?" *The New York Times,* May 27, 2009 (nytimes.com/2009/05/28/garden/28repair.html).

28. "Industry Statistics for 2008," *PSA Update,* newsletter of the Professional Service Association newsletter, April 2009 (psaworld.com/ASN_Update_04-09.pdf).

29. Shoe Service Institute of America website: ssia.info/about.asp.

30. Gena Terlizzi, "Shoe Repair Shops Boom During Tough Economic Times," KTKA, February 16, 2009 (ktka.com/news/2009/feb/16/shoe_repair_shops_boom_during_ tough_economic_times/).

31. Vance Packard, *The Waste Makers* (New York: David McKay, 1960), p. 119.

32. John Roach, "Plastic-Bag Bans Gaining Momentum Around the World," *National Geographic News,* April 4, 2008 (nationalgeographic.com/news/2008/04/080404 -plastic-bags.html).

33. "Irish Bag Tax Hailed as Success," BBC News, August 20, 2002 (news.bbc.co.uk/1/hi/ world/europe/2205419.stm).

34. Daniel Imhoff, *Paper or Plastic* (San Francisco: Sierra Club Books, 2005), p. 139.

35. "The Decline of Refillable Beverage Bottles in the U.S.," Container Recycling Institute (container-recycling.org/facts/glass/decline.htm).

36. *Beverage Containers: US Industry Forecasts for 2012 and 2017,* summary, Freedonia Group, November 2008 (reportbuyer.com/industry_manufacturing/chemicals_industry/beverage_containers.html).

37. "Bottle Bill Resource Guide," Container Recycling Institute (bottlebill.org/about/whatis.htm).

38. "H.R. 2046—Bottle Recycling Climate Protection Act of 2009," OpenCongress (opencongress.org/bill/111-h2046/show).

39. "Bottle Bill Opponents," Container Recycling Institute (bottlebill.org/about/opponents.htm).

40. "Bottle Bill Toolkit," Container Recycling Institute (toolkit.bottlebill.org/opposition/opponents.htm).

41. "Keep America Beautiful: A History," Container Recycling Institute (toolkit.bottlebill.org/opposition/KABhistory.htm).

42. Chadd De Las Casas, "Playing Indian: The Iron Eyes Cody Story," Associated Content, October 15, 2007 (associatedcontent.com/article/404817/playing_indian_the_iron_eyes_cody_story_pg2.html?cat=38).

43. Ted Williams, "The Metamorphosis of Keep America Beautiful," *Audubon,* March 1990.

44. "Key Vote for National Recycling Coalition," *BioCycle,* vol. 50, no. 7, July 2009, p. 6.

45. Bette K. Fishbein, *Germany, Garbage and the Green Dot: Challenging a Throwaway Society* (Philadelphia: Diane Publishing, 1996), p. 46.

46. Ibid., p. 36.

47. *Extended Producer Responsibility,* Clean Production Action, 2003, p. 28 (cleanproduction.org/library/EPRtoolkitFINAL.pdf).

48. Deanne Toto, "Green with Envy: Germany's Green Dot program continues generating good collection numbers," *Recycling Today,* October 2004 (thefreelibrary.com/Green+with+envy%3a+Germany's+Green+Dot+program+continues+generating . . . -a0123753975).

49. "Summary of Germany's packaging take-back law," Clean Production Action, September 2003, p. 3 (cleanproduction.org/library/EPR_dvd/DualesSystemDeutsch_REVISEDoverview.pdf).

50. Garth T. Hickle, "The Producer Is Responsible for Packaging in the European Union," *Package Design Magazine,* 2006 (packagedesignmag.com/issues/2006.11/special.producer.shtml).

51. Spiegelman and Sheehan, *Unintended Consequences,* p. 5.

52. "History of Waste," Product Policy Institute (productpolicy.org/content/history-waste).

53. Spiegelman and Sheehan, *Unintended Consequences,* p. 2.

54. "Fees," Product Policy Institute (productpolicy.org/content/fees).

55. Construction Materials Recycling Association website: cdrecycling.org.

56. "Mission Statement," Rebuilders Source (rebuilderssource.coop//index.php?option=com_content&task=view&id=14&Itemid=32).

57. Personal correspondence with Glenn McRae, May 2009.

58. "Waste Minimization, Segregation, and Recycling in Hospitals," Healthcare Without Harm, October 2001 (72.32.87.20/lib/downloads/waste/Waste_Min_Seg_Recyc_in_Hosp.pdf).

59. "Waste Management," Healthcare Without Harm (72.32.87.20/us_canada/issues/waste/) and Paul Connett, "Medical Waste Incineration: A mismatch between prob-

lem and solution," *The Ecologist Asia,* vol. 5, no. 2, March/April 1997 (bvsde.paho .org/bvsacd/cd48/mismatch.pdf).

60. "Electronics," Clean Production Action (cleanproduction.org/Producer.International .Europe.Electronics.php).

61. "Problem: Electronics Become Obsolete Quickly," Electronics TakeBack Coalition (computertakeback.com/problem/made_to_break.htm).

62. "Poison PCs and Toxic TVs," Silicon Valley Toxics Coalition, p. 9. Based on data from Microelectronics and Computer Technology Corporation's *Electronics Industry Environmental Roadmap,* 1996.

63. *E-Waste: The Exploding Global Electronic Waste Crisis,* Electronics TakeBack Coalition, p. 8 (computertakeback.com/legislation/Ewaste%20Briefing%20Book.pdf).

64. "Problem: Electronics Become Obsolete Quickly."

65. "Facts and Figures on E-Waste Recycling," Electronics TakeBack Coalition (computer takeback.com/Tools/Facts_and_Figures.pdf).

66. Ibid.

67. Brandon Sample, "Prisoners Exposed to Toxic Dust at UNICOR Recycling Factories," *Prison Legal News,* July 15, 2009 (prisonlegalnews.org/displayArticle.aspx?artic leid=20750&AspxAutoDetectCookieSupport=1).

68. Elena H. Page and David Sylvain of the National Institute for Occupational Safety and Health report on the health and safety investigation of the Federal Prison Industries (UNICOR) electronics recycling program at Federal Bureau of Prisons institutions in Ohio, Texas, and California in a July 16, 2008, letter to Randall Humm, investigative counsel, U.S. Department of Justice (peer.org/docs/doj/08_28_7_ elkton_prison_niosh_report.pdf).

69. Sample, "Prisoners Exposed to Toxic Dust at UNICOR Recycling Factories."

70. Michelle Chen, "E-waste: America's Electronics Feed the Global Digital Dump," The Women's International Perspective, April 26, 2009 (thewip.net/contributors/2009/04/ ewaste_americas_electronics_fe.html).

71. Personal correspondence with Jim Puckett, February 2009.

72. "Environmentalists and Consumer Groups Applaud Dell's Policy on E-Waste Export," Electronics TakeBack Coalition, May 12, 2009 (computertakeback.com/ media/press_releases_dell_export_poliy.htm).

73. "States Are Passing E-Waste Legislation," Electronics TakeBack Coalition (electron icstakeback.com/legislation/state_legislation.htm).

74. "The e-Steward Solution," e-Stewards (e-stewards.org/esteward_solution.html).

75. "The State of Garbage in America 2008," *BioCycle,* vol. 49, no. 12, December 2008, p. 22 (jgpress.com/archives/_free/001782.html).

76. Van Jones, *The Green Collar Economy* (San Francisco: Harper One, 2008), p. 7.

77. Landfill Operation Management Advisor website: loma.civil.duth.gr/.

78. "Fresh Kills Park Project Introduction," New York City Department of City Planning, 2007 (nyc.gov/html/dcp/html/fkl/fkl_index.shtml).

79. Landfill Operation Management Advisor website: loma.civil.duth.gr/.

80. Catherine Brahic, "Atlas of hidden water may avert future conflict," *New Scientist,* October 24, 2008 (newscientist.com/article/dn15030-atlas-of-hidden-water-may -avert-future-conflict.html).

81. In the *Federal Register,* February 5, 1981, the U.S. Environmental Protection Agency first stated its opinion that all landfills will eventually leak: "There is good theoretical and empirical evidence that the hazardous constituents that are placed in land disposal facilities very likely will migrate from the facility into the broader environment. This may occur several years, even many decades, after placement of the waste in the

facility, but data and scientific prediction indicate that, in most cases, even with the application of best available land disposal technology, it will occur eventually." More than a year later, on July 26, 1982, the EPA again put its opinions into the *Federal Register,* emphasizing that all landfills will inevitably leak: "A liner is a barrier technology that prevents or greatly restricts migration of liquids into the ground. No liner, however, can keep all liquids out of the ground for all time. Eventually liners will either degrade, tear, or crack and will allow liquids to migrate out of the unit," vol. 46, no. 24, p. 32284.

82. "Waste Identification," U.S. Environmental Protection Agency (epa.gov/osw/hazard/wastetypes/wasteid/index.htm).

83. Daniel Steinway, "Trashing Superfund: The Role of Municipal Solid Waste in CERCLA Cases," *The American Lawyer's Corporate Counsel Magazine,* November 1999 (library.findlaw.com/1999/Nov/1/130490.htm).

84. "Additive to reduce cows' methane emissions on innovation shortlist," The Low Carbon Economy (lowcarboneconomy.com/community_content/_low_carbon_news/5073).

85. "Landfills Are Dangerous," Environmental Research Foundation (rachel.org/en/node/4467). This summary cites twenty-one different studies including: 1. State of New York Department of Health, *Investigation of Cancer: Incidence and Residence Near 38 Landfills with Soil Gas Migration Conditions, New York State, 1980–1989* (Atlanta, Ga.: Agency for Toxic Substances and Disease Registry, June 1998); 2. Lynton Baker, Renee Capouya, Carole Cenci, et al., *The Landfill Testing Program: Data Analysis and Evaluation Guidelines* (Sacramento, Calif.: California Air Resources Board, September 1990); 3. M. S. Goldberg et al., "Incidence of cancer among persons living near a municipal solid waste landfill site in Montreal, Quebec," *Archives of Environmental Health,* vol. 50, no. 6 (November 1995); 4. L. D. Budnick et al., "Cancer and birth defects near the Drake Superfund site, Pennsylvania," *Archives of Environmental Health,* vol. 39, no. 6 (November 1984); 5. K. Mallin, "Investigation of a bladder cancer cluster in northwestern Illinois," *American Journal of Epidemiology,* vol. 132, no. 1, supplement (July 1990); 6. J. Griffith et al., "Cancer mortality in U.S. counties with hazardous waste sites and ground water pollution," *Archives of Environmental Health,* vol. 44, no. 2 (March 1989); and 7. Martine Vrijheid, Ben Armstrong, et al., *Potential Human Health Effects of Landfill Sites; Report to the North West Region of the Environment Agency* (London: Environmental Epidemiology Unit, London School of Hygiene and Tropical Medicine, March 1998).

86. Daphne Wysham, "Good News, There's a Climate Bill—Bad News, It Stinks," originally published by Alternet.org (no-burn.org/article.php?id=711), and Kate Sheppard, "Everything You Always Wanted to Know About the Waxman-Markey Energy/Climate Bill," *Grist,* June 3, 2009 (grist.org/article/2009–06–03–waxman-markey-bill-breakdown/).

87. "Organic Materials," U.S. Environmental Protection Agency (epa.gov/osw/conserve/materials/organics/index.htm).

88. "Zero Waste: Composting," SFEnvironment (sfenvironment.org/our_programs/topics.html?ti=6).

89. Personal correspondence with Robin Plutchok, program manager at Stopwaste.org, August 2009.

90. "Managing MSW in Nova Scotia," *BioCycle,* February 1999, vol. 40, no. 2, p. 31.

91. "The State of Garbage in America" *BioCycle,* vol. 47, no. 4, April 2006, p. 26 (jgpress.com/archives/_free/000848.html).

92. Peter Montague, "The Modern Solution to Pollution is Dilution," *Rachel's Democracy*

and Health News, no. 996, January 29, 2009 (precaution.org/lib/09/waste_dispersal .090129.htm).

93. *Inventory of Sources and Environmental Releases of Dioxin-Like Compounds in the United States for the Years 1987, 1995, and 2000,* final report, United States Environmental Protection Agency, EPA/600/P-03/002f, November 2006. And *Waste Incineration: A Dying Technology,* Global Alliance for Incinerator Alternatives/Global Anti-Incinerator Alliance, 2003 (no-burn.org/article.php?id=276). Additional information and sources can be found at "Dioxin Homepage," EJnet.org (ejnet.org/dioxin/).

94. Michelle Allsopp, Pat Costner, and Paul Johnston, *Incineration and Human Health— State of Knowledge of the Impacts of Waste Incinerators on Human Health,* Greenpeace Research Laboratories, University of Exeter, 2001; Jeremy Thompson and Honor Anthony, *The Health Effects of Waste Incinerators: 4th Report,* British Society for Ecological Medicine, 2006 (ecomed.org.uk/publications/reports/the-health -effects-of-waste-incinerators); M. Franchini, M. Rial, E. Buiatti, and F. Bianchi, "Health effects of exposure to waste incinerator emissions: A review of epidemiological studies," *Annali dell'Istituto Superiore di Sanità,* vol. 40, no. 1, 2004, pp. 101– 15; N. Floret, E. Lucot, P. M. Badot, et al., "A municipal solid waste incinerator as the single dominant point source of PCDD/Fs in an area of increased non-Hodgkin's lymphoma incidence," *Chemosphere* vol. 68, no. 8, 2007, pp.1419–26; T. Tango, T. Fujita, T. Tanihata, et al., "Risk of adverse reproductive outcomes associated with proximity to municipal solid waste incinerators with high dioxin emission levels in Japan," *Journal of Epidemiology,* vol. 14, no. 3, 2004, pp. 83–93.

95. Paul Connett, from his white paper "Waste Management as if the Future Mattered," 1990.

96. Personal correspondence with Paul Connett, June 2008.

97. Personal correspondence with Mike Ewall, May 2009.

98. Global Alliance for Incinerator Alternatives/Global Anti-Incinerator Alliance website: no-burn.org.

99. "Incinerators in Disguise," Global Alliance for Incinerator Alternatives/Global Anti-Incinerator Alliance (no-burn.org/article.php?list=type&type=132).

100. U.S. Environmental Protection Agency, eGRID 2000 database, cited in *Zero Waste for Zero Warming: GAIA's Statement of Concern on Waste and Climate Change,* Global Alliance for Incinerator Alternatives/Global Anti-Incinerator Alliance, December 2008 (no-burn.org/article.php?id=567).

101. Sherry Greenfield, "Trip to PA convinces Jenkins that Frederick should build incinerator," Gazette.net, May 20, 2009 (gazette.net/stories/05202009/frednew174253 _32537.shtml).

102. Brenda Platt, *Resources up in Flames,* Global Alliance for Incinerator Alternatives/ Global Anti-Incinerator Alliance, April 2004, p. 12 (no-burn.org/downloads/ Resources up in Flames.pdf).

103. *Wasting and Recycling in the United States,* Grass Roots Recycling Network, 2000 (grrn.org/order/w2kinfo.html).

104. Information packet from a visit to the Davis Street Transfer Center in May 2009, compared to the data provided in Greenfield, "Trip to PA convinces Jenkins that Frederick should build incinerator."

105. Platt, *Resources up in Flames,* p. 14.

106. T. Rand, J.Haukohl, and U. Marxen, *Municipal Solid Waste Incineration: Requirements for a Successful Project,* World Bank technical paper no. 462, The World Bank, June 2000, p. 25.

107. Personal correspondence with Paul Connett, June 2008.

108. "What is TURA," Toxics Use Reduction Institute (turi.org/turadata/what_is_tura).

109. Jay Pateakos, "'Green' Light: City company recognized for helping environment," *The Herald News*, June 8, 2009 (heraldnews.com/homepage/x313680023/Green-light).

110. Ken Geiser and Joel Tickner, "When haste makes toxic waste," *The Boston Globe*, July 14, 2009 (boston.com/bostonglobe/editorial_opinion/oped/articles/2009/07/14/when_haste_makes_toxic_waste/).

111. "A Basic Guide to Exporting—International Legal Considerations," Unz and Co. (unzco.com/basicguide/c9.html).

112. Halina Ward, "Corporate accountability in search of a treaty?" briefing paper, The Royal Institute of International Affairs, May 2002 (chathamhouse.org.uk/files/3033_corporate_accountability_insights.pdf).

113. "Thor Chemicals and Mercury Exposure in Cato-Ridge, South Africa" (umich.edu/~snre492/Jones/thorchem.htm), using data from the series of articles by Bill Lambrecht for the *St. Louis Post-Dispatch* between 1989 and 1994.

114. Ibid.

115. Ibid.

116. "A Thor Chronology," *groundWork*, vol. 9, no. 3, September 2007 (groundwork.org.za/Newsletters/September2007.pdf).

117. "South Africa: Chemical cleanup begins," *Pambazuka News*, iss. 168, August 5, 2004 (pambazuka.org/en/category/environment/23609).

118. Tony Carnie, "Poison concerns for Inanda Dam," *The Mercury* [South Africa], October 15, 2008.

119. *Advising and Monitoring the Clean Up and Disposal of Mercury Waste in Kwazulu-Natal, South Africa: The Case of Thor Chemicals*, groundWork, May 2005 (Zeromercury.org/projects/Proposal_EEB_Thor_Chemicals_Final_revised_new_webvs.pdf).

120. James Ridgeway with Gaelle Drevet, "How Thousands of Tons of Philadelphia's Toxic Waste Ended Up on a Haitian Beach and What the City of New York Is Doing About It," *The Village Voice*, January 13, 1998 (ban.org/ban_news/dumping_on_Haiti.html).

121. Personal correspondence with Senior Litigation Counsel Howard Stewart, of the U.S. Department of Justice, Environmental Crimes Section, June 1989.

122. Website of the Basel Convention on the Control of Transboundary Movements of Hazardous Wastes and Their Disposal: basel.int/.

123. "Milestones in the Convention's History," Basel Convention (basel.int/convention/basics.html).

124. Heather Rogers, *Gone Tomorrow: The Hidden Life of Garbage* (New York: New Press, 2005), p. 170.

125. Neil Seldman, "The New Recycling Movement, Part 1: Recycling Changes to Meet New Challenges," Institute for Local Self-Reliance, October 2003 (ilsr.org/recycling/newmovement1.html).

126. *Municipal Solid Waste in the United States 2007 Facts and Figures*, U.S. Environmental Protection Agency, p. 1.

127. Ibid., p. 16.

128. "Recycling Means Business," Institute for Local Self-Reliance (ilsr.org/recycling/recyclingmeansbusiness.html).

129. "Mobil Chemical Corporation," abstract, World Resources Institute Sustainable Enterprise Program, 1992 (pdf.wri.org/bell/abstracts/case_1–56973–155–1_abstract_version_english.pdf). Another Mobil spokesperson said, "[Degradable bags] are not an answer to landfill crowding or littering . . . Degradability is just a marketing tool . . . We're talking out of both sides of our mouths because we want to sell bags. I

don't think the average consumer even knows what degradability means. Customers don't care if it solves the solid-waste problem. It makes them feel good." Quoted in Carl Deal, *The Greenpeace Guide to Anti-Environmental Organizations* (Berkeley: Odonian Press, 1993), p. 9.

130. "Mobil, FTC to settle 'environmental' claims for its Hefty trash bags," *Boston Globe*, July 28, 1992. Also see Keith Schneider, "Guides on Environmental Ad Claims," *New York Times*, July 29, 1992.

131. Rogers, *Gone Tomorrow*, p. 174.

132. Personal correspondence with Paul Connett, June 2008.

133. Anne Underwood, "10 Fixes for the Planet," *Newsweek*, April 14, 2008 (newsweek .com/id/130625?tid=relatedcl%20).

134. "What Is Zero Waste?" Grass Roots Recycling Network (grrn.org/zerowaste/ zerowaste_faq.html).

135. Personal correspondence with Monica Wilson, international co-coordinator for Global Alliance for Incinerator Alternatives/Global Anti-Incinerator Alliance, August 2009.

136. Brenda Platt, David Ciplet, Kate M. Bailey, and Eric Lombardi, *Stop Trashing the Climate*, Institute for Local-Self Reliance, the Global Alliance for Incinerator Alternatives/Global Anti-Incinerator Alliance, and Eco-Cycle, June 2008, p. 2 (stoptrashing theclimate.org/fullreport_stoptrashingtheclimate.pdf).

137. "Milestones on the Zero Waste Journey," Zero Waste New Zealand Trust (zerowaste .co.nz/default,724.sm).

138. John Coté, "S.F. OKs toughest recycling law in U.S.," *San Francisco Chronicle*, June 10, 2009 (sfgate.com/cgi-bin/article.cgi?f=/c/a/2009/06/10/MN09183NV8.DTL).

139. Ibid.

140. Zero Waste Kovalam website: zerowastekovalam.org.

141. From a speech by Jayakumar Chelaton at a meeting of international waste activists in Penang, Malaysia, in 2003.

Epilogue: Writing the New Story

1. Robert Putnam, *Bowling Alone* (New York: Simon & Schuster, 2000), p. 20.

2. Ibid., p. 21.

3. Colin Beavan, post from the No Impact Man blog on March 21, 2008 (noimpactman. typepad.com/blog/2008/03/like-falling-of.html). See his book for more: Colin Beavan, *No Impact Man: The Adventures of a Guilty Liberal Who Attempts to Save the Planet, and the Discoveries He Makes About Himself and Our Way of Life in the Process* (New York: Farrar, Straus and Giroux, 2009).

4. Michael Maniates, "Going Green? Easy Doesn't Do It," *The Washington Post*, November 22, 2007 (washingtonpost.com/wp-dyn/content/article/2007/11/21/AR20071121 01856.html).

5. John Talberth, Clifford Cobb, and Noah Slattery, *The Genuine Progress Indicator 2006*," Redefining Progress, p. 9 (rprogress.org/publications/2007/GPI%202006 .pdf).

6. Personal correspondence with John Talberth, July 2009.

7. Associated Press, "Global Arms Spending Up, Study Shows," *The New York Times*, June 9, 2009 (query.nytimes.com/gst/fullpage.html?res=9B05E2DD1530F93AA357 55C0A96F9C8B63).

8. National Priorities Project website: nationalpriorities.org.

9. *The Happy Planet Index 2.0: Why good lives don't have to cost the earth*, The New Economics Foundation, 2009, p. 28.

10. National Priorities Project Cost of War counters: costofwar.com.
11. Ibid.
12. Elisabeth Rosenthal, "Amazon Culture Withers as Food Dries Up," *The New York Times,* July 24, 2009 (nytimes.com/2009/07/25/science/earth/25tribe.html).
13. Sarah van Gelder, "The Next Reformation," an interview with Paul Hawken, *In Context: A Quarterly of Humane Sustainable Culture,* no. 41, Summer 1995 (context .org/ICLIB/IC41/Hawken1.htm).
14. Lester Brown, *Plan B 3.0: Mobilizing to Save Civilization* (New York: W.W. Norton & Co., 2008), p. 7.
15. Personal correspondence with Dave Batker, July 2009.
16. Juliet Schor, "Downshifting to a Carbon Friendly Economy," in *Less Is More: Embracing Simplicity for a Healthy Planet, a Caring Economy and Lasting Happiness* (Canada: New Society Publishers, 2009), p. 231.
17. "Americans Eager to Take Back Their Time," Take Back Your Time Poll highlights, Center for a New American Dream, August 2003 (newdream.org/about/polls/time poll.php).
18. Schor, "Downshifting to a Carbon Friendly Economy," p. 233.
19. David Wann, "Why Isn't This Empire Sustainable?" in *Less Is More: Embracing Simplicity for a Healthy Planet, a Caring Economy and Lasting Happiness* (Canada: New Society Publishers, 2009), p. 217.
20. "More of What Matters Poll," Center for a New American Dream, September 2004 (newdream.org/about/polls.php).
21. Influenced especially by the work of Paul Hawken, the Global Scenario Group convened by the Stockholm Environment Institute, Tim Jackson of the Sustainable Development Commission, and ecological economist Hermann Daly.
22. Wann, "Why Isn't this Empire Sustainable?" p. 217.
23. Penny Herscher, "Will the Rising Personal Savings Rate Boom the US Recovery?" *The Huffington Post,* January 13, 2009 (huffingtonpost.com/penny-herscher/will-the -rising-personal_b_157526.html).
24. "National Voter Turnout in Federal Elections 1960–2008," Infoplease.com, from the Federal Election Commission, based on data from Congressional Research Service reports, Election Data Services Inc., and state election offices (infoplease.com/ipa/ A0781453.html).
25. Paul Hawken, "Commencement: Healing or Stealing?" 2009 commencement address at the University of Portland (up.edu/commencement/default.aspx?cid=9456).

ACKNOWLEDGMENTS

Over the last twenty years, many dedicated and knowledgeable people all over the world helped me understand elements of the Story of Stuff.

Davis Baltz, Charlotte Brody, Barry Castleman, Gary Cohen, Tracy Easthope, Ken Geiser, Lois Gibbs, Judith Helfand, Michael Lerner, Stacy Malkan, Pete Myers, Peter Orris, Arlene Rodriguez, Kathy Sessions, and Sandra Steingraber educated me about the environmental health impacts of toxic chemicals. Marni Rosen and Sharyle Patton helped me conduct my own body burden testing and Ted Schettler helped me analyze the results.

Bradley Angel, Paul Connett, Pat Costner, Charlie Cray, Jorge Emmanuel, Mike Ewall, Rick Hind, Josh Karliner, Gary Liss, Glenn McRae, Pierre-Emmanuel Neurohr, Brenda Platt, Elizabeth Royte, Neil Seldman, and Alan Watson have spent two delightful decades talking trash with me. Hats off to Martin Bourque, Eric Lombardi, Dan Knapp, Jack Macy, and Dave Williamson, visionary leaders from whom I learned about the practical implementation of reuse, composting, and recycling programs. Beverly Thorpe and Bill Sheehan taught me about Extended Producer Responsibly (EPR). Thanks to them I no longer walk around the house cleaning up after my daughter: she now cleans up after herself, since—as EPR teaches—her mess is her responsibility. Bharati Chaturvedi, Juan Rosario, Omar Freilla, Heeten Kalan, Laila Iskandar, Jayakumar Chelaton, Shibu Nair, Merci Ferrer, Damu Smith, and David Pellow taught me that solutions must include a commitment to not wasting people alongside not wasting resources.

Many people shared stories about their personal experiences resisting oil and coal extraction around the world: Oronto Douglas, MaryAnn Hitt, Robert Shimeck, Owens Wiwa, Ka Hsaw Wa, Steve Kretzman, and Mike Roselle. Payal Sampat, Pratap Chatterjee, and Danny Kennedy taught me about mining. Lafcadio Cortesi, Daniel Katz, Josh Martin, Todd Paglia, Mike Brune, Randy Hayes, and Tyson Miller shared their vast knowledge of forestry and paper issues. Patricia Jurewicz did the same for cotton production and Mike Shade for all things PVC. Thanks also to my supply-chain guru Dara O'Rourke, and to Gary Ruskin and Vance Packard, who educated me about the advertising industry. Ted Smith, Sheila Davis, and Robby Rodriguez provided me with more information about electronics than even the most powerful iPod could hold.

Colin Beavan, John DeGraaf, Tim Kasser, Alan Durning, Michael Maniates, Tom Princen, Vicki Robbins, Juliet Schor, and the indomitable Betsy Taylor all helped me understand that for many of us, living with less really is more satisfying.

Thanks to the hundreds of people who opened their homes, welcomed me into their communities and shared their stories with me during my years of tracking factories and dumps. There are far too many to name here, but they include Bobby Peek in South Africa, Ralph Ryder in the U.K., Tomori Balasz in Hungary, Von Hernandez in the Philippines, Madhumitta Dutta, Bittu Sahgal, Praful Bidwai, and Nityanand Jayaraman—the Indian journalist who accompanied me on so many factory investigations that he once called me his greatest occupational hazard—in India. Many of the people I worked with around the world are members of GAIA, an international network of people in eighty-one countries working for safe, just alternatives to incineration. To GAIA, I offer especially heartfelt thanks.

Thanks to the economists who made me realize that the study of economics is both fascinating and essential: Dave Batker, Josh Farley, David Korten, Pritam Singh, John Talberth, and especially Jeffrey Morris, who spent hours exploring the nearly infinite externalized costs associated in making a modern-day consumer product.

I deeply appreciate the people who shared their knowledge about solutions and alternatives: Bryony Schwan and Janine Benyus for their teachings on biomimicry, Beverly Bell for documenting that other worlds are possible, and John Warner for articulating and advancing Green Chemistry.

In addition to the invaluable expertise shared by those working in specific issue areas, I also want to thank those who taught me to look at the big picture, who helped me to connect the dots. First and foremost, Patrick Bond at the University of KwaZulu Natal in Durban, South Africa, who read through this manuscript and provided invaluable critiques and comments throughout. Additionally, Maude Barlow, John Cavanagh, Gopal Dayaneni, Ellen Dorsey, Anwar Fazal, Tom Goldtooth, Paul Hawken, Van Jones, Rita Lustgarten, Jerry Mander, Donella Meadows, Peter Montague, Ralph Nader, Bobby Peek, Meena Raman, Mark Randazzo, Katie Redford, John Richard, Satinath Sarangi, and Robert Weissman.

I am forever grateful that my first real job was with an organization whose default response was "let's do it" rather than "but that might not work." Jim Vallette, Heather Spalding, Kenny Bruno, Connie Murtagh, Jim Puckett, Marcelo Furtado, Von Hernandez, Veronica Odriozola, Kevin Stairs, Dave Rapaport, Peter Bahouth, and others in Greenpeace's Toxic Trade Team taught me how a handful of people, whose sense of possibility far outweighed a sense of limitations could tackle a problem as sinister and widespread as international waste trafficking.

I am grateful to Idelisse Malave, one of the first to see the potential of the Story of Stuff project, and her colleagues at the Tides Center Cathy Lerza and Chris Herrera, for their invaluable guidance and support.

The 20-minute internet film that first brought the Story of Stuff to over 8 million people (and counting) worldwide would not have been possible without the genius creative team at Free Range Studios: Producer Erica Priggen, Director Louis Fox, Animator extraordinaire Ruben DeLuna along with Jonah Sachs, Emily Weinstein, Liz Kuehl and Ross Nover. Free Range's Amy Hartzler and Chris Brunell also helped with the images for this book cover.

I am grateful to the Funders Workgroup for Sustainable Production and Consumption, who provided encouragement, support and friendship in getting this message out: Jennie Curtis, Stuart Clarke, Scott Denman, Jon Jensen, Daniel Katz, Cathy Lerza, Jenny Russell, Ina Smith, Don Weeden, Darryl Young, Pam Allen, Nikhil Aziz, Tim Crosby, and Valentine Doyle.

The staff of the Story of Stuff Project—especially Allison Cook and Michael O'Heaney—kept our project moving forward while I focused on writing this book. Their skill and dedication is unsurpassed. I am also grateful to the members of the Story of Stuff Advisory Board (Stuart Baker, Jennie Curtis, Omar Freilla, Ken Geiser, Michael Maniates, Erica Priggen, Beverly Thorpe, Darryl Young) and the Community Board (Lorna Apper, Nikhil Aziz, Andy Banks, Colin Beavan, Bill Bigelow, Gary Cohen, Lafcadio Cortesi, Josh Farley, Reverend Harper Fletcher, Ilyse Hogue, Danny Kennedy, Mateo Nube, Dara O'Rourke, Richard Oram, David Pellow, Maritza Schafer, Bryony Schwan, Robert Shimeck, Ted Smith, Betsy Taylor, Pamela Tuttle, Aditi Vaidya, Monica Wilson). Scott Denman, Jeff Conant, Nathan Embretson, Babken DerGrigorian, Chris Naff, and Jodi Solomon have also contributed greatly to the SOS Project.

Thanks to those who provided funding for the Story of Stuff Project: the 11th Hour Project, the Artnz Family Foundation, the Jenifer Altman Foundation, the Fund for the Environment and Urban Life, Garfield Foundation, Grassroots International, The Overbrook Foundation, Johnson Family Foundation, Wallace Global Fund, Lia Fund, Park Foundation, Singing Field Foundation, Solidago Foundation, Peter Buckley, Jack Paxton, and many individual donors. Thank you for making our work possible.

I am immensely grateful to the many thousands of viewers of Story of Stuff who wrote letters and emails to me sharing the insights and insights that the film inspired.

Acknowledgments

A special thanks to Raffi Cavoukian, for making me laugh and for always reminding me to honor children. A society that truly honors our children, as Raffi advocates, would never permit waging war to secure oil or putting neurotoxins in furniture.

Experience is the best teacher and I have learned about the invaluable benefits of living in community by experiencing it day in and day out. I thank the people with whom I share backyards, bikes, garden tools, meals, adventures, and love: Bill Barclay, Andre Carothers, Faik Cimen, Lafcadio Cortesi, Adam Dawson, Cathy Fogel, Maureen Graney, Bryon and Cindy Hann, John Harvey, Andrea Hurd, Firuzeh Mahmoudi, Deborah Moore, Sloane and Nick Morgan, and Joanne Welsch.

While I worked on weekends, researching the data about how Americans work too much and neglect their families, a team of friends whisked my daughter away and kept her entertained. Thanks to Jane Fry, Lisa Hunter, Christie Keith, Josue Revolorio, Danny Kennedy, Miya Yoshitani, Jeremiah Holland, Michelle Hammond, Michael Cohen, Leigh Raiford, Erick Matsen, Zephania Cortesi, Joe Leonard, Rebecca Fisher, and above all my mother, Bobbie Leonard, who over the years has always cared for my daughter while I traveled, sometimes even accompanying me with my daughter in tow for a truly unique intergenerational holiday: grandmother, mother, and toddler heading off to the PVC factory.

My book agent, Linda Loewenthal, skillfully guided me through the world of book publishing. My editor, Wylie O'Sullivan, at Free Press was a cheerful source of feedback as the book came together. Dominick Anfuso and Sydney Tanigawa provided invaluable guidance and support. Karen Romano and Suzanne Donahue made sure that the production of the book was as environmentally friendly as possible. Researcher Marcia Carroll found facts and figures far beyond Google's reach, and Renee Shade also helped track down specific data for this book. Patrick Bond, Alan Watson, and Ken Geiser provided valuable comments on specific chapters in this book.

There is one person without whom this book really could not have been written: Ariane Conrad. Ariane collaborated with me, in a role she describes as a book doula, throughout the long months of labor and successful delivery of this book. Ariane's intellectual and logistical contributions were significant and I am delighted that the result is not just *The Story of Stuff* book but a treasured new friend. Thank you Ariane.

HOW WE MADE THIS BOOK

Our intent in creating this book was to use as few toxic materials as possible, to minimize the carbon footprint, and to avoid waste. To that end the manuscript was almost entirely designed and edited electronically. Review copies were offered to readers as downloadable e-galleys, and a very limited number of publicity copies were printed on 100 percent post-consumer waste recycled fiber.

The book was printed on Rolland Enviro100 Print, a 100 percent post-consumer fiber paper that is processed chlorine-free. The text plates were recycled after use and the ink used in this book contains more than 20 percent renewable resources, including soy and other vegetable-based oils. All of our adhesives for the case glues are solvent free. The case boards were created with 100 percent recycled fiber. The jacket was printed with vegetable-based inks and was printed on 100 percent post-consumer waste stock. Of the materials used in the creation of this book, including the printing plates and paper waste, 90 percent were recycled.

Any unused inventory or returned books will be recycled.

INDEX

ABOUT THE AUTHORS

Annie Leonard, born in Seattle in 1964, learned to love nature in the forests of the Pacific Northwest. When as a college student in New York City she saw her beloved trees turned to wastepaper and packaging, she followed them to the world's largest dump, and found her calling. After a stint doing graduate work at Cornell University in upstate New York, she spent nearly two decades tracking international waste trafficking and fighting incineration around the world, first as an employee of Greenpeace International from 1988–1996. She later worked in Ralph Nader's Washington office for Essential Action, and then for the Global Alliance for Incineration Alternatives (GAIA), Health Care Without Harm and The Sustainability Funders. In 2007 she created *The Story of Stuff,* a video that summarized her learnings from two decades on the international trail of waste. It has been watched over 7 million times—and counting—and translated into over a dozen languages. In 2008, she was one of *TIME* magazine's Heroes of the Environment. She lives in the San Francisco Bay area with her daughter, in a community committed to sustainability and sharing.

Ariane Conrad, aka the Book Doula, is a writer, editor, and activist. She co-authored the *New York Times* bestselling *The Green Collar Economy* by Van Jones (Harper One, 2008) and *HOOPING* by Christabel Zamor (Workman Publishing, 2009). Visit her at bookdoula.com.